THOMAS PAINE

Also by Craig Nelson

The First Heroes: The Extraordinary Story of the Doolittle Raid—America's First World War II Victory

I am Gentlemen

on account of the other proposal

Yr. Obliged Humble Servt.

T Paine

THOMAS PAINE

Enlightenment, Revolution, and the Birth of Modern Nations

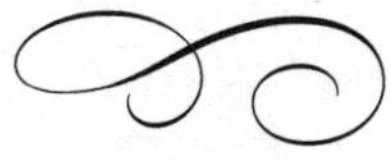

Craig Nelson

P
PROFILE BOOKS

First published in Great Britain in 2007 by
PROFILE BOOKS LTD
3A Exmouth House
Pine Street
London EC1R 0JH
www.profilebooks.com

First published in the United States in 2006 by
Viking Penguin, a member of the Penguin Group (USA) Inc.

1 3 5 7 9 10 8 6 4 2

Set in Adobe Garamond
Designed by Francesca Belanger

Printed and bound in Great Britain by
Clays, Bungay, Suffolk

A CIP catalogue record for this book is available from the British Library.

ISBN-10: 1 86197 638 0
ISBN-13: 978 1 86197 638 3

The paper this book is printed on is certified by the © 1996 Forest Stewardship Council A.C. (FSC). It is ancient-forest friendly. The printer holds FSC chain of custody SGS-COC-2061

Not to have knowledge of what happened before you were born is to be condemned to live forever as a child.

—CICERO

The penalty good men pay for not being interested in politics is to be governed by men worse than themselves.

—PLATO

There have been so many writers who dominated a period and then slipped off. History is like some gigantic beast—it simply wriggles its back and throws off whatever is on it.

—ARTHUR MILLER

A Note

Writers of the eighteenth century did not believe that consistency in spelling, capitalization, punctuation, or italics was a mark of literacy. I have used modern versions of their work so that today's reader will not imagine them fusty, old-fashioned, or poorly educated, opinions that would have horrified them. The American founding fathers, British progressives, and French revolutionaries who are the subjects of this book, after all, considered themselves a forward-thinking global avant-garde, absolutely modern, who believed with all their hearts that they had in their power to begin the world over again.

As we now know, this is exactly what they did.

Acknowledgments

Anyone who writes history depends, in great measure, on the kindness of librarians, and the key figures in the world of Paine scholarship have been remarkably kind, gracious, and professional toward me:

Valerie-Anne Lutz, J. J. Ahern, Roy Goodman, and Elaine Delduca, the Library of the American Philosophical Society, Philadelphia; Bruce Kirby, Manuscript Division, the Library of Congress, Washington, D.C.; Jean Archdeacon and Janet Broughton, Ambrose Barker Paine Collection, Norfolk County Council Library, Thetford; Esme Evans and Ann Mills, the Sussex Archaeological Society Library, Lewes; Andrew Lusted and Anne Hart, the East Sussex Records Office, Lewes.

I owe a great deal of thanks to the women who helped extensively with research in France: Mona Ghuneim, for her reconnoitering with the Institut d'Histoire de la Révolution Française, Université de Paris, and Katharine Coit, for her investigations at the Bibliothèque Nationale and the Ministère des Affaires Etrangères.

I'm grateful for my big-hearted and hardheaded agent, Stuart Krichevsky;
for my dazzling American editor, Rick Kot;
für meinen grossen Schatz, Dan Golden.

Contents

1. The Mission of Atonement

JUST BEFORE DAYBREAK on or about September 25 in the year 1819, a fifty-six-year-old Englishman by the name of William Cobbett found himself twenty-two miles due north of New York City, stumbling pink-faced and ardent through the wild blackness of Westchester, followed by his son, J.P., and a hired hand. The night was dank and blind and crowded with the raucous blur of a thousand unseen creatures, for though the myriad flocks and herds of the New World would in time be annihilated for their fur, their meat, and the carnal pleasure of taking a life, at that moment the continent was as awash in wildlife as an African dream—bald eagles nested along the Manhattan riverbanks, and catamounts prowled the outskirts of Greenwich Village. As Cobbett and his men scurried forward into the darkness, they found themselves engulfed by the moans of frogs, the rasps of crickets, the pierce of owls, the bark of foxes, the mourning of wolves.

Burdened by a large box and an assortment of picks and shovels, the men made their way across the border of the French Protestant refuge of New Rochelle, hindered by using as few torches as possible in order to travel unnoticed. Even so, at the nearby tavern owned by Charity Badeau, her son, Albert, heard the men in the dead of night and alerted the authorities. Now Cobbett and his men could hear a group of local magistrates in the distance, approaching.

They hurried along as well as could be managed, helped by their leader's knowing exactly where his quarry lay, having traced the route numerous times before in daylight hours. Finally he and his men arrived at their destination and hurriedly began to dig.

Even taking into account that era's Renaissance style of gentlemanly pursuits—exemplified by printer, natural philosopher, essayist, businessman, inventor, civil servant, and diplomat Benjamin Franklin—William Cobbett had pursued a significant range of trades over the course of one lifetime. Soldier, publisher, Tory, radical, Commons deputy, essayist, and Long Island farmer (who loathed the potato but championed the rutabaga), he is primarily known today for *Rural Rides,* an ode to bucolic Albion:

> I knew that my road lay through a hamlet called Churt, where they grow such fine bennet-grass seed. There was a moon; but there was also a hazy rain. . . . I am here got into some of the very best barley land in the kingdom; a fine, buttery, stoneless loam, upon a bottom of sand or sandstone. Finer barley and turnip-land it is impossible to see.

Regardless of such reveries on beloved turnip lands, Cobbett was in the flesh a bare-knuckled, go-for-broke political gladiator, perennially struggling to change the mass beliefs of humankind. He was that type of man whose emotions fattened until they became intolerable, and something had to be done, especially when it came to righting social injustice. Cobbett would have his first great political epiphany in 1792 when, as a twenty-nine-year-old sergeant major, newly retired from the British army, he followed the House of Commons' debate on whether to raise taxes to pay soldiers three shillings a week. The men were already supposed to be receiving that sum, but endemic graft meant they got only about half that, and Secretary at War George Yonge had decided that the answer was to increase revenue instead of trying to stop the service's long-standing corruption. Cobbett, made bitter from his years in the army by his own commanders' habitual larceny, challenged this position with *The Soldier's Friend,* a pamphlet exploring the history of state-sanctioned bunco. His Majesty's government replied by throwing *Soldier's* publisher James Ridgeway into prison for four years, and forcing the new author to flee the country.

Cobbett arrived in the United States to find a nation "exactly the contrary of what I expected . . . the land is bad, rocky . . . the seasons are detestable . . . the people are worthy of the country—cheating, sly, roguish. . . . Instead of that perfect freedom, and that amiable simplicity, of which PAINE had given me so flattering a description, I found myself placed under a set of petty, mean, despots, ruling by the powers given them by a perversion of the law of England." In Philadelphia he taught English to Parisians fleeing the French

Revolution; their horrific accounts, combined with his own infinite disappointment in the ways of American democratic government, threw Cobbett's political beliefs into a full-throttle reverse. He opened a printshop (a business incorporating the entire eighteenth-century media universe of letters, broadsides, newspapers, pamphlets, magazines, and books), decorated it with portraits of King George III, and, under the byline "Peter Porcupine," wrote such rabble-rousing commentary as calling democracy "a despotism of the many over the few" and Benjamin Franklin "a whore-master, a hypocrite and an infidel." His cantankerous and rabidly pro-British, pro-Federalist *Porcupine's Gazette* quickly became North America's most widely read periodical. In 1797 he referred to Philadelphia scion and American founding father Benjamin Rush as "Doctor Sangrado," and denounced his widespread use of bloodletting as a form of medical Terror. Rush sued for libel and (perhaps assisted by the judge's close friendship with Rush's attorney) won an astounding $5,000—around $400,000 today. Forced to shut down *Porcupine's Gazette,* Cobbett tried to replace it with *The American Rush-Light; by the Help of which, Wayward and Disaffected Britons may see a Complete Specimen of the Baseness, Dishonesty, Ingratitude, and Perfidy of Republicans, and of the Profligacy, Injustice, and Tyranny of Republican Government,* but this did not satisfy Rush or the court, and he fled jurisdiction once again.

Returning to London, Cobbett issued both *The Porcupine (Fear God: Honour the King)* and *Cobbett's Political Register,* which went undelivered until he stopped refusing to make kickback payoffs to Britain's Post Office Secretary. When Cobbett then decried the army's use of flogging, he was tried and found guilty of sedition, and was sentenced to two years' confinement in Europe's most notorious prison, Newgate. By the time of his release, the man had come to believe that he had spent his American years living in a fool's paradise, blind to the debauched march of English history. Now he found that Britain's wealthy had only gotten richer and its working class had fallen further into poverty; he saw the starving poor riot for food, and the government do nothing except order soldiers to beat the mobs into a cowed retreat. He now viewed Whitehall as a repulsive and degenerate system of graft and patronage controlled by oligarchs and plutocrats, a system he called the "Thing," a Thing that was turning Englishmen away from the nation's great traditions of honor and virtue into a wholly self-interested horde of beasts.

Cobbett was baffled and aggrieved. How had this happened to his great nation? How could it be remedied? He found an answer in *The Decline and Fall of the English System of Finance,* an essay linking Britain's never-ending warmongering to her escalating national debt, crushing taxes, and overreliance on paper money. *Decline and Fall*'s author ominously predicted that the Bank of England would fail, and when the following year the bank indeed suspended cash payments, Cobbett realized that he had found the political and philosophical fount he had been looking for all his life. "At his expiring flambeau," he would explain just before he died, "I lighted my taper."

By this time Cobbett had grown a torso as burly as in any John Bull legend, topped by bushy, snow-white hair and equally bushy, snow-white eyebrows, along with the burnt skin of a weekend farmer, pink as a Christmas ham. He had become England's most popular journalist, selling forty thousand copies of the weekly *Political Register* at a price workingmen could afford. The government responded to this achievement by passing Gagging Acts and a suspension of habeas corpus, forcing him once again to leave England for the United States. He returned to what he now believed was an American paradise, mercifully untainted by the English Thing.

Just a few decades before, there had existed a coterie of men (and one woman) known variously as progressives, radicals, philosophes, *illuministi,* and founding fathers, who had come to the fantastical notion that civilization could be improved through the application of human reason and science. This group of modern thinkers, united through their constant interactions in the Republic of Letters, believed they had it in their power to begin the world over again, to end relentless poverty and widespread ignorance while destroying the mindless and oppressive power of parasitic monarchs and idle aristocrats. In time, through their efforts, the lives of millions of ordinary people would be dramatically improved, and many of their febrile dreams, once widely ridiculed, would become so commonplace that today it is a struggle to appreciate the dramatic labor of their births.

By the early nineteenth century, however, their era of profound hope was in eclipse, its astounding, brilliant figures either dead, ridiculed, or wholly ignored. The citizens of America had entirely repudiated their own founding fathers, turning away from the Enlightenment's optimistic vision of progress for the future, belief in the infinite powers of natural philosophy, and admiration for ancient Rome's republican heroes, in favor of evangelical religion, land speculation, bargain corn whiskey, kaleidoscopes, and a style of clothing and interior decorating that would come to be known by historians as "American Fancy." The European avant-garde, who had once hoped to drive out corrupt monarchies and establish democratic republics, had in turn been silenced by the reigns of Terror, Bonaparte, and England's Pitt the Younger.

While a Tory Federalist living in Philadelphia, Cobbett had attacked this group of do-gooders, claiming that their "humanity, like that of all the reforming philosophers of the present enlightened day, is of the speculative kind. It never breaks out into action." Two decades later, he would in fact evolve into one of these reforming philosophers himself, carrying on the utopian missions of the previous century in an attempt to destroy the Thing and restore England to a golden age of selfless virtue. In returning to his progressive roots, he would have an almost religious conviction that the fount that had awakened him politically and philosophically one full and final time was in fact the true father of the United States—not a general, but a writer (for before the sword, there is always the word), and not just any writer, but the most famous and popular author of the entire eighteenth century.

During the final years of Thomas Paine's life William Cobbett had been one of his most public and brutal foes, using *Porcupine's Gazette* to attack him on issue after issue. "How Tom gets a living now, or what brothel he inhabits, I know not," he wrote during Paine's last years in physical and professional decline. "Whether his carcass is at last to be suffered to rot on the earth, or to be dried in the air, is of very little consequence. Whenever and wherever he breathes his last, he will excite neither sorrow nor compassion; no friendly hand will close his eyes, not a groan will be uttered, not a tear will be shed. Like Judas he will be remembered by posterity; men will learn to express all that is base, malignant, treacherous, unnatural and blasphemous, by the single monosyllable, PAINE."

Having witnessed the turns of history in the years since Paine's death, however, Cobbett had undergone a profound conversion: "Any man may fall into error, but a fool or a knave will seldom acknowledge it. . . . I saw Paine first pointing the way, and then leading a nation through perils and difficulties of all sorts, to independence and to lasting liberty, prosperity and greatness." Cobbett had become certain that his erstwhile nemesis had been right about everything all along, and he in turn was now Thomas Paine's most devoted acolyte. He immediately became a friend to Mme. Bonneville, the woman who had inherited Paine's literary estate, and worked to ensure that all of the great man's writing would be safeguarded, and eventually published. He interviewed as many friends and acquaintances as possible in order to produce a definitive Paine biography, doing penance for having been the American publisher of Francis Oldys's *The Life of Thomas Paine,* a slanderous attack subsidized by the British government.

What Cobbett could not undo or scarcely bear was Paine's debased reputation. How could the American people ignore this hero, who had convinced their ancestors to renounce the depraved government of their homeland and build a new world . . . this author, who had conceived and written the very principles on which their nation was founded . . . this theorist, whose writings were the very essence of what it meant to be an American . . . this man, who had fought so publicly for decades over the United States' very right to exist as something beyond an abused and belittled colony? At the same time, the citizens of Britain were rejecting this visionary who had been threatened with execution, and who had suffered lifelong exile from his native country, solely because he attempted to gain political powers for the common Englishman for the first time in that nation's history.

William Cobbett arrived at one conclusion. If no one else would put things right, then he, who had participated so eagerly in everything that was wrong during his early Tory years in America, would have to make amends. He would perform one heroic, glorious act of atonement that would startle the world and reignite humanity's appreciation for the extraordinary ideas and writings of Thomas Paine.

The Porcupine had insinuated what he was about to attempt in upstate New York through letters and in the *Political Register:* "Paine lies in a little hole under the grass and weeds of an obscure farm in America. There, however, he shall not lie, unnoticed, much longer. . . . These bones will effect the reformation of England in Church and State. . . . Never will England be what it ought to be until the marble of [First Minister William] Pitt's monument is converted into a monument to the memory of Paine. . . . He belongs to England. His fame is the property of England; and, if no other people will show that they value that fame, the people of England will."

Cobbett had decided that he would exhume the decade-old corpse of Thomas Paine from his long-forgotten grave on deserted New Rochelle farmland. He would then sail with it to London, and there construct the grand mausoleum that he fervently believed the greatest hero of the century truly deserved.

The digging, even with the coming of first light, was difficult. Finally the deteriorating cadaver was fully unearthed, and transferred to a box less unwieldy than its mahogany casket. Cobbett then decided that he could not live without the headstone, and took that as well. As the local sheriffs drew closer, the three men ran, fumbling with their cargo, barely outracing the deputies to New Rochelle's Hudson River docks. Cobbett and J.P. then returned to Hyde Park, their family farm on Long Island, to make final preparations—as the house had burned down the year before, they had to sleep in a tent—and the following week they sailed on the *Hercules,* with the corpse, to England. During a customs inspection at Liverpool on November 21, 1819, Cobbett opened his various bits of luggage and, revealing the body, announced, "There, gentlemen, are the mortal remains of the immortal Thomas Paine." (Apparently he had decided not to continue on to London with the stone, as James Dow revealed in a letter to a progressive New York periodical, *The Truth-Seeker,* on August 8, 1909: "Since October 1819, the [Paine] gravestone has been in the quiet and continuous custody of the Rushton family in this city. It has never been publicly exhibited, and is regarded as an heirloom. . . . The gravestone was presented by William Cobbett to Edward Rushton between the 31st Oct, 1819 and the 28th Nov. . . . The widow [of Edward Rushton's son] possesses the stone, and is indisposed to restore it to the public.")

As Cobbett and his luggage passed through Bolton, the town crier announced the arrival of Mr. Thomas Paine, and was consequently jailed for nine weeks. When Cobbett at last arrived in London and explained to the world his grand vision, the reaction was not at all what he had hoped. The English government refused permission for his plans for a "colossal statue in bronze" of Paine. When his workingmen readers then failed to rally to the cause to force Whitehall to reconsider, Cobbett decided to exhibit the bones for an entry fee of one tuppence to raise money for his "fund for reform," and to fashion Paine's hair around metal rings to wear in his honor. Nothing came of these schemes, however. The incident instead turned into a national joke, with the English Tory press taunting Cobbett as a "resurrection man," referring to those who made a living by supplying medical schools with cadavers of dubious origins, and Lord Byron himself quatrained, "In digging up your bones, Tom Paine, Will Cobbett has done well; You visit him on earth again, He'll visit you in hell." The scandal would become so well known in its day that it generated an endless series of political cartoons ridiculing Cobbett, as well as a popular nursery rhyme:

Poor Tom Paine! there he lies;
Nobody laughs and nobody cries;
Where he has gone or how he fares;
Nobody knows and nobody cares.

Such attitudes would foreshadow the next two centuries of public thinking about the man who was once considered the most important political writer of his century. Though "Poor Tom" was a founder of both the United States and the French Republic, the creator of the phrase "United States of America," and the author of the three biggest bestsellers of the eighteenth century, he is known today by the educated public primarily through biographies for children. At the same time, since he wholeheartedly followed a motto that life should be "a daring adventure, or nothing," his personal drama and historic achievements have inspired a never-ending chain of advocates, apostles, and cultists.

For centuries after his death Paine would be remembered as a filthy, poverty-stricken, drunken wastrel and an unoriginal thinker—an image engineered by his great foes, the American Federalist Party of John Adams and the British government of King George III. In fact, in his lifetime he was considered on intellectual par with the giants of his century, and far from being impoverished, he left an estate worth nearly a million dollars in today's money. He clearly had a charm, a style, and an intelligence that others found overpoweringly attractive, since he rose from the lowest ranks of working-class England to the highest levels of the era's global intellectual society, becoming a friend (or an ally) to the century's greatest luminaries: Benjamin Franklin, George Washington, Thomas Jefferson, Benjamin Rush, James Monroe, Georges-Jacques Danton, Jacques-Pierre Brissot, Antoine-Nicolas de Condorcet, William Blake, Joseph Priestley, Richard Price, William Godwin, and Mary Wollstonecraft. Indeed, though from the last years of his life to the present day, Paine has been considered one of the most controversial figures in American history, nearly all of his writings reflect the consensus opinion of his Enlightenment peers. He has been quoted in admiration by figures as diverse as Ronald Reagan, Walt Whitman, Richard Perle (the intellectual father of the American war in Iraq), Andrew Jackson, and Abraham Lincoln—and all of them are right to claim him. Thomas Edison thought Paine "the equal of Washington in making American liberty possible; where Washington performed, Paine devised and wrote," while among his detractors was Teddy Roosevelt, who pronounced him nothing but "a dirty little atheist." John Adams at first told Thomas Jefferson that "history is to ascribe the American Revolution to Thomas Paine," but later would dismiss him as "a disastrous meteor." In fact, when his momentous era began to be known by the title of Paine's last great work, Adams would protest with his signature melodramatic flair (a key talent for an eighteenth-century trial lawyer):

> I am willing you should call this the Age of Frivolity as you do, and would not object if you had named it the Age of Folly, Vice, Frenzy, Brutality, Daemons, Buonaparte, Tom Paine, or the Age of the Burning Brand from the Bottomless Pit, or anything but the Age of Reason. I know not whether any man in the world has had more influence on its inhabitants or affairs for the last thirty years than Tom Paine. There can be no severer satyr on the age. For such a mongrel between pig and puppy, begotten by a wild boar on a bitch wolf, never before in any age of the world was suffered by the poltroonery of mankind, to run through such a career of mischief. Call it then the Age of Paine.

Adams's screed came at the end of decades of philosophical conflict between the two men—both he and Paine loved out-and-out warfare—but the significance he ascribes to his opponent was patently true. Paine's writings were a fundamental source for European and American ideas of society and government. Almost everything about America and Americans that is globally admired today is found in his work; almost every issue he raised is still at issue in our own times; almost every argument in which he engaged—most obviously his verbal duel with Edmund Burke over whether "ordinary" human beings are civilized enough to govern themselves—is still being argued more than two hundred years later. And, if the journalistic credos of speaking truth to power, comforting the afflicted, and afflicting the comfortable have a godhead, that would have to be Paine, whose writing was so provocative and so uncompromising that he faced the gibbet and the blade everywhere he published—in England, and in France, and in the United Colonies.

Practically every human detail about the seventeenth century's lodestone figure, Isaac Newton, is now lost to us, even the specifics of his physical appearance. The same is almost true of Paine, the vast majority of whose documents were either deliberately or accidentally destroyed, and who shared with Newton the status of having created such fundamental theory that today it is nearly impossible to understand his ideas as the revolution in thinking they once were. History rises from primary documents, but in Paine's case these have been decimated, while the key secondary sources include a propagandist hired by the British government, a onetime Paine ally writing for vengeance, and a besotted acolyte overwhelmed by love for his subject. During the last years of Paine's life, he would have an all-too-common writer's dispute with New York newspaper editor James Cheetham, a dispute that became so heated he would use his celebrity to uncommonly (and somewhat deservedly) attack his editor's professionalism. Cheetham would wait until the week of the official announcement of Paine's death, and then take his vengeance with a biography of vicious slurs. Under the guise of a fair and balanced journalist, he sent a query letter to a near-lifelong Paine friend; Joel Barlow replied with a description of the difficulties Cheetham would face in composing his life:

> If this piece of biography should analyze his literary labors, and rank him as he ought to be ranked among the brightest and most undeviating luminaries of the age in which he has lived—yet with a mind assailable by flattery, and receiving through that weak side a tincture of vanity which he was too proud to conceal; with a mind, though strong enough to bear him up and to rise elastic under the heaviest load of oppression, yet unable to endure the contempt of his former friends and fellow-laborers, the rulers of the country that had received his first and great services. . . . If you are disposed and prepared to write his life, thus entire, to fill up the picture to which these hasty strokes of outline give but a rude sketch with great vacuities, your book may be a useful one. . . . It is said he was always a peevish intimate . . . but Thomas Paine . . . was one of the most instructive men I ever have known. He had a surprising memory and

> brilliant fancy; his mind was a storehouse of facts and useful observations; he was full of lively anecdote, and ingenious, original, pertinent remarks upon almost every subject.

At the same time, another Paine contemporary would warn, "The name is enough. Every person has ideas of him. Some respect his genius and dread the man. Some reverence his political, while they hate his religious, opinions. Some love the man, but not his private manners. Indeed he has done nothing which has not extremes in it. He never appears but we love and hate him. He is as great a paradox as ever appeared in human nature."

2. Begotten by a Wild Boar on a Bitch Wolf

It is an ironic symmetry of history how Thomas Paine was carried out of America, for his nearly lifeless body had similarly arrived in the New World between December 7 and 12, 1774, its condition a result of eighteenth-century maritime travel, when a ten- to thirteen-week, 3,500-mile Atlantic crossing was so perilous that prudent men ensured their wills were in order before embarking. Traveling to the other side of the world meant facing the threats of marine storms, becalmings, icebergs, pilot error, and rotted food, not to mention state-sanctioned buccaneering. Ships were blown off course to find themselves making land in the West Indies or North Africa; it was such an arduous journey that on his first crossing, John Adams would provision himself, his son John Quincy, and their servant with "ink, paper, account books, twenty-five quill pens, a dozen clay pipes, tobacco, . . . a pocket-size pistol; . . . two hogs, two 'fat sheep,' six dozen chickens and five bushels of corn, fourteen dozen eggs, a keg of rum, a barrel of madeira, four dozen bottles of port wine, tea, chocolate, brown sugar, mustard, pepper, a box of wafers, a bag of Indian meal, and a barrel of apples." The year of Paine's crossing, one brigantine took three months to reach the New World; more than one hundred of its passengers (one-third the manifest) died of starvation, their bodies shedded to Atlantic tombs.

Added to these perils was the era's woeful state of medical science, unchanged since Galen's second-century theory of humors, which attempted to cure all physical and mental illness through a balance of black bile, yellow bile, phlegm, and blood. The state-of-the-art medical school, the University of Edinburgh, had in its pharmacy every cure known to modern science, including ant eggs; frog sperm; pigeon blood; spiderwebs; human skulls; a choice of horse, pig, or peacock feces; and mummies. One of the era's richest men, Matthew Boulton, was prescribed peacock dung, along with mistletoe, elk claw, camphor, and seahorse teeth to cure his adored wife Mary's hysterics (epilepsy). Mary died. Life expectancy then was 36.6 years, with a fifth of women perishing through childbirth. One terrible but not atypical example of infant mortality was the family of the artist Goya; his wife, Josefa, became pregnant twenty times, gave birth to seven children, and saw only one of them survive to adulthood.

Under such conditions, spending nine weeks in close contact with 120 German and English indentured servants sailing in steerage from England to Philadelphia was perilous in and of itself. One of only five cabin passengers on his voyage, Thomas Paine described his experience in a March 4, 1775, letter to his benefactor:

> I did not sail in the vessel I first intended, it not having proper conveniences, but in the London Packet, Captain Cooke. The exchange was much for the worse. A putrid fever [probably louse-carried epidemic typhus] broke out among the servants, having an 120 on board, which though not very fatal, was dismal and dangerous. We buried five, and not above that number escaped the disease. By good Providence we had a Doctor on board, who entered himself as one of the servants, otherwise we must have been in as deplorable a situation, as a passage of nine weeks could have rendered us. Two cabin passengers escaped the illness owing I believe to their being almost constantly seasick the first three weeks. I had no serious illness but suffered dreadfully with the fever. I had very little hopes that the Captain or myself would live to see America. Dr. Kearsley of this place, attended the ship on her arrival, and when he understood that I was on your recommendation he provided a lodging for me, and sent two of his men with a chaise to bring me on shore, for I could not at that time turn in my bed without help.

With debilitating headaches, fever, chills, nausea, and fatigue, and a rash covering his entire body, the nearly comatose Paine was convinced he would die before seeing anything of the New World, and in fact was so delirious with fever that he was initially unaware that he had successfully traversed the Atlantic and arrived at the docks of Philadelphia. At this critical moment he received medical attention due to a packet of letters of recommendation written by that same benefactor, which very likely saved his life. Dr. John Kearsley not only arranged to have two men hoist Paine ashore in a blanket, but would give him room and board for six weeks of recovery, during which time the feverish Paine would continue to need help just to turn over in bed. How an itinerant staymaker, taxman, grocer, teacher, widower, and divorcé, who'd relentlessly failed in everything personal and professional he had ever attempted, acquired these letters, and how he ended up delirious with fever on the shores of William Penn's Quaker utopia, is a story so preposterous it could only be true.

The January 29, 1737, birth of Thomas Pain (as he would spell it until becoming famous, "Paine" being more commonly used in the United Colonies) was a biological miracle, a Rousseau dream, and an English class-system nightmare. His forty-year-old Anglican mother, Frances, was the daughter of a Thetford lawyer so popular and successful that he would be named Town Clerk, cementing the family's status in the local elite. Pain's twenty-nine-year-old Quaker father, Joseph, on the other hand, was a master craftsman so poor he would have to borrow money from his spinster sister-in-law to afford the local grammar school's fees for Thomas's supplies. The adult Paine would display evidence of having been an only child, with his dazzling precocity, occasional self-absorption, characteristic self-esteem, a well-developed sense of entitlement, and an active internal life.

The Pains (or Paynes, as the name variously appears in government documents) lived in a small thatch-roofed home on Bridgegate Street in a neighborhood known as "the Wilderness," close by the county of Norfolk's medieval jail hewn from black flint, and within view of the slight rise in elevation of Gallows Hill. The most popular entertainment of the age was the thrill of the hangman's noose, with executions the only public holidays for workers besides Christmas and Easter, thus allowing apprentices, servants, and the working poor to mull the consequence of villainy. As eighteenth-century England had two hundred crimes punishable by death, with theft the most common capital offense, and executions meted out even when the accused was starving, and even for remarkably petty gains (a handkerchief; twenty shillings; a box of tea), the Court of Common Pleas hearings, known as the Lent Assizes, held every March at Thetford's Guildhall, would be crowded with thousands of locals and holidaymaking tourists hoping for a good courtroom drama, followed by the Christian justice of a public hanging. Every spring, scores of hooded peasant convicts arrived to face the branding iron, life imprisonment, transport to the outlying colonies, or a session on the ducking stool at the river Thet. Those refused such mercies of the court would be led to the chalk ridge overlooking the Pain cottage, their bodies left to swing for an hour as the townspeople watched and laid wager as to the time of their passing.

The Pains lived among the two thousand farmers, unskilled laborers, indentured servants, apprentices, journeymen, master craftsmen, merchants, and gentry of Thetford, a thousand-year-old East Anglia town built at the confluence of the rivers Thet and Little Ouse (pronounced "Ooze"), seventy-eight miles northeast of London on the border of Norfolk and Suffolk at the dead center of the Brecklands, in Britain's swollen eastern belly. The Brecks see little rainfall, but host a great acreage of river, pond, lake, and marshland teeming with beaver, otter, whinchat, stone curlew, nightjar, and hen harrier, against a landscape of heath, pines, lichens, heather, cattail, reed, sedge, valerian, and devil's-bit scabious. In the twelfth century, local farmers so overgrazed their sheep and rabbits that the area suffered immense sandstorms for the next five hundred years, and those inland dunes can still be seen. Today the region is home to paper mills and turkey farms and a thriving community of expatriate Portuguese, but in Pain's day it was a center of malt grain and metalwork—blacksmiths, whitesmiths, and foundries—thanks to its terribly infertile but rich-in-clay soils. ("Brecklands" means, literally, pasture that must lie fallow, or in break, for nine years every ten.) Only the twentieth-century's application of irrigation, fertilizer, insecticide, and herbicide would make the area suitable for wide-scale agriculture; in the eighteenth century, farmers relied on oats, groats, and goats. The Danes had established Thetford as East Anglia's capital, and the Normans had made it their holy see, but in 1095 the county government moved to Norwich, and the town, with barges to the Great Ouse and service on the post road to London, became a place sailed by and ridden through on the river or road to somewhere else.

As was true in England as a whole, 5 percent of Pain's neighbors were aristocrats and gentry (doctors, lawyers, and landowning yeomen and clergy), while 95 percent were rural paupers trying to survive the enclosure movement, when common folk were suddenly forbidden to graze their herds, hunt, or forage on 3.4 million acres of now private grounds. Eventually this measure would transform English agriculture and provide a year-round supply of fresh meat, but in the short term it meant destitution for those who had depended on those no longer communal lands. The century's closing years would force Norfolk's agrarian poor, like many rural Europeans, into rioting and looting for food.

Pain's childhood home was a pocket (or "rotten") borough, its electorate controlled by the local aristocrats, the Graftons, who resided at the forty-mile-in-circumference property Euston Hall, and who paid the salaries and expenses of Thetford's mayor, alderman, mace-bearer, sword-bearer, and its two members of Parliament. Of the town's two thousand citizens, thirty-one could vote, which was representative of the country as a whole, with its population of five million and its suffrage of six thousand, erratically applied. When one particularly esthetic Grafton decided that the village of Euston was interfering with the beauty of the view from his bedroom window, he simply had the entire town and its inhabitants removed.

Thomas Pain was baptized and confirmed in the Church of England, and would call himself Anglican until his first years in America. As a child, however, he regularly accompanied his father, Joseph, to services at the Quaker meetinghouse. Many of the adult Paine's progressive notions would be ascribed to these early experiences, even though he would often find himself at odds with the Friends, fiercely attacking the loyalist Quakers in Pennsylvania during the American Revolution, and noting that "if the taste of a Quaker could have been consulted at the Creation, what a silent and drab-colored Creation it would have been! Not a flower would have blossomed its gayeties, nor a bird been permitted to sing." When his own pet bird died, the eight-year-old author, at an age when many of his schoolmates were statistically perishing, composed his first writing to survive history, an epitaph with a suitably Quaker admonition:

Here lies the body of John Crow,
Who once was high but now is low;
Ye brother Crows take warning all
For as you rise, so must you fall.

The Pains attended a meetinghouse on Cage Lane, so named since adjacent to the dissenters' building were the cage, pillory, and stocks for the condemned overflow of Thetford prison. During Quaker services, young

Thomas would have been surrounded by the "sadd colours"—autumnal greens, dun wheats, and wintry barks—of the congregants' clothing, while listening to prayer and testimony intermingled with bellowing wails, screams for mercy, and the taunts of locals having a grand old time tormenting the criminals on public display next door.

Having been raised in two religions simultaneously during a period when competing doctrines waged armed warfare against one another could have triggered Paine's adult tendency to question all received wisdom. However, such an upbringing was not all that uncommon, and one of his few surviving memories about this issue seems to prove that, in the battle over young Thomas's beliefs, neither Friend nor Anglican would prevail:

> I well remember, when about seven or eight years of age, hearing a sermon read by a relation of mine, who was a great devotee of the church, upon the subject of what is called Redemption by the death of the Son of God. After the sermon was ended, I went into the garden, and as I was going down the garden steps (for I perfectly recollect the spot) I revolted at the recollection of what I had heard, and thought to myself that it was making God Almighty act like a passionate man, that killed his son, when he could not revenge himself any other way; and as I was sure a man would be hanged that did such a thing, I could not see for what purpose they preached such sermons. This was not one of those kind of thoughts that had anything in it of childish levity; it was to me a serious reflection, arising from the idea I had that God was too good to do such an action, and also too almighty to be under any necessity of doing it. I believe in the same manner to this moment; and I moreover believe, that any system of religion that has anything in it that shocks the mind of a child, cannot be a true system.

At the age of six, Thomas began attending the local grammar school, where his parents' class differences would become manifest. Father Joseph was a master craftsman staymaker, engineering the rigid foundation garment that created the heaving-bosomed, wasp-waisted shape of every desirable eighteenth-century Englishwoman. Stays were made from leather or linen, with ribs of paste, steel, or whalebone; they came as pairs laced together up the sides with ribbon (according to how much air a woman wished to breathe), and resembled body armor. Like a bodice, they were designed to be seen, with the poorest women wearing nothing else but a skirt, while the majority would at least have a mantua, a dress with upper folds exposing a coordinated pair of stays. As was the case with all artisans, Pain's primary creditors and most significant customers were local merchants, aristocrats, and gentry. When the economy soured and the bills of the well-to-do went unpaid, artisans were the first to be thrown into debtors' prison. By 1759, the twenty thousand incarcerated had so overwhelmed London's Fleet penitentiary for debtors that there was no room for the newest convicts, who were ordered instead to live nearby. They were comparatively lucky; Fleet's annual mortality rate was one-fourth its population.

The son of an artisan would typically expect to receive only a basic education in reading, writing, math, measuring, and bookkeeping, with perhaps some specialized teaching, depending on the field for which he would apprentice. As the grandson of a lawyer, however, Thomas would additionally be expected to become fluent in Latin—grammar in the eighteenth century meant Latin grammar—and to learn rhetoric, geometry, logic, dancing, and at least a smattering of Greek, all in preparation for college and then a career in the law, the church, or the healing arts. (There were exceptions to this standard, memorably for that son of a glover, William Shakespeare.) Pain would spend six years at Thetford Grammar, so it seems his parents were hoping that their only child would escape the frightful economics of craftsmanship—like those of so many of that era's independent artisans, the Pain family business drifted at a permanent edge of falter—and the adult Paine would remember that as a child "the natural bent of my mind was to science," which would seem to give Latin every educational priority, but "my father being of the Quaker profession, it was my good fortune to have an exceedingly good moral education, and a tolerable stock of useful learning. Though I went to the grammar school, I did not learn Latin, not only because I had no inclination to learn languages, but because of the objection the Quakers have against the books in which the language is taught. But this did not prevent me from being acquainted with the subjects of all the Latin books used in the school."

At the age of twelve, with the family able to afford no other options—it cost one hundred guineas to apprentice with a London grocer, three hundred pounds to join a brewery or pharmacy, and six hundred for banking or surgery—Thomas ended his formal education and his one chance to escape the destiny of his father's class, and began an apprenticeship in staymaking.

Just as his seven years of learning to custom-fit foundation garments came to an end, however, the world went to war. Like all global conflicts, this one began as an insignificant quibble, when in 1753 a twenty-one-year-old future friend of Paine's, who had recently inherited the rank of major in the Virginia militia when his half brother died of tuberculosis, was sent on a mission. British Virginia had heard rumors that the French were constructing forts along the western territories of the Ohio River, and the colony's governor sent this boy—volunteering for his first military assignment—to deliver a letter demanding that they immediately withdraw. The young major returned to the capital with the news that the French had refused to comply, and after a promotion to lieutenant colonel, he and a battalion were ordered to march to the Monongahela to reinforce British troops guarding the frontier.

As the redcoats tramped slowly through the wilderness, the area's locals—twenty thousand Iroquois—kept them informed of what lay ahead, especially the fearful rumor that the French had already defeated the British at the fort that was their destination. Just before they reached the river, Iroquois chieftain Half-King sent word that a party of French soldiers was waiting just ahead of them, and that his warriors would be glad to help the British kill them all.

On May 28, 1754, at 7 a.m., forty Virginians and twelve Iroquois assaulted thirty Frenchmen, killing ten, in a battle lasting fifteen minutes; the lieutenant colonel wrote his little brother that "I heard the bullets whistle and, believe me, there is something charming in the sound." In fact, these Frenchmen were not aggressive soldiers but diplomatic agents, and the young man who, with that attack, started what would become the first global war was George Washington. Two years later, Prussia's Frederick the Great invaded Saxony, and these minor skirmishes triggered an epic clash of France, Austria, Saxony, Sweden, and Russia against Prussia, Hanover, and Great Britain, with battlefields in Europe, Africa, and India, on the oceans, and in the New World. In the end, the key to victory in the Seven Years War would turn out to be an enormous strategic debt incurred by the rheumy-eyed first minister of England, William Pitt, the "Great Commoner" Whig for whom Pittsburgh is named. With colonials paid to fight in America and Prussians hired for Germany, Pitt both protected his king's ancestral homeland of Hanover on one continent, and made Britain the world's foremost colonial power on the other.

Like all wars, this one provided a cornucopia of opportunity for fearless young men, offering any number of positions that did not require fluency in Latin or fluidity in sewing. Just after those first Saxony battles in the summer of '56, perhaps additionally inspired by the recently popular adventures of Robinson Crusoe and Gulliver, Thomas Pain left home: "Raw and adventurous, and heated with the false heroism of a master who had served in a man-of-war [his grammar school teacher], I began the carver of my own fortune." Soon after he arrived in London, a notice in the *Daily Advertiser* caught his eye: "To cruise against the French, the *Terrible* Privateer, Captain William Death. All gentlemen sailors, and able-bodied landmen, who are inclinable to try their fortune, as well as serve their King and country, are desired to repair on board the said ship." Pain was making his way to the docks to sign up for the romantic life of a buccaneer when he heard someone calling his name. It was his father, Joseph, who'd tracked him down through tips from his fellow master craftsmen. Joseph was able to convince his son to reconsider a career on the high seas, which likely saved his life, for immediately after entering the Channel, the *Terrible* fell under assault from a French privateer, the *Vengeance;* only 17 English crewmen survived while more than 150 died, including Captain Death himself.

Joseph, however, either could not or did not persuade Thomas to return with him to Thetford. Instead, in the wake of a strike—London tailors and staymen having formed England's first union in 1720—the younger Pain was able to acquire a position under master craftsman John Morris amid the bars and brothels of Hanover Street in Covent Garden, directly adjacent to the Hogarth-immortalized slum of St. Giles's. Then, on January 17, 1757, he returned to the docks, ready again for the great gamble of his age, signing on to crew for Captain Mendez and the *King of Prussia.* Instead of suffering the dreadful fate of the *Terrible, Prussia* went on to capture the treasure of eight enemy vessels in as many months, with Pain returning to London on August 20 in triumph. His extant documents mention almost nothing about this wartime service, and it is unknown how he "retired" after a mere six months, but *Prussia*'s record of conquest would mean at least thirty pounds in commission (around $5,000 today)—a grand fortune for a young man just beginning to make his way in the world.

Thomas Pain would so fall in love with the city of London at this moment that he would return to it again and again, even at the peril of his freedom. A tall-for-his-era five feet nine inches, he had a striking face, with wavy brown hair and such dazzling blue eyes he was convinced that with one look, any woman would fall hopelessly in love with him. Pain's nose, however, was strikingly bulbous, and eventually it would be suffused with a skin condition, perhaps rosacea. The young-man-about-London could now afford to exchange his Thetford country-bumpkin homespun for proper clothing: linen shirt with a front ruffle of lace; damask coat lined with silk; waistcoat embroidered with gold or silver thread; knee breeches; garters; silk stockings; leather shoes with silver buckles; and a felt hat. As far as we know, Pain never used ceruse (a white lead powder used to camouflage the scars of smallpox), mouse skins to accentuate his eyebrows, or randomly applied beauty marks (popular with both sexes at the time), and he certainly never aspired to the fashions of the rich, such as Massachusetts import-export titan John Hancock, with his lavender suits, mink coats, and blinding yellow phaeton. With a little more luck, however, it is certain that Pain the vain optimist would have commissioned a full-length portrait in those salad years, posing with one leg fully twisted, the heel facing the viewer, and showing to the fullest extent possible that era's symbol of male power: the calf.

Our common impression of the eighteenth century is drawn from the perspective of a man such as Hancock: a life of eternal Mozart and minuet, plectrum and brocade, of winking fans and dying candlelight. In fact, the age of revolution offered more than a few compelling reasons to revolt. For every maquillage-bearing Versailles minion, there was an abrasive, monochromatic Puritan heretic, and nowhere can this duality be seen more emphatically than in the homes of the very rich. Though the century's most popular colors were relentlessly pallid—dim blues, faint roses, pale grays, those autumnal "sadd colours," with beige, ivory, and bleach white leading all, the latter seen in both male and female faces, pancaked into rigor mortis eclipse, as well as on talc-dusted, snowy wigs made from horsehair, goat hair, human hair, and duck feathers—the upper crust did not follow this tonal scheme with their decorating. Georgian architects mandated a strict nub of geometric precision for the exteriors of buildings (including double-squared façade widths that always equaled the heights of the chimneys). The interiors, however, were not executed with the same austere minimalism. Walls were painted in lurid, fruity glosses—acid lemons, screaming apricots, aquatic limes—or outfitted in embossed leathers and scenic mock flock wallpapers.

Unlike most successful privateers, Thomas Pain did not spend all his winnings on clothes, gin, and women; instead, "As soon as I was able I purchased a pair of globes, and attended the philosophical lectures of Martin and Ferguson, and became afterwards acquainted with Dr. Bevis, of the society called the Royal Society, then living in the Temple, and an excellent astronomer." Historians have long wondered exactly how this lower-class rarely-do-well became the most popular author of the eighteenth century and famed citizen of the world. He did it, we now know, in a signature American fashion—a rigorous course of self-improvement leading to personal reinvention—inspired by one of the most remarkable transformations of thought in world history. Thomas Pain would spend only a few years in London, but they would make of him a central figure in the creation of the modern world.

When this twenty-year-old returned to that city of 650,000 souls in 1757, he was immediately confronted by all that made his time such a staggering dichotomy, for London then contained the dazzling heights of Western civilization directly alongside a vertiginous maw of human depravity. Great sophistication, elegance, and beauty were found in the squares of Berkeley, Bloomsbury, Cavendish, and Grosvenor, the sites of an existence so elevated that Talleyrand would explain it by saying that if one had not lived as an aristocrat before the French Revolution, one could never know the full sweetness of life. At the same time, squalor, stench, and filth infected the slums of Whitechapel, St. Giles's, Cheapside, and Houndsditch (so named for being the preferred final resting place of city pets), along with grotesque amounts of pollution. "If I would drink water," Tobias Smollett reported, "I must quaff the mawkish contents of an open aqueduct, exposed to all manner of defilement; or swallow that which comes from the river Thames, impregnated with all the filth of London and Westminster—human excrement is the least offensive part of the concrete, which is composed of all the drugs, minerals and poisons used in mechanics and manufacture, enriched with the putrefying carcasses of beasts and men, and mixed with the scourings of all the washtubs, kennels and common sewers."

For entertainment, bluebloods might spend the evening strolling across the concert halls, pavilions, tents, ruins, promenades, and supper booths of the pleasure gardens of Ranelagh or Vauxhall, or perhaps enjoy the antics of the mentally ill offered up at the Hospital of St. Mary of Bethlehem (Bedlam), followed by dinner and a whore at the popular London bagnios, highly recommended as a great bargain by none other than Casanova: "A rich man can sup, bathe and sleep with a fashionable courtesan . . . it makes a magnificent debauch and only costs six guineas." There were more wholesome entertainments, of course; John Adams's daughter, Nabby, would remember a London vaudeville show starring a "learned pig, dancing dogs, and a little hare that beats a drum."

The hoi polloi, meanwhile, could enjoy bare-knuckled boxing, cockfights, dogfights, and one very popular game of chance, cockshailing, which involved throwing a club at a chicken tied to a distant post, with the successful executioner winning the well-tenderized bird. A visit to the Tower zoo cost a mere sixpence, while a few pence less paid for a spot at the bear-, bull-, and badger-baiting haunts outside Bloomsbury. If you were too poor to afford even that, there were many pleasures that cost nothing at all, such as throwing garbage at the prisoners held in the stocks of Charing Cross, enjoying the screams at the whipping station at Bridewell, and watching the final dance of the hangman's noose at Newgate.

The most popular sport of the eighteenth-century London poor, however, remained constant: full-fledged rioting. These episodes of democratic rout had become so frequent that British army troops were stationed nearby to assist the remarkably ineffectual municipal constables in quelling the violence against property. While working in London, Ben Franklin once wrote, "Do you Englishmen then pretend to censure the colonies for riots? Look at home!!! I have seen within a year, riots in the county about corn, riots about elections, riots about workhouses, riots of colliers, riots of weavers, riots of coalheavers, riots of sawyers, riots of sailors, riots of Wilkites, riots of government chairmen, riots of smugglers. . . . In America if one mob breaks a few windows, or tars and feathers a single rascally informer, it is called REBELLION: troops and fleets must be sent, and military execution talked of as the decentest thing in the world. Here indeed one would think riots part of the mode of government."

At the same time, no matter how stringently the Hanoverians kept adding to their list of crimes deemed worthy of execution, it seemed to have little effect on urban miscreants. Novelist and magistrate Henry Fielding said of London that "the whole appears as a vast wood or forest, in which a thief may harbour with as great security as wild beasts do in the deserts of Africa or Arabia." One of the era's underworld potentates, Jonathan Wild, was believed to have seven thousand employees; there was one prostitute for every twelve men, with girls beginning that line of work when they reached the age of consent (twelve)—if, of course, they managed to reach that age. Almost 60 percent of Londoners would die before the age of ten, with more than nine thousand children perishing from drinking gin in 1751 alone (a year when one-quarter of all the homes in St. Giles's sold homemade *eau de genièvre*). The city's 1758 Bill of Mortality is a striking account of this suffering:

> Christened: 14,209
> Buried: 17,576
> Whereof have died under two years of age: 5,971
> Between two and five: 1,795
> five and ten: 717
> ten and twenty: 556
> twenty and thirty: 1,362
> thirty and forty: 1,589
> . . . [Of] Convulsion: 4,417
> Consumption: 3,411
> Fever, Malignant Fever, Scarlet Fever, and Purples: 2,472
> Small pox: 1,273

With such extremes in their capital, is it any wonder that the London rich would spend the last years of the eighteenth century reading French news of guillotines and heads on pikes and wondering, in growing panic, when they would be similarly set upon by their own starving masses?

At the very moment that Thomas Pain arrived in London, however, he would find that alongside the squalor and inequity the discoveries of the Renaissance were culminating in a two-hundred-year apex, escaping the confines of the academy, the clergy, and the nobility to become a part of the very fabric of everyday urban life. Technology, society, science, and politics were each undergoing a staggering upheaval that would reorder the course of history, producing in the midst of this barbaric, feudal society what could only be considered a wholly new culture, including a wholly new way of thinking, and a wholly new religion—a religion of light.

Just as Petrarch had announced in the fourteenth century that the era of ignorance and darkness was over and that an era of renewal, of renaissance, was about to begin, so did one eighteenth-century philosopher after the next in Pain's time proclaim the imminent birth of an entirely new world. In time, a global avant-garde of highly educated, hardworking progressives dedicated to making the most of their lives through a program of self-improvement, education, communication, invention, pragmatism, natural philosophy, and virtue gathered in communities of correspondence as each, in turn, underwent a great awakening, an Enlightenment. As their intellectual and spiritual Renaissance ancestors had done, these eighteenth-century moderns traveled across continents and oceans to meet and debate; turned conversation into an art form; and strove to tolerate (if not even assimilate) contrary opinion in a universal search for truth among cosmopolitan gentlemen. The humanists had rescued the great works of classical Rome and Greece from monk-controlled athenaeums; the enlighteneds would learn Cicero, Seneca, Catullus, and Tacitus from these scrolls, and use their words for direction and inspiration. The intellectual and spiritual connection between the elites of the Medici and Georgian centuries was so powerful, in fact, that one historian would call the American Revolution "the last great act of the Renaissance."

If the educated of this era rejected aristocracy by birth to create their own cliques of merit, meeting through clubs, societies, friends, and acquaintances, then the biggest clique of all was a global effort of moderns carried on through correspondence—John Locke's Republic of Letters—reading one another's books, pamphlets, and articles, as well as an endless exchange of quill-scratched missives. In a sense, writing a letter was an eighteenth-century form of media; you expected that, besides the recipient, everyone in his or her family would read your letter; everyone nearby who knew you would also want a look; very likely, the friend carrying the letter for you (and anyone he might run into along the way) would read it; and, if you were a public figure, the recipient's local newspaper would publish it. The volume of correspondence was stupefying. Princeton University currently expects to finish publishing Thomas Jefferson's 75 volumes of papers, consisting of the estimated twenty thousand letters he sent and the thirty thousand he received, in 2026; Harvard's Adams Family Papers, meanwhile, are expected to total 150 volumes. It is clear, in fact, that the epistolary stalwarts of this era wrote letters convinced that we, today, would be reading them as well. They sensed that they were on the stage of history, that the future would be watching.

Everyone knew one another in this remarkably small world. In May of 1771, to take one example, Benjamin Franklin decided to meet in person his correspondents in the British Midlands. He visited a marble works, Joseph Priestley, caverns, a silk mill, Erasmus Darwin, an ironworks, James Watt, the Bridgewater Canal, and Matthew Boulton in his Soho Manufactory—in other words, nearly every key figure of England's Industrial Revolution. One London publisher, Joseph Johnson, meanwhile, would include among his authors Thomas Paine, Erasmus Darwin, John Aiken, Thomas Erskine, Henry Fuseli, William Godwin, Richard Price, Joseph Priestley, Mary Wollstonecraft, William Hazlitt, Thomas Robert Malthus, and William Wordsworth. One author, Immanuel Kant, offered a primer to those hoping to join this new global movement:

> Enlightenment is man's leaving his self-caused immaturity. Immaturity is the incapacity to use one's intelligence without the guidance of another. . . . Sapere Aude! ["dare to know," citing Roman poet Horace] Have the courage to use your own intelligence! is therefore the motto of the enlightenment. . . . All that is required for this enlightenment is freedom; and particularly the least harmful of all that may be called freedom, namely, the freedom for man to make public use of his reason in all matters. . . . The question may now be put: Do we live at present in an enlightened age? The answer is: No, but in an age of enlightenment. Much still prevents men from being placed in a position or even being placed into position to use their own minds securely. . . . Eventually, the government is also influenced by this free thought and thereby it treats man, who is now more than a machine, according to his dignity.

Kant was able to have a worldwide bestseller with this essay through a singular Renaissance invention, the printing press. The eighteenth century would transform printing, publishing, and writing into commerce, with the invention of hot metal type and the extraordinary new popularity of reading itself. This last development, without which the Enlightenment would never have existed, was in large part generated by a remarkably unlikely source, none other than the great scourge of the papists. A cornerstone of Martin Luther's doctrine was that everyone, even the lowliest of women and children, should be able to commune directly with God by reading the Bible. In his wake, churches of the sixteenth and seventeenth centuries began widespread instruction in literacy. By the eighteenth, many European state governments would take over this responsibility, with the result that a huge swath of the public would become literate. Autobiographical essays were published on the great revolution in thinking, imagination, and social status brought forth by learning to read; illiterates were, for the first time, considered mentally suspect. When the fourteen-year-old William Cobbett first saw Jonathan Swift's *A Tale of a Tub* in a store window, he spent every pence he had to get it: "the book was so different . . . it delighted me beyond description, and it produced what I have always considered a sort of birth of intellect." East London cooper Will Crooks found a used *Iliad* selling for a tuppence, and decided to take a browse: "What a revelation it was to me! Pictures of romance and beauty I had never dreamed of suddenly opened up before my eyes. I was transported from the East End to an enchanted land. It was a rare luxury for a working lad like me just home from work to find myself suddenly among the heroes and nymphs of ancient Greece." Some historians have even come to think that this mass eruption of literacy marked the very origins of adulthood itself, noting that in such pre-eighteenth-century painters as Brueghel, a whole town's population is in the street at dusk, playing the games of children. After Luther, there would be two kinds of Europeans: those initiated into the illuminating world of print, and those still playing with hoops.

As the century progressed, the number of books published in England would mushroom from six thousand in 1620 to twenty-one thousand in the 1710s and fifty-six thousand in the 1790s, while newspaper sales would rise from two and a half million in the 1710s to twelve million in the 1770s and sixteen million by 1801. Advances in printing technology transformed publishing to a new scale of economy and gave rise to the era's favored method of public discourse, the pamphlet, the medium employed in years to come by the Enlightenment's premier evangelist, Thomas Paine. This same economy would also make possible a new overnight sensation: the library. Previously, a middle- or working-class family might own a Bible, some other inspirational spiritual volumes, and a few business necessaries, such as almanacs, and read them over and over. Now they subscribed to circulation libraries or created their own collections by patronizing booksellers, whose shops became a nexus where the educated met and socialized. Before 1710, a monopoly on copyrights had been owned by London stationers, and writers were either independently wealthy or beholden to patrons. England then amended its law, so that publishers now had to pay authors for rights. Before 1710, there were no printer/publishers outside London; by the 1790s, there would be a thousand, based in more than three hundred towns and cities, while the number of men employed in the London printing business exploded from 198 in 1668 to 3,365 in 1818. Oliver Goldsmith observed that his fellow authors "no longer depend on the great for subsistence; they have now no other patrons but the public, and the public, collectively considered, is a good and generous master" (Goldsmith wrote bestsellers).

Europeans were now reading both because they had to and for pleasure. The term "autobiography" first appeared, and novels (such as *Tristram Shandy* and the world's first celebrity author, Laurence Sterne) revealed the beginnings of modern psychology in portraiture. Henry Fielding would declare in *The History of Tom Jones, a Foundling* (1749) that "I am, in reality, the founder of a new province of writing, so I am at liberty to make whatever laws I please therein." The first science fiction, the first children's books, and the first magazine exclusively for women were introduced, as was Johnson's *Dictionary of the English Language* (1755) and the *Encyclopaedia Britannica* (1768), these latter serving as testament to the boom not just in reading but in self-education, an Enlightenment hallmark.

In the entry "encyclopédie" of the *Encyclopédie,* Denis Diderot explained that his purpose was "to collect all knowledge scattered over the face of the earth . . . and to transmit this to those who will come after us, so that . . . our children, by becoming more educated, may at the same time become more virtuous and happier, and that we may not die without having deserved well of the human race." In such a spirit did gentlemen across Europe produce volume after volume, attempting to establish an ordering of *everything,* from Johnson's *Dictionary* to Erasmus Darwin's *Zoonomia* to Joseph Priestley's *History of Electricity* and Uppsala botanist Carolus Linnaeus's *Systema Naturae,* in which he invented the genus/species classification and naming system used in biology today. (Linnaeus would additionally hold a place in history for convincing Europeans that there were no such things as dragons.)

This rise in literacy and publishing cascaded into an explosive era of innovation. From 1660 to 1760, England granted around sixty patents per decade; from 1760 to 1790, the average jumped to 325. The first restaurants appeared; the systems of Fahrenheit and Celsius were invented; hospitals that actually tried to cure the sick (instead of merely offering beds for them to die in) were constructed. Stores stopped being addendums to workshops and became the forerunners of today's retail, in which shopping would be considered a pleasurable activity. Opening in 1759 to display the oddments collected by Sir Hans Sloane, the British Museum offered displays "not only for the inspection and entertainment of the learned and the curious, but for the general use and benefit of the public." This made it the first public museum, even though it was a difficult venue for workingmen to enjoy, being closed on weekends and holidays, and tickets taking months to obtain. (In its first year only sixty visitors were allowed to peer inside.)

Reading for education and pleasure was creating one kind of cultural revolution; addictive drugs would initiate the other. The seventeenth century had been for England a hundred years of violent tumult, with two civil wars; a "glorious" revolution; ongoing battles with the rest of Europe; endless civil disorder over religion (practically no English stained glass survives today, as it was shattered in the anti-Catholic rages of the Reformation and the civil wars); a countrywide siege of alcoholism from the introduction of gin; a 1665 epidemic of bubonic plague that killed a hundred thousand Londoners in that year alone; and a cataclysmic fire in 1666 that destroyed thirteen thousand London buildings, nearly the entire city. All this had taken a great toll on the political power of both the king and the noble families, as well as on the public reputation of anyone inclining toward political or spiritual extremism. The rising European middle class—mechanics and merchants both—had had enough, as captured in the lifelong motto of Talleyrand: *"Surtout, pas de zèle!"* ("Above all, no zealotry!")

For the first time, a new gentry could afford to indulge in the latest imported addictions—Linnaeus proposed naming hot cocoa "the drink of the gods"—as well as the time to enjoy such pleasures as cooking with sugar, snuffing tobacco, quaffing rum, infusing tea, eating chocolates, and most especially, drinking coffee. Originating in Constantinople and first popular in England with Protestants abstaining from anything and everything under Cromwell, the institution of the coffeehouse expanded dramatically. In 1663, there were 82 London coffeehouses; by 1734, there were 551. As the century turned, it brought with it an almost natural evolution, from coffee drinking, to conversation, to business opportunities, to business meetings—an evolution that would essentially draw the very society of London itself out of the courts of the boorish Hanoverians and into the coffeehouses, chocolate houses, and taverns of the middle class (which became nicknamed "tattling universities"). Soon enough, men like-minded in business or hobby began making regular appearances at set locations and turned them into clubs.

There were clubs specializing in poetry, foreign affairs, politics, singing, and farting. Import-export traders working the Baltic gathered at the Threadneedle Street coffeehouse, while James Boswell and Ben Franklin joined fellow "Honest Whigs" to pay eighteen pence every other Thursday at St. Paul's for beer, punch, or wine, Welsh rarebit, and apple puffs. One coffeehouse, New Jonathan's, attracted a club of bankers who eventually became the London Stock Exchange. Artisans gathered at the Robin Hood tavern to pay sixpence for beer and a chance to say anything a mind could produce (as long as it did not exceed five minutes). Even as small a burg as Glasgow was blessed with the Pig, the Grog, the Accidental, the Hodge-Podge, and the What-You-Please clubs. Some gatherings were dazzling in their membership: politician Edmund Burke, playwright Oliver Goldsmith, painter Joshua Reynolds, historian Edward Gibbon, and economist Adam Smith could be found at Dr. Johnson's Literary Club, meeting at the Turk's Head on Gerrard Street in Soho. The favored club of the Duke of Grafton, Paine's childhood aristocrat, was the Kit-Cat, named for a popular style of mutton pie, and frequented by power Whigs—Lord Chancellor Somers, the Duke of Marlborough, and the first Earl of Orford, Sir Robert Walpole—as well as such writers as Steele, Addison, and Congreve.

Beyond its impatience with zealots and its caffeinated temperance, this new and enlightened society championed tolerance, diversity, psychology, economics, reason, logic, courtesy, manners, and an elevated sense of urban bonhomie. Its members, however, needed a guide to make their way through this revolutionary new world, and they found it in an anthology of decades-old newspapers. Conceived by Kit-Cat Club associates Richard Steele (hoping to escape bankruptcy) and Joseph Addison (seeking a way out of academe) and published six days a week from 1711 to 1714, the *Spectator* would have a profound effect on the century's new meritocrats, as it would be read during its greatest years by a quarter of the population of London, and its complete bound edition would ever afterward be thought an essential element of every educated Englishman's library. Considered the first periodical to enjoy true mass readership, the *Spectator* was nothing like a magazine or newspaper of today; instead of the latest news on the most glamorous celebrities, it focused on the celebration of ideas, presented in a series of essays written almost entirely by Addison and Steele, portraying the life of modern London as it hurtled inexorably away from the ancien régime and toward a regime of consumers who worked for a living, all inspired by Horace's encomium *ex fumo dare lucem,* "to turn the darkness light."

Members of the Spectator Club—prudent, dignified merchant Sir Andrew Freeport; courageous retired soldier Captain Sentry; kind, foppish man-about-town Will Honeycomb; and eccentric, athletic country squire Sir Roger de Coverley—discoursed on the way to improve the happiness of all through a system of urbane courtesies and ethics greatly inspired by the philosophies of Aristotle and Locke. Writing from every coffee shop in the land (perhaps in a bid to match Voltaire's habit of fifty cups a day) was the paper's and this new society's éminence grise, Mr. Spectator, the prudent yet worldly-wise urbanite who was fascinated by and tolerant of every human foible, whose education spanned the great books both ancient and modern, who could always make an analogy of current events from his wide-ranging travels in foreign lands, and whose commentary on London society regularly employed nature's gift of human reason to propose the correct behavior and elevated standards suitable for the cosmopolitan citizens of the world—that is, the readers of the *Spectator.*

Rebuking Hobbes's vision of humanity as like a vulpine mob snarling over the smallest inch of gristle, Addison and Steele envisioned the society of tomorrow as polite, relaxed, peaceful, and good-natured as the regular denizens of London's café society, moderate businessmen who enjoyed their work, their reading, and one another. Even Boswell aspired to follow in Mr. Spectator's footsteps, since "a person of imagination and feeling, such as the Spectator finely describes, can have the most lively enjoyment." If happiness had a definition with this coterie, it would be the eudaemonism of Aristotle, as recapitulated by Locke: "I will faithfully pursue that happiness I propose to myself, all innocent diversions and delights, as far as they will contribute to my health, and consist with my improvement, condition, and my other more solid pleasures of knowledge and reputation,

I will enjoy." This pursuit of happiness is one of many Aristotle/Locke/*Spectator* notions that would appear in various significant documents, sixty years later, on the other side of the world.

Addison's Mr. Spectator was an apostle, bringing the ideas of the Enlightenment from the aristocrats and the academics to the middle and working classes, a position that would one day be assumed by Thomas Paine, who at the height of his fame would lead the life of a real-world Mr. Spectator, while a great many of Paine's "radical" ideas can be found, fifty years before, in the "good and gentle" newspaper's columns. Addison would also become something of an unacknowledged founding godfather of the United States, both through the Lockean notions cultivated in his essays for the paper and through his post-*Spectator* work as a playwright. His drama *Cato,* the story of a virtuous senator fighting corruption, treason, and Julius Caesar in a last desperate plea for the final days of the Roman Republic, would become George Washington's moral and dramatic lodestone, first read with the great love of his life, the married Sally Fairfax, and so admired that he would have it performed during the brutal winter of Valley Forge to inspire his troops. When the Americans ultimately triumphed, but his officers threatened a coup d'état against Congress over the nation's inability to pay their salaries, Washington used *Cato*'s act 3, scene 5 tactics in facing down his own mutineers (both left their audiences crying with guilt). John Adams had a favorite *Cato* motto—"We cannot insure success, but we can deserve it"—and Addison's writing is remembered today mostly through the *Cato* allusions of Patrick Henry (the original announcing, "It is not now a time to talk of aught but chains or conquest, liberty or death"), and Nathan Hale's paraphrase:

> How beautiful is death, when earn'd by virtue!
> . . . what pity is it
> That we can die but once to serve our country. . . .

Throughout the course of his writings, Paine would again and again take to heart Addison and Steele's utopian visions of liberty, equality, and sociability as the underpinnings of enlightened liberal democratic government. Even his epochal argument with Edmund Burke over the French Revolution and the course of human history could be argued to have originated with the arcadia espoused by *Spectator.* Siding with Paine in that dispute means believing (or hoping) that an entire nation might be politically capable of being as civilized, educated, and rational as the customers of an eighteenth-century coffeehouse. Paine would cite Addison at various times, though there is no conclusive proof that he read the *Spectator;* in fact, there are few surviving instances of Paine's saying that he read anything at all, which has led some historians to believe that he was a political-science idiot savant. In fact, Paine's typical refusal to cite his sources likely resulted from a trend in rhetoric at that time, where it was believed more convincing to rely on one's own reason than to cite a prior authority. It is implausible that he took part in the Enlightenment in London and the Revolution in Philadelphia, and impressed such a panoply of his era's great thinkers, without having read the same books that everyone else he knew had read. His closest, most famous friends during those years—Benjamin Franklin, Thomas Jefferson, and George Washington—were all Addison and *Spectator* acolytes, who did not just read the bound periodicals again and again, but would quote them and allude to them in letters, speeches, and conversations throughout their lives. Ultimately, it is not that the *Spectator* held the same concepts as Paine as that its pages offered up an ambience of utopian virtue for the new world in which his ideas would be born, a modern life blessed by public service, compassion, insight, sympathy, reason, benevolence, and merit, a life whose spirit Paine would strive to fulfill.

The young Thomas Pain's life in London café society revolved around his profound interest in natural philosophy, the key Enlightenment enthusiasm that would sweep through every social class. The most ardent students of nature were in fact artisans, those self-employed master craftsmen and wage-earning journeymen like Pain who made, in that preindustrial era, pretty much everything money could buy, a group we remember today from such names as Waterman, Webster, Thatcher, Sawyer, Sherman, Mason, Miller, Draper, Chandler, Cooper, and Cutler. In the eighteenth century, they called themselves "mechanics," and their great hero was the world's most celebrated self-made mechanic, Benjamin Franklin, who in *Poor Richard's Almanack* delineated their shared ideology: hard work, fortitude, thrift, patience, prudence, economy, moderation, sobriety, and self-improvement (qualities that could just as easily have been enumerated by Addison). While aristocratic enthusiasts pursued a mania for collecting barometers and thermometers, balances and forceps, quadrants and astrolabes, telescopes, microscopes, and orreries (mechanical versions of the solar system, with the known planets, modeled in brass and silver, rotating and revolving through a crank of gears), mechanics could make their own scientific devices, and knew how to both modify and improve them for their own inquiries in what by 1833 would be called "science," but was then known as natural philosophy.

This side of the Enlightenment revolution began when an itinerant academic, Bremen scholar-linguist-tutor Henry Oldenburg, working for Lady Ranelagh at Oxford, fell naturally into conversation with her brother, chemist Robert Boyle, and his friends, mathematicians John Wilkins and John Wallis, and astronomer-architect Christopher Wren. The group decided to turn their casual get-togethers into formal weekly meetings (another club), which Oldenburg called the Invisible College, but when Charles II gave them a charter in 1662, they became known as the Royal Society, with Oldenburg using his knowledge of nearly every European language to translate reports from Paris (on the controversial new method of blood transfusion), Herefordshire (advances in cider), York (Martin Lister on biology), and Delft (from his discovery by microscope that twenty hairs reached one-thirtieth of an inch, today we know that the wig of the father of microbiology, Antoni van Leeuwenhoek, was made of angora). Oldenburg published a collection of these letters in 1665 as *Philosophical Transactions: Giving some Account of the Present Undertakings, Studies, and Labours, of the Ingenious in many Considerable Parts of the World*—the first scientific journal.

Before Oldenburg's publication and the Royal Society's efforts (along with those of the other Invisible Colleges in Paris, Rome, Berlin, and Florence), the various occupations closely guarded their professional knowledge. Becoming a printer, cooper (barrel-maker), doctor, or clockmaker meant learning the secret methods of each profession, kept from outsiders by universities, guilds, and apprenticeships. Now having your new discovery published gave you the ownership—*and* the credit. For the first time, everyone wanted to be the originator of new ideas, and to tell the world of his accomplishments. If a natural philosopher wanted to contribute to Oldenburg's *Philosophical Transactions,* however, he had to do so in a whole new style of language. Journal editors urged their contributors to forgo the century's excruciatingly rococo style and oratory in favor of "a close, naked, natural way of speaking; positive expressions; clear senses; a native easiness; bringing all things as near the Mathematical plainness, as they can: and preferring the language of Artisans, Countrymen, and Merchants, before that, of Wits, or Scholars"—a style to be found in the prose of Thomas Paine.

One of Oldenburg's correspondents would spend his lifetime preferring *not* to publish his findings, especially his obsessive experiments with the alchemy of quicksilver (mercury), which would bring about his death. At the time of his first approach to Oldenburg, this natural philosopher was a Trinity College student using the simplest of tools to discover that light was composed of bendable rays (thus beginning the science of spectroscopy), and that white light was made from every color in the world instead of being the absence of all tint, as common sense might indicate. At one point, he slipped a bodkin between his eyeball and its bone, to reshape the eye's curvature and note the results. Proofs of these findings, along with the invention of the reflecting telescope (his was six inches long), brought him academic membership in the Royal Society, but it would be his response to a question posed by Edmund Halley and Christopher Wren about the geometries of planetary orbits that would make him the preeminent figure of his age.

Many historians date the start of "the long eighteenth century" to England's Glorious Revolution of 1688, and end it with the defeat of Napoleon, but they are a year tardy, for it is 1687 and the publication of this reply that would ignite the epoch. After reading this book, Voltaire would name him the greatest man who ever lived and announce to the Académie française that "we are all his disciples now," while Alexander Pope would declaim:

> Nature, and Nature's Laws lay hid in Night:
> God said, Let Newton be! and All was Light.

Isaac Newton's *Mathematical Principles of Natural Philosophy (Principia Mathematica)* explained how the force that pulls an apple from the tree also binds the moon to the earth (and attracts all objects to one another), governs the motion of the tides, times the arrival of the seasons, and shapes the elliptical movements of heavenly bodies. He combined Kepler's ideas of orbits with Galileo's on rotation to uncover the laws of attraction (gravity), and used the method of fluxions (calculus) to show how the entire universe operated like a machine, rationally and orderly, according to mathematical principles. Pythagoras had insisted the universe was a plenitude of numbers;

Principia revealed a cornucopia of formulae rising from the farthest reaches of the cosmos. In its wake, a great many moderns would no longer believe in an Old Testament God who was vengeful, mysterious, and inscrutable but in a Newtonian First Being eminently visible in the glorious benevolence of nature and the astounding beauty of the cosmos. As *Principia* itself would announce, "This most beautiful system of the sun, planets and comets, could only proceed from the counsel and domination of an intelligent and powerful Being . . . eternal and infinite, omnipotent and omniscient; that is, his duration reaches from eternity to eternity." Thomas Paine would in time suffer two hundred years of condemnation for writing a variation on these religious principles.

After Newton and the exhortations of Francis Bacon ("Knowledge is power"), Immanuel Kant ("Dare to know!"), and England's Royal Society (*Nullius in Verba;* i.e., "Take no one's word for it; see for yourself"), moderns came to believe that the forces of the universe were no longer divine mysteries to be forever withheld from mortals but phenomena that, by means of scientific experiments, could be elucidated by anyone. Across the continent and its various territorial possessions, any man who considered himself a gentleman bought or hand-tooled his own set of scientific instruments and conducted experiments, to see for himself—experiments that could be repeated and verified by others. In London, Pain, raised and trained as a mechanic, joined these Newtonians with gusto, arguing with them in coffeehouses; reading the newest scientific publications; regularly attending evening lectures (many at those same coffeehouses) on the properties of air, the behavior of comets, the ingredients of light, and the engineering of pendulums; and watching eidophysicons (magic-lantern slide shows), globes, and orreries, as well as demonstrations of the powers of electricity, gas, chemicals, and magnets. "Every person of learning is finally his own teacher," he said. "I seldom passed five minutes of my life however circumstanced in which I did not acquire some knowledge." Drinking, smoking, and arguing in St. Paul's Coffee-House at the Club of Honest Whigs into all hours of the night, he likely met such fellow moderns as dissenting minister Richard Price and pastor, natural philosopher, and political scientist Joseph Priestley, along with Benjamin Martin—spectacle-maker, mathematician, fossil collector, globe maker, editor of the *General Magazine of Arts and Sciences,* and designer of cometariums (showing their elliptical orbits), tellurions (showing the earth rotating and orbiting the sun), and lunariums (displaying phases and motions of the moon)—and James Ferguson—Scottish astronomer, mechanical engineer, portrait painter, and author of the enormously popular *Astronomy Explained upon Sir Isaac Newton's Principles, and made easy to those who have not studied Mathematics.* One of Ferguson's neighbors, with whom he was collaborating on the design of a new timepiece, was the revered Benjamin Franklin himself.

The moderns, however, did not limit their studies to mere "physicks" and "opticks"—the Enlightenment inspired them to question, debate, and ponder all received ideas, to reconsider all axiomatic opinion; the revolution of Newton had upended both cosmology and received wisdom. If the very movement of the heavenly spheres was determined by a simple act of gravity and not the manipulations of an unseen, benevolent Almighty, after all, weren't there other laws to be uncovered by gentlemen—laws of biology, sociology, even, perhaps, government? Could civilization be reengineered to more closely resemble the extraordinary workings of the celestial heavens? Could the balance of forces that perfectly holds the moon to the earth be applied to human society?

Within a hundred years, the coffee-shop and lecture-hall patrons of Pain's London milieu would become a commanding presence in Europe's social hierarchy, but in the England of his youth the vast majority of merchants and mechanics were barely one step above menservants and housemaids. Though Pain's childhood may have been fiscally meager, father Joseph did earn enough to keep the family fed and clothed in Thetford for his entire lifetime, achieving far greater success than the average craftsman, who was forced to migrate continually from village to town to hamlet in a vain attempt to eke out a living and escape the constant threat of debtors' prison. Such was to be the destiny of the young adult Thomas Pain, compelled for the next eleven years into recurrent poverty and wanderings under the pitiless gaze of an indifferent Albion. He would be so traumatized by this period in his life that when he made various proposals in the future for the welfare state, he always included among the beneficiaries, along with the poor and the aged, young adults just leaving their parents' home for the first time.

By 1758 Pain had exhausted his privateer earnings and was forced to leave London for work in Dover as a journeyman staymaker. The next year, with a ten-pound loan ($1,500 today) from his employer, Mr. Grace, he tried to start his own staymaking business in the town of Sandwich. There, on September 27, 1759, he wed Mary Lambert, maid to the wife of a prominent woolen-draper, and an orphan. Paine would later write the poem "What Is Love?"

> 'Tis that delightsome transport we can feel
> Which painters cannot paint, nor words reveal
> Nor any art, we know of, can conceal.
> Canst thou describe the sun-beams to the blind?
> Or make him feel a shadow with his mind?
> So neither can we by description shew
> This first of all felicities below.

Almost immediately after their wedding, Pain's staymaking business collapsed, Mary got pregnant, and they moved to Margate for her health and, very likely, to escape his creditors. She went into an early labor. As was all too common, neither she nor the child survived. Pain, twenty-three, wrote that "there is neither manhood nor policy in grief."

He moved back to Thetford to live with his parents and, perhaps inspired by Mary's tales of her beloved father, spent the next fourteen months studying to follow in his footsteps and enter the ranks of the Excise—inspectors of coffee, tea, chocolate, tobacco, and alcohol, who collected what Dr. Johnson defined as "a hateful tax levied upon commodities and adjudged not by the common judges of property but wretches hired by those to whom excise is paid." Excisemen (whose ranks in time would also include the poet Robert Burns) were loathed by common folk and menaced by the kingdom's twenty thousand owlers (smugglers), who knew that capture and conviction would mean a hanging, and who treated crown officials accordingly. The position paid so poorly that it inspired every sort of corruption, as well as requiring the applicant to prove his baptism and confirmation in the Church of England, and to call upon the social connections of any and all relations (in Pain's case, his prominent-in-Thetford maternal grandfather, Thomas Cocke).

By December 1762 he had passed the exam and was assigned to gauge casks in Grantham. On August 18, 1764, he was promoted to the Alford Out-Ride in Lincolnshire, fighting Dutch gin owlers along the coast and becoming so familiar with this landscape that he would one day recommend it to Napoleon as a good location for invading England and overthrowing George III: "as level as a bowling-green, and approachable in every part. The shore is a clear firm sand, where a flat-bottomed boat may row dry aground." The underpaid excisemen regularly accepted a shopkeeper's word instead of making a direct assessment; in July 1765, after less than a year on the job, Pain was accused of doing exactly this, and was fired. The details are murky, but there is evidence he was caught up in the corrupt practices of his superior, William Swallow, and scapegoated.

Pain decided to return to staymaking in the town of Diss, but lost or quit that position and tried again to get by in London. The only work he could find was as a private schoolteacher, but the salary (around half of what he had made as a taxman) was not enough to live on. On July 3, 1767, in the first letter of his that survives to the present day, Pain wrote to the Excise ministry, begging to be rehired: "In humble obedience to your honors' letter of discharge bearing date of August 29, 1765, I delivered up my commission and since that time have given you no trouble. I confess the justice of your honors' displeasure and humbly beg to add my thanks for the candor and lenity with which you at that unfortunate time indulged me. And though the nature of the report and my own confession cut off all expectations of enjoying your honors' favor then, yet I humbly hope it has not finally excluded me therefrom, upon which hope I humbly presume to entreat your honors to restore me."

On February 29, 1768, his petition was granted, and he was posted to the town of Lewes (pronounced "Lewis"), population five thousand, where he would live for the next six years. It was a harsh assignment, for the southeast seaboard was popular with tobacco, tea, silk, and brandy smugglers working the Kent and Sussex beaches with Dutch gin and French imports. At the same time, Lewes was (and still is) one of the most perfect of all English country towns, sitting high in the Sussex hills, eight miles inland to the east of Brighton, with a steep pitch to its streets and a port on the Big Ouse River, surrounded by an English dream of high and wooded hills fronting a green and pleasant pastureland for sheep, cattle, and horses, with the river offering salmon, trout, and eel. The adult Paine would repeatedly question the legitimacy of the British dynasty by recalling its brutal origins in the Norman invasion, an interest that may have sprung from the imposing Norman-era castle that still dominates the town's skyline.

If Pain had been exposed to an insider's view of British government in the corruption-prone patronage position of exciseman, and to an outsider's view of not-so-good-or-gentle John Bull growing up a half-Quaker in Thetford, he was exposed very quickly in Lewes to a radical view of his nation's history, which may have laid the groundwork for his lifelong philosophy. The town was known as a center of political and religious dissent starting in 1264, when Simon de Montfort and the Greyfriars Priory monks negotiated the Mise of Lewes from Henry III, considered the start of representational government in Britain. During the Civil War, the region was an active foe of the throne, consistently electing antiroyalist radical dissenters to the Commons. At the monarchy's restoration, Cromwell's son Richard evaded capture by setting sail from Lewes.

In Lewes Pain quickly made a lifelong friend of Thomas "Clio" Rickman, nicknamed for history's muse, and such an Enlightenment modern that his children would be christened Washington, Franklin, Rousseau, Petrarch, Volney, and Paine. Through Rickman's accounts, a Paine biography is allowed to turn from vague conjecture to the personal opinions of a very enthusiastic eyewitness, with Rickman describing Pain's "eye, of which the painter could not convey the exquisite meaning, [as] full, brilliant, and singularly piercing; it had in it the 'muse of fire.'" Rickman would remember his friend as a popular man-about-town with an outgoing, friendly, and quick-to-charm personality, the men of Lewes "being entertained with his witty sallies, and informed by his more serious conversations. . . . In politics he was at this time a Whig, and notorious for that quality which has been defined perseverance in a good cause and obstinacy in a bad one. He was tenacious of his opinions, which were bold, acute, and independent, and which he maintained with ardour, elegance, and argument."

Pain would find in Lewes something of the life he missed in London, joining the Headstrong Club, which met regularly for an evening's meal and a night of arguing over local and national affairs at the White Hart Inn, and frequently winning its informal prize—"General of the Headstrong War"—for the measure of his oratory. Standing before an audience hanging on his every word, Pain discovered the essence of his talent and the rhetorical foundation for the work that would make him famous. He loved the logic of debating, the thrill of stunning a crowd (not to mention his opponents) into silence, and especially he loved to dazzle with style and erudition, wholly the results of his own efforts in becoming a self-made man.

The first surviving Pain mention of politics was in Lewes in 1773 when, after an afternoon round of bowls, one of the town's patriarchs remarked that he considered Prussia's Frederick the Great "the right sort of man for a king for he has a deal of the devil in him." Pain wondered "if a system of government could not exist that did not require the devil."

The only other direct evidence of Pain's political life during his first thirty-seven years in England is a poem, "Farmer Short's Dog Porter: A Tale"—the story of a man who refuses to vote the way that the local powers that be insist he must. When borough magistrates cannot conceive of a crime to charge him with to force a change of heart, their attentions turn to his dog:

> That he, this dog, did then and there
> Pursue, and take, and kill a hare;
> Which treason was, or some such thing,
> Against our Sovereign Lord the King.

The authorities convicted Porter of sedition, and the dog was hanged.

During Pain's years in Lewes, a great and endless political struggle captivated the entire nation, and its central figure was John Wilkes. Son of a maltster, parliamentarian for Aylesbury, and member of the notorious Hell-Fire Club, Wilkes loved nothing more than to attack King George III and his ministers—along with George's very own mother—in the pages of his newspaper, the *North Briton*. The government replied by having Wilkes thrown into the Tower, but the lord chief justice ruled this a violation of his parliamentary privilege, and he was released. Asked at the time to define the limits of free speech in Britain, Wilkes said, "I cannot tell, but I am trying to find out."

The government would not be stopped. While Wilkes was visiting his daughter in Paris for Christmas (and recovering from a duel), Lord Sandwich led a successful campaign to have him expelled from the House of Commons. Now stripped of privilege, Wilkes was quickly tried and convicted of seditious libel and, when he decided not to return from France, declared an outlaw. After running out of money, however, he was forced to come home, where he immediately won a seat in Parliament for Middlesex and turned himself over to the authorities, who responded with a sentence of two years' imprisonment. Wilkes sought a pardon, and Whitehall arranged to expel him from the Commons once again. His bravery against the state had made him one of the most popular figures in Britain, however, and he was immediately restored to his seat by the voters of Middlesex.

The story of John Wilkes was a dramatic illustration of government corruption abridging the sacred and traditional rights of a free Englishman, and it would resonate strongly with the American founders, including Thomas Paine. Additionally, Paine would seem to inherit something of Wilkes's style of provocation, with the bons mots of both men passed along at every level of society. While attacking George III, Wilkes was invited to play a game of cards. He replied, "Do not ask me, for I am so ignorant that I cannot tell the difference between a king and a knave." When Sandwich predicted that Wilkes would die from the pox or the gibbet, Wilkes responded, "That depends, my lord, whether I embrace your mistress or your principles."

In Lewes, Pain received an annual excise salary of fifty pounds ($8,500 today), and reported to Thomas Scrace, who both oversaw nine excisemen and managed the Headstrong Club's haunt, the White Hart Inn. It's likely that Scrace introduced Pain to another city elder, who was looking for a tenant for his spare bedroom at Bull House, just up the street from the tavern. If there were any qualms about taxman Pain living with Samuel and Esther Ollive and four children over their store, which sold "Tobacco, Snuff, Cheese, Butter, and Home-made Bacon, with every article of Grocery (Tea excepted)," the great bulk of which he would be taxing, there is no record of Pain, Scrace, or Ollive making comment.

Like Pain, Ollive pursued two religions simultaneously, attending services under the nonconformist minister at Westgate Chapel next door to Bull House, while also keeping a pew at St. Michael's, directly across the street. Though his business was even more financially precarious than Joseph Pain's, Samuel Ollive was a respected town elder who was required to be a member of the Church of England to hold his post, as was Pain with the Excise. Samuel even served as one of Lewes's two constables (or town managers), and was a member of both St. Michael's Vestry (a church society that aided widows, orphans, and the poor through parish assessments) and the Society of Twelve, a governing body of the local elite. With Samuel's introduction, Pain joined both organizations, but no records survive of his involvement with local politics, save one legal matter involving a dripping roof.

The two men became so close that when Samuel died in July 1769, Pain tried helping the widow Ollive with the business in his off-hours. It was peculiar enough that an exciseman was living with a tobacconist; now he *was* a tobacconist, though for propriety's sake (whose it cannot be determined) he removed himself from Bull House. Eventually, on March 26, 1771, the thirty-four-year-old Pain married Samuel's only daughter, the twenty-four-year-old Elizabeth, but the marriage was never consummated. Pain never said why, telling Clio Rickman, "It is nobody's business but my own. I had cause for it, but I will name it to no one." Perhaps the Ollive nuptials were considered a business proposition by everyone concerned; it was not so unusual in that time (nor is it in ours). The parish record of their union refers to Pain as a "Bachelor," leading some historians to conclude that he hid his first marriage from everyone in Lewes, though perhaps it is more plausible to imagine that the same clerk who misspelled the bride as "Olive" was equally careless with the groom's marital status. There is another point of interest with this document, for one theory of why Pain changed his name to Paine after the worldwide success of *Common Sense* has to do with the flourish he always used at the end of his signature, one that can be seen clearly on these banns. So many mistook the decoration for a final "e" that perhaps he just acquiesced to the alternative spelling.

By this time, Pain not only was popular with the men of Lewes but had also become an admired and respected figure among his fellow taxmen. The story's details are unknown, but the ridiculous scale of excise salaries was clearly a subject of regular discussion among the service's employees, and when their financial condition seemed unbearable and they decided to act, they chose Pain to represent them. Clio Rickman reported that "in 1772 the excise officers throughout the kingdom formed a design of applying to Parliament for some addition to their salaries. Upon this occasion, Mr. Paine, who by this time, was distinguished among them as a man of talent, was fixed upon as a fit person, and solicited to draw up their case, and this he did in a very succinct and masterly manner."

Pain worked day and night to draft his colleagues' petition, *The Case of the Officers of Excise,* before the legislature. Its quality is exemplary, and its argument thoroughly convincing. The vivid imagery and caustic prose that would be a later hallmark aren't yet in evidence, but, following the style of the Royal Society and a Newtonian's love of logic and reason, the voice of the novice author is startlingly modern and remarkably ahead of its time—clear, forthright, plainspoken, and completely lacking the era's usual reliance on endless classical citation, rococo oratory, and convoluted sentence structure. It would also be one of the first published essays in England to argue that if a government does not wish to take care of its poor for humane reasons, it might wish to do so for the pragmatic purpose of lowering crime rates: "Poverty, in defiance of principle, begets a degree of meanness that will stoop to almost anything. . . . He who never was an hungered may argue finely on the subjection of his appetite; and he who never was distressed may harangue as beautifully on the power of principle. But poverty, like grief, has an incurable deafness, which never hears; the oration loses all its edge; and *'To be, or not to be'* becomes the only question."

The response among his colleagues was electric. Excisemen were treated with contempt by every level of British society, and Pain, by explaining their crucial standing within the economic scheme of British government, gave them a stirring reason to feel proud—an inspirational element that would appear in all his major works. Each taxman was convinced to contribute three shillings, totaling five hundred pounds, to print four thousand copies of *The Case of the Officers of Excise,* with the rest of the funds covering Pain's costs of traveling to London to present their case. There, his remarkable sense of nerve inspired him to forward a copy to the most celebrated Englishman of letters of that moment, Oliver Goldsmith, the playwright whose *She Stoops to Conquer* was about to become London's talk of the town. Not only did Goldsmith agree to have dinner with Pain, but the two began a long friendship, and Goldsmith would be only one of many celebrated figures in Pain's new London circle. The nervy Pain was developing a striking agility at inspiring the help and friendship of rich and well-connected men. One of his great supporters in the Excise, actively encouraging him on his mission to Parliament, was a fourteen-year commissioner of the Excise board, George Lewis Scott, who had known George III as a child and who had originally met Pain during his first years in London. Sharing with him a keen interest in natural philosophy and mathematics, Scott would introduce Pain to a group of friends that included historian Edward Gibbon, author Samuel Johnson, and the United Colonies' premier colonial agent.

On this third stay in London Pain spent two years waiting for a final decision from the government on the case of the Excise, having to take what jobs he could get as a private tutor after the stipend contributed by his fellow taxmen was exhausted. During that time, the tobacco and grocery business he had inherited from Samuel Ollive, run by Elizabeth and her mother in his absence, was slowly but surely going bankrupt. No letters between London and Lewes survive to explain exactly what happened—Pain would merely say later that "trade I do not understand"—but the most direct conclusion would be that the distracted child who could not learn Latin was now letting his business collapse while hobnobbing with the greats.

As would be expected by anyone more astute (or more cynical) than Pain, all of his great efforts on behalf of the poor taxmen came to naught. Between the public's loathing of the Excise and the government's interest in paying its employees as little as possible, this noble campaign was a fool's errand, no matter how beautifully written and carefully argued its petition. In an era when medieval guilds were on the decline and the general acceptance of trade unions was almost one hundred years in the future, the governing board saw *The Case of the Officers of Excise* not as a reasonable petition for a decent livelihood but as an insurrection to be put down immediately. Pain could not accept this explanation and would imagine other, more dramatic factors at play, explaining years later that his cause was undone as "the King, or somebody for him, applied to Parliament to have his own salary raised a hundred thousand pounds a year, which being done, everything else was laid aside."

Far worse, however, was to come. On April 8, 1774, Pain's long absence from his post without official leave led the Board of Excise to relieve him of his duties, whereupon he was subject to immediate arrest for debt. On April 14 of that year, a notice appeared in the *Sussex Weekly Advertiser; or, Lewes Journal:* "To be sold . . . all the Household Furniture, Stock in Trade and other Effects of Thomas Pain, Grocer and Tobacconist, near the West Gate in Lewes; Also a Horse Tobacco and Snuff Mill, and with all the Utensils for cutting Tobacco and grinding Snuff, and two unopened Crates of Cream-Colour Stone Ware." Immediately after, Pain and Elizabeth separated, with Pain receiving thirty-five pounds in exchange for agreeing to "not at any time thereafter claim or demand the said monies which [Elizabeth] should be entitled to at the time of the sale of the said House in Lewes aforesaid, or any of the Monies Rings Plate Clothes Linen Woolen Household Goods or Stock in Trade which the said Elizabeth should or might at any time thereafter buy or purchase or which should be devised or given to her or she should otherwise acquire."

At a time when married women were expressly denied property rights, this was an unusually enlightened outcome, but it poses one more unanswered question about Pain and his second wife. Neither party would ever seek a final divorce, and neither would ever remarry, though they would both live into their seventies and die a mere eight months apart. When Pain in later life learned that the Ollives were having financial troubles, he would anonymously send Elizabeth money, and when Elizabeth had the opportunity to pocket a tidy sum by agreeing to take part in the British government's drive to vilify her ex-husband, she would categorically refuse. Like his fellow British philosophers Isaac Newton, Adam Smith, and David Hume, Pain would, as far as we know, have no further romantic or sexual relationships with anyone for the rest of his life, and he would adamantly refuse to discuss the topic, as his French publisher, Nicolas de Bonneville, remembered: "Thomas Paine did not like to be questioned. He used to say, that he thought nothing more impertinent, than to say to anybody: 'What do you think of that?' On his arrival at New York, he went to see General [Lee]. After the usual words of salutation, the general said: 'I have always had it in mind, if I ever saw you again, to ask you whether you were married, as people have said.' Paine not answering, the general went on: 'Tell me how it is.' 'I never,' said Paine, 'answer impertinent questions.'" Paine's only surviving comments about this aspect of his life would appear in a magazine article, "Reflections on Unhappy Marriages"—"As ecstasy abates, coolness succeeds, which often makes way for indifference, and that for neglect. Sure of each other by the nuptial bond, they no longer take any pains to be mutually agreeable. Careless if they displease, and yet angry if reproached; with so little relish for each other's company that anybody else's is more welcome, and more entertaining . . ."—as well as in a 1789 letter to the newly wed Kitty Nicholson Few:

> Though I appear a sort of wanderer, the married state has not a sincerer friend than I am. It is the harbor of human life, and is, with respect to the things of this world, what the next world is to this. It is home; and that one word conveys more than any other word can express. For a few years we may glide along the tide of youthful single life and be wonderfully delighted; but it is a tide that flows but

> once, and what is still worse, it ebbs faster than it flows, and leaves many a hapless voyager aground. I am one, you see, that have experienced the fate I am describing. I have lost my tide; it passed by while every thought of my heart was on the wing for the salvation of my dear America, and I have now, as contentedly as I can, made myself a little bower of willows on the shore that has the solitary resemblance of a home. Should I always continue the tenant of this home, I hope my female acquaintance will ever remember that it contains not the churlish enemy of their sex, not the inaccessible cold hearted mortal, nor the capricious tempered oddity, but one of the best and most affectionate of their friends.

With the near-simultaneous collapse of his petition to Parliament, the bankruptcy of his business, the second firing by his employer, and the separation from Elizabeth Ollive, Pain was now at his life's first great abyss. He did not know it at the time, but this seemingly unconquerable mountain of failure would force him to risk all, to take a very great leap of faith that would lead to his immortality. As William Cobbett described it, "A little thing sometimes produces a great effect; an insult offered to a man of great talent and unconquerable perseverance has in many instances produced, in the long run, most tremendous effects; and it appears to me very clear that some beastly insults, offered to Mr. Paine while he was in the Excise in England, was the real cause of the Revolution in America; for, though the nature of the cause of America was such as I have before described it; though the principles were firm in the minds of the people of that country; still, it was Mr. Paine, and Mr. Paine alone, who brought those principles into action."

Beyond his own talent, charisma, and education, one reason why Thomas Pain was able to make so many friends in such high places in London was a new idea then making its way through the world: meritocracy, what Thomas Jefferson would call a "natural aristocracy," one based on talent and sweat instead of the luck of birth. Meritocracy would become so ingrained in the eighteenth-century enlightened mind that it would become a literary plot point, most famously appearing in one of the era's signature works, *The Marriage of Figaro,* wherein a worthless aristocrat is taught a lesson by his far nobler valet. (Beaumarchais, the author of the original *Figaro,* will play a very interesting role in the future life of Thomas Paine.)

The upheaval in belief of meritocracy was accompanied by another full-throttle reversal, the Enlightenment's extravagant optimism, based on a faith in an ever-improving future of eternal human progress. At a time when European religions were teaching that human beings were meant to wait for death and heaven to achieve pleasure and contentment, the moderns believed (against all evidence to the contrary) that the First Being who had created the glories of nature and the infinite mysteries of the human mind was clearly a benevolent force, and that human life was not intended to be an eternal vale of tears (or per Hobbes, "solitary, poor, nasty, brutish, and short") but something meant to be enjoyed. *Carpe diem* was even inscribed in the town square sundial of Lewes. Adam Smith, remembered wrongly today as a hard-hearted Darwinian precursor, believed that "the happiness of mankind, as well as of all other rational creatures, seems to have been the original purpose intended by the Author of nature, when he brought them into existence." A common theme of eighteenth-century documents is an endlessly bubbling optimism about the future, "the best of all possible worlds."

Perhaps it was his tremendous nerve, his faith in meritocracy, and that propulsive optimism that inspired the young taxman Pain to write Oliver Goldsmith and to carry on with his hopeless mission to Parliament, and to do what he would do now. After separating from Elizabeth Ollive and auctioning off all his earthly possessions, he returned to London, where he made his way to 36 Craven Street to meet with George Lewis Scott's dear friend, that highly regarded British-American colonial agent, the sharp-nosed and tight-lipped Benjamin Franklin, and almost immediately after, set sail for the New World, the promised land of final refuge, lost causes, second chances, and childhood dreams, as Pain remembered: "I happened when a schoolboy to pick up a pleasing natural history of Virginia, and my inclination from that day of seeing the western side of the Atlantic never left me."

Sometime between December 7 and 12, 1774, unable to walk because of the ravaging fever of typhus, Pain would be carried in a blanket onto the docks of Philadelphia, where his real life story would begin, the story of a life that he would start with but two assets. One would be his history with the London Newtonians; half of the population of Philadelphia, with 30 to 40 percent of its wealth, would turn out to be fellow mechanics, pursuing enlightened ideas. The other asset would be a cache of letters written by

Benjamin Franklin to the most important men in the New World, including his son-in-law, Richard Bache ("Beech"):

> The bearer Mr Thomas Pain is very well recommended to me as an ingenious worthy young man. He goes to Pennsylvania with a view of settling there. If you can put him in a way of obtaining employment as a clerk, or assistant tutor in a school, or assistant surveyor, of all of which I think him very capable, so that he may procure a subsistence at least, till he can make acquaintance and obtain a knowledge of the country, you will do well, and much oblige your affectionate father.

This simple letter marks the beginning of a remarkably close friendship that would last for the rest of Benjamin Franklin's life. After the great American hero lost both of his own sons—Francis, who died of smallpox as a child, and William, who abandoned his father to join the British during the Revolution—the bereaved father will turn again and again to Paine, calling him his "adopted political son." In turn, Paine will discuss with Franklin all that he writes and all that he invents. Over the years, they will grow more and more alike, coming to agree on nearly all matters large and small—becoming so close, in fact, that many believed that Paine's first great work, *Common Sense,* was wholly Franklin's notion.

Franklin and Paine were both born near the bottom rungs of Anglo-American society. Both had acquired an advanced education by their own efforts, and both believed in cultivating an elegant and stylish simplicity as an outward manifestation of republican ideals, traits they would share with the great American autodidact George Washington, to whom Franklin at his death would bequeath a humble crab-tree walking stick. Franklin was remembered as being notoriously argumentative as a young man; Paine would be accused of having a similar temper, and especially (and fatally for his political career in America) a marked inability to compromise.

Franklin and Paine fell in synch politically on almost every issue, from considering the best form of government to be composed of one legislature as democratically elected as feasible (though Paine would eventually come to see the benefits of bicameral systems), to launching public attacks on the institution of slavery. They were of exactly the same mind when it came to religion, though Franklin did not fully share Paine's almost spiritual devotion to human reason, dryly commenting that "so convenient a thing it is to be a reasonable creature, since it enables one to find or make a reason for everything one has a mind to do." Paine would regularly forgo royalties to more widely distribute his writings, just as Franklin would never patent his lightning rod or stove (and would never make a penny from either) so that their designs could be shared beneficially by all. The family member Franklin loved most, his grandson Benjamin Franklin Bache (known as Benny), would eventually become Paine's American publisher.

Paine lacked the experience of his benefactor's decades of training in commerce, civil service, and international diplomacy, which all contributed to form Franklin's notorious persona: reserved, impassive, and unforthcoming; he was a businessman, a politician, and a deal-maker above all else. Both Franklin and Washington vigorously created and brandished their public images and a granite restraint that were essential keys to their success as politicians, and though both would become two of his closest American friends, Paine never achieved this level of self-control. Spurred on by his massive nerve, he loved to provoke. Believing in the Enlightenment as an absolute truth, he would become as much an Apostle of the Light as any Saint Paul could ever be, and just as unyielding in his beliefs and as sanctimonious with those of less pristine dedication. Paine would in time make of himself the Enlightenment's greatest missionary, carrying the thoughts of the patrician avant-garde to the great mass of merchants and artisans. At the same time, he would be a living embodiment of Poor Richard, the secret personality that Franklin had hidden away for the sake of his business and his country, an outrageously controversial and very public savant who shocked the lesser-educated into imagining a new world in which they had a serious role in the affairs of state, and assaulted the corruption of power in the ancien régime across two continents.

In America, Thomas Pain will reinvent himself as Thomas Paine, and Thomas Paine will become Benjamin Franklin unleashed.

3. Pragmatic Utopians

"A LITTLE THING sometimes produces a great effect," remarked William Cobbett; "an insult offered to a man of great talent and unconquerable perseverance has in many instances produced, in the long run, most tremendous effects." Three hundred years before this comment, there lived a very different young man named William, a full-lipped, basset-eyed youth so devoted to his religious calling that he was imprisoned, repeatedly, for his spiritual beliefs. On August 14, 1670, when the twenty-six-year-old William Penn arrived for Sunday service, he discovered that the authorities had padlocked his church's doors. As his fellow parishioners argued about what they should do and where they should go, William preached out in the streets, drawing an audience of hundreds—until he was arrested once again, this time on the fabricated charge of inciting a riot.

Almost directly following this acquittal, William's father, a turncoat admiral of the English seas, passes on, leaving him a grand fortune, including a debt of sixteen thousand pounds (three million dollars today) owed by the very king of the land himself. That monarch, the restored Charles II, offered to give William a parcel of distant territory in lieu of cash, to which William eventually agreed, after deciding to use these lands for a "holy experiment" he would call Sylvania. The king instead believed that the colony should be forever inscribed as a memorial and a monument to his very good friend, the boy's monarchist father. They arrived at a compromise.

Pain's March 4, 1775, letter to Benjamin Franklin, recounting his first three months in the Quaker eden of Pennsylvania, is only the third letter of his that survives:

I was six weeks on shore before I was well enough to wait on [Franklin's son-in-law] Mr. Bache with your favor, but am now thank God perfectly recovered. . . . I attribute the disease to the impurity of the air between decks, and think ventilation would prevent it, but I am convinced it cannot remove the disease after it has once taken place.

I observe in Dr. Priestley's late experiments on air and your letter thereon, that vegetation will recover air rendered noxious by animal substances decaying in it, to its former purity. Query, whether it will recover air rendered impure *by respiration only.* If it does, it seems to indicate that air either has no vivifying spirit, or does not lose it, by passing through the lungs, but acts only as a cleanser, and becomes foul by carrying off the filth—i.e., not by what it loses but by what it gains. I have not the treatise by me, and may perhaps have made a useless remark.

[Franklin's son William] is removed to Amboy. I have not yet waited on him. Your countenancing me has obtained me many friends and much reputation, for which, please to accept my sincere thanks. I have been applied to by several gentlemen to instruct their sons, on very advantageous terms to myself, and a printer and bookseller here, a man of reputation, and property a Robert Aitken, has lately attempted a magazine, but having little or no turn that way himself, has applied to me for assistance. He had not above 800 subscribers, when I first assisted him. We have now upwards of 1500 and daily increasing. I have not yet entered into [salary negotiations] with him. This is only the second number, the first I was not concerned in. I beg your acceptance of one of the enclosed, and request you to present the other to my good friend, Mr. [George Lewis] Scott, to whom I intend to address a letter when I can have time and opportunity to entertain him with a few amusing particulars.

I have not time Sir to copy this letter fair, as I have a long one to write to my father wherefore I beg you to accept it as it is, and should he request you to take charge or forward a letter to me, from him, I entreat your kindness thereon.

Please to present my duty to Mr. Scott as early as you conveniently can.

I am, Honored Sir, Your much obliged Humble Servant,

THOMAS PAIN.
opposite the London Coffee House
Front Street

Pain had needed six weeks of bed rest in the home of Dr. Kearsley before he was able to find his own lodging and approach Franklin's relatives with his letters of introduction. In London, he had told the senior Franklin that in America his "particular design was to establish an academy on the plan they are conducted in and about London," so Bache (who worked in marine insurance, but had many contacts through his father-in-law) introduced him to various members of Philadelphia society, some of whom gave him work tutoring their children. It was a start, and came just in time, for he was running out of the small savings he had received through the Ollive bankruptcy and the termination of his marriage.

Regardless of what Franklin may have told him, Pain undoubtedly arrived in Pennsylvania filled with the encyclopedia of conflicting New World dreams known by all educated Europeans. Cornelius de Pauw, philosopher to the court of Frederick II, had sadly written in 1768 that "it is a great and terrible spectacle to see one-half of the globe so disfavored by nature that everything found there is degenerate or monstrous," with America being a "vast and sterile desert" home to "astonishingly idiotic" humans with dogs that never barked. Others described the obverse, imagining a great wilderness of awesome beasts, peopled by incorruptible savages.

At that moment in 1775, with a population of thirty thousand, Philadelphia was the largest, wealthiest, and most beautiful city in America. Though over one hundred miles from the ocean, it was the third largest port in the world after London and Liverpool, with two miles of Delaware riverside wharfage serving as the nexus between England, the Caribbean, and the natural resources (mainly lumber and wheat) of the Delaware Valley. There was endless traffic, not so much of horse and carriage but of barge, bark, cutter, dinghy, dory, ketch, schooner, scow, shallop, skiff, and sloop. For Quaker, Welsh, Moravian, Scotch-Irish, and Palatine German immigrants (who numbered one-third of the colony and who would one day be known as "Pennsylvania Dutch"), it offered the ultimate colonial allure of religious tolerance and fertile land. They in turn made it the most cosmopolitan city in the Western Hemisphere.

Newcomers were charmed by the modern grid of Philadelphia's streets, designed by William Penn himself—so rational, so enlightened, and so unlike the "wherever the cows may roam" style of Old World byways. Due to its industrious immigrants, the Quakers, Ben Franklin, and the vast civic energies of the Penn family, the city was blessed with a library, a hospital, a fire company, a medical school, seven newspapers, and brick walkways lit by whale-oil-fired street lamps. In his *Lettres philosophiques,* Voltaire would proclaim that the English had brought to America everything great about Great Britain, while the Quakers had created "that golden age of which men talk so much and which probably has never existed anywhere except in Pennsylvania." Even today, standing amid the restored brickwork, traces of two-centuries-old Philadelphia can be glimpsed, a brave symbol of English civilization erected against the dark frontiers of the wild, wild west.

Not everything was as golden as Voltaire imagined, however, and Pain found aspects of the colonies considerably unlike any New World eden foretold by Rousseau. "American," after all, was at the time a wholly pejorative term, referring to a provincial, backward, and inferior person or thing; a hillbilly cracker. In Philadelphia, Boston, and New York, America's three largest ports, packs of hogs still foraged through the streets, garbage piled up into repulsive hillocks, and clouds of stinging mosquitoes and biting flies chased sailors all the way from the docks to the whorehouses. The food was primitive, the colonial breakfast and supper consisting of cereal mashes, while the dinner, served between noon and three, was a boiled-for-hours stew that might include wild turkey, raccoon, deer, turtle, lobster, or goose. The Massachusetts colony was at the time offering a hundred pounds for Indian scalps taken from males over the age of twelve, while female scalps brought fifty pounds. Nowhere on the continent could be found a bank or currency of any kind; promissory notes, credit, and barter were the sole means of exchange.

The settlers of the United Colonies were such a motley lot that at the very moment of Pain's arrival, in fact, the entire continent teetered at the edge of civil war. Throughout the opening decades of the American Republic, one writer after the next would assuredly predict that this raging heterogeneous mix of class, religion, traditions, food, and beliefs, of Quakers, Anglicans, Baptists, Congregationalists, Presbyterians, Jews, Catholics, Lutherans, Mennonites, Moravians, and Calvinists, of Swedes, Germans,

Dutch, French, Scots, Irish, Welsh, English, Africans, and Amerindians, would never cohere into a unified nation. Though two-thirds of colonial America had come from one tiny island, and the vast majority of them from a very narrow socioeconomic range, they had, in every other way measurable, absolutely nothing in common.

Most of the Quakers living in Penn's promised land (today's Pennsylvania, New Jersey, and Delaware) had emigrated from the Pennine Moors in England's North Midlands, that wild and desolate Brontë countryside of *Wuthering Heights* and *Jane Eyre*. They believed that food was given by God for nourishment, not pleasure, and developed a taste for all things boiled, from dumplings to puddings, complemented with meat jerkies, cream cheeses, fried scrapple, and citrus curds. They believed in the spiritual equality of women, going so far as to allow the weak sex to minister and missionize, with one female evangelist even attempting to spiritually conquer the Ottomans through the conversion of Sultan Mehmed IV in his very own palace. The Friends' permissiveness with children was also considered strange, especially their disdain for corporal punishment, while in sexual matters, they were more puritan than the Puritans, and disapproved of everything from dancing to such "needless" games (which Pennsylvania law forbade) as "prizes, stage plays, cards, dice, may games, masques, revels, bull-baitings, cock-fightings, bear-baitings and the like."

The great majority of Massachusetts Puritans, meanwhile, had sailed from Pain's own neighborhood of East Anglia—Norfolk, Suffolk, and Essex—and, like the Friends, were solidly middle-class, needing to achieve that level of prosperity to be able to afford their crossing. Their "Norfolk whine" would become a Yankee twang, their saltbox architecture would be as commonplace in the New World as it had been in the Old, and when it came to cuisine, as David Hackett Fischer, the great historian of this migration, noted, "For three centuries, New England families gave thanks to their Calvinist God for cold baked beans and stale brown bread, while lobsters abounded in the waters of Massachusetts Bay and succulent game birds orbited slowly overhead. Rarely does history supply so strong a proof of the power of faith."

Americans living in the South, on the other hand, had been more or less personally selected to emigrate by the royal governor of Virginia. In a reign that lasted for thirty-four years, Sir William Berkeley enticed aristocrats to the New World with such great success that in the Cromwell era of 1650–70,

Virginia's population grew from fifteen thousand to seventy thousand. Unlike nearly all other immigrant groups, southern Cavaliers had supported the king in the Civil War, were Church of England in faith, and had been raised on baronial estates. The vast majority came from the southwest countryside known today from Thomas Hardy novels, where a precursor of the American southern accent could be heard. When this immigrant nobility had poor luck (and not much sport) hunting native American foxes, they imported English red ones. Unlike the Quakers, with their boiled cuisine, southerners loved frying, especially chicken, along with roast beef, hominy (a cousin to grits), and pleb, a mix of leaves, salted meat, and wild herbs, not unlike today's southern staple of collard greens. While every New England Yankee strove for a reputation as a hard worker, Virginians strove to appear as leisured gentlemen who never needed to sweat, regardless of how much they actually toiled. Differing attitudes about the necessity of working for a living—with the rich finding it distasteful, and the dissenting middle class believing it ennobling—would become a touchstone of the age of revolution.

The two-hundred-mile-long Chesapeake Bay, shared by Virginia and Maryland, was banked by remarkably fertile soil, and the richest immigrants bought up tidewater property immediately. After trying sugar, tobacco, silkworms, and vineyards, farmers in the Carolinas finally settled on rice and indigo (the eighteenth-century source of all that is blue), but the great plantations of Maryland and Virginia refused to diversify, all steadily increasing their economic dependence on tobacco and on the London merchants who purchased their crops, borrowing greater and greater sums from overseas creditors to stay afloat—the standard business model of southwest England. Thomas Jefferson's nonchalance about money—he shopped to the point of mania, and spent his adult life sunk in debt—was for men of his background no idiosyncrasy but a cultural heritage. Those same tidelands that could be cultivated into bounteous plantations, however, were home to enteritis, typhoid fever, amoebic dysentery, yellow fever, and the revenge of Africa: malaria, transmitted by *Plasmodium falciparum* journeying with the slave ships. Virginians would come to be characterized by Europeans as lazy, irritable, and quick to anger—all known effects of aquatic pestilence.

The last quarter of the eighteenth century would see the arrival of what could be thought of as the anti-Cavaliers—a huge migration of impoverished families (more than 50,000 from the north of England, 75,000 from western Scotland, and 150,000 from northern Ireland) fleeing economic rupture, political struggle, and endemic violence at the United Kingdom's borderlands to settle in the frontiers of the New World: the Pennsylvania backcountry, Appalachia, and the South's western outbacks. They imported variations on their north of England food—potatoes, whiskey, cornmeal mush (another grits forebear), and clabber (spoilt milk, curds, and whey)—as well as their language, with slang such as "cracker," "redneck," and "hoosier" originating at the border of England and Scotland, where cracker meant "a low and vulgar braggart," redneck was a "Presbyterian" (or any dissenter), and hoosier an overgrown, uncultured lout. Though Paine would never have much direct association with this group, they would for a time produce one Paine-styled philosophical ally after the next to take the stage of American history, including Patrick Henry and Andrew Jackson.

Is it any wonder that these disparate immigrants and their descendants had as little to do with one another as possible? They did share a few traits, one being the New World miracle of corn—eaten by cattle, goats, hogs, sheep, horses, poultry, and people; its stalks turned to fodder; its husks stuffed into mattresses; its cobs transformed into handles and pipes. Another shared taste was a direct result of the era's medical science, which meant that even the crudest New World backwoodsman knew to dig a well uphill from a privy, but not even a Harvard summa cum laude knew why. Water and milk were known sources of intestinal disorders (for many, fatal intestinal disorders), and therefore were disliked; instead, Anglo-Americans preferred boiled teas, coffees, chocolates, and fermented beer (most of which was watered down to between 0.5 and 1 percent alcohol, coincidentally just enough to keep it from carrying typhoid, cholera, and dysentery), along with molasses rum, peach brandy, apple cider, gin, and flip (beer mixed with sugar, molasses, or dried pumpkin). Why did the Pilgrims settle in Massachusetts instead of continuing on south, as originally planned? They had run out of beer.

It is impossible to imagine an odder muddle of two million human creatures, thrown together at the very edge of the civilized world. At least in the mother country, when it came to the crucial tenets of earth and lucre, there were centuries-old traditions of inheritance and caste and yeomen and husbandry to follow, and when it came to politics, there was the great pride in being a free son of Britain. Unlike subjects of the tyrannical monarchs of France, Spain, and the German states (whose legislatures—Etats-Généraux, Cortes, and various diets—had all but vanished), English citizens had a Parliament to represent them (even though it was controlled for centuries by landed aristocrats), and various rights and freedoms as bulwarks against the greed and corruption of kings and bluebloods. In America, however, Whitehall had created a distorted mirror where the grand traditions of Albion did not quite apply, and whose inhabitants wielded far more political power and sophistication in their little outposts than the great majority of Englishmen did at home.

The startling political differences began at the very outset, when New World landowners needed to offer something beyond spiritual refuge to get Britons to emigrate. In addition to extravagant descriptions of awaiting paradises and luxuriant farmlands, a key element of the sales pitch was a charter of enticements. William Penn's "Concessions . . . or Fundamental Rights" of West New Jersey, for example, offered such terms as "no men nor number of men upon earth hath power or authority to rule over men's conscience in religious matters" and no man "shall be deprived or condemned of life, limb, liberty, estate, property . . . without a due trial and judgment passed by twelve good and lawful men of his neighborhood." Brave the Atlantic, other contracts promised, and anyone with fifty acres (available to newcomers at extremely favorable rates) would have the right to vote for the provincial assembly. Come to the New World, many offered, and you will pay no taxes beyond what you and your fellow colonists agree on.

Across the centuries, British law had granted suffrage based on land, but this provision, which limited the British electorate to a mere one-fifth of the population, would have decidedly different consequences in America, where two-thirds were property owners who voted, greatly broadening the political involvement of the working and middle classes, and dramatically strengthening the power of the legislature. The colonial government employees may have been appointed by king and Parliament, but king and Parliament were thousands of miles away, as historian Paul Rahe described: "The appointed governors soon discovered that in America the legislature really was supreme, in part as a consequence of the reforms pressed on the Board of Trade in the late 1690s by John Locke, in part as a result of local initiative and legislation, and in part as the governors had very little in the way of patronage to influence the deliberations of the colonial assemblies. There were no rotten boroughs in the New World; those who represented a given locality paid close attention to the sentiments of their constituents. . . . Where visitors from the continent of Europe were inclined to suppose that they had seen in England the future of the human race, well-to-do Americans who crossed the Atlantic were prone to think that they had made a journey into the distant past."

A decided lack of attention paid to these dramatic advances in colonial living is just one example of how wholly uninterested the British were in directly managing any of their overseas empire, beyond regulating commerce. Beginning with Charles II's restoration, the navigation (or mercantile) laws of the kingdom required everything exported from the North American colonies (hides and lumber, tar and turpentine, tobacco and indigo, iron and copper, pitch and potash) to pass through English ports before being sold elsewhere, and all imports to British America (anything and everything manufactured) to do likewise. If colonials wanted to buy something French or Spanish instead of English, they would have to pay 25 to 40 percent extra for the privilege, just because they were colonists, and these were only the basic rates of a dizzying and ever-changing encyclopedia of tariffs and restrictions and law. Americans were allowed to trap beavers and minks, but not to make anything from their furs to sell. They could dig and ship pig ore, but not export metalwork. They could not export anything knitted or woven. They could not sell hats. The entire point of Adam Smith's 1776 *An Inquiry into the Nature and Causes of the Wealth of Nations* was an attack on the foolishness of governmental interference in the economy in general and the mercantile system in particular. Additionally, these always evolving laws meant that while the great mass of English citizens paid little attention to the doings of Whitehall, every American who worked for a living needed to follow the minutiae of overseas government policy. With the strike of a pen, the whims of King George and his pocket Parliament could destroy everything they had.

When Pain arrived in 1774, the richest tenth of Philadelphia's citizens owned more than 50 percent of its wealth, and followed the English tradition of spending winters in urban town homes and the rest of the year in country estates. Half of the city, however, was mechanics, who followed the news of changes in British mercantile law as closely as anyone in the shopkeeping or import trades. Three years before Pain's arrival, master craftsmen had deserted the Franklin-directed Quaker Society political organization over disagreements with city merchants on British import law, in order to form their own mechanics-only group, the Patriotic Society. Pain would join his fellow workingmen there, as well as eating, drinking, and debating at the Indian Queen, an American version of Lewes's Headstrong Club or London's Honest Whigs.

But Pain met more than mechanics as he browsed the titles of the Philadelphia Library Company and attended lectures hosted by the American Philosophical Society, where he would eventually be accepted as a member. Founded in 1743 for "the promoting of useful knowledge, especially as it respects the agriculture, manufactories, and natural history of North America," this United Colonies rendition of the Royal Society was the headquarters for the greatest of American intellectuals, including such future Pain friends as clockmaker, surveyor, state treasurer, astronomer, and first director of the U.S. Mint David Rittenhouse. As his study of Newton and his personal charisma had brought Pain such friends as Scott and Franklin in London, so now, alongside the introductions of Richard Bache, it would bring him to the heart of Philadelphia's burgeoning enlightened society.

The most important Philadelphian in Pain's life after Ben Franklin, however, would turn out to be a man he met while visiting the printshop and bookstore next to his riverside rooming house on the corner of Front and Market streets. Robert Aitken was its owner, and Pain spent so much time there that on January 10, 1775, the two fell into conversation. Pain greatly impressed Aitken (who had himself arrived in the New World from Scotland just a few years before), to the point where the printer decided to offer him a job as executive editor of his brand-new magazine.

Clad in a blue paper cover under the motto *Fuval in sylvis habilare* ("Happy it is to live in the woods"), *Pennsylvania Magazine; or, American Monthly Museum* would at first follow the strict formula of almost every other eighteenth-century publication, with their overriding tone of smothering pleasantness. Maidens, flowers, glades, and scampering forest creatures made regular appearances, while disputatious essays on religion or politics were strictly forbidden. A typical issue would additionally include such up-to-the-minute concerns as an explication of the constitution of beavers, a biography of Voltaire, a land-surveying mathematical puzzle, an essay on suicide, the announcement of a new machine for generating electricity, treatises on self-improvement and the inexorable law of progress, current Philadelphia commodity prices, the text of the Continental Congress's writ to George III, and extensive descriptions and illustrations of the latest and most exciting European inventions, the latter being must-reads for Philadelphia moderns, those American Philosophical Society members who would become Pain's personal friends and political allies in the decade to come.

The first issue, fifty-two pages long, appeared on January 24, 1775, and sold six hundred copies. Within a few months of Pain's stewardship, however, *Pennsylvania Magazine* would attract more than fifteen hundred paid subscribers, making it the most widely read New World periodical. The new editor's first article, "The Magazine in America," outlined his aspirations: "The two capital supports of a magazine are utility and entertainment. The first is a boundless path, the other an endless spring. . . . I have no doubt of seeing, in a little time, an American magazine full of more useful matter than I ever saw an English one: Because we are not exceeded in abilities, have a more extensive field for enquiry; and, whatever may be our political state, *Our happiness will always depend upon ourselves*. . . . I consider a magazine as a kind of bee-hive, which both allures the swarm, and provides room to store their sweets. Its division into cells, gives every bee a province of its own; and though they all produce honey, yet perhaps they differ in their taste for flowers."

About half of each issue was written by three men: lawyer Francis Hopkinson, College of New Jersey (today Princeton) president John Witherspoon, and Pain, who used such pseudonyms as Justice and Humanity, Humanus, Atlanticus, Vox Populi, and Aesop, at first to make the magazine seem to have more contributors than it actually did (a common practice for every European and American publication), but eventually as a cover for his more treasonous and incendiary material. Besides "The Magazine in America," he would contribute "Description of a New Electrical Machine" and "A Mathematical Question Proposed" for the January issue; "Useful and Entertaining Hints on the Internal Riches of the Colonies," "The Critic and the Snowdrop," and "New Anecdotes of Alexander the Great" for February; "Reflections on the Life and Death of Lord Clive," "The Monk and the Jew," and "The Death of General Wolfe" for March; and "A New

Method of Building Frame Houses," "Cupid and Hymen," and "An Account of the Burning of Bachelor's Hall" for April. Some later Paine critics would find in the brevity of his three famous works evidence of laziness; considering the volume of essays he produced in the first months of *Pennsylvania Magazine,* however, it is hard to imagine a more industrious editor and contributor.

Years later Isaiah Thomas interviewed publisher Aitken for his *History of Printing in America.* By then Aitken and Pain were no longer speaking, having waged a very bitter and very public battle over salary and title, and this may have colored Aitken's reminiscence:

> On one of the occasions, when Paine had neglected to supply the material for the magazine, with a short time of the day of publication, Aitken went to his lodgings, and complained of his neglecting to fulfill his contract. Paine heard him patiently, and coolly answered, "You shall have them in time." Aitken expressed some doubts on the subject, and insisted on Paine's accompanying him and proceeding immediately to business, as the workmen were waiting for copy. He accordingly went home with Aitken, and was soon seated at the table with the necessary apparatus, which always included a glass, and a decanter of brandy. Aitken observed, "he would never write without that." The first glass put him in a train of thinking; Aitken feared the second would disqualify him, or render him intractable; but it only illuminated his intellectual system; and when he had swallowed the third glass, he wrote with great rapidity, intelligence and precision; and his ideas appeared to flow faster than he could commit them to paper. What he penned from the inspiration of the brandy, was perfectly fit for the press without alteration, or correction.

For the first time in his life, Thomas Pain had found an occupation that fully matched his talents and his aspirations. He was almost immediately a tremendous success, both with the magazine's readership and with his own ever-expanding social sphere. He admitted that he had found the "one kind of life I am fit for, and that is a thinking one, and, of course, a writing one." The consequences of this second round of apprenticeship reversed thirty-seven years of failure and psychologically transformed him. Pain would no longer be that callow boy who couldn't bring himself to learn his

Latin or that selfish excise officer who let his family business collapse as he sought glory in the big city. He was now a man thoughtful in his private life, and sedulous in his profession, while pursuing the holy grail of eighteenth-century moderns: *virtue.*

What heaven is for Christians, virtue was for those educated in the values of the Enlightenment. With its origins in *vir,* the Latin word for man, and considered the ultimate goal of every meritocrat, *virtù* was originally translated as "public spirit," for, as described by a line of philosophers from Aristotle to Montesquieu, it referred to someone so devoted to civic service that he became famous in his lifetime, and after death was remembered by history for his great and generous work. Machiavelli had warned that democratic states depended on the virtue of their citizens, for if a love of power inspired "factions" to pursue private interests in lieu of the greater good, or if *fortuna* (an epicene lust for riches and luxury) defeated *virtù,* corruption and tyranny would be the inevitable result. Time and again across the years of revolution and republic, the American founding fathers would worry that their reputations were being sullied, despite their assiduous efforts at leading lives of sterling virtue.

A key point of this ethic was to first become so successful in business as to satisfy the financial needs of one's family that one could then afford the charity of public service, but Pain, like Samuel Adams (who lived in such poverty that he needed the donations of friends to be dressed properly as a delegate to the 1774 Continental Congress), omitted that step. Instead, he would leap directly to relinquishing a great fortune in order to more widely spread the teachings of the Enlightenment to improve the lives of future  generations. When, at the start of his writing career, he was not fairly reimbursed as the world's bestselling author due to living in the copyright-free American frontier, Pain would entirely forgo all royalties, which made it possible to reduce the cover price so that almost anyone could afford his pamphlets. He described his new character to one of his closest friends: "You will say that in this classification of citizens I have marked no place for myself; that I am neither farmer, mechanic, merchant nor shopkeeper. I believe, however, I am of the first class. I am a *farmer of thoughts,* and all the crops I raise I give away."

Just as he had so ardently converted to the causes of Newton and the Enlightenment in London, Pain now became more of an American than any native son. As an editor, he regularly sought to publish articles on more substantive issues, including attacks on cruelty to animals and the barbaric tradition of dueling. It was long believed that Pain also wrote one of the most famous articles ever published in *Pennsylvania Magazine,* "An Occasional Letter on the Female Sex," one of the first arguments in favor of women's rights in America. It has since been shown that he did not write the piece, but that it appeared under his editorship shows the type of progressive modern work he and Aitken were championing. In his role as printer and businessman, Aitken at times, however, refused to go forward with some of the more avant-garde material, and Pain would have to turn to the *Pennsylvania Journal* or the *Ledger* to publish them. One of these pieces was cowritten with Thomas Pryor in November 1775, "Experiments for Making Saltpeter in Private Families," saltpeter being a crucial component of gunpowder. Another was one of the first public attacks on slavery. Philadelphia's slave auctions were held in an outdoor shed across the street from Pain's own room, and would-be bidders could inspect the merchandise at the London Coffee House next door. Seeing this inspired Pain to publish a shocking essay, years ahead of its time, that assaulted every excuse for the trade and demanded immediate emancipation for all Africans in every colony:

> Our traders in men (*an unnatural commodity!*) must know the wickedness of that slave-trade, if they attend to reasoning, or the dictates of their own hearts. . . . They show as little reason as conscience who put the matter by with saying—"Men, in some cases, are lawfully made slaves, and why may not these?" So men, in some cases, are lawfully put to death, deprived of their goods, without their consent; may any man, therefore, be treated so . . . ? Nor is this plea mended by adding—"They are set forth to us as slaves, and we buy them without farther inquiry, let the sellers see to it." Such man may as well join with a known band of robbers, buy their ill-got goods, and help on the trade; ignorance is no more pleadable in one case than the other; the sellers plainly own how they obtain them. But none can lawfully buy without evidence that they are not concurring with men-stealers; and as the true owner has a right to reclaim his goods that were stolen, and sold; so the slave, who is proper owner of his freedom, has a right to reclaim it, however often sold. . . . Is the barbarous enslaving our inoffensive neighbours, and treating them like wild beasts subdued by force, reconcilable with

> the divine precepts? Is this doing to them as we would desire they should do to us? If they could carry off and enslave some thousands of us, would we think it just?—One would almost wish they could for once; it might convince more than reason, or the Bible.

African Slavery in America was so vigorous, intemperate, and influential that five weeks after its publication, on April 14, 1775, Philadelphians formed the Pennsylvania Society for the Relief of Negroes Unlawfully Held in Bondage, the first abolitionist organization in the Western Hemisphere. The nerve of this essay, the same kind of nerve that had inspired the younger Pain to present himself to Oliver Goldsmith, in time triggered a chain reaction, one eventually leading to Pain's becoming Paine, as Dr. Benjamin Rush remembered: "I met him accidentally in Mr. Aitkin's bookstore, and was introduced to him by Mr. Aitkin. We conversed a few minutes, and I left him. Soon afterwards I read a short essay with which I was much pleased, in one of Bradford's papers, against the slavery of the Africans in our country, and which I was informed was written by Mr. Paine. This excited my desire to be better acquainted with him."

One of the first to champion inoculations for children and humane treatment for the mentally ill (instead of condemning them for being possessed by devils), the hawk-eyed Benjamin Rush believed that all disease had one source—overactive blood—making him one of medical history's most enthusiastic purgers. A scion of Philadelphia who attended medical school at the famed University of Edinburgh, Rush would be a signer of the Declaration of Independence, a surgeon for the Continental Army, treasurer of the U.S. Mint under his dear friend President John Adams, and one of the cofounders of the Pennsylvania Society for Promoting the Abolition of Slavery, the successor to the organization formed in the wake of Pain's essay. Rush would be a principal of both organizations, and publish essays as an ardent abolitionist, while continuing to own slaves himself.

Dr. Rush was, like Pain, immersed in Enlightenment thinking, strong-willed, and always ready to say exactly what was on his mind. They differed, however, in that the physician was one of America's founding-father workaholics, keeping to an early-to-bed, early-to-rise clock of Presbyterian discipline and disdaining (as much as possible in that era) liquor. Pain, on the other hand, loved meeting with friends for talking, debating, and drinking at all hours of the night; he slept away the mornings, and thoroughly enjoyed a good afternoon nap. Rush and Pain's friendship became very close very quickly, however, through their shared feelings and beliefs on science, abolition, and the education of women, and on the most pressing issue of the day: the recent dawn, in blood, of the colonial civil war.

What would eventually be called the American Revolution had its roots in the same state crisis—chronic, staggering war debt—that had been a key ingredient of the English civil wars and would become a foundation of the French Revolution. Though England had won the Seven Years War, annual government expenses had risen from £6.5 million to £14.5 million, with a final debt of £140 million ($25 billion today). Clearly state revenue needed to be dramatically increased, but when the government had merely applied a new tax on cider, mobs had run riot in the streets, for Britons were already being taxed as much as they could stand. Americans, however, were very lightly tariffed by empire standards, and could provide a new and worry-free source of income, as colonials could not destroy London property or vote anyone out of Parliament.

First Minister George Grenville had decided in 1765 to institute a new colonial excise on anything made of paper—newspapers, magazines, almanacs, licenses, contracts, leases, wills, bills of lading, playing cards—and dice. This Stamp Act seemed straightforward enough, but in reply, Virginia burgess Patrick Henry announced that if the government of George III wished to pursue unconstitutional policies, Americans would do for him what Cromwell had done for Charles I, and Brutus for Caesar. The colonials had in fact begun arguing over this matter the year before, when West Indies sugar barons seemed on the verge of bankruptcy and Parliament decided to support them by charging North Americans additional tariffs on sugar, rum, and molasses. Besides the terrific popularity of rum across the Atlantic seaboard, sugar had become such a critical element of the local diet that a number of import-export men, notably Boston's John Faneuil and John Hancock, began smuggling untariffed sugar products. Local customs officers responded by issuing writs of assistance and sending in sheriffs to search the houses, warehouses, and boats of anyone who was suspected of breaking the law. When Faneuil and Hancock were arrested, they hired James Otis for the defense; he both attacked the legality of the writs and announced in the middle of the trial that "taxation without representation is tyranny!" When it was explained to Otis that, though the colonists may not have direct representatives in Parliament, they did have *virtual* representatives, just like the great majority of British subjects who were not allowed to vote, he replied that the answer was to end virtual representation by granting the right of voting to all.

One of the greatest of the Stamp Act opponents was the glaring-eyed Samuel Adams, a distant cousin to John, whose life and ideas would in many ways directly parallel Paine's at the same time that John Adams would become Paine's great political and philosophical antagonist. Just as Paine communicated the revolutionary ideas of the Enlightenment to the middle and working classes and even to the illiterate, Sam Adams spoke directly with Boston's workingmen in their taverns and clubs, explaining the politics of liberty and the policies of mercantilism. Both Paine and Adams had worked for the British government as taxmen and for United Colonies legislatures as clerks, both were exceedingly righteous in pursuing a life of virtue in service to the public good, and both were decades ahead of their time in their political thinking. As a member of the Continental Congress, Adams would be the first in the federal government to avidly support Paine's *Common Sense.* In 1765, meanwhile, the Americans pursued a startlingly effective consumer boycott of British goods, organized by Samuel Adams, which convinced merchants to prominently display signed nonimportation agreements; merchants who did not sign were listed in the local papers as "Enemies to American Liberty." In Boston a horde of mechanics, innkeepers, fishermen, and merchants, led by Adams and calling itself the Sons of Liberty, savaged the houses of various crown officers. Boston's Sons were famous for their regular and effective mass demonstrations, but they were not the only mobs turning to the streets. The Dr. Kearsley who had tended to Pain on his arrival in the New World was attacked by a rebel pack in Philadelphia for his loyalist views, and died from his injuries.

However rational the series of boycotts, protests, mob rebellions, and outright warfare that became the American Revolution seemed to many United Colonists, they completely baffled Europeans. If the colonials wished to retain the rights of free Englishmen, the general Old World thinking went, they needed to contribute their fair share to the costs of running an empire. Even today, the historical summaries offered by most American schools almost suggest that the Revolution and the founding of the United States were undertaken on the slightest of pretexts, a quarrel about nothing more than tax and tea. As always, however, the real reasons are far more interesting.

There were so many issues triggering the American Revolution, in fact, that the conflict could be described as one in which each individual rebel had his or her own reason for revolt. There were cynical rationales, such as the financial windfall that massively indebted southern plantation owners would reap by defaulting their British creditors, or the money that could be made by land speculators if the boundary for westward migration drawn by First Minister Grenville was effectively erased. There were issues of legal precedent, such as those settlement charters that forbade anyone but colonial legislatures to levy taxes. Most significantly, however, there were four elements that caused such a dramatic rift between Whitehall and Philadelphia that it became virtually impossible for Britons and British Americans to find common ground. These four factors—an English history of civil unrest, an Enlightenment-inspired questioning of power, a popular analysis of incipient state corruption, and an ever-growing class rage—would become elemental motifs in the work of Thomas Paine.

By the time of Paine's arrival in Philadelphia, American moderns, just like their European colleagues, had spent decades in the faint yellow glow of candlelit coffee shops arguing over the essential tenets of science, society, politics, government, and religion. One of those arguments, a question that led directly to the rise of modern nations and provoked much of Paine's work, was: Why should we have kings? Moderns began considering this revolutionary quandary partly as a result of the mind-bending revelations of Newton, but also because of the recent calamitous course of English history. The crown and legislature had spent six decades at war over God and mammon, notably in the case of Charles I, who was eventually defeated by the military prowess of Oliver Cromwell, convicted of treason as "a Man of Blood," and executed. The country no longer had its God-given Majesty, and England was no longer a kingdom, but a commonwealth.

This shocking development was accompanied by an upheaval in philosophy. For the first time in twelve hundred years, the continent-wide belief in the divine right of kings (that monarchs are given their throne by the will of God, and that anyone opposing royalty was in rebellion against God Himself) was faltering. In 1651 Thomas Hobbes, in his *Leviathan,* had declared that kings did not require a benediction from God but only from their citizens, and that instead of pursuing his own glory, a monarch must direct his government to create as much happiness for as many citizens as possible. Hobbes prescribed that civil and criminal laws were to be made congruent with the laws of nature, and as unalike in every other way as Hobbes was from Paine, all these notions would be regular leitmotifs in Paine's writing.

In *An Essay Concerning Human Understanding* and *Two Treatises on Government,* John Locke crafted something of a reply to and an elaboration on *Leviathan:*

> Because monarchs are prey to delusions of grandeur, they are especially vulnerable to the flattery of crafty priests who encourage tyranny and promote ambition, revenge, covetousness, and many another irregular passion by persuading them of three things: that kings rule not on the basis of their subjects' consent but as the Lord's anointed; that they are not subject to judgment by any earthly power, and that they have been singled out by God himself to stamp out heresy and instill in their subjects the one, true faith. . . . When a ruler stops maintaining the welfare of his subjects, when he wields the power of the government against the people, when he allows Parliament and his ministry to become corrupt and a foe of human liberty, he is nothing but a tyrant, and it is the people's right to remove him.

Both of Locke's key works were enormous bestsellers throughout the British Empire, in some years surpassed only by the Bible in sales, and his ideas would become cornerstones in the curricula of American universities, as Locke's disciples, the "Real Whigs," published variations on his work, including John Trenchard and Thomas Gordon (*Cato's Letters*); James Harrington (*Commonwealth of Oceana, the Excellency of a Free State*); Algernon Sidney (*Discourses Concerning Government*); and Richard Price (*Observations of the Nature of Civil Liberty*). Many of these men would share a number of myths and axioms, especially the idea that power always corrupts, as explained by historian Bernard Bailyn:

> What lay behind every political scene, the ultimate explanation of every political controversy, was the disposition of power . . . meaning the dominion of some men over others, the human control of

> human life . . . and its endlessly propulsive tendency to expand itself beyond legitimate boundaries. . . . It is everywhere in public life, and everywhere it is threatening, pushing, and grasping; and too often in the end it destroys its benign—necessarily benign—victim. . . . Power's natural prey, its necessary victim, was liberty, or law, or right. . . . Mankind as a species was incapable of withstanding the temptations of power, with power always and everywhere having a pernicious, corrupting effect.

Some historians have commented on Thomas Paine's "anger," as if this emotion were unusual for its time and place. Many British Americans, in fact, found reason enough to be righteously enraged. Part of this colonial fury stemmed from a diminishing tolerance for class distinctions, for alongside the decline in faith in the divine right of kings came a fundamental questioning of the inherent superiority of aristocrats. Europeans had for centuries imagined society and government as one intertwined creature, part of the cascading hierarchy of the universe today called the Great Chain of Being. They believed God's immense creative force had given rise to creatures large and small, populating the heavens and the earth, with a God-anointed niche for each, from angel to man to ape to earthworm. There was even (portrayed most vividly by Dante) a hierarchy of the afterlife. As late as 1825 Samuel and Sarah Adams would note in *The Complete Servant* that "the supreme lord of the universe has, in his wisdom, rendered the various conditions of mankind necessary to our individual happiness: some are rich, others poor—some are masters, and others servants," while even Charles Darwin, in his *Descent of Man* (1871), noted that some creatures were "lowly in the scale of nature."

Every country had the form of a grand human pyramid, England's being topped by the king and the queen and the royal family; followed by around two hundred peers; supported by titled knights, esquires, and various aristocrats holding a coat of arms; followed by university-trained ministers, physicians, and lawyers; merchants, traders, and businessmen; artisans; yeomen and husbandmen; and the great base of peasants and urban poor. Each level of this pyramid was conceived as almost a wholly distinct species, with the line dividing bluebloods and plebeians especially sharply drawn. No one seemed to consider this arrangement particularly unfair, as everyone occupied his God-given link in the Great Chain of

Being. The Enlightenment undermined this myth with the new attitudes of those hardworking businessmen and artisans who were now prosperous beyond the traditions of their class, who were proud of their success, who felt that they deserved recognition and respect, and who began believing far more in meritocracy than in aristocracy. As European society offered daily reminders that one's status in life was determined by an accident of birth rather than by talent and efforts—that all men were not, in fact, created equal—the anger of the new mercantile class over this social inequity grew.

Americans, particularly, were treated with disdain by government officials, by social "betters," and by Britons as a whole, because of their colonial status, often viewed as a crude mob not so very different from the "Hindoos" of India. In nearly every discussion of English politics that survives from the decades leading to war, the king is portrayed as the father, England as the motherland, and the British Americans as nothing but children. Various politicians would engineer policy based on this unfortunate analogy, one side seeing unruly teenagers (the colonists who refused to pay certain tariffs) as delinquents requiring a firm hand (military force), and the other attributing such misbehavior to bad parenting (incompetence in Parliament and the ministries). In the early 1770s David Hume would remember a conversation with Lord Bathurst: "Nations, as well as individuals, had their different ages, which challenged a different treatment. . . . You have sometimes, no doubt, given your son a whipping: and I doubt not, but it was well merited and did him much good: yet you will not think proper at present to employ the birch: the colonies are no longer in their infancy."

In London, provincial agent Benjamin Franklin was repeatedly insulted by the secretary of state for the colonies, and then publicly humiliated by the solicitor general before the entire Privy Council; some of his biographers have come to believe that these snubs were responsible for his taking a commanding role in the Revolution. Franklin's adopted political son, Thomas Paine, suffered constant slights throughout the course of his life because of his humble origins. He expressed his own class acrimony solely through his public writing; there is little vitriol in his correspondence (with the exception of one very famous letter to George Washington) and none in the surviving accounts of his personal behavior, where he is commonly described as moody but not ferocious. He was, however, clearly blessed with that enduring proletarian resentment toward the attitudes of pretentious "betters" who were belittling or condescending in the presence of anyone not of their class. In his writing Paine greatly enjoyed undermining the self-styled grandeur of would-be seigneurs, taking them down more than a few notches.

When in time Paine was attacked by the English government, he was accused of "leveling," an epithet most significantly applied to a group of political reformers that philosophically link the English civil wars, the writings of Thomas Paine, and the guarantee of rights in the American and French constitutions. In 1637 clothier John Lilburne met a Puritan minister by the name of John Bastwick, and Lilburne would remember the encounter for the rest of his life, as Bastwick had no ears: they had been axed off as punishment for his criticizing the papist leanings of the archbishop of Canterbury. This outrageous injustice revolutionized Lilburne's political views; he swore to fight personally for a better society and became known as "Freeborn John" for a series of articles on the natural rights of soldiers—or, more accurately, on the fact that they had no rights. With fellow pamphleteer Richard Overton (who had written that "by natural birth all men are equally and alike born to like propriety, liberty and freedom"), silk weaver William Walwyn, Colonel Thomas Rainborough, and barrister John Wildman, Lilburne formed a new political party that became known as the Levellers; its announced goals included universal franchise, full religious toleration, equality of all before the law, trial by jury, full press freedom, graduated taxes, capital punishment restricted to murderers, no imprisonment for debts, a maximum interest rate of 6 percent, free trade, and a termination of hereditary rule—that is, the end of monarchy and the House of Lords. Almost every demand of the wildly radical Leveller program would in time be championed by Thomas Paine and by the American and French Revolutions.

In 1766 the quixotic George III—who as a youth had been reproached by his mother with "Be a King, George! Be a King!"—replaced Lord Grenville with Charles Townshend, who in turn replaced the hated internal Stamp Act with external tariffs on nearly every import the Americans bought. Townshend would use this new revenue in a manner the colonies judged especially pernicious: to pay the salaries of royal colonial officials, which had previously been overseen by American legislatures. A Parliament acting in concert had then passed an egregious corollary law granting the legislature the power "to bind

America in all cases whatsoever." Paine would describe the American reaction to this binding: "The Declaratory Act left [Americans] no rights at all; and contained the full grown seeds of the most despotic government ever exercised in the world . . . and what renders this act the more offensive, is, that it appears to have been passed as an act of mercy; truly then may it be said, that the *tender mercies of the wicked are cruel.*" Parliament additionally required colonials to house troops as requested by the British army—a clear violation of English law. When protests against this erupted in New York, Whitehall responded by dissolving the province's assembly.

Even colonials who had ridiculed the Americans' outrage over a sugar tax now found reason for alarm. What had once seemed an absurdly paranoid colonial fear, that seemingly insignificant taxes actually marked the beginnings of a government drunk with power trying to enslave its provinces, was now viewed as prescient.

By 1767, Americans had used another round of consumer boycotts to cut British imports in half, and Townshend's excises were repealed, but the battle between England and America reignited in May of the following year, when the sloop *Liberty* landed in Boston and reported to customs that she was carrying a cargo of twenty-five pipes (around three thousand gallons) of Madeira wine, a figure notably below her capacity. One month later, customs inspector Thomas Kirk reported that he was nailed shut inside a *Liberty* cabin while the crew unloaded smuggled casks. After crown officials had the boat seized, a mob gathered, beating various customs employees, stealing the Madeira, setting the commission's boat on fire, and overall proving so threatening and intractable that the state governor had the royal officers and their families escorted for their protection to the safety of the British gunboat *Romney*. *Liberty* owner John Hancock was charged with smuggling, but, with John Adams defending him, the government was eventually forced to drop all charges.

Simultaneously, the crown began regular patrols of Boston's harbor with warships and its streets with a thousand British soldiers. A cannon was pointed directly at the Massachusetts Bay Colony's House of Representatives; soldiers walked through the streets swinging cutlasses, tearing rips into trousers and nicks into shoulders, and randomly jabbing civilians with the butts of their bayonets. One British captain, coming upon some slaves one night after a bout of drinking, screamed, "Go home and cut your masters' throats!" Fighting regularly broke out between soldiers and civilians, and rumors began circulating that a massacre was forthcoming at any moment, during which Boston would be destroyed.

On March 5, 1770, the Boston Customs House was guarded by a solitary redcoat. A mob of colonials spontaneously gathered, taunting him. When British reinforcements arrived, the Americans pelted them with oyster shells, rocks, icicles, sticks, and snowballs, daring them to retaliate. The British opened fire, killing five. Samuel Adams and Paul Revere designed and distributed a print throughout the colonies commemorating this Boston Massacre. Twelve thousand attended the victims' funeral. No one would defend the British soldiers at trial, except for John Adams, who argued self-defense. Seven were acquitted, and two were convicted of manslaughter, establishing Adams's professional reputation.

Three years of relative peace followed, until 1773, when the East India Company, facing bankruptcy, raised tea prices to three shillings a pound. Americans began smuggling in two-shilling Dutch tea, and Parliament struck back, giving East India a monopoly on American distribution, eliminating the added fees (and jobs) of independent colonial wholesalers. Consumers enjoyed the benefits of this price war, but influential merchants believed that if this latest tactic worked, Parliament would be able to assume tyrannical control of any aspect of American commerce and could cripple any colonial business at will. Boston accordingly voted to ban the import of British tea.

In late 1773 four British tea ships arrived in the harbor, and were told to depart. They refused. On December 16 between forty and fifty men, their faces blackened with burnt cork to pass as Mohawks, shouted war whoops as they attacked the ships, axing 342 crates and dumping £10,000 ($1.5 million today) worth of tea into Boston harbor. The next morning, floating islands of leaves had to be pushed by sailors out of the harbor to keep the traffic lanes clear, and sodden mounds clogged the Massachusetts beaches all the way to Dorchester.

Horrified by this loss of property (an issue so profound in British culture that Locke's description of the rights of man had included "life, liberty, and property"), Parliament enacted in the spring of 1774 the Coercive Acts, closing Boston harbor to all commerce, moving its customhouse to Plymouth and its provincial government to Salem, allowing Massachusetts criminals to be brought to England for trial, enabling the British army to seize unoccupied buildings to house its troops, putting colonial juries under the control of crown officials, outlawing town meetings, changing the elected assembly to a crown-appointed one, and stationing four thousand British troops in the town of seventeen thousand. A gleeful George III proclaimed, "The die is now cast. The colonies must either submit, or triumph."

In September 1774 colonial legislators had decided that if they allowed the Coercive Acts to stand, similar dictates would be enacted across all of British America. With delegates from every colony save Georgia, the first Continental Congress met at Carpenter's Hall in Philadelphia, drinking toasts at their opening-night dinner to the "union of Britain and the colonies on a constitutional foundation." John Adams came to an immediate assessment of his fellow delegates: "We have not men fit for the times. We are deficient in genius, in education, in travel, in fortune—in everything." The next day's first speech was delivered by Virginia's Patrick Henry, who startled everyone by concluding that "I am not a Virginian, but an American."

Congress asked Parliament to restore the rights of all Englishmen (elective assemblies and juries of peers), to agree that only the colonists could tax themselves, and to remove all standing armies. They gave the British government a one-year deadline to accept, or face a continent-wide series of boycotts. Pain considered all this as "a kind of lawsuit. I supposed the parties would find a way either to decide or settle it. I had no thoughts of independence or of arms. The world could not then have persuaded me that I should be either a soldier or an author. If I had any talents for either, they were buried in me, and might ever have continued so, had not the necessity of the times dragged and driven them into action. I had formed my plan of life, and conceiving myself happy, wished everybody else so."

In response to Congress's writ, William Pitt the Elder submitted a motion to the House of Lords to withdraw English troops from Boston, saying, "When your lordships look at the papers transmitted from America, when you consider their decency, firmness and wisdom, you cannot but respect their cause and wish to make it your own." It was defeated, 68 to 18. Accompanied by Edmund Burke, he then introduced a compromise bill to the Commons, but it too was voted down. Most Britons considered the American requests patently ridiculous, a view held by Dr. Samuel Johnson in *Taxation No Tyranny: An Answer to the Resolutions and Address of the*

American Congress: "We are told, that the subjection of Americans may tend to the diminution of our own liberties; an event, which none but very perspicacious politicians are able to foresee. If slavery be thus fatally contagious, how is it that we hear the loudest yelps for liberty among the drivers of Negroes?"

On April 18, 1775, learning that British troops were marching from Boston to seize a store of gunpowder and arrest John Hancock and Samuel Adams, a militia of around 250 Americans gathered in Concord and headed toward Lexington to stop them. Seeing they were outnumbered by 600 British soldiers, the Minutemen withdrew into the woods. The next morning they mistook British fires for Concord being torched, and shooting broke out. Two Americans died and one was wounded, while three British were killed, with four wounded.

The English retreated to Lexington, where they found seventy-seven Americans holding the commons. The colonists were ordered to withdraw, and they did, but the British, hearing a shot whose source has never been determined, opened fire, killing eight and wounding nine. During their return to Boston (without Adams, Hancock, or gunpowder), the redcoats were repeatedly attacked by hidden snipers.

On May 10, 1775, the second Continental Congress began deliberations at Pennsylvania's State House. John Adams moved that every colony immediately create its own local government, and pressed his fellow delegates to consider independence from Britain, a position that fellow delegate Benjamin Rush remembered made him "an object of nearly universal scorn and detestation." Congress instead voted to ask the king for relief. After news arrived that Massachusetts governor Thomas Gage had issued pardons to all rebels except John Hancock and Samuel Adams—for their heads, the English offered a reward of five hundred pounds ($85,000 today)—Congress made Hancock their president and George Washington commander of the Continental Army.

This civil war split the country almost exactly in two. In Massachusetts and Virginia, rebels were the majority; in New York and Georgia, loyalists were; while the very divided Carolinas endured an endless series of skirmishes. When accounts of the events at Lexington and Concord reached Boston, Dr. Joseph Warren called for volunteers to form a new American army, and twenty thousand men assembled at Harvard Yard in Cambridge. When this news reached London, King George announced to American secretary Lord Dartmouth that America was now either a colony or an enemy. When it reached Philadelphia, it wholly transformed the life of Thomas Pain. He himself knew that this was his personal turning point, saying that "when the country, into which I had just set my foot, was set on fire about my ears, it was time to stir. It was time for every man to stir. Those who had been long settled had something to defend; those who had just come had something to pursue; and the call and the concern was equal and universal." He published more and more incendiary pieces in the *Pennsylvania Magazine,* deepening the rift with Aitken. He also came to feel that the magazine's social prominence at the heart of colonial life, along with its extraordinary jump in circulation, justified his no longer being treated as an apprentice earning fifty pounds a year (the exact sum of the excise salary that he had denounced before Parliament), and he demanded a contract and improved pay. Aitken did not agree, and they would argue about content, position, and money for the next twelve months.

Responding to the vast Quaker consensus that pacifists could not support revolt against the throne, Pain's first comment on the British-American conflict was the debut of his famously choleric prose. "Thoughts on Defensive War" (*Pennsylvania Magazine,* July 1775) beautifully turned Britain's "colonists as children" argument against itself:

> I am thus far a Quaker, that I would gladly agree with all the world to lay aside the use of arms, and settle matters by negotiation; but unless the whole will, the matter ends, and I take up my musket and thank heaven he has put it in my power. Whoever considers the unprincipled enemy we have to cope with, will not hesitate to declare that nothing but arms or miracles can reduce them to reason and moderation. They have lost sight of the limits of humanity. The portrait of a parent red with the blood of her children is a picture fit only for the galleries of the infernals. From the House of Commons, the troops of Britain have been exhorted to right, not for the defense of the natural rights, not to repel the invasion of the insult of enemies; but on the vilest of all pretences, gold.

That October Thetford's Whig lord, the Duke of Grafton, resigned from Parliament when his fellow legislators refused to negotiate with the Americans, and editor Pain published African-American poet Phillis Wheatley's ode to George Washington leading "freedom's heaven-defended race," which she had sent to the general and he had forwarded to the *Pennsylvania Magazine.* This was perhaps the start of a near-lifelong friendship between the general and the journalist:

> Proceed, great chief, with virtue on thy side,
> Thy ev'ry action let the goddess guide.
> A crown, a mansion, and a throne that shine
> With gold unfading, WASHINGTON! be thine.

On October 18 Pain reappeared as "Humanus" in the *Pennsylvania Journal* with his most provocative article to date, "A Serious Thought." Responding to those like Johnson who ridiculed Virginian slave owners now demanding liberty for themselves, it offered a preview of what was to come:

> When I reflect on the horrid cruelties exercised by Britain . . . that ever since the discovery of America she hath employed herself in the most horrid of all traffics, that of human flesh, unknown to the most savage nations, hath yearly (without provocation and in cold blood) ravaged the hapless shores of Africa, robbing it of its unoffending inhabitants to cultivate her stolen dominions in the West—when I reflect on these, I hesitate not for a moment to believe that the Almighty will finally separate America from Britain. Call it independency or what you will, if it is the cause of God and humanity it will go on.

Throughout the summer and fall of 1775 Pain spent less and less time editing and contributing to *Pennsylvania Magazine* as his relationship with Aitken collapsed. The quarrel grew so bitter that at one point the two men agreed to have their differences arbitrated by third parties, but Aitken at the last minute refused even this gesture. A group of allies offered to financially back Pain with his own magazine, but he, for reasons unknown, declined, perhaps because he was already consumed with drafting a major essay on the history of the American colonies and their position within the British Empire.

According to his very-late-in-life and not entirely accurate memoirs, Benjamin Rush was greatly involved with the crafting of this article, providing the idea for the title, finding the printer, and even originally planning to write it all himself. After he published a piece attacking slavery, however, Rush's medical practice was so damaged that he felt he could not be publicly identified with another incendiary stance. Pain easily could, for after all, Rush thought, what did *he* have to lose (besides being hanged for sedition):

> I suggested to him that he had nothing to fear from the popular odium to which such a publication might expose him, for he could live anywhere, but that my profession and connections . . . tied me to Philadelphia. . . . He readily assented to the proposal, and from time to time he called at my house, and read to me every chapter of the proposed pamphlet as he composed it. I recollect being charmed with a sentence in it, which by accident, or perhaps by design, was not published. It was as follows, "Nothing can be conceived of more absurd than three millions of people flocking to the American shore, every time a vessel arrives from England, to know what portion of liberty they shall enjoy." When Mr. Paine had finished his pamphlet, I advised him to show it to Dr. Franklin, Mr. Rittenhouse, and Mr. Samuel Adams, all of whom I knew were decided friends to American independence. I mention these facts to refuse a report that Mr. Paine was assisted in composing his pamphlet by one or more of the above gentlemen. They never saw it until it was written and then only by my advice.

Though it is true that Pain originally wanted the title "Plain Truth" and Rush instead suggested "Common Sense," the doctor's account is not wholly plausible. Pain, after all, needed no intermediary to discuss his work with Benjamin Franklin, while Rush had absurdly commented on the writing of this essay on independence and republicanism that "there were two words which [I had warned him] to avoid by every means as necessary to his own safety and that of the public—independence and republicanism." Additionally, if Rush did not understand the danger in publishing such seditious and treasonous material, Pain certainly did:

> It cannot at this time a day be forgotten that the politics, the opinions and the prejudices of the country were in direct opposition to the principles contained in that work. And I well know that in

> Pennsylvania, and I suppose the same in other of the then provinces, it would have been unsafe for a man to have espoused independence in any public company and after the appearance of that pamphlet it was as dangerous to speak against it. It was a point of time full of critical danger to America, and if her future well being depended on any one political circumstance more than another it was in changing the sentiments of the people from dependence to Independence and from the monarchial to the republican form of government; for had she unhappily split on the question, or entered coldly or hesitatingly into it, she most probably had been ruined.

Rush's memoir offers only a half-glimpsed picture of the process that Pain followed in developing *Common Sense* and all his major works. Missing to us today from the documentary record is one very significant part of the author's life—the hours spent daily (or nightly) in conversation with his fellow moderns. These talks included international news, local gossip, and debates on the issues of the day; the news and gossip ending up in his letters, and the debates in his essays. This is not to say that his pamphlets were produced by committee, or that every one of his contemporaries agreed with everything in them, but it is patent that Pain assimilated the conversations and correspondence with his many friends and allies into his work. He would remember discussing *Common Sense* with Ben Franklin as, "In October, 1775, Dr. Franklin proposed giving me such materials as were in his hands towards completing a history of the present transactions [the Anglo-American conflict], and seemed desirous of having the first volume out the next spring. I had then formed the outlines of *Common Sense,* and finished nearly the first part; and as I supposed the doctor's design in getting out a history was to open the new year with a new system, I expected to surprise him with a production on that subject much earlier than he thought of."

The paucity of documents revealing the evolution of Paine's ideas has led to a profound misconception of him. Instead of assessing them as radical manifestos, as they generally are today, it would be more accurate to view the great majority of Paine's lasting works as core treatises of the Enlightenment. *Common Sense, Rights of Man,* and *The Age of Reason,* after all, do not stray far outside the beliefs of Franklin, Washington, Jefferson,

Rousseau, Condorcet, Smith, Price, Priestley, Godwin, and Wollstonecraft. This is not to say that Paine was unoriginal or less radical than he is now judged; it is to say that everyone in his global modern circle had sensibilities as progressive as his own. The American founding fathers, especially, are now remembered as less extreme that they actually were; nostalgia and patriotism have rendered them safe and domesticated. Ben Franklin is now a wizened polymath who flew kites; Thomas Jefferson, a quirky inventor who perhaps loved too much; John Adams, a churchgoing, salt-of-the-earth Yankee. Paine's subject matter may have been scandalous, his writing style spicy and pugnacious, and his utopian vision an inspiration to progressives across history, but the biggest bestselling author of the eighteenth century was not generally considered a wild, black-sheep extremist in his own time—otherwise, he would never have been so popular with such a broad readership, or been the friend or ally of every significant figure in the eighteenth-century fight against tyranny and for the greater good. What was truly radical about him, in fact, was wholly a matter of class; he explained modern, patrician ideas in essays that any plebeian  could read and understand. He was the Enlightenment's great Mercury, and in time, exactly for this immense popularity, he would be convicted of treason.

Common Sense appeared in the form of a pamphlet, the most popular style of eighteenth-century publishing, as it offered a medium for anyone who could afford the cost of paper and a printshop's fees. Pamphlets had no binding or cover, and were affordable for almost any would-be author; most consisted of between twenty and eighty loosely sewn pages, with the longest pamphlets about the length of today's romance novels or classic mysteries. Costing about a shilling and therefore far less expensive than books, pamphlets were just the right length for explaining a position in detail, as well as for being read aloud to the illiterate, an important consideration for those wanting to reach the widest audience. (There is new evidence, in fact, that Jefferson inscribed pause marks in copies of the Declaration of Independence to aid in public performances.) One later pamphleteer, George Orwell, would call these booklets "a one-man show. One has complete freedom of expression, including, if one chooses, the freedom to be scurrilous, abusive, and seditious; or, on the other hand, to be more detailed, serious and 'high-brow' than is ever possible in a newspaper or in most kinds of periodicals . . . it can be produced much more quickly than a book, and . . . can reach a bigger public."

The writing in *Common Sense* was part Enlightenment inspirational—proclaiming the present as the propitious moment for America to become a New World model of government and society, as well as a beacon of freedom and human progress—and part bilious attack. Though Pain never seemed to regard himself as a missionary of Enlightenment principles (such a notion being fundamentally contrary to rationalist natural philosophy), *Common Sense* would, like all of his major works, be structured very much like a traditional pulpit sermon. There is the oral quality of the prose, which seems styled to be read aloud; the dramatic portrayal of imminent dangers facing the audience; and the answer, an exhortation to action (which, in the case of *Common Sense,* meant war, not prayer). The Enlightenment urged human beings to search for ways to improve the lot of all people, everywhere; Pain's consistent metaphor elevated the American citizen as someone equipped to wield such power, now.

As plutocrats, the great majority of the American founding fathers were understandably concerned with mercantilism, customs, navigation law, tariffs, and land charters. *Common Sense,* instead, attacked all that was feudal in the Europe of the eighteenth century, notably its hereditary thrones and privileges of class. Pain took an idea that Englishmen on both sides of the Atlantic cherished—that theirs was the best government in the world, as it balanced the competing powers of monarch, gentry, and commoner against one another, pitting the throne against the House of Lords against the House of Commons—and detonated it. For those fervently believing that kings offered stability through their absolute rule, Pain deftly parried that "the whole history of England disowns the fact. Thirty kings and two minors have reigned in that distracted kingdom since the conquest, in which time have been (including the Revolution) no less than eight civil wars and nineteen rebellions." He so cleverly and so logically strung together his causes and effects of society and government, employing such Real Whig concepts as the inherent equality of human beings and the inanity of inherited power, that North American readers could find no fault with his argument, one that would dissolve colonial fealty to King George III.

Another key to the great popularity and influence of *Common Sense* was Pain's ability to address the colonists' greatest fears by appealing to their noblest aspirations, especially with his insistence that tyrants, monarchs, and legislators had no power unless the citizens of a state granted it to them—that the world's greatest power lay within the united action of ordinary people. According to *Common Sense,* there was no question that, in a war against the greatest military power of its time, the free citizens of America would triumph. Historian Bernard Bailyn explained the force of *Common Sense* by calling it "a work of genius—slapdash as it is, rambling as it is, crude as it is. . . . One had to be a fool or a fanatic in early January 1776 to advocate American independence. Everyone knew England was the most powerful nation on earth . . . and that a string of prosperous but weak communities along the Atlantic coast left uncontrolled and unprotected would quickly be pounced on by rival European powers. . . . Why should one want to destroy the most successful political system in the world, which guaranteed both liberty and order, under which America had flourished? . . . There is something extraordinary in this pamphlet and in the mind and imagination of the man who wrote it, something bizarre, outsized, unique."

Real Whig James Harrington's "The Grounds and Reasons of Monarchy Considered" (with its attacks on hereditary succession) and scientist-philosopher-clergyman Joseph Priestley's "An Essay on the First Principles of Government" (with its ideas on the evolution of representational democracies) were clear forebears to *Common Sense,* and Pain told John Adams that his history of kings and the Bible was inspired by John Milton's *Defence of the People of England* and *Tenure of Kings and Magistrates;* he credited his arguments in favor of independence to James Burgh's "Political Disquisitions" of 1775. The author likely was familiar with both the Royal Society's dicta on prose and with William Duncan's *Elements of Logick,* which convinced a number of Anglo-American writers and speakers to forgo the classical rhetoric of Cicero in favor of one based on Newton, nature, and mathematics, in the laying out of one's argument from only "self-evident" propositions.

Regardless of his many sources, Pain's ability to seize readers' attention and the confrontational style of his prose were uniquely his own. For those accustomed to the era's standard baroque emollients of endless allusion and the subjunctive case, Pain's decidedly plainsong argot must have appeared harsh, stark, raw, and unsettling. For contrast, consider a fair representation of mainstream eighteenth-century prose in this single sentence of Priestley's "First Principles of Government":

> In the largest states, if the abuses of government should, at any time be great and manifest; if the servants of the people, forgetting their masters, and their masters' interest, should pursue a separate one of their own; if, instead of considering that they are made for the people, they should consider the people as made for them; if the oppressions and violations of right should be great, flagrant, and universally resented; if the tyrannical governors should have no friends but a few sycophants, who had long preyed upon the vitals of their fellow citizens, and who might be expected to desert a government, whenever their interests should be detached from it: if, in consequence of these circumstances, it should become manifest, that the risk, which would be run in attempting a revolution would be trifling, and the evils which might be apprehended from it, were far less than these which were actually suffered, and which were daily increasing; in the name of God, I ask, what principles are those, which ought to restrain an injured and insulted people from asserting their natural rights, and from changing, or even punishing their governors that is their servants, who had abused their trust; or from altering the whole form of their government, if it appeared to be of a structure so liable to abuse?

Common Sense could be considered the first American self-help book, the help being for those who could never imagine life without a monarch. The king was then viewed not just as an executive of the state but as the very reflection of the nation, the God-given pater to whom even the lowliest of subjects could appeal in time of need. Cromwell's republic was not remembered fondly in Pain's time; many believed that a throneless nation was like a body without a head, that in such systems total anarchy and chaos would necessarily result.

Pain announced not only that there did not exist a divine right of kings, but that the proof lay within the pages of the Bible itself, and that the king/Lords/Commons balance of powers was nothing but a theatrical performance, helping subjects believe the myth of their system's fairness and equity, when in fact it was corrupt and oligarchic. He explained that adults do not require any fatherly king (or mother country) to oversee them; they only need the rule of law. He attacked the very limited suffrage offered to British citizens through absurdly high property requirements (to date, Pain had yet to own fifty pounds' worth of property and could not vote) and the allocation of districts that kept English suffrage firmly in the hands of the elite. He proclaimed the benefits of American independence before anyone else was brave enough to speak of such matters in public. He directly focused the inchoate rage of the British-American middle class against crown bureaucrats and aristocratic disdain. He sparked the Declaration of Independence, and inspired colonials to see themselves not as traitors or as mere defenders of English constitutional history but as pioneers and forefathers struggling to create a better world for future generations. Most crucially, he transformed an unfocused and confusing civil war into an ennobling crusade of good confronting evil, following a course both difficult and frightening, but ending with a triumph that was inevitable:

Common Sense

The cause of America is, in a great measure, the cause of all mankind. . . .

Some writers have so confounded society with government, as to leave little or no distinction between them; whereas they are not only different, but have different origins. Society is produced by our wants, and government by our wickedness; the former promotes our happiness positively by uniting our affections, the latter negatively by restraining our vices. . . .

Society in every state is a blessing, but government, even in its best state, is but a necessary evil; in its worst state an intolerable one; for when we suffer, or are exposed to the same miseries by a government, which we might expect in a country without government, our calamity is heightened by reflecting that we furnish the means by which we suffer! Government, like dress, is the badge of lost innocence; the palaces of kings are built on the ruins of the bowers of paradise. . . .

I know it is difficult to get over local or long standing prejudices, yet if we will suffer ourselves to examine the component parts of the English constitution, we shall find them to be the base remains of two ancient tyrannies, compounded with some new republican materials.

First—The remains of monarchical tyranny in the person of the king.

Secondly—The remains of aristocratical tyranny in the persons of the peers.

Thirdly—The new republican materials, in the persons of the commons, on whose virtue depends the freedom of England.

The two first, by being hereditary, are independent of the people; wherefore in a constitutional sense they contribute nothing towards the freedom of the state.

To say that the constitution of England is a union of three powers reciprocally checking each other, is farcical, either the words have no meaning, or they are flat contradictions.

To say that the commons is a check upon the king, presupposes two things.

First—That the king is not to be trusted without being looked after, or in other words, that a thirst for absolute power is the natural disease of monarchy.

Secondly—That the commons, by being appointed for that purpose, are either wiser or more worthy of confidence than the crown. . . .

But there is another and greater distinction for which no truly natural or religious reason can be assigned, and that is, the distinction of men into kings and subjects. Male and female are the distinctions of nature, good and bad the distinctions of heaven; but how a race of men came into the world so exalted above the rest, and distinguished like some new species, is worth enquiring into, and whether they are the means of happiness or of misery to mankind. . . . One of the strongest natural proofs of the folly of hereditary right in kings, is, that nature disapproves it, otherwise she would not so frequently turn it into ridicule by giving mankind an ass for a lion. . . .

This is supposing the present race of kings in the world to have had an honorable origin; whereas it is more than probable, that could we take off the dark covering of antiquity, and trace them to their first rise, that we should find the first of them nothing better than the principal ruffian of some restless gang, whose savage manners or preeminence in subtlety obtained him the title of chief among plunderers; and who by increasing in power, and extending his depredations, overawed the quiet and defenseless to purchase their safety by frequent contributions. . . .

England, since the conquest, hath known some few good monarchs, but groaned beneath a much larger number of bad ones, yet no man in his senses can say that their claim under William the Conqueror is a very honorable one. A French bastard landing with an armed banditti, and establishing himself king of England against the consent of the natives, is in plain terms a very paltry rascally original. It certainly hath no divinity in it. . . .

The most plausible plea, which hath ever been offered in favor of hereditary succession, is, that it preserves a nation from civil wars; and were this true, it would be weighty; whereas, it is the most barefaced falsity ever imposed upon mankind. The whole history of England disowns the fact. Thirty kings and two minors have reigned in that distracted kingdom since the conquest, in which time there have been (including the Revolution) no less than eight civil wars and nineteen rebellions. . . .

In England a king hath little more to do than to make war and give away places; which in plain terms, is to impoverish the nation and set it together by the ears. A pretty business indeed for a man to be allowed eight hundred thousand sterling a year for, and worshipped into the bargain! Of more worth is one honest man to society, and in the sight of God, than all the crowned ruffians that ever lived.

Thoughts of the present state of American Affairs

. . . I have heard it asserted by some, that as America hath flourished under her former connection with Great Britain, that the same connection is necessary towards her future happiness, and will always have the same effect. Nothing can be more fallacious than this kind of argument. We may as well assert, that because a child has thrived upon milk, that it is never to have meat, or that the first twenty years of our lives is to become a precedent for the next twenty. . . .

But Britain is the parent country, say some. Then the more shame upon her conduct. Even brutes do not devour their young; nor savages make war upon their families; . . . to say that reconciliation is our duty, is truly farcical. The first king of England, of the present line (William the Conqueror) was a Frenchman, and half the peers of England are descendants from the same country; wherefore by the same method of reasoning, England ought to be governed by France. . . .

let a Continental Conference be held, in the following manner, and for the following purpose . . . to frame a Continental Charter, or Charter of the United Colonies; (answering to what is called the Magna Charta of England) fixing the number and manner of choosing members of Congress, members of Assembly, with their date of sitting, and drawing the line of business and jurisdiction between them: always remembering, that our strength is continental, not provincial: Securing freedom and property to all men, and above all things the free exercise of religion, according to the dictates of conscience; with such other matter as is necessary for a charter to contain. Immediately after which, the said conference to dissolve, and the bodies which shall be chosen conformable to the said charter, to be the legislators and governors of this continent for the time being: Whose peace and happiness, may God preserve, Amen. . . .

But where says some is the king of America? I'll tell you Friend, he reigns above, and doth not make havoc of mankind like the Royal [Brute] of Britain. Yet that we may not appear to be defective even in earthly honors, let a day be solemnly set apart for proclaiming the charter; let it be brought forth placed on the divine law, the word of God; let a crown be placed thereon, by which the world may know, that so far as we approve of monarchy, that in America THE LAW IS KING. For as in absolute governments the king is law, so in free countries the law ought to be king; and there ought to be no other. . . .

It is the custom of nations, when any two are at war, for some other powers, not engaged in the quarrel, to step in as mediators, and bring about the preliminaries of a peace: but while America calls herself the subject of Great Britain, no power, however well disposed she may be, can offer her mediation. Wherefore, in our present state we may quarrel on for ever. . . . Were a manifesto to be published, and dispatched to foreign courts, setting forth the miseries we have endured, and the peaceable methods we have ineffectually used for redress; declaring, at the same time, that not being able, any longer to live happily or safely under the cruel disposition of the British court, we had been driven to the necessity of breaking

> off all connection with her; at the same time assuring all such courts of our peaceable disposition towards them, and of our desire of entering into trade with them. Such a memorial would produce more good effects to this Continent, than if a ship were freighted with petitions to Britain. . . .
>
> Should an independency be brought about . . . we have every opportunity and every encouragement before us, to form the noblest, purest constitution on the face of the earth. We have it in our power to begin the world over again.

Rush acted as Pain's agent, approaching one Philadelphia printer after the next with the manuscript, but no one dared publish it. Pain at the time remembered that the Americans' "attachment to Britain was obstinate, and it was at that time a kind of treason to speak against it. They disliked the ministry, but they esteemed the nation. Their idea of grievance operated without resentment, and their single object was reconciliation." Even after King George had declared the colonies to be in a state of rebellion, the Pennsylvania and New Jersey assemblies instructed their congressional delegates to do nothing that might further distance America from England. In London Ben Franklin assured William Pitt that he had heard nothing in favor of breaking away to form a new nation "from any person drunk or sober."

Rush finally settled with a Scots printer on Third Street, Robert Bell, who remembered that "when the work was at a stand for want of a courageous typographer, I was then recommended by a gentleman nearly in the following words: 'There is Bell, he is a Republican printer, give it to him, and I will answer for his courage to print it.' " For being so courageous, Bell demanded that if there was a financial loss, Pain would be liable; that if there were profits, he would take half; and that he would charge an outrageous two shillings cover price (about fifteen dollars today). With no other stationers willing to go forward, Pain agreed to Bell's terms, but was slightly less courageous than the publisher. The first printing of *Common Sense* had Bell's name on it but not Pain's (or Paine's); instead, the title page announced only that it was "written by an Englishman."

Bell printed one thousand copies on January 10, 1776—the same day that King George denounced the colonies to Parliament—and sold them all within days. Pain calculated that he was owed thirty pounds for his half-share, but Bell claimed instead that there were no profits whatsoever, and that in fact Pain owed him £29 12s 1d. The publisher also refused to include in the second printing revisions the author made in reply to the loyalist criticisms of Pennsylvania's many Quakers (pamphleteering gave rise to an industry of its own, where a publication was answered by its political opponents in the press or in their own pamphlets, and the original author would then answer back in revised editions or sequels). Pain was enraged. He paid Bell's demanded sum, and then approached another printer, paid for a run of six thousand, and arranged for brothers William and Thomas Bradford to sell them at a price of one shilling, undercutting Bell (whose success with the first edition was so remarkable that it emboldened his fellow stationers). Pain then forswore all royalties, and donated his profits to George Washington's Continental Army, to be used for mittens: "As my wish was to serve an oppressed people, and assist in a just and good cause, I conceived that the honor of it would be promoted by my declining to make even the usual profits of an author." The Bradford edition's cover clearly stated, "by Thomas Paine."

The combination of an author charitably renouncing what would become a significant fortune to keep the cover price attractively low, and the public street brawlings of printers Bell and the Bradfords, resulted in a marketing strategy of rapt genius. Bell launched an advertising campaign in the *Pennsylvania Evening Post,* dismissing the Bradford edition as similar to his "in figure and utility as much as a British shilling in size and value resembleth a British half crown." The Bradfords in turn explained that Bell's machinations were depriving American troops of their mittens. The controversy only spurred sales of both editions. When Bell then replied with ads attacking the author, Paine responded by publicly repudiating his own copyright, thereby giving *any* colonial printer the right to issue his own edition. The various ad campaigns, charges, and countercharges set off a response that would enflame the whole of the United Colonies. Across the seaboard, colonial printshops printed and distributed knockoffs in New York, Salem, Hartford, Lancaster, Albany, Providence, and Norwich; by the end of the month, a German translation appeared, and by the end of April, French editions were available in Quebec. John Adams noted that *Common Sense* was "received in France and in all of Europe with rapture," eventually appearing in Warsaw, London, Edinburgh, Newcastle, Rotterdam, Copenhagen, Berlin, Dubrovnik, and Moscow.

Many of these European editions deleted Paine's comments on the foolishness of hereditary rule, and none remitted to the author any royalties. It was, in fact, impossible for a successful author to make any money in America, since there was no true copyright in force, and the minute a piece of writing was seen to have favor with the public, it was pirated and sold throughout the colonies with all revenues kept by the stationers. In this lawless atmosphere, what Paine (or any other author) needed for financing was a patron. As the apostle of the Enlightenment, however, one of Paine's great targets of attack was the absurdity of inherited wealth and title, with the side effect of closing off that potential avenue of income. In time, he would address the perils of his copyright-free nation in a letter that may have had some bearing on the American Constitution's inclusion of "Congress shall have Power . . . To promote the Progress of Science and useful Arts, by securing for limited Times to Authors and Inventors the exclusive Right to their respective Writings and Discoveries":

George Washington
Philadelphia
2 April 1783
Sir

Understanding that Congress has it in contemplation to recommend to the States the passing of a law for the security of literary property, I take the liberty of troubling Congress, with an anecdote which will serve to shew the necessity of such a measure.

On the recommendation of Doctor Rush, I gave the manuscript copy of the pamphlet Common Sense to a certain printer of this city and as I did not intend to have any trouble with the work after it was printed, and had conceived it proper toward supporting the reputation of the principles of the pamphlet contained, that no parts of the profits arising from the sale should come into my hands, I, therefore gave one half of the clear profits to the printer over and above his charge of printing—and the other half, I gave by my own hand to Mr. Thomas Pryor and Mr. Joseph Dean both of this city, to be received by them and disposed of to any public purpose they might choose, the particular thing mentioned was to purchase woolen mittens for the soldiers then going to the Quebec Expedition. The printer not only kept the whole profits of the first edition, which he still retains [illegible] but in the course of two or three days printed [a] second edition, and on my expressing some surprise at his doing it without my knowledge, as I intended making additions to it, he very bluntly told me—I had no business with it.

I am
Your Excellency's
Most Obt and very hble Sevt
Thomas Paine

America would not have a copyright law until 1790—a statute that owed its existence primarily to the strenuous efforts of Paine's great friend Joel Barlow—and it would solely concern charts, maps, and books. Previously, the nation had followed English common law in considering literary output a form of property, but, as in England, the actual law benefited the owner of the printing press—the stationer—more than it did the author. The attitude of early American colonials toward their authors was perhaps summed up by Virginia's royal governor Sir William Berkeley, who commented in 1671, "I thank God there are no free schools nor printing, and I hope we shall not have these [for a] hundred years; for learning has brought disobedience, and heresy, and sects into the world, and printing has divulged them, and libels against the best government. God keep us from both."

Common Sense made Thomas Paine America's first bestselling author. By the end of that year of 1776, between 150,000 and 250,000 copies were sold, at a time when the American population stood at three million—the equivalent in per capita of selling thirty-five million copies of a single title today. Aitken's store by itself sold seven dozen in its first two weeks, and a mere ten days after Bell's first printing, copies were on sale in Virginia and Massachusetts. It would have the greatest public impact on American history of any piece of writing, with *Uncle Tom's Cabin* following a close second. In time, half the nation either read it or had it read to them. A Connecticut reader marveled that "you have declared the sentiments of millions. Your production may justly be compared to a land-flood that sweeps all before it. We were blind, but on reading these enlightening works the scales have fallen from our eyes; even deep-rooted prejudices take to themselves wings and flee away. . . . The doctrine of independence hath been in times past, greatly disgustful; we abhorred the principle—it is now become our delightful theme, and commands our purest affections." A citizen of Massachusetts remembered the public frenzy: "I believe no pages was ever more eagerly read, nor more generally approved. People speak of it in rapturous praise." A Bostonian commented that "independence a year ago could not have been publickly mentioned with impunity. . . . Nothing else is now talked of, and I know not what can be done by Great Britain to prevent it."

Paine found himself carried forward by the immense wave of his book's popularity into the heart of New World society. If *Common Sense* isolated the fears and the angers of the average colonist and focused them into a strategy for the future, its impact was tenfold for the men who would face charges of treason as the American founding fathers. *Common Sense* would lead directly to the Declaration of Independence and the Articles of Confederation, and among the United Colonies' elite now in favor of separation from Britain Paine was both a celebrity and a sage.

General Charles Lee wrote George Washington to ask, "Have you seen the pamphlet *Common Sense*? I never saw such a masterly irresistible performance. It will, if I mistake not, in concurrence with the transcendent folly and wickedness of the Ministry, give the *coup-de-grace* to Great Britain. In short, I own myself convinced, by the arguments, of the necessity of separation." Washington in turn reported that "the sound doctrine and unanswerable reasoning contained in the pamphlet *Common Sense* will not leave members [of Congress] at a loss to decide upon the propriety of separation. . . . [It is] working a wonderful change in the minds of many men," while John Adams called the pamphlet "a tolerable summary of the arguments which I had been repeating again and again in Congress for nine months," and passed on the rumor that the author's "name is Paine, a gentleman about two years from England—a man who, General [Charles] Lee says, has genius in his eyes." Adams would later write Thomas Jefferson that "every post and every day rolls upon us independence like a torrent. . . . History is to ascribe the American Revolution to Thomas Paine," while Jefferson commented that "no writer has exceeded Paine in ease and familiarity of style, in perspicuity of expression, happiness of elucidation, and in simple and unassuming language."

Paine would explain his pamphlet's muscular appeals in a January 14, 1779, letter to Henry Laurens, president of Congress: "I saw the people of this country were all wrong, by an ill-placed confidence. After the breaking out of hostilities I was confident [that British] design was a total conquest. . . . I think the importance of [*Common Sense*] was such that if it had not appeared, and that at the exact time it did, the Congress would not now have been sitting where they are. The light which that performance threw upon the subject gave a turn to the politics of America which enabled her to stand her ground. Independence followed in six months after it, although before it was published it was a dangerous doctrine to speak of, and that because it was not understood."

The book aroused such depths of passion that when New Yorkers learned that printer Samuel Loudon was going to issue a critical rejoinder, concluding that Paine "unites the violence and rage of a republican with all the enthusiasm and folly of the fanatic," forty *Common Sense* advocates forced their way into Loudon's printshop, demanding to know who had written the attack. The printer claimed to not know the author's name, and the mob responded by pushing their way into his office, seizing the fifteen hundred copies already manufactured, assembling at the common, and burning them.

One of the most serious challenges to *Common Sense* came as a series of eight letters published in various Pennsylvania newspapers by "Cato," assumed to be the College of Philadelphia provost, the Reverend Dr. William Smith. Arguing that Paine and his fellow rebels were wildly overreacting to what was in fact a minor quarrel between Britain and America, Smith accused those proposing independence of being secretly allied with France or Spain, and predicted that a democratic republic would bring with it a cataclysm of unforeseen perils. His arguments were so influential that a group of Philadelphians, including Rittenhouse and Franklin (who had arrived on May 5 to serve as a delegate to the second Continental Congress), pooled their resources to hurry Paine home from New York City, where he was visiting General Charles Lee, to respond. Paine would answer Smith in a series of letters signed "The Forester," the pseudonym of a political essayist from his days in Lewes.

A great controversy in those early years of democratic republics was the question: Where should the fulcrum of power between the governors and the governed be placed? *Common Sense* moved it dramatically to the side of the citizen, arguing that as many adult males as possible should be eligible to vote; that elections should be held annually to quell corruption; that power should be reduced for officeholders and strengthened for Congress, which should be enlarged (he estimated a need for 390 legislators); and that the great power of government be held in one elected legislature for the nation and one for each individual province (a position favored by Franklin and followed in Pennsylvania).

These suggestions found little favor with the melodramatic John Adams. After *Common Sense* had turned him from a voice in the wilderness to a commanding presence in the mainstream of Congress, Adams would at first give great praise to, and then in time turn completely against, Paine:

> In the course of this winter appeared a phenomenon in Philadelphia, a star of disaster, a disastrous meteor, I mean Thomas Paine. He came from England, and got into such company as would converse with him, and ran about picking up what information he could concerning our affairs. . . .
>
> [*Common Sense*'s] arguments in favor of independence I liked very well; but . . . his arguments from the Old Testament were ridiculous. . . . The other third part relative to a form of government I considered as flowing from simply ignorance and a mere desire to please the democratic party. . . . I regretted to see so foolish a plan recommended to the people of the United States. . . . I dreaded the effect so popular a pamphlet might have among the people and determined to do all in my power to counteract the effects of it. . . . It is the fate of men and things which do great good that they always do great evil, too. "Common Sense," by his crude, ignorant notion of a government by one assembly, will do more mischief, in dividing the friends of liberty, than all the Tory writings together. . . . It was so democratical, without any restraint or even an attempt at any equilibrium or counterpoise, that it must produce confusion and every evil work.

Adams was that sort of man who felt the need to compete with everyone he met, and since those Adams met included George Washington, Benjamin Franklin, Thomas Jefferson, Alexander Hamilton, and other titans of his century, it is easy to imagine how difficult this must have been. Adams will in time have many terrible things to say about Paine, just as he had many dreadful things to say about nearly everyone he ever knew save Abigail, and it is a benefit to remember not only that Adams used the rhetorical melodrama favored by every eighteenth-century attorney, but that one of Adams's great boyhood heroes was the Roman lawyer and orator Cicero, and that in emulation of that classical republican, Adams embraced the pleasures of floridity, of being a cascading font of words, surging in torrents from his pen or his lips. Scholars John Ferling and Lewis E. Braverman have additionally proposed that the second American president was a victim of the overactive thyroid of Graves' disease, noting his painfully owl-like eyes, history of mental breakdowns, lifelong irritability, and fits of paranoia. As biographer James Grant would describe it, Adams's hatreds were "throbbing, intricately constructed, and obsessive."

For various reasons, Adams would be especially roused to vitriol with each publication of Thomas Paine's, to the point where he would respond, in writing, as the anti-Paine. It is possible to see in the conflict between these two every essential argument at the heart of democratic republics. After copies of the American Constitution arrived in Europe in 1787, Adams and Jefferson argued over its many points, with Adams finally stating that the key point distinguishing him from Paine's ideological brother was that "you are afraid of the one, I, the few. . . . You are apprehensive of monarchy; I, of aristocracy." In fact, what Adams really feared was not aristocracy but mob rule, the tyranny of the many and the power of the demagogue, and he would respond to *Common Sense* with *Thoughts on Government,* calling for two legislative bodies, an independent judiciary, and a veto-wielding chief selected by the legislatures in order to counter "democratic tyranny" and ensure that government was the bailiwick of "a few of the most wise and good."

After *Thoughts* was published, Adams reported that "Mr. Thomas Paine was so highly offended with it that he came to visit me at my chamber at Mrs. Yard's [boardinghouse] to remonstrate and even scold me for it, which he did in very ungenteel terms." The lawyer held firm to his belief that a multipart system would follow the British model in solving the great riddle posed by the Real Whigs: preventing tyranny from accruing to any one person or branch of government. Paine's real criticism of Adams, however, was that a public attack on *Common Sense* by so respected a patriot could only help reinforce the American loyalist faith in King George. They fought terribly, and eventually to the ruin of their friendship. Until the Revolution was won, though, Paine and Adams remained on good terms, the hatred of their common foe outweighing their personal differences.

On June 7, 1776, Virginian Richard Henry Lee, a forty-four-year-old ally of Samuel Adams, moved that Congress issue *Common Sense*'s recommendations of a conference to draft a constitution for the new nation, laws to bypass the United Kingdom and promote trade with the rest of Europe, and, most important, what Paine called in *Common Sense* "a manifesto to be published" announcing "that these United Colonies are, and of right ought to be, free and independent states, that they are absolved from all allegiance to the British Crown, and that all political connection between them and the state of Great Britain is, and ought to be, totally dissolved."

Congressional committees were named to prepare the documents for foreign alliances, colonial unity, and independence from Britain; the independence committee included Ben Franklin, John Adams, and a thirty-two-year-old, thin-skinned and redheaded Virginian, who constantly loved to sing or hum, and who had been raised in a life of such immense wealth that his first childhood memory was of being carried, on a pillow, by a slave to his grandfather's plantation. Though hundreds of thousands of pages have been written on this man, there is so much we will never know about him: were his eyes hazel, green, or blue? Was his complexion clear or freckled? Did he speak with an English or southern accent? Just before his death, he was described by Daniel Webster as "above six feet high, of an ample long frame, rather thin and spare. His head, which is not peculiar in its shape, is set rather forward on his shoulders, and his neck being long, there is, when he is walking or conversing, an habitual protrusion of it. It is still well covered with hair. . . . His eyes are small. His chin is rather long, but not pointed, his nose small, regular in its outline, and the nostrils a little elevated. His mouth is well formed and still filled with teeth; it is generally strongly compressed, bearing an expression of contentment and benevolence. His limbs are uncommonly long, his hands and feet very large, and his wrists of a most extraordinary size. His walk is not precise and military, but easy and swinging; he stoops a little, not so much from age, as from natural formation. When sitting he appears short, partly from the disproportionate length of his limbs. His general appearance indicates an extraordinary degree of health, vivacity, and spirit."

Thomas Jefferson had just arrived in Philadelphia that May of 1776, having postponed his trip after suffering six weeks of searing migraines. According to *Common Sense,* the key point of the independence manifesto should be to promote the drive for American liberty as a cause greater than just a quarrel within the boundaries of the British Empire, and it should encourage support for the American rebellion against a monarchy from other

European nations (which were themselves monarchies). In the Declaration of Independence, Jefferson would carry this idea forward, as well as blame King George for American slavery (another Paine motif). In fact, there are so many common elements between Paine's first American writings and the Declaration that some historians have claimed that Paine himself secretly wrote it, or that Jefferson copied him so thoroughly that it amounted to the same thing.

Though no documentary record exists today, Paine and Jefferson likely met at this time, and they would become friends for life, a bond for Paine second in importance and strength only to that with Benjamin Franklin. These three men would come to illustrate the remarkable paradox at the heart of American political life, a paradox that the founding fathers would create from their Enlightenment heritage of Locke and Newton. Beginning with Franklin and Washington, every successful American leader throughout the nation's history would balance the pragmatic with the utopian. Where Franklin the master politician would be almost entirely pragmatic, Paine would be too fervidly utopian in ways that would not just damage him financially, but imperil him physically. Though his "political father" was easily the foremost American negotiator of both the colonial and revolutionary eras, Paine would never be capable of Franklin's easy way with flattery and finesse, or his method of drawing a blank curtain over his own personality in service to compromise and politics, whether for business or for the nation. Paine would instead always be too ardent with his religion of the light, a Savonarola of reason and liberty, and as inept a political operator as any fervid Christian saint.

Jefferson, nearly Franklin's equal in political legerdemain, would be tormented for his entire life by the conflicting demands of pragmatic utopianism, of balancing need with desire, freedom and state, meritocrats and common men, independence and slavery. Bernard Bailyn would comment that "he remained throughout his long career the clear voice of America's Revolutionary ideology, its purest conscience, its most brilliant expositor, its true poet, while struggling to deal with the intractable mass of the developing nation's everyday problems. In this double role—ideologist and practical politician, theorist and pragmatist—he sought to realize the Revolution's glittering promise, and as he did so he learned the inner complexities of these ideals as well as their strengths. . . . He hoped, with increasing confidence, that the common sense of the people and their innate idealism would overcome the obstacles and somehow resolve the ambiguities, and that America would fulfill its destiny—which was, he believed, to preserve, and to extend to other regions of the earth, 'the sacred fire of freedom and self-government,' and to liberate the human mind from every form of tyranny." The success or failure of any leader in U.S. history can be judged through his or her successes or failures at reaching the pragmatic utopian paradox that remains at the heart of the American experiment.

In the summer of 1776 Paine lobbied the Tory-dominated Pennsylvania Assembly and the fractious Continental Congressmen to support the Jefferson committee's manifesto. The Assembly vacillated on the matter, but on July 2, three of Pennsylvania's five delegates voted with the majority of Congress to form a new nation, and after news reached Congress that Britain was preparing to invade New York City, the Declaration ultimately won by a unanimous vote. When it was then published and distributed, Samuel Adams reported from Boston that "the people seem to recognize this resolution as though it were a decree promulgated from heaven." After it appeared in London, England's minister plenipotentiary secretly purchased the services of sixteen thousand German mercenaries for £522,628.

Another congressional committee formed in the wake of Lee's various *Common Sense* motions was one to encourage European support of the American cause. The Committee of Secret Correspondence—Benjamin Harrison, John Dickinson, Thomas Johnson, John Jay, and Benjamin Franklin—at first met regularly with M. Bonvouloir, a spy working for the court of Versailles, and soon employed as a European agent Silas Deane, a one-term Connecticut congressman whose overseas business as a merchant gave him cover to carry letters for the traitors. From France, Deane reported back to the Committee that "*Common Sense* has been translated, and has a greater run, if possible, here than in America." M. Dubourg, Franklin's publisher in Paris, introduced Deane to the comte de Vergennes, the French foreign minister, who was intrigued by the thought of working with America as a means of extracting revenge against the British for the Seven Years War. Vergennes in turn put Deane in touch with Caron de Beaumarchais, a watchmaker, playwright, and spy for the French court, who was establishing a money-laundering operation in support of the United Colonies.

4. Hell Is Not Easily Conquered

When Parliament ignored the Continental Congress's deadline for restoring the colonists' rights as Englishmen, the Americans tried making a direct appeal to the mercies of the throne. Good King George III responded by attacking his own subjects with the largest expeditionary force in British history. Under the command of Admiral Sir Richard Howe, an armada of 138 ships and thirty-two thousand troops began to anchor at Sandy Hook, New Jersey, on July 3, 1776, joining the admiral's landed brother, General William Howe; Canada's General Sir Guy Carleton (with ten thousand troops); and the Carolinas' Admiral Peter Parker (with two thousand). The colonial rebels—in John Adams's estimate, a mere one-third of the American population—defended themselves with both state militias and a national army, Washington's Continental, whose combined force at any one moment rarely exceeded twenty thousand men.

When news of Howe's flotilla reached Philadelphia, Congress insisted that Washington defend New York City. It was, politically, a touchingly naive civilian notion—the feisty little New Worlders giving an immediate drubbing to the might that was England—but strategically it was a general's nightmare. New York's terrain of ocean, inlets, rivers, and islands made it ideal for attack by a great navy, and impossible for troops on the ground to hold. Washington decided the answer would be to split his forces, stationing the great majority at Brooklyn Heights, which he thought might be defensible.

On August 27, Washington watched through a telescope as the British invaded Long Island, storming every outlying post and killing, wounding, or capturing more than fifteen hundred Americans, stopping just short of the trenches defending the Heights. It was a gruesome rout. One British soldier reported that "the Hessians and our brave Highlanders gave no quarter; and it was a fine sight to see with what alacrity they dispatched the rebels with their bayonets after we had surrendered them so that they could not resist."

On the thirtieth, General Howe sent a scouting party to investigate why gunfire from the American fortifications had fallen silent. The men reported back that it was because they had been abandoned. All night and into that very morning, hidden by impenetrable fogs, Washington had commandeered every boat available to evacuate the entire American army across the river and into Manhattan.

At four in the morning on September 15 the British began their assault on New York City. Americans on the first line of defense fled at the mere sound of the enemy's gunships, while others held up their hands in surrender to attacking Hessians, only to be shot in the face. In the retreat to Harlem Heights Washington's volunteers deserted en masse, until only ten thousand troops remained. Within twelve hours the British were marching down Broadway, cheered on by Tory locals.

After hearing relentlessly terrible news from the front lines, Thomas Paine decided he needed to do more than just write and politic from the safety of Philadelphia. He and his musket joined the Pennsylvania Associators, a.k.a. General Roberdeau's Flying Camp, a group of volunteers "flying" into action wherever they might be needed, which at that moment was Amboy, New Jersey, where it was rumored that British forces would be immediately invading. When no redcoats appeared the Associators disbanded, many quitting the cause on the spot after seeing the overwhelming number of British troops unloading in a never-ending flotilla of dinghies from their mass of warships to their fortifications on Staten Island across Raritan Bay.

Paine, however, traveled north to Fort Lee, where on September 19, 1776, General Nathanael Greene, commander of New Jersey's Fort Lee and New York's Fort Washington, which guarded opposing banks of the Hudson River, made him an aide-de-camp and appointed him brigadier. A well-fed, lame, and asthmatic Quaker who would fight by Washington's side throughout the war, Greene was ranked as designated successor should the commander in chief be captured or killed. (Washington's other second was another Paine friend and fan, General Charles Lee, whose less than pleasant disposition brought him the Native American nickname of "Boiling Water.") Greene's wife, Kitty, was Washington's favorite dancing partner, and on many camp nights at Valley Forge and Morristown, Nathanael and Martha sat and talked while George and Kitty danced into the morning light.

Through General Greene Paine was introduced to nearly every American involved in the Revolution whom he had not already met through Franklin or through the immense fame of *Common Sense*. His most significant new friend was a brown-haired, gray-eyed officer whose nose was stippled with the scars of smallpox. Both physically enormous and enormously self-controlled—those who had witnessed his raging temper firsthand would come to prefer his icy disdain—George Washington had "so much martial dignity in his deportment that . . . there is not a king in Europe that would not look like a *valet de chambre* by his side," as Rush described him. Paine and Washington's personal and professional friendship would endure for decades. They shared many ideals: just as Paine had donated all his *Common Sense* profits to the Continental Army, so George Washington refused to accept salaries for the positions of both commander in chief and president. The general was notoriously plainspoken, and Paine's uncluttered prose found great favor with him. They also shared much personally, such as a love of horses, with Washington considered the finest horseman of his time.

Having quickly decided that the rebels needed to back their army and its leader with unquestioned devotion, Paine became Washington's most loyal supporter, both publicly in the press and privately with the civilians running the nation. To the general, a man very much interested in the polish of his reputation, both for his own time and for history, this was a crucial gift, and something only Paine, with his great popularity, reputation, and puffer's talents, could offer. While the writer had a practical rationale for his unwavering stance—he "could see no possible advantage, and nothing but mischief, that could arise by distracting the army into parties"—Paine also very much liked Washington as a man, and greatly admired his zeal for virtue. These feelings were returned by a commander who knew he needed soldiers both on and far from the killing fields.

As time would quickly prove, Paine was not much of a military man; General Greene wrote his wife, Kitty, that in camp, "Common Sense and Colonel Snarl [Cornwell] are perpetually wrangling about mathematical problems," and stories circulated about Paine's less-than-military bearing causing inspiration to such practical jokers as a Major Blodget, who carefully hid Paine's boots and wig and then called out an alarm in the middle of the night so that everyone could watch the fun. While carrying out his military assignments Paine also worked as a correspondent for the Philadelphia papers, and wrote the most significant journalism of this war. When the British next attacked in a series of skirmishes that forced the Americans to retreat to White Plains and then to North Castle, a soldier in the fighting on October 27, Alexander Graydon, said that "the celebrated Thomas Paine . . . happened to witness the proceeding from Fort Lee, and gave us a handsome puff in one of the Philadelphia papers."

Even the most optimistic American rebel leader knew the United Colonies could never defeat Britain alone. Congress approached John Adams and Thomas Jefferson to act as emissaries to the most promising ally—the court of Versailles—and both declined, perhaps one reason being that a transatlantic crossing risked an encounter with a legion of British gunships whose greatest achievement would be the capture of a famous American rebel for treason. Paine's close friend and onetime president of Congress, Henry Laurens, would be apprehended in 1780 while sailing to Holland to negotiate American loans; he would remain imprisoned in the Tower of London for fifteen months, and eventually freed in exchange for Cornwallis.

The man who did accept Congress's assignment was the seventy-year-old Benjamin Franklin. Because of the dangers, news of his departure on October 27, 1776, was kept strictly confidential. There was so much treachery within the American cause, however, that the information was almost immediately passed on to British authorities in New York. That Franklin arrived safely in France on December 21 was a remarkable piece of good fortune, as was the fact that the Americans could not possibly have sent a more suitable representative, for the French welcomed Franklin as if they were receiving the visitation of a living saint, especially the seigneurs of Paris, who had made an immense bestseller of *Poor Richard's Almanack*, and had become eager followers of the ideas of Voltaire, Montesquieu, Diderot, and Rousseau. One Frenchman noted, "He was not given the title Monsieur; he was addressed simply as Doctor Franklin, as one would have addressed Plato or Socrates." The comte de Ségur summed up the Franklin bewitchment as "Nothing was more astonishing than the contrast between the luxury of Paris, the elegance of our fashions, the splendor of Versailles, all those living survivals of the autocratic pride of Louis XIV, the polite but arrogant loftiness of our great nobles—with the almost peasant clothes, the simple but proud deportment, the outspoken but honest language, the uncurled and unpowdered hair . . . which seemed suddenly to transport to Paris in the middle of the decadent and servile civilization of the eighteenth century a philosopher of the time of Plato or a republican of the age of Fabius or Cato." Franklin's popularity in France became so clamorous that it thoroughly annoyed Louis XVI, who gave the Franklin-besotted duchesse de Polignac a Sèvres chamberpot with Franklin's portrait engraved on the inside.

That the American master of lightning and scourge of tyrants was so habitually unassuming only added to his immense appeal. He would describe, at being honored by France's Academy of Sciences and London's Royal Society, feeling just like a little girl, knowing she owns a new pair of beautiful silk garters, even if no one else can see them. However simple his manner, he was nevertheless not one to suffer slights. When refused a request to dine with the author of *The History of the Decline and Fall of the Roman Empire*—Edward Gibbon believing the colonists to be nothing but a pack of traitors—Franklin sent word that he would be happy to serve as a source for Gibbon's next great opus, *The History of the Decline and Fall of the British Empire.*

Despite the warmth of his reception, Franklin believed the job he had been sent by Congress to fulfill—obtaining financial and military aid, either gratis or loaned, from the courts of Europe—was hopeless. The press, the news from back home, and the gossip at the salons were filled with admiration for the American cause, accompanied by a sober acknowledgment of the inevitability of British triumph. These sentiments would only grow after the reports of Washington's cavalcade of loss. To European eyes, the outcome of this colonial insurrection, noble though it might be, was patently clear.

On November 16, 1776, George Washington, Nathanael Greene, and Thomas Paine watched from across the Hudson as General Charles Cornwallis captured Fort Washington and its 2,858 men. Greene had sworn to his commander that the post could be held, and now the Continental Army had, in one day, lost one-fifth of its troops. Six thousand British and Hessian soldiers then attacked Fort Lee on the twentieth, and the Americans fled, in chaos, to Hackensack.

On December 1 the enlistment contracts for soldiers from Maryland

and New Jersey expired. Two thousand men refused to reenlist, abandoning the cause. All other contracts would terminate by year's end.

On December 3 the British took Newport, Rhode Island, and, five days later, Trenton, New Jersey. One fine example of Paine's devotion to Washington was his optimistic account of this dreadful news for Philadelphia readers: "This retreat was censured by some as pusillanimous and disgraceful; but, did they know that our army was at [the] time less than a thousand effective men, and never more than 4000—that the number of the enemy was at least 8000—exclusive of their artillery and light horse—that this handful of Americans retreated *slowly* above 80 miles with losing a dozen men—and that suffering themselves to be forced to an action, would have been their entire destruction—did they know this, they would never have censured it at all—they would have called it prudent—posterity [will] call it glorious—and the names of Washington and Fabius will run parallel to eternity."

On December 10 Washington wrote to his cousin Lund (Mount Vernon's caretaker), "I tremble for Philadelphia. Nothing in my opinion, but General Lee's speedy arrival, who has been long expected, though still at a distance (with about three thousand men), can save it." Charles Lee, who had told John Adams that Paine had "genius in his eyes," was in fact deliberately not making haste, hoping that Washington's floundering would force Congress to replace him as commander in chief. Three days later the British captured Lee, and Washington would write Lund, "Your imagination can scarce extend to a situation more distressing than mine. Our only dependence now is upon the speedy enlistment of a new army. If this fails, I think the game will be pretty well up, as from disaffection and want of spirit and fortitude, the inhabitants, instead of resistance, are offering submission and taking protection from [British General] Howe in Jersey."

On December 13 Washington and a mere 5,000-man Continental Army retreated to the west side of the Delaware River, directly across from Trenton, where the general was forced to send Congress a message that the nation's capital was imperiled, and that they must immediately evacuate. He began a series of guerrilla tactics—small parties crossing the river into the Jerseys to worry Hessian outposts—and an operation of espionage in the form of double agent John Honeyman, who reported the German troop positions to Washington, while telling the Germans that the colonial army was too small and bedraggled to be a threat. Washington then wrote his adjutant, Joseph Reed, about his desperate gamble to keep the cause alive:

> Christmas Day at night, one hour before day, is the time fixed for our attempt on Trenton. For Heaven's sake, keep this to yourself, as the discovery of it may prove fatal to us; our numbers, sorry I am to say, being less than I had any conception of: but necessity, dire necessity, will—nay, must—justify any attempt.

When Paine arrived at camp, senior officers (perhaps including the general) took him aside to insist that the country needed him writing more than fighting. Paine agreed and walked thirty-five miles to Philadelphia, expecting to be captured at any moment during the eleven-hour trek. British forces knew all too well who "Common Sense" was.

Paine arrived to find Philadelphia in chaos. News of defeat after defeat had frightened the vast majority of residents into flight, and morale had collapsed; Paine noted "the deplorable and melancholy condition the people were in, afraid to speak and almost to think, the public presses stopped, and nothing in circulation but fears and falsehoods." British troops were just across the Delaware River, ready at any moment to march into the city and force the American capital to surrender. Tory Philadelphians were preparing to welcome General Howe and his men as saviors. The Continental Congress had removed to the backwater hamlet of Baltimore. It was, Paine said, "the very blackest of times . . . when our affairs were at their lowest ebb and things in the most gloomy state."

He frantically began writing the first of what would eventually number a series of thirteen pieces, one in honor of each colony. He immediately knew just what Americans needed to hear in that time of terror and invasion, a time he called *The American Crisis*. As with *Common Sense,* he rallied his countrymen, evoking the Revolution as a cause far greater than any disagreement over tariffs. With his first *Crisis,* he ennobled each and every citizen rebel into a heroic agent of destiny, and of history. In the prose style that had already made him famous around the world, he promised to "bring reason to your ears, and, in language as plain as A, B, C, hold up truth to your eyes." Finally, Paine used every weapon in his propagandist's arsenal to upend the great advantage Britain held in its favor—fear. In the America of 1776, everywhere they looked, Americans saw reasons to be profoundly afraid—afraid of what the redcoats would do to them, their families, and their property; afraid of losing their British Empire and their British citizenship; afraid of what this new homemade government would do, and what it would require. Paine answered all of these vague and paralyzing terrors in a mere eight pages.

The *Pennsylvania Journal* published this first *Crisis* the week before Christmas, and printers Melchior Steiner and Carl Cist rushed eighteen thousand copies into the streets at a minimal cost. Once again Paine relinquished his share of profits in order to sell at the lowest possible price and achieve the greatest public good. Other printers immediately distributed their own versions throughout each colony. This was, after all, the first new work from America's most famous, most admired, and bestselling author. One pamphlet made its way back to the very source of Paine's inspiration—the banks of the Delaware River.

At dusk on December 23, 1776, General Washington ordered his officers to gather their men into small squads and read aloud what Paine had written. In twenty-one months of fighting, the rebels had not achieved one notable victory. Out of five thousand remaining troops, the general knew that in six days, fifteen hundred contracts would expire.

The American Crisis

These are the times that try men's souls. The summer soldier and the sunshine patriot will, in this crisis, shrink from the service of their country; but he that stands it now, deserves the love and thanks of man and woman. Tyranny, like hell, is not easily conquered; yet we have this consolation with us, that the harder the conflict, the more glorious the triumph. What we obtain too cheap, we esteem too lightly: it is dearness only that gives every thing its value. . . .

As I was with the troops at Fort Lee, and marched with them to the edge of Pennsylvania, I am well acquainted with many circumstances, which those who live at a distance know but little or nothing of. . . . I shall not now attempt to give all the particulars of our retreat to the Delaware; suffice it for the present to say, that both officers and men, though greatly harassed and fatigued, frequently without rest, covering, or provision, the inevitable consequences of a long retreat, bore it with a manly and martial spirit. All their wishes centered in one, which was, that the country would turn out and help them to drive the enemy back. Voltaire has remarked that King William never appeared to full advantage but in difficulties and in action; the same remark may be made on General Washington, for the character fits him. There is a natural firmness in some minds which cannot be unlocked by trifles, but which, when unlocked, discovers a cabinet of fortitude; and I reckon it among those kind of public blessings, which we do not immediately see, that God hath blessed him with uninterrupted health, and given him a mind that can even flourish upon care. . . .

I once felt all that kind of anger, which a man ought to feel, against the mean principles that are held by the Tories: a noted one, who kept a tavern at Amboy, was standing at his door, with as pretty a child in his hand, about eight or nine years old, as I ever saw, and after speaking his mind as freely as he thought was prudent, finished with this unfatherly expression, "Well! give me peace in my day." Not a man lives on the continent but fully believes that a separation must sometime or other finally take place, and a generous parent should have said, "If there must be trouble, let it be in my day, that my child may have peace"; and this single reflection, well applied, is sufficient to awaken every man to duty. . . .

Let it be told to the future world, that in the depth of winter, when nothing but hope and virtue could survive, that the city and the country, alarmed at one common danger, came forth to meet and to repulse it. . . .

I thank God, that I fear not. I see no real cause for fear. I know our situation well, and can see the way out of it. . . . It is great credit to us, that, with a handful of men, we sustained an orderly retreat for near an hundred miles, brought off our ammunition, all our field pieces, the greatest part of our stores, and had four rivers to pass. None can say that our retreat was precipitate, for we were near three weeks in performing it, that the country might have time to come in. Twice we marched back to meet the enemy, and remained out till dark. The sign of fear was not seen in our camp.

For two days Washington's men prepared for their mission. Then, on Christmas, they awoke to hailstorms driving the banks of the Delaware River, which by nightfall quieted into a steady sleet. Though the river was a mere three hundred yards wide, between the darkness, the ice floes crowding the river, and a heavy current, it took four thousand men nine hours to make the crossing, the last of them arriving on the Jersey shore at three in the morning on December 26.

The password for this battle was "victory or death." Trenton meant an additional five-mile hike through a blizzard, and the soldiers did not reach it before sunlight endangered their assault. More than a few of the Americans who marched their way to face a great and determined foe were either barefoot or had their feet tied up only in rags or cowhide. They left smeared tracks of blood across the icy road.

Waiting for them in Trenton were not British redcoats but Hessian mercenaries from the German states of Frankfurt and Kassel, known for their midnight blue uniforms, ponytails hanging to the waist, and mustaches dyed in bootblack. The British had warned their German employees about these colonial foes with such tales as, if caught, the Hessians could expect to be spit-roasted over an open fire like suckling pigs, their flesh eaten, their skin used for drumheads. What the English had failed to caution them about, however, was indulgence in the grand German Christmas tradition of drinking until stupefied, though this turned out to be much less of a factor in the battle to come than that the newly arrived mercenaries had spent a week on twenty-four-hour alerts and were exhausted.

As the Continental Army split into battalions to attack from three different directions (a strategy the commander would later reveal was inspired by Indian raids), Washington heard the worst possible news. Without orders, an underling had sent a group of scouts ahead into town. They had encountered six Germans, and shots had been fired, giving the enemy twelve hours of warning. There would be no surprise in this assault.

At 7:45 a.m. the first of the Americans reached Trenton, only to discover thousands of Germans sleeping soundly. The mercenaries' commander, Colonel Johann Gottlieb Rall, had been so convinced of his forces' superiority over the lowly Americans that he had dismissed the gunfire and his wounded sentries, and had even cancelled the customary patrols along the Delaware River due to the bad weather. When a Tory farmer spotted the rebel army approaching and ran to Rall with a message containing the news, the colonel stuck the farmer's note in his pocket. He was too busy enjoying dinner to read it.

Between Christmas drinking, sentry exhaustion, and commander arrogance, the three American battalions seemed to appear suddenly in the middle of Trenton all at once. Firing with musket and cannon and striking with bayonet, they screamed, "*These* are the times that try men's souls!" The fight lasted all of ninety minutes. Every Hessian regiment surrendered, a total of nearly one thousand prisoners, and Colonel Rall was mortally wounded. The full American casualties: four dead, four injured.

Cornwallis would recover the town by January 2, almost trapping the whole of the Continental Army. The Americans would escape in the middle of the night (just as they had in Brooklyn), and would go on to win another decisive battle at Princeton. For colonial civilians these victories were seen as proof that Americans could defeat the terrifying Hessian mercenaries, and that they might very possibly triumph against King George after all. The province of New Jersey, long on the verge of surrendering to the British, now supported the fight for independence, as did a growing majority of other Americans. The country for the first time was rallying to Congress and its army, and the cause of liberty was saved from a premature collapse. Perhaps more important, between Paine's inspiring manifesto, a ten-dollar bonus supplied by Philadelphia financier Robert Morris, and impassioned pleading from General Washington ("your country is at stake, your wives, your houses, and all that you hold dear"), almost fourteen hundred farmer-citizens would agree to extend their service contracts, and many more would sign on to fight; one said that *these are the times that try men's souls* was "in the mouths of everyone going to join the army." As the war would ultimately be responsible for the deaths of twenty-five thousand Americans, the greatest percentage of the population in U.S. history except for the Civil War, the cause required an endless stream of fresh recruits.

Prussia's Frederick the Great called "the achievements of Washington and his little band of compatriots" at Trenton and Princeton "the most brilliant of any recorded in the history of military achievements." The American struggle, which had seemed so desperate before Trenton, now carried a whiff of hope.

These are the times that try men's souls marked the start of what can only be considered a triumphant era in the life of Thomas Paine. *The American Crisis* solidified his reputation in the pantheon of colonial letters, and he became one of the renegade nation's most admired and beloved public figures.

Instead of turning complacent from this universal acclaim, however, he rededicated his life to fighting for the American cause. At the moment that Paine was writing the first *Crisis,* Admiral Sir Richard Howe announced that, in exchange for an agreement of reconciliation, the king of England would offer full pardons to all. Paine thought he could help Americans consider how they might respond to this offer with *American Crisis II,* which used remarkably acid prose to describe the supplicating overlord, as well as offering a promise that a good dose of patience would surely end in victory for "The United States of America"—this being the first published use of that phrase:

> The Republic of Letters is more ancient than monarchy, and of far higher character in the world than the vassal court of Britain; he that rebels against reason is a real rebel, but he that in defense of reason rebels against tyranny has a better title to "Defender of the Faith," than George the Third. . . .
>
> "The United States of America," will sound as [importantly] in the world or in history, as "the kingdom of Great Britain"; the character of General Washington will fill a page with as much lustre as that of Lord Howe: and the Congress have as much right to command the king and Parliament in London to desist from legislation, as they or you have to command the Congress. . . .
>
> It has been the folly of Britain to suppose herself more powerful than she really is, and by that means has arrogated to herself a rank in the world she is not entitled to: for more than this century past she has not been able to carry on a war without foreign assistance. . . . As a nation she is the poorest in Europe; for were the whole kingdom, and all that is in it, to be put up for sale like the estate of a bankrupt, it would not fetch as much as she owes; yet this thoughtless wretch must go to war, and with the avowed design, too, of making us beasts of burden, to support her in riot and debauchery, and to assist her afterwards in distressing those nations who are now our best friends.

Paine followed almost immediately with another "puff"—really a hymn to the military genius of George Washington and a reproof of the vile conduct of the barbarian invaders—in the January 29, 1777, *Pennsylvania Journal.*

While even the most ardent of rebels would over time be ambivalent about their army's commander, Paine would remain throughout the course of the war, both publicly and privately, steadfastly loyal.

Tories and redcoats were not the only dangers that the rebels had to take into account during the years of revolution. Besides his burst of writing and publishing, Paine served as a secretary to the United States Council of Safety from January 21 until the end of March, negotiating new treaties with Iroquois chief Last Night at the First Reformed Church in Easton, Pennsylvania. The Indian leader had seen the great might of British warships, but observed, "The King of England is like a fish. When he is in the water, he can wag his tail; when he comes on land, he lays down on his side." Paine would come to believe that "the English government had but half the sense this Indian had."

On April 17, after being nominated by John Adams, Paine won congressional appointment, at a monthly salary of seventy pounds, to be secretary of the Committee of Foreign Affairs (previously the Committee of Secret Correspondence). This federal assignment set him at the very nexus of power between the two men he most admired, George Washington and Ben Franklin. April 19 was the anniversary of Concord-Lexington, and to mark the occasion Paine addressed those who were not yet wholeheartedly supporting the new nation with *Crisis III:* "To know whether it be the interest of the continent to be independent, we need only ask this easy, simple question: Is it the interest of a man to be a boy all his life? . . . But what weigh most with all men of serious reflection are, the moral advantages arising from independence: war and desolation have become the trade of the old world; and America neither could nor can be under the government of Britain without becoming a sharer of her guilt, and a partner in all the dismal commerce of death."

The colonists suffered a terrible setback on July 6, when Fort Ticonderoga fell to General John Burgoyne. On hearing the news, King George jubilantly told his wife, "I've beat them, I've beat all the Americans!" Then on September 11, Washington lost the battle of Brandywine, English forces began their march on Philadelphia, and Congress was again forced to evacuate. Paine tried to rally the nation once again, with *Crisis IV:* "It is not a field of a few acres of ground, but a cause, that we are defending, and whether we defeat the enemy in one battle, or by degrees, the consequences will be the same. . . . We are not moved by the gloomy smile of a worthless king, but by the ardent glow of generous patriotism. We fight not to enslave, but to set a country free, and to make room upon the earth for honest men to live in."

Paine bravely procrastinated until the very last moment to leave Philadelphia, and instead of joining his friends in Lancaster and Bordentown, he again followed the front, reaching the Continental Army on October 4, the very day that Washington lost the battle of Germantown. Historians have cited this engagement as one more example of General William Howe's failing to press his advantage, to administer one final coup de grâce. The Howe brothers were in fact caught in an untenable situation, being a general and an admiral attempting reconciliation, to regain colonial hearts and minds. That King George III would insist on continuing the fight no matter what he was told by his officers on the ground would directly inspire the drafters of the American Constitution to grant the power of war solely to Congress.

The morning after the disaster of Germantown, Paine had breakfast with Washington, and later wrote Franklin with news from the front in a letter that (taking into account Paine's native optimism) offers vivid details about day-to-day life in a nation under siege:

> My dear Sir,
>
> . . . Mr. Gross in his English Antiquities mentions fire arrows being used for disabling or destroying fleets but the extract which I have seen, gives me no description how the machine was constructed by which they were thrown. . . . I have made a draft of a bow, something on the plan of the steel cross by which I think [it] will [be possible to] throw an iron arrow across the Delaware. I [propose enclosing] the fire in a bulb near the top. I have shewn it to Mr Rittenhouse who joins me in getting one made for experiment. . . .
>
> On Friday the 19th about one in the morning the first alarm of [the British crossing into the outskirts of Philadelphia] was given, and the confusion, as you may suppose, was very great. It was a beautiful still moonlight morning and the streets as full of [fleeing] men women and children as on a market day. . . .
>
> I set off for German Town about 5 next morning. The skirmishing with the pickets began soon after. I met no person for several

miles riding, which I concluded to be a good sign; after this I met a man on horseback who told me he was going to hasten on a supply of ammunition, that the enemy were broken and retreating fast, which was true. I saw several country people with arms in their hands running cross a field towards German Town, within about five or six miles, at which I met several of the wounded on wagons, horseback, and on foot. I passed Genl. Nash on a litter made of poles, but did not know him. I felt unwilling to ask questions lest the information should not be agreeable, and kept on. About two miles after this I passed a promiscuous crowd of wounded and otherwise who were halted at a house to refresh. Col. Biddle D.Q.N.G. was among them, who called after me, that if I went farther on that road I should be taken, for that the firing which I heard ahead was the enemy's. I never could, and cannot now learn, and I believe no man can inform truly the cause of that day's miscarriage.

The retreat was as extraordinary. Nobody hurried themselves. Every one marched his own pace. The enemy kept a civil distance behind, sending every now and then a shot after us, and receiving the same from us. . . . The army had marched the preceding night 14 miles and having full 20 to march back were exceedingly fatigued. They appeared to me to be only sensible of a disappointment, not a defeat, and to be more displeased at their retreating from German Town, than anxious to get to their rendezvous. . . .

I breakfasted next morning at Genl. W. Quarters, who was at the same loss with every other to account for the accidents of the day. I remember his expressing his surprise, by saying, that at the time he supposed every thing secure, and was about giving orders for the army to proceed down to Philadelphia; that he most unexpectedly saw a part (I think of the artillery) hastily retreating. This partial retreat was, I believe, misunderstood, and soon followed by others. The fog was frequently very thick, the troops young and unused to breaking and rallying, and our men rendered suspicious to each other, many of them being in red. A new army once disordered is difficult to manage, the attempt dangerous. . . .

Genl. Washington keeps his station at the Valley Forge. I was there when the army first began to build huts; they appeared to me like a family of beavers; every one busy; some carrying logs, others mud, and the rest fastening them together. The whole was raised in a few days, and is a curious collection of buildings in the true rustic order. . . .

Mr. & Mrs. Bache are at Mainheim, near Lancaster; I heard they were well a few days ago. . . . Miss Nancy Clifton was there, who said the enemy had destroyed or sold a great quantity of your furniture. Mr. Duffield has since been taken by them and carried into the city, but is now at his own house. I just now hear they have burnt Col. Kirkbride's, Mr. Borden's, and some other houses at Borden Town.

Despite their lack of decisive victories, the brothers Howe had succeeded in capturing Manhattan, Long Island, Staten Island, and Rhode Island, and now controlled the crown jewel of the New World. On September 26 the British army paraded down Philadelphia's Market Street to flag-waving hosannas from loyalist supporters. While Washington and his five thousand men settled into Valley Forge, with officers openly fighting one another and a horrific winter killing a quarter of their troops, British forces spent nine months housed in prodigal comfort, supported at every turn by magnanimous Tories.

If news of the loss of the capital was demoralizing to Americans, it was a terrible blow to the efforts of their colonial agents in Europe. When one Frenchman offered Ben Franklin condolences, Franklin responded with the only defense he had—wit—insisting, "You mistake the matter. Instead of Howe taking Philadelphia, Philadelphia has taken Howe." Franklin knew, however, that to gain any European support for the American cause, Washington and his rebel army would have to prove themselves in the field with a signal victory.

If it is barely conceivable how the Anglo-American cousins went to war, it is almost incomprehensible why the colonists wanted to overthrow both the British Empire and the English form of government entirely, along with centuries of society and culture. That they were willing to confront the military wrath of George III, and then be governed by a system that they were inventing from extremely thin scratch, is confounding, especially in light of such founders as John Adams and Alexander Hamilton insistently proclaiming

Britain's constitutional monarchy as the finest government in the history of the world.

There are three explanations for this attitude, the first being that the British system was thought to depend on a three-tiered state of monarch, nobles, and plebeians balancing one another in a harmony of power. As the colonists now considered monarchs and toffs repugnant and were hoping to create a meritocratic instead of an aristocratic society, they came to believe that the traditional form of state would fail, and that a New World required a new government based on Enlightenment principles of liberty and the educated citizen.

A second reason can be found in the example set by the colonists' neighbors, whose civil rights made the rights of Englishmen seem feeble by comparison. The colonial era was a time when American Indians and Europeans became fully integrated as a community, with full and common relationships not only of business and of government but of friendship and intermarriage. As a child, John Adams met the chiefs of the Punkapaug and Neponsit when they came to visit his father, and Paine would come to know a number of aboriginal men over the course of his American life, and make constant reference in his work to the natural wisdom of Native American political philosophy.

The most significant Amerindians in the Northeast were the Iroquois, whose confederation of Mohawk, Tuscarora, Onondaga, Oneida, Cayuga, and Seneca tribes was governed by a constitution, the Great Law of Peace, and headed by a Great Council of fifty representative sachems, with local powers reserved to chiefs and intertribal issues to the Council. Their constitution made insistent reference to the need for imposing limits to power, as well as to the individual's consent to be governed. One anonymous missionary complained, "All these barbarians have the law of wild asses—they are born, live, and die in a liberty without restraint; they do not know what is meant by bridle and bit." The French explorer baron de Lahontan explained that the Iroquois "valued themselves above anything that you can imagine, and this is the reason they always give for it, that one's as much master as another, and since men are all made of the same clay there should be no distinction or superiority among them." All of these complaints would be echoed in European assessments of Americans during the first years of the United States, and innumerable principles of the Great Law of Peace would surface in the U.S. Constitution.

The most significant reason for British Americans to believe in a democratic republic, however, began in the childhood dreams of the men who would turn the notions of European philosophes into an operating bureaucracy. If boys today hope to grow up to be movie or music stars, or titans of business, the boys who would become the American founding fathers dreamed of modeling themselves on classic Roman orators. The Latin that Thomas Paine never learned in grammar school had been wholeheartedly studied by everyone else he knew, most of whom were the first of their families to attend college (such as Rush and both Adamses) and needed Latin fluency and a working knowledge of Greek to be accepted into King's College (today's Columbia), the College of New Jersey (Princeton), Yale, William and Mary, or Harvard. Those American moderns like Paine who had not been raised on the classics—notably Franklin and Washington—would, like Paine, catch up with English translations later in life. They had to know their Tacitus, Sallust, Cicero, Livy, Virgil, and Plutarch, as the eighteenth century was obsessed with the Roman Republic in the years 509–27 BCE, when it shone in august glory. To the Enlightened mind, that epoch was nothing less than a paradise of liberty, virtue, and justice from which the England of the Hanoverian Georges had fallen like a tottered golem.

The Roman Republic was so idolized, in fact, that the moderns considered Julius Caesar (who, they believed, ended it) one of the greatest villains in world history, a tyrant so vile that the most painful epithet hurled at Washington during his tumultuous second term as president would be "American Caesar!" The young John Adams practiced declaiming Cicero's speeches aloud to himself in his college rooms at night, while Thomas Jefferson revealed a few years before his death that "I feel a much greater interest in knowing what has happened two or three thousand years ago than in what is now passing," and believed that the neoclassical architecture of state buildings inspired American citizens to thoughts of civic virtue and noble democracy. To his new bride, Dolley, James Madison offered a wedding gift of necklace and earrings with stones carved to represent great moments in Roman history. George Washington modeled himself on Cato, the republican senator who stood up to imperial corruption, as well as on Cincinnatus, who devoted himself to his country during a time of national peril but relinquished power and retired to his farm after the crisis was averted. In his biography of Washington, Parson Weems proclaimed the first American president "as pious as Numa, just as Aristides, temperate as Epictetus, and patriotic as Regulus. In giving public trusts, impartial as Severus; in victory, modest as Scipio—prudent as Fabius, rapid as Marcellus, undaunted as Hannibal, as Cincinnatus disinterested, to liberty firm as Cato, and respectful of the laws as Socrates."

In 1709, an Italian woman was digging a well for her garden when the earth gave way. She fell into what turned out to be a four-storied Roman theater, which professional excavation revealed to be part of the cities of Herculaneum and Pompeii. By 1748 the news of these exhumations enlarged the passion for all things Roman far beyond those who had spent their teen years immersed in dead tongues, transforming Europe and America into continents of ardent classicists.

The books (actually papyri) found at Herculaneum were in Greek, the language of first-century Roman intellectuals, and focused on the ideas of Epicurus, who insisted that human beings need not worry about the gods (who provided models of perfection to which we should aspire, but who were completely uninterested in our petty lives) or about what might happen to us after death. Our only concern should be with avoiding pain and living life to the fullest through the principle of *carpe diem* (seize the day), the epigram found circling the sundial in the center of the town of Lewes and sanctified by Horace in his *Odes* with *Nunc est bibendum, nunc pede libero pulsanda tellus* ("Now is the time to drink, now the time to dance footloose upon the earth"). By "living life to the fullest" Epicurus did not mean "the pleasure of profligates"; he was referring, rather, to Aristotle's *eudaimonia,* the good life, the pursuit of happiness, a mixture of sociable companionship (or *fraternité*), conversation, contemplation, and what modern psychology calls "flow," the state of being so enraptured in what you are doing that time flies by and nothing else matters. Some would describe *eudaemonia* as the peace in knowing that you had done the best you could with the life you had; Solon would instruct to "call no man happy until he is dead." Despite this irony, Epicurus would be seen as the constant eighteenth-century antagonist to the Hobbesian, Puritan brimfire notion of a bestial life that must be endured in the hopes of an afterlife of celestial delights. The poet Lucretius's encomium for Epicurus—*qui genus humanum ingenio speravit* ("he who surpasses the human race by his genius")—would be carved into the pedestal of Isaac Newton's statue at Trinity College.

The rage for Epicurus would additionally collide with the eighteenth century's equally great fondness for his philosophic nemesis, Zeno of Citium, master of stoicism. The key to human happiness, Zeno insisted, was to understand that the universe is infused with order and reason, and human beings must live orderly and reasonably, congruent with nature's laws. They must overcome blind passions (to a stoic the source of all evil) while practicing self-control, frugality, simplicity, selflessness, honor, justice, and fortitude, as well as using their unique strengths in service to something greater than themselves. The reward for this virtue is not heaven, but fame—a sterling reputation among one's friends, and then to be remembered across human history. Zeno would further Diogenes' notion of *cosmopolites*—citizens not of individual nations, but of the world—and his most famous Roman adherents would be Seneca and Marcus Porcius Cato (the Younger), subject of playwright Joseph Addison. Beloved Cicero, meanwhile, studied the philosophies of both Epicurus and Zeno, among others, and tried to blend them all into a philosophic epiphany, notably to answer the great question of the classical age: is death something to fear? If fear of death could be ended, Roman philosophers believed, then tyrants would be stripped of all power. Cicero finally concluded that, even if the soul was immortal (as Zeno maintained), it was foolish superstition to believe it would spend eternity in Hades; and if the soul was mortal (as Epicurus taught), then death would bring the loss of all feeling, and there would be no reason to fear something that could not be felt.

The opposing philosophies of Zeno and Epicurus became keystone motifs in the debates of the revolutionary era, and in the works of Thomas Paine. The Enlightenment moderns were additionally devoted to the principle that a country based on the empyrean ideas of the classical world could simultaneously restore that heroic and virtuous era and precipitate "a new order of the ages"—*novus ordo seclorum*—as it proclaims, in the words of Virgil, on the back of the American dollar bill. There was a grave threat to this utopian vision, however, that had precedent in the history of Rome's collapse, another eighteenth-century obsession that reached fever pitch with the 1776 publication of Edward Gibbon's one-and-a-half-million-word bestseller, *The History of the Decline and Fall of the Roman Empire.* The tyranny that ended Roman democracy began with barely noticeable conspiracies against liberty, and so destroyed the virtue, generosity, public spirit, and manliness of the nation's citizens that the greatest of empires collapsed into oblivion. The founding fathers were so inspired by this history that a tea tax judged reasonable by Whitehall was, for them, the first step in the road to slavery, and with their constitutional convention they would attempt to engineer a government that could resist decline and fall in the ways described by Gibbon.

If Thomas Paine was one of the least classically educated of all his friends and acquaintances, he made lifelong amends for that lack. His writings, noted for their appeal to the "common man," made reference to Plato, Socrates, Aristotle, Diogenes, Herodotus, Democritus, Scipio, Aristides, and Epamimondas, and he himself employed such pseudonyms as Atlanticus, Humanus, Aesop, Vox Populi, and Comus. Like many, however, Paine could not help but comment on the mixed blessings of the era's worship of the classical age: "How strangely is antiquity treated! To answer some purposes, it is spoken of as the times of darkness and ignorance, and to answer others, it is put for the light of the world."

The military triumph that every American prayed for finally arrived, but not from George Washington. Following General Howe's long-pursued strategy to take control of the Hudson River and cut off New England and New York from the rest of the United Colonies, British general John Burgoyne and his nine thousand troops marched south from Canada, having to axe their way through the forests and construct forty bridges to cross the wilderness. On July 6 Burgoyne took Fort Ticonderoga, from which he continued on to Albany. From a high bluff over the Hudson River, American generals Horatio Gates and Benedict Arnold were able to determine the British position and then mount a U-shaped counterattack of more than ten thousand patriots at the town of Saratoga. Their strategy was so successful that on October 17, 1777, at 11 p.m., Burgoyne was forced to surrender.

What is it in human nature that, when a great foe is defeated, the victors turn on one another? Gates's and Arnold's breathtaking achievement would in just such a way bring to a head the first of the great and many feuds between the American founding fathers. Washington's string of military failures had made such civilian leaders as Benjamin Rush, Richard Henry Lee, John and Samuel Adams, and Thomas Mifflin openly question his professional competence, and in the wake of Gates's great victory, their criticism turned virulent. Some of them circulated an anonymous pamphlet,

Thoughts of a Freeman, which worried that "the people of America have been guilty of idolatry in making a man their God." John Adams began to publicly suggest that "Washington got the reputation of being a great man because he kept his mouth shut" (not a trait anyone would ascribe to Adams), and to believe that the lack of decent shoes among Continental soldiers was due to Washington's insistence on pointless marching. In time he came to believe that if the commander in chief won the war he would use his enormous popularity to turn himself into a dictator. Adams complained of the general's cautiousness by directly attacking Paine's praise of Washington with, "I am sick of Fabian systems [Fabius being a Roman general known as 'the delayer' for his patience] in all quarters!"—even though he well knew that "Fabian systems" eventually triumphed over Hannibal in the Punic Wars.

In the midst of this conflict came a letter from one Thomas Conway, an Irishman who had performed heroically under fire at Brandywine and had been referred by European colonial agent Silas Deane. Deane had told Conway that a man of his talents would quickly rise up the ranks of the Continental Army, and Conway was now requesting a promotion directly from Congress that would catapult him over many of his superiors. South Carolina congressman Henry Laurens regularly kept his son John, a member of Washington's staff, fully informed of the anti-Washington talk from "actors, accommodators, candle snuffers, shifters of scene and mutes." Laurens may have been the source for Washington's learning of Conway's letters, resulting in the general directly telling one of the anti-Washington group, congressman Richard Henry Lee, that this particular soldier deserved no promotion. On December 13, however, the anti-Washington forces held sway as Congress promoted Conway to both major general and inspector general.

On the nineteenth, Conway and General Horatio Gates met with Congress at York to debate the future of the leadership of the Continental Army. Appearing in Washington's defense was the commander's most loyal ally besides Thomas Paine and Alexander Hamilton, the marquis de Lafayette. Knowing that the American rebels were hoping for Benjamin Franklin, Arthur Lee, and Silas Deane to arrange a full range of military and financial aid from King Louis XVI, Lafayette explained to Congress that, to the French mind, Washington was America, and America, Washington, and the court of Versailles would not accept another commander in his place. Lafayette himself knew that this was not yet true, but Congress did not, and as French aid was crucial for American victory, Washington's position was for the time secured.

Paine joined Lafayette in privately defending Washington against "the Conway Cabal" to his fellow American patricians, while publicly promoting the commander in the public mind by linking his military operations in Pennsylvania to Gates's in New York. He had spent ten months traveling on various missions to gather information for both General Greene and the Pennsylvania Assembly, wandering the colony's back roads, living as a refugee and sleeping at the homes of various friends while avoiding the British and their helpful Tory locals. Most of Paine's friends and the province's government had evacuated to Lancaster, and in time he joined them, living with David Rittenhouse in the home of gunsmith William Henry. If Paine was a man liked either very much or not at all, Henry's son, John Joseph, fell into the not-at-all camp, remembering that "Paine would walk of a morning until 12 o'clock; come in and make an inordinate dinner. The rising from table was between two and three o'clock. He would then retire to his bed-chamber, wrap a blanket around him, and in a large arm chair, take a nap, of two or three hours—rise and walk. These walks and his indolence, surprised my parents. . . . His remissness, indolence or vacuity of thought caused great heart-burning among many primary characters."

In fact, Paine's next major essay, *Crisis V,* was composed on those walks about Lancaster, as he would explain:

> When a party was forming, in the latter end of seventy-seven and beginning of seventy-eight, of which John Adams was one, to remove Mr. Washington from the command of the army, on the complaint that he did nothing, I wrote the fifth number of the *Crisis,* and published it at Lancaster (Congress then being at Yorktown, in Pennsylvania), to ward off that meditated blow; for though I well knew that the black times of seventy-six were the natural consequence of his want of military judgment in the choice of positions into which the army was put about New York and New Jersey, I could see no possible advantage, and nothing but mischief, that could arise by distracting the army into parties, which would have been the case had the intended motion gone on:

To General Sir William Howe . . .

The utmost hope of America in the year 1776, reached no higher than that she might not then be conquered. She had no expectation of defeating you in that campaign. Even the most cowardly Tory allowed, that, could she withstand the shock of that summer, her independence would be past a doubt. You had then greatly the advantage of her. You were formidable. . . . When I look back on the gloomy days of last winter, and see America suspended by a thread, I feel a triumph of joy at the recollection of her delivery, and a reverence for the characters which snatched her from destruction. To doubt now would be a species of infidelity, and to forget the instruments which saved us then would be ingratitude. The close of the campaign left us with the spirit of conquerors. . . .

To the Inhabitants of America . . .

America has surmounted a greater variety and combination of difficulties, than, I believe, ever fell to the share of any one people, in the same space of time, and has replenished the world with more useful knowledge and sounder maxims of civil government than were ever produced in any age before. Had it not been for America, there had been no such thing as freedom left throughout the whole universe. . . . We may justly style it the most virtuous and illustrious revolution that ever graced the history of mankind.

Early in 1777 First Minister Lord North sent General Clinton, the Earl of Carlisle, and William Eden to America to offer the colonials anything they wanted to end the conflict—except independence. When Congress replied that they would only negotiate "such terms of peace as may consist with the honor of independent nations," the English delegates tried to bring their suit directly to the American public. Paine would answer them with *American Crisis VI:*

What sort of men or Christians must you [British delegates] suppose the Americans to be, who, after seeing their most humble petitions insultingly rejected; the most grievous laws passed to distress them in every quarter; an undeclared war let loose upon them, and Indians and negroes invited to the slaughter; who, after seeing their kinsmen

> murdered, their fellow citizens starved to death in prisons, and their houses and property destroyed and burned; who, after the most serious appeals to heaven, the most solemn abjuration by oath of all government connected with you, and the most heart-felt pledges and protestations of faith to each other; and who, after soliciting the friendship, and entering into alliances with other nations, should at last break through all these obligations, civil and divine, by complying with your horrid and infernal proposal. Ought we ever after to be considered as a part of the human race? Or ought we not rather to be blotted from the society of mankind, and become a spectacle of misery to the world?

On November 27, Clinton, Carlisle, and Eden conceded that their efforts had failed, and returned to London to announce that the Americans were determined to form a separate nation.

The French aid that Lafayette had promised in order to save Washington, meanwhile, was already under way. Before even the publication of the Declaration of Independence, King Louis XVI had sent the colonists a million livres. Then, in January 1778, three French ships carrying money and military supplies for the American rebel army set sail for Philadelphia. The machinations that resulted in an absolute monarch supporting the cause of a democratic republic, and initiated the sailing of those ships, would put Thomas Paine at the center of the American Revolution's greatest scandal.

5. The Silas Deane Affair

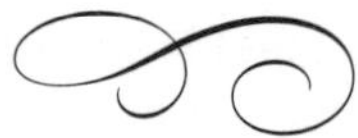

If Britain's tax scheme to subsidize the costs of the Seven Years War triggered the American Revolution, France's bitterness at losing that war would become the linchpin of American triumph. In the summer of 1775, French foreign minister Charles Gravier, comte de Vergennes, sent royal agent Pierre Augustin Caron de Beaumarchais to London undercover to gather more detailed information on the Anglo-American quarrel. Beaumarchais reported back that "all sensible people in England are convinced that the English colonies are lost to the mother country, and that is my opinion too." One of the people Beaumarchais met was Arthur Lee, who for many years served as Benjamin Franklin's London assistant and was now acting as an agent for the American Congress's Committee of Secret Correspondence (to be known when Paine was its clerk as the Committee of Foreign Affairs). A Virginian who had stepped in at the last minute to replace Thomas Jefferson in this posting, Lee met Beaumarchais at a dinner given by London mayor John Wilkes (the same Wilkes whose battles with Whitehall were such an inspiration to Paine in Lewes and Americans in Philadelphia). This proved to be the beginning of a long and difficult relationship that would not end well, with Beaumarchais remarking on "the bilious Arthur Lee, with his yellow skin, green eyes, yellow teeth and hair always in disorder."

There are those living through turning-point eras who embody their spirit, and Caron was such a man. Trained by his watchmaker father to carry on in the family business, the young artisan had barely finished his apprenticeship when, at the age of twenty-two, he invented a wholly new escapement. When a rival horologist stole his design, Caron took their dispute to the French newspapers and then to the Academy of Sciences, where he was vindicated. This self-generated *publicité* brought him to the notice of Mme. de Pompadour, who ordered a watch, as did her paramour, which enabled Caron to now refer to himself as "Watchmaker to the King."

At the court of Versailles he met a Mme. Franquet. When her royal auditor husband died of typhoid, he married her, used her inheritance to purchase an office of royal secretary, and became de Beaumarchais. Within a year she too was dead, and Beaumarchais married a Mme. Lévêque, who also tragically died, inspiring court gossips to wonder if perhaps this particular artisan was also well versed in the constitution of poisons. Besides making watches, overseeing his newly inherited investments, and giving harp lessons to the king's sisters, the indefatigable Beaumarchais additionally worked as a playwright, creating two works that would remain popular in France for centuries, while becoming famous elsewhere as the source of operas by Rossini and Mozart.

Le barbier de Séville and *Le mariage de Figaro* feature in Figaro a variation of Beaumarchais himself, not as a royal watchmaker but as a lowly servant whose diligence, shrewdness, and decency bring justice and mercy to the complicated love lives of immoral aristocrats while showing them their place in the modern (meritocratic) world. It is easy to hear the voice of Caron when, at the turning point of one dramatic scene, Figaro assails Count Almaviva with "Just because you're a great lord, you think you're a genius. Nobility, fortune, rank, position—you're so proud of these things. What have you done to deserve so many rewards? You went to the trouble of being born, and no more."

The Parisian theatergoers who made these plays so immensely successful in the first place were, of course, French aristocrats themselves. Not everyone saw them as merely a delightful way to spend an evening, however; for *Mariage,* Louis XVI would have Beaumarchais imprisoned at St. Lazare, while Napoleon would proclaim it the "revolution already in action." But those troubles and distinctions (as well as revolutionary years spent in exile) lay far in the future; for now, Beaumarchais's great passion besides playwrighting was in working for that same King Louis as a spy, seizing and destroying publications of political attacks on the French state in England and Holland, including one affront to Mme. Du Barry, and another to Marie Antoinette. It was on such an espionage mission to London, in fact, that he met Arthur Lee, who convinced him of the absurd idea that the Americans were going to win their spat with Britain. Beaumarchais took all this into account, and decided there must be a way he could support the enlightened republican cause and make a good deal of money, all at the same time.

After further conversations with Arthur Lee and French foreign minister Vergennes, Beaumarchais began a new corporation, Roderigue Hortalez et Cie (Hortalez being his undercover alias), to covertly funnel aid to the Americans from England's great rivals, the Bourbon courts of Spain and France. The company's secrecy—it was, in truth, a money-laundering front—was critical, as neither court wished to directly reignite a war with Britain, and neither monarch could appear to publicly support republican democrats rebelling against another monarch. Vergennes would reason with his king that "if the colonies are determined to reject the sovereignty of His Britannic Majesty, it would not be in the interest of France to see them reduced by force," while Beaumarchais would point out that to "sacrifice a million to put England to the expense of a hundred millions, is exactly the same as if you advance a million to gain ninety-nine." Eventually an exuberant Arthur Lee informed the Committee of Secret Correspondence that France would be sending the American republicans five million livres in gold and materials. In actuality, on May 2, 1776, Vergennes prepared documents for the throne authorizing a million livres in gold to be paid to Beaumarchais, another million to come from the Spanish, and a third from the moneylenders of Europe. Beaumarchais divvied the three million among three ships, which sailed to the French West Indies after Vergennes had learned of the American victories at Trenton and Princeton. However secret its operation, however, every Hortalez move was uncovered by British agents, and only one ship, with one million livres, reached the colonial rebels.

Two months later Silas Deane arrived in France to begin his new assignment as America's commercial agent for Europe. Deane got this appointment even though he had never before been overseas, and could neither speak nor read French. He was, however, the man who had supplied the Green Mountain Boys in their 1775 conquest of Fort Ticonderoga, was a longtime backer of the American cause, and proved to be remarkably assiduous. Immediately on arriving in Europe, Deane met with Vergennes, who on July 17, 1776, referred him to Beaumarchais. The French government and Arthur Lee told Deane that the million livres that had arrived in Philadelphia was a gift. Beaumarchais, however, insisted that it was a loan, for which Beaumarchais would receive a 10 percent commission.

As Deane himself was to be paid a 5 percent commission on his overseas transactions, he had reason to believe Beaumarchais instead of Lee and Vergennes.

Every American rebel agent working in Europe at the time found himself besieged by would-be volunteers for the Continental Army, and Deane was no exception. Washington would become annoyed with the useless recruits arriving from Europe with Deane letters of recommendation—with one remarkable exception, a redheaded nineteen-year-old by the name of Marie Joseph Paul Yves Roch Gilbert du Motier, a French dragoon captain wealthy enough to pay for the American rank of major general and to offer his services to the Continental Army gratis. Like Vergennes, Motier was allying himself with the American cause in revenge for the Seven Years War, though his case was more personal, as his father, a colonel, had been killed in battle. He had heard wonderful things about the Americans from one of their most ardent supporters in Europe, the Duke of Gloucester—King George III's younger brother—and had defied a direct order from King Louis XVI forbidding his volunteering. "I am persuaded that the human race was created to be free and that I was born to serve that cause," was his motto, which perfectly suited this disciple of Voltaire. He traveled the seven hundred miles from Charleston to Philadelphia (writing his wife along the way that "the United States is the most marvelous land on earth"), and on his arrival, Washington felt compelled to apologize for the starving and naked condition of his troops: "We must be embarrassed to show ourselves to an officer who has just left the French Army." The marquis de Lafayette replied, "I am here to learn, not to preach or teach." He would become as much a son to Washington as the general would ever have, and a great friend to Thomas Paine, with whom he would wage two revolutions on opposite sides of the world.

In France, regardless of Beaumarchais's interest in the making of great sums of money, his grave industriousness was a tremendous aid to the American cause. Over the war years, Hortalez would sail between twelve and forty ships from various French ports to aid the colonists. At the end of 1777, however, M. De Francey, a Hortalez agent, appeared before Congress with a bill of 4.5 million livres and a letter signed by Silas Deane testifying to the accuracy of this sum. Congress wrote to its French representatives—Deane, Lee, and Franklin—for an explanation, and though a reply was sent, the letter never arrived.

During his months of working for the American foreign office in Europe, Arthur Lee had come to learn that, in addition to his government post, Silas Deane was employed by American financier Robert Morris as a commercial agent, and Lee soon after became convinced (from some not so convincing evidence) that Deane was a fraud and a war profiteer, which accusation he swiftly made to various U.S. congressmen, most notably his two older brothers. When Deane sent the American legislature a letter of bona fides signed by Franklin, Arthur Lee in turn accused Franklin of also profiting from the conflict. Though the era was fairly lax about mixing business and statecraft, it was nonetheless a particularly damning charge. Not only did it violate the eighteenth-century stoic view of selfless devotion to the greater good as a key element of virtue, but so many Americans had already gotten so rich from the Revolution that such leaders as John Adams feared that even if independence was won, the nation was certain to fracture into a civil war of rich versus poor.

On December 8 Deane was recalled to Philadelphia; he was replaced by Adams, who, like Deane, had never previously been outside the United States and could neither speak nor read French. Benjamin Franklin, meanwhile, used the news of Gates's and Arnold's American triumph over Burgoyne at Saratoga to conjure a monumental bit of political derring-do. The American victory had stunned Europe so deeply that German princes from that moment on refused to contract with Westminster for additional mercenaries, and the king of France wrote the king of Spain that "the destruction of the army of Burgoyne . . . [has] totally changed the face of things. . . . I have thought . . . having consulted upon the propositions which the insurgents make, that it was just and necessary to treat with them to prevent their reunion with the mother country." One of France's great philosophes, the encyclopedist Denis Diderot, was inspired to proclaim, "May these brave Americans, who would rather see their wives raped, their children murdered, their dwellings destroyed, their fields ravaged, their villages burned, and rather shed their blood and die than lose the slightest portion of their freedom, prevent the enormous accumulation and unequal distribution of wealth, luxury, effeminacy, and corruption of manners, and may they provide for the maintenance of their freedom and the survival of their government!"

Franklin exploited the shock of Saratoga to inform all of Europe that it was merely the beginning of the end for George III's American empire, and that the Howe brothers' surrender was imminent. When British first minister North immediately sent a representative offering everything but independence, Franklin had the nerve to reply, "You have lost by this mad war, and the barbarity with which it has been carried on, not only the government and commerce of America, and the public revenues and private wealth arising from that commerce, but what is more, you have lost the esteem, respect, friendship and affection of all that great and growing people, who consider you at present, and whose posterity will consider you, as the worst and wickedest nation upon earth." North's emissary was only one of many visitors, however, to Franklin's Hôtel de Valentinois apartment on the rue Basse in the town of Passy (between Paris and Versailles), which hosted, by turns, numerous British agents as well as Vergennes's secretary, Conrad Alexandre Gérard. Gérard offered generous military assistance and just as generous commercial treaties, while British Secret Service Parisian chief Paul Wentworth conveyed a letter to Franklin that the king was now indeed pondering the question of American independence. Franklin met openly with all, making no effort to shield his correspondence and meetings from spies, which he assumed were everywhere (as they were). After intercepting the materials of various British agents, the French assumed that Franklin was in final negotiations for an Anglo-American reunion, which only intensified their efforts, while the escalation of France's offers convinced the anxious English that Versailles and Philadelphia were on the verge of a great tactical, commercial, and political agreement.

On February 6, before Adams had even left the United States, Franklin negotiated a Franco-American alliance pledging that neither country would stop fighting Britain until America's freedom as a nation had been secured. When in March news of Franklin's treaty reached the United States, the British immediately retreated from Philadelphia to defend New York City against what they foresaw as an imminent French naval assault. On April 13, 1778, seventeen French vessels under the command of Admiral Charles Hector, comte d'Estaing, left Toulon for the New World. On the passenger list were Conrad Alexandre Gérard, who had been appointed French minister to the United States, and Silas Deane, who returned home to find that he, Caron de Beaumarchais, and Hortalez had ignited a federal crisis.

Arriving at Bordeaux on March 30, 1778, meanwhile, John Adams learned that he had yet another reason to dislike Thomas Paine:

> The French naturally had a great many questions to settle. The first was, Whether I was the famous Adams [meaning cousin Samuel]? . . . The pamphlet entitled *Common Sense* had been printed in the "Affaires de Angleterre et de l'Amérique," and expressly ascribed to Mr. Adams, the celebrated member of Congress—*le célèbre member du congres.* It must be further known that, although the pamphlet, *Common Sense,* was received in France and all of Europe with rapture, yet there are certain parts of it that they did not choose to publish in France. The reasons of this any man may guess. *Common Sense* undertakes to prove that monarchy is unlawful by the Old Testament. They therefore gave the substance of it, as they said; and paying many compliments to Mr. Adams, his sense and rich imagination, they were obliged to ascribe some parts of it to republican zeal. When I arrived at Bordeaux, all that I could say or do could not convince anybody but that I was the fameux Adams. . . . When I arrived in Paris . . . I found great pains taken, much more than the question was worth, to settle the point that I was not the famous Adams. There was a dread of sensation. . . . It was settled, absolutely and unalterably, that I was a man of whom nobody had ever heard before—a perfect cipher; a man who did not understand a word of French, awkward in his figure, awkward in his dress; no abilities, a perfect bigot and fanatic.

Franklin immediately put Adams up at his Passy château, and got his son, John Quincy, accepted into the boarding school attended by his grandson, Benny. These, it seems, were the only kindnesses that any of the Americans in Paris would ever offer one another. Arthur Lee told Adams that "Franklin was beneath contempt," while Franklin, on April 3, 1778, wrote Arthur Lee a letter, which he never sent: "If I have often received and borne your magisterial snubbings and rebukes without reply, ascribe it to . . . my pity for your sick mind, which is forever tormenting itself with its jealousies, suspicions and fancies that others mean you ill, wrong you or fail in respect for you. If you do not cure yourself of this temper, it will end in insanity, of which it is the symptomatic forerunner, as I have seen in several instances. God preserve you from so terrible an evil; and for his sake pray suffer me to live in quiet." Adams's opinion of Franklin, meanwhile, would, over time, sour to a curdle:

> I can have no dependence on his word. I never know when he speaks the truth and when not. If he talked as much as other men and deviated from the truth as often in proportion as he does now, he would have been the scorn of the universe long ago. . . . The history of our Revolution will be one continued lie from one end to the other. The essence of the whole will be that Dr. Franklin's electrical rod smote the earth and out sprang General Washington. That Franklin electrified him with his rod, and thence forward these two conducted all the policy, negotiations, legislatures and war.

In turn, Franklin would eventually say of Adams that "those who feel pain at seeing others enjoy pleasure and are unhappy because others are happy, must daily meet with so many causes of torment, that I conceive them to be already in a state of damnation. . . . [Adams] means well for his country, is always an honest man, often a wise one, but sometimes and in some things, is absolutely out of his senses."

In Philadelphia, Deane testified before Congress on August 9 and 15. When asked to produce his accounting ledgers, he replied that he had not brought them along, as "having placed my papers and yours in safety, I left Paris . . . in full confidence that I should not be detained on the business I was sent for." In spite of the fact that, five months earlier, a letter from Lee, Franklin, and Deane had arrived at Congress confirming that "no repayment will ever be required from us for what has already been given either in money or military stores," Deane again insisted that the Hortalez bill should be paid, as well as the costs of his return voyage, which had been loaned by Beaumarchais.

The Silas Deane affair split the American government exactly in half, with Arthur Lee, his brothers Richard Henry and William, Timothy Matlock, Samuel Adams, and Thomas Paine arrayed against Robert Morris, Gouverneur Morris, John Jay, Robert Treat Paine, Matthew Clarkson, and William Duer. Their battle would mark the beginnings of feral party politics in American government, and the split was, for most of the men involved, irreconcilable and lifelong, even though (or perhaps especially because) the evidence was confusing and the testimony contradictory. The rancor of the various pro- and anti-Deane factions in Congress grew increasingly severe, until that body's president, Henry Laurens, was forced to resign, replaced by Deane ally John Jay.

The split in opinion remained so even and so intractable, however, that it incapacitated the legislature. Deane asked to testify before Congress once again, and was turned down; he waited to be either accused or exonerated, but even after months had passed, nothing was decided. Finally, Deane took matters into his own hands with "The Address of Silas Deane to the Free and Virtuous Citizens of America," published in the December 5 *Pennsylvania Packet,* which attacked the character of Arthur Lee and the competence of the American government. Until that time, the argument over Deane had been kept within the halls of Congress, as both sides feared that any publicity (or the wrong decision) would undermine both the alliance with France and the tottering public spirit of a besieged United States. Richard Henry Lee would remark of Deane's article that "the single publication of the libel on the 5th of December had done more injury to the American cause than a reinforcement of 20,000 men to the [enemy's] general could have produced," while John Adams, in France, wrote, "It appeared to me like a dissolution of the constitution. . . . [Deane] ought to be hunted down for the benefit of mankind."

Paine, who believed in principle over realpolitik (and was, after all, donating the whole of his *Common Sense* earnings to the war effort), was incensed that anyone was making money through his political connections—which Paine thought Deane was doing with Robert Morris—or that anyone would try to extort money from the new country's impoverished government—which Paine believed Deane was doing with Beaumarchais. Alongside the Lees, he worried that the agent's greed might endanger the goodwill of Louis XVI, and that the mix of commerce and government practiced by Deane and the Morrises would lead to a nation controlled by wealthy oligarchs, precisely the sort of aristocratic vermin that American moderns were hoping to annihilate through a democracy of virtuous citizens.

Paine became so angry that he responded to Deane's charges with a series of essays published in the *Pennsylvania Packet* on December 15, December 29, January 2, and January 5. Besides attacking Deane's unpatriotic behavior, his lack of civic virtue, and the financial shenanigans of his allies, Paine insisted that a public inquiry be made into Robert Morris's chairing of the committee supplying the Continental Army, which contracted with Morris's own firm for more than half a million dollars:

> If Mr. Deane or any other gentleman will procure an order from Congress to inspect an account in my office, or any of Mr. Deane's

> friends in Congress will take the trouble of coming themselves, I will give him or them my attendance, and show them in handwriting which Mr. Deane is well acquainted with, that the supplies he so pompously plumes himself upon were promised and engaged, and that as a present, before he ever arrived in France. . . . Those who are now [our] allies, prefaced that alliance by an early and generous friendship; yet that we might not attribute too much to human or auxiliary aid, so unfortunate were these supplies that only one ship out of three arrived; the *Mercury* and *Seine* fell into the hands of the enemy.

Paine's virtuous zealotry and energetic lack of self-restraint backfired, however, for in announcing that "those who are now allies, prefaced that alliance by an early and generous friendship," he in effect revealed that America had received French assistance before the two countries' treaties had been recognized. This not only publicly embarrassed the French government but also threatened to undermine the Franco-American alliance. Though it was widely known in both Philadelphia and Versailles that Britain was aware of the details of the first Hortalez mission long before Paine had divulged its secret, the French minister to Philadelphia (and Deane ally) Gérard nevertheless immediately demanded that Paine publicly reverse himself. When the next Paine article appeared without any amends, however, Gérard went that same day to Congress to insist it immediately undertake "measures suitable to the circumstances." President of Congress John Jay issued a letter repudiating the actions of his secretary to the Committee of Foreign Affairs, while Deane supporter Gouverneur Morris attacked him on the floor of Congress as being unfit to serve the American government:

> What would be the idea of a gentleman in Europe of Mr. Paine? Would he not suppose him to be a man of the most affluent fortune, born in this country of a respectable family, with wide and great connections, and endured with the nicest sense of honor? Certainly he would suppose that all these pledges of fidelity were necessary to a people in her critical circumstances. But, alas, what would he think, should he accidentally be informed, that this, our Secretary of Foreign Affairs, was a mere adventurer from England, without fortune, without family connections, ignorant even of grammar.

When the controversy became public, many Paine enemies took the opportunity to denounce his actions as unpatriotic. In the *Pennsylvania Evening Post,* an anonymous poem concluded:

> So you, great Common Sense,
> did surely come
> From out the crack
> in grisly Pluto's bum.

And at least twice he was beaten in the streets by Deane supporters.

At the same time that French minister Gérard was demanding Congress take action, however, he was also negotiating directly with Paine in an effort to co-opt him, as he discussed in a January 17 letter to Vergennes:

> When I had denounced to Congress the assertions of M. Payne [as the French would always spell his name], I did not conceal from myself the bad effects that might result to a head puffed up by the success of his political writings, and the importance he affected. I foresaw the loss of his office, and feared that, separated from the support which has restrained him, he would seek only to avenge himself with his characteristic impetuosity and impudence. All means of restraining him would be impossible, considering the enthusiasm here for the license of the press, and in the absence of any laws to repress audacity even against foreign powers. The only remedy, my lord, I could imagine to prevent these inconveniences, and even to profit by the circumstances, was to have Payne offered a salary in the King's name, in place of that he had lost. He called to thank me, and I stipulated that he should publish nothing on political affairs, nor about Congress, without advising with me, and should employ his pen mainly in impressing on the people favorable sentiments towards France and the Alliance, of the kind fittest to foster hatred and defiance towards England. He appeared to accept the task with pleasure. I promised him a thousand dollars per annum, to begin from the time of his dismission by Congress. He has already begun his functions in declaring in the Gazette that the affair of the military effects has no reference to the Court and is not a political matter. You know too well the prodigious

> effects produced by the writings of this famous personage among the people of the States to cause me any fear of your disapproval of my resolution.

Even though he would most likely write of his own volition exactly what Gérard wanted, and even though he was now facing serious financial difficulties, Paine decided there might be a conflict of interest in working as an American political essayist for the court of Versailles, and turned the offer down, all of which he explained in another *Packet* article: "Mr. Gérard through the medium of another gentleman made me a very genteel and profitable offer. My answer to the offer was precisely in these words: 'Any service I can render to either of the countries in alliance, or to both, I ever have done and shall readily do, and Mr. Gérard's esteem will be the only compensation I shall desire.' "

In the wake of the French minister's complaints, Paine and his publisher were called before Congress and asked if Paine was the writer of the articles printed under the name *Common Sense.* They both responded yes and were dismissed. The next day, Paine wrote to the legislature: "From the manner in which I was called before the House yesterday, I have reason to suspect an unfavorable disposition in them towards some parts in my late publications. What the parts are against which they object, or what those objections are, are wholly unknown to me." After five days of debate, in a motion seconded by Gouverneur Morris, Congress voted whether or not to relieve Paine of his clerkship. The result was a tie, and again a vote was called, and again the count was a deadlock. The pro- and anti-Paine forces were just as perfectly split as were the pro- and anti-Deane factions. Eventually, John Jay tried to solve this conundrum by publicly claiming that Louis XVI "did not preface his alliance with any supplies whatever sent to America."

What is painfully revealed by the documents of this incident is that Paine did not really comprehend that he had done anything wrong. Democracy, he believed, meant a government transparently open to its citizens; with his actions he had attempted to counter Silas Deane's public fabrications and treasonous attacks on the reputation of what was, in his mind, a new and precarious Congress. The anti-Paine legislators were furious that he had upset the French, but were perhaps additionally angry that he had taken their dispute outside the "club"; in addition, many ideological foes had been looking for a reason to rid themselves of Paine's overly democratical notions and his Enlightenment sanctimony. How much the citizens of a republic should know of their government's business would remain a profound source of debate for the next two hundred years of American history.

Besides being by turns voluble and taciturn, manic and depressive, and a little too quick to trumpet his own talents, Paine was famously oversensitive and easily hurt (such sensitivity was at times a virtue, for as Clive James has noted, "Thin skin, after all, is what a writer is in business to have"). Like Deane, Paine heard nothing from Congress, and the next day, for these reasons and more, he, like Deane, took matters into his own hands, and he resigned.

The loss of this position was a severe blow. Being secretary to the Committee of Foreign Affairs gave Paine a center seat, directly at the intersection of Washington and Franklin, in the war for independence and the founding of the United States. Eventually, he would have to write at least two letters explaining what had happened. Considering how relentlessly optimistic and ebullient he usually was (even when writing the *Crises*), these letters reveal how deeply he had fallen into a depression blurring into paranoia. He was severely afflicted with this immense grief for a number of months, and would, some years later in Paris, suffer a resurgence so crushing it would lead to his reputation for being a drunkard:

TO HIS EXCELLENCY GENERAL WASHINGTON
PHILADELPHIA, January 31st, 1779.
SIR:

Hearing that you leave this place tomorrow I beg you to accept a short reason why I have not waited on you.

I have been out nowhere for near these two months. The part I have taken in an affair that is yet depending, rendered it most prudent in me to absent myself from company lest I should be asked questions improper to be answered, or subject myself to conversation that might have been unpleasant. That there has been foul play somewhere is clear to every one—and where it lies, will, I believe, soon come out.

Having thus explained myself, I have to add my sincere wishes for your happiness in every line of life, and to assure you, that as far

> as my abilities extend I shall never suffer a hint of dishonor or even a deficiency in respect to you to pass unnoticed.
>
> I have always acted that part, and am confident that your virtues and conduct will ever require it from me as a duty as well as render it a pleasure.

He wrote similarly to Franklin:

> I have lately met with a turn, which, sooner or later, happens to all men in popular life, that is, I fell, all at once, from high credit to disgrace, and the worst word was thought too good for me. But so sudden is the revolution of public opinion that the same cause which produced the fall recovered me from it.
>
> Mr. Deane is here. He is certainly not the man you supposed him to be when you wrote your recommendatory letters of him. He published a most inflammatory address in the newspapers of the 5th of December last, which, by the means of a party formed to support it, obtained such an ascendancy over all ranks of people, that the infatuation was surprising. . . . The clamor against Congress was violent, and as I saw no prospect of it abating, I gave, after ten days, an answer to it; hoping thereby to stay the rage of the public till the matter could be calmly understood. . . . The dispute has been a disagreeable one, but the imposition had it passed would have been still worse, and it will serve to show to the enemy that the Congress are not the absolute leaders of America.

In time Robert Morris would be forced to admit that he and Deane were, just like Deane and Beaumarchais, running independent commercial ventures while simultaneously working for the American government. Then, in 1780, Silas Deane left America for Europe, where he would later be paid by the British government to write letters urging reunion, to be published in the British-controlled New York City papers, as Paine would report in a November 26, 1781, letter to Franklin's grandnephew, Jonathan Williams:

> Your former friend Silas Deane has run his last length. In France he is reprobating America, and in America (by letters) he is reprobating France, and advising her to abandon her alliance, relinquish her

> independence, and once more become subject to Britain. . . . Mr. Robt. Morris assured me that he had been totally deceived in Deane, but that he now looked upon him to be a bad man, and his reputation totally ruined. Gouverneur Morris hopped round upon one leg, swore they had all been duped, himself among the rest, complimented me on my quick sight—and by Gods says he nothing carries a man through the world like honesty.

After Silas Deane's death, his heirs sued the American government for compensation, and received $35,000. When archives of King George's letters were released in 1867, however, it was revealed that Deane had in fact been working as a British informant for the whole of the Revolution, holding regular midnight meetings in France at the Place Vendôme with agent Paul Wentworth (who described the American contingent in Paris as "Dr. Franklin is taciturn, deliberate, and cautious; Mr. Deane is vain, desultory, and subtle; Mr. Arthur Lee, suspicious and indolent"). It is unclear whether or not Deane knew that his secretary, Edward Bancroft, was also working as a British spy, for four hundred pounds a year.

Like Deane's heirs, Beaumarchais would eventually be paid as well. In 1786 a congressional accounting produced certain promissory notes, signed by the king of France and vetted by Franklin, amounting to three million livres, but only two million had been deposited in the United Colonies' French bank accounts. On January 25, 1787, Franklin would explain to Congress that "I conjecture it must be money advanced for our use to M. de Beaumarchais, and that it is a *mystére du cabinet,* which perhaps should not be further enquired into. . . . It may well be supposed that if the Court furnished him with the means of supplying us, they may not be willing to furnish authentic proofs of such a transaction so early in our dispute with Britain." Arthur Lee and some of his Philadelphia contingent would accuse Franklin of keeping this one million for himself, but after Franklin's death a receipt from Beaumarchais would be found, exonerating him.

Paine's intransigence (or principle) in the Deane affair would cause him lingering damage. He managed to repair his relationships with most of Deane's supporters, especially after the traitorous letters urging reunion with England were published, but John Jay turned against him, as did the Baches, Franklin's daughter and son-in-law; Sarah wrote her father that "there never was a man less beloved in a place than Paine is in this, having at different times disputed with everybody. The most rational thing he could have done would have been to have died the instant he had finished his *Common Sense,* for he never again will have it in his power to leave the world with so much credit." In time, Franklin would call Arthur Lee "the most malicious enemy I ever had," but he never begrudged Paine for siding with the anti-Deane forces, and the two would remain extremely close for the rest of Franklin's life.

There is no better illustration of the great paradox of Thomas Paine than that, in the wake of the Deane affair, he would never again be employed by the U.S. government. For a man who suffered periods of financial drought, whose closest friends included Benjamin Franklin, George Washington, and Thomas Jefferson, this was astonishing. If John Adams, famous for turning so heated in debate that he would "flip his wig" and hurl it at his opponent, could have a near-lifelong political career what element in Paine's character prevented him from doing likewise? However admired and even loved he was by some of the greatest men of his age, others just as passionately found him impudent, obnoxious, self-absorbed, impetuous, conceited, and disputatious, and accordingly made efforts to undermine him. It is also apparent that he was not all that interested in or capable of engaging in the day-to-day maneuvers of realpolitik. He was clearly enraptured by ideas and values, not coalitions and compromise. The result of this disparity in theory and practice was that Thomas Paine, one of the great political essayists in world history, would fail at politics, both in the New World and the Old.

If the Deane affair ended up turning such propertied men as John Jay and Gouverneur Morris against Paine, it just as decisively turned Paine against them. In one of his most fascinating but little-known essays, "A Serious Address to the People of Pennsylvania on the Present Situation of Their Affairs," published in the *Packet* of December 1778, he discussed various issues surrounding the still controversial Pennsylvania constitution, while slyly making jabs at the American nouveaux riches. Inspired by his reading of *An Inquiry into the Nature and Causes of the Wealth of Nations,* Paine came to theorize that labor was the true source of all capital, while property, without consumers to buy it or farmers to harvest it, was worth absolutely nothing in and of itself. He feared that if America fell into extremes of rich and poor, it would be corrupted to the point where virtue would be suffocated, ending charity, as well as any other desire to contribute to the public good, leaving a society with nothing supporting it beyond what is today called Darwinian capitalism. He postulated that if only the propertied were allowed the vote, the poor and the plebeian would no longer consider themselves citizens, and the rich would be forced to be the nation's sole backbone and defense. At the same time, however, he reiterated the Enlightenment ideology that a republic must be composed of educated, selfless citizens or it would fall into the hands of craven mobs.

Paine was not the only official relieved of his duties by Congress during this time, for Arthur Lee and John Adams were informed that they were no longer needed in France. Adams took the news poorly, writing to Abigail, "The Congress have not taken the least notice of me. . . . They never so much as bid me come home, bid me stay, or told me I had done well or done ill. . . . The scaffold is cut away, and I am left kicking and sprawling in the mire. It is hardly a state of disgrace that I am in but rather of neglect and contempt." His removal meant a promotion for Franklin, and Paine sent him a note to mark the honor: "I congratulate you on your accession to the State of Minister Plenipotentiary. Could you have lived to fill a particular point in the circle of human affairs, it would have been that to which you are now so honorably called. We rub and drive on, all things considered, beyond what could ever be expected, and instead of wondering why some things have not been done better, the greater wonder is we have done so well."

The following month John Adams fell into a violent disagreement with his cousin Samuel over the drafting of the Massachusetts state constitution. Samuel wanted to follow the outlines of Pennsylvania's charter, written at a convention chaired by Franklin, which had led to perhaps the most democratic government in human history. The Pennsylvania constitution extended voting rights to all males (free, Caucasian, and over the age of twenty) who had lived and paid taxes in the state for at least one year; the greatest power in its government was held by a single legislature, whose assemblymen did not need to own property to run for office. When Paine backed Samuel Adams, John commented that "Paine's wrath was excited because my plan of government was essentially different from the silly projects that he had published in his *Common Sense*. By this means I became suspected and unpopular with the leading demagogues and the whole Constitutional Party in Pennsylvania"; he would later take a gibe at

Franklin, writing that he "did not even make the constitution of Pennsylvania, bad as it is." When Pennsylvania's charter became the model for the revolutionary government of France, Adams suggested that it had sowed the seeds of the Terror and the guillotine, writing of Condorcet and the duc de la Rochefoucauld that they "owed their final and fatal catastrophe to this blind love" of the suspect constitution. His rancor stemmed from the belief, shared by such other wealthy founding fathers as John Dickinson and Robert Morris, that such a charter could only lead to mob rule and demagogues. They wanted instead to emulate the British model of separation of powers, at the state level meaning a balance of governor, senate, and house of representatives, with those hoping to serve as senators first showing significant ownership of property as proof of their wisdom and education, much like the members of England's House of Lords. In what must have been a shock to them all, Paine (who changed his mind on many key issues over the course of his life) eventually came to think that a unicameral legislature might not be the best form of government after all. In a September 20, 1786, letter to the *Pennsylvania Gazette,* he would say that "a single legislature, on account of the superabundance of its power, and the uncontrolled rabidity of its execution, becomes as dangerous to the principles of liberty as that of a despotic monarch."

For the United States as a whole, John Adams's theories of government would, in general, prevail, and many onlookers would question how democratic and representative American government could actually be following the British, Harrington, Adams et al. models. French minister Anne-Robert-Jacques Turgot commented:

> The fate of America is already decided. Behold her independence beyond recovery. But will she be free and happy? . . . I am not satisfied. . . . I observe that by most of the [state] constitutions the customs of England are imitated without any particular motive. Instead of collecting all authority into one [legislature] . . . they have established different bodies, a body of representatives, a council, and a governor, because there is in England a House of Commons, a House of Lords, and a King. They endeavor to balance these different powers, as if this equilibrium, which in England may be a necessary check to the enormous influence of royalty, could be of any use in republics founded upon the equality of all the citizens.

Turgot's letter enraged Adams, who responded in 1787 with the three-volume *Defence of the Constitutions of the Government of the United States of America Against the Attack of M. Turgot, in His Letter to Dr. Price, Dated the Twenty-Second Day of March, 1778.* (In the small world that was the Republic of Letters, that same Dr. Price would in turn inspire Adams's political cousin, Edmund Burke, to publish *Reflections on the Revolution in France,* which would serve as impetus for Paine's *Rights of Man.*) In *Defence,* Adams would "contend that the English Constitution is in theory the most stupendous fabric of human invention, both for the adjustment of its balance and the prevention of its vibrations, and that the Americans ought to be applauded instead of censured for imitating it so far as they have. . . . In this society of Massachusettensians . . . there are persons descended from some of their ancient governors, counsellors, judges. . . . This natural aristocracy . . . is a fact essential to be considered in the institution of a government. . . . The only remedy is to throw the rich and the proud into one group, in a separate assembly."

After immediately reading all three volumes of *Defence,* Thomas Jefferson commented, "Can anyone read Mr. Adams' defense of the American constitutions without seeing he was a monarchist? . . . [Adams] was for two hereditary branches and an honest elective one; [Hamilton] for a hereditary king with a house of lords and commons, corrupted to his will and standing between him and the people." Franklin, Paine, and their like-minded Philadelphia colleagues responded to *Defence* by founding the Society for Political Enquiries to discuss ways in which the American government could be made more representative and democratic; but during the Constitutional Convention of 1787, Pennsylvania delegate Benjamin Rush honored the profound influence of Adams's treatise, saying that it "has diffused such excellent principles among us that there is little doubt of our adopting a vigorous and compounded federal legislature. Our illustrious minister in this gift to his country has done us more service than if he had obtained alliances for us with all the nations of Europe."

As a national charter, the American Constitution was a dramatic breakthrough for egalitarian democracy, with no property restrictions placed on voters; a House of Representatives adjusted through census taking to stymie rotten boroughs; and the end of titled nobility. At the same time, only one chamber of Congress was chosen through direct democracy; the president was named by an electoral college; senators were selected by their state's leg-

At Thetford Grammar School, Thomas Paine first discovered the glories of the New World but failed to learn Latin, which consigned him in his early professional life to sewing ladies' undergarments.

ABOVE: The twenty-year-old Paine's visit to London in 1757 introduced him to the Enlightenment and began his lifelong program of self-education in natural philosophy.

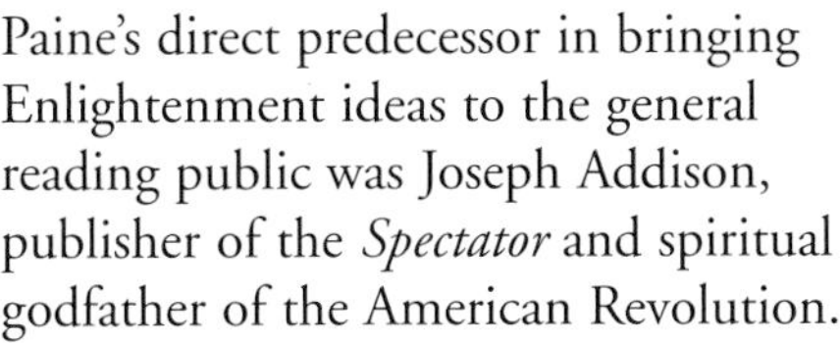

Paine's direct predecessor in bringing Enlightenment ideas to the general reading public was Joseph Addison, publisher of the *Spectator* and spiritual godfather of the American Revolution.

When Paine was an exciseman posted to the town of Lewes, his skill in debate was first noticed by the members of the Headstrong Club, which met regularly at the White Hart Inn (now Hotel).

Raised as both Quaker and Anglican, Paine married his second wife, Elizabeth Ollive, at St. Michael's, the church across the street from the home he shared with the Ollive family in Lewes.

Lewes's castle and bowling green, the latter the site of Paine's first known political quip. When a player mentioned Frederick the Great as "the right sort of man for a king for he has a deal of the devil in him," Paine wondered "if a system of government could not exist that did not require the devil."

Paine's life changed dramatically on his arrival in Philadelphia, where he met fellow modern thinkers, wrote one of America's first antislavery essays, and became the editor of *Pennsylvania Magazine.*

Paine's political father was Benjamin Franklin, who gave him letters of introduction to the grandees of Philadelphia.

COMMON SENSE;

ADDRESSED TO THE

INHABITANTS

OF

AMERICA,

On the following intereſting

SUBJECTS.

I. Of the Origin and Deſign of Government in general, with conciſe Remarks on the Engliſh Conſtitution.

II. Of Monarchy and Hereditary Succeſſion.

III. Thoughts on the preſent State of American Affairs.

IV. Of the preſent Ability of America, with ſome miſcellaneous Reflections.

Man knows no Maſter ſave creating HEAVEN,
Or thoſe whom choice and common good ordain.

THOMSON.

PHILADELPHIA;

Printed, and Sold, by R. BELL, in Third-Street.

MDCCLXXVI.

The immense popularity of *Common Sense* inspired American independence from Britain and became the template for Paine's future writings. The pamphlet was so controversial that the first edition, seen here, was credited to "an Englishman."

Paine's years as a political essayist were ruled by two Georges: his friend and idol, Washington (shown here in the wake of victory at Princeton, a success helped by Paine's *American Crisis*), and his nemesis, King George III.

When America's bestselling author could not make a living from writing, he turned to civil engineering—designing a single-span iron bridge—and when no one in the United States would build his bridge, he returned to Europe.

While a prototype of his bridge was being manufactured, Paine stayed near the ironworks at the home of British politician Edmund Burke. Their friendship would end with the revolution in France, with Burke attacking it and Paine defending it.

Rights of Man made its author one of the most celebrated figures in all of Europe, so much so that he could afford to have his portrait (as seen on the book's jacket) rendered by the master George Romney. Those wanting to honor Paine in their homes less expensively than with a Romney bought a variation, such as this 1865 study by the Parisian artist Winkler.

The English government first responded to *Rights of Man* by commissioning an attack biography (BELOW) by onetime Maryland resident George Chalmers, writing under a pseudonym. As Paine's insights became more and more popular, inspiring a broad range of Englishmen to question their government, the attacks grew more severe. When Paine then released *Rights of Man, Part the Second,* which directly criticized the monarchy, he was charged with seditious treason.

Humbly dedicated to the Jacobine Clubs of France & England
"These are your Gods, O Israel!"
"Fathom & a half! Fathom & a half! Poor Tom!"
"THE RIGHTS OF MAN; _or_ TOMMY PAINE, the little American Taylor, taking the Measure of the CROWN, for a new Pair of Revolution-Breeches.

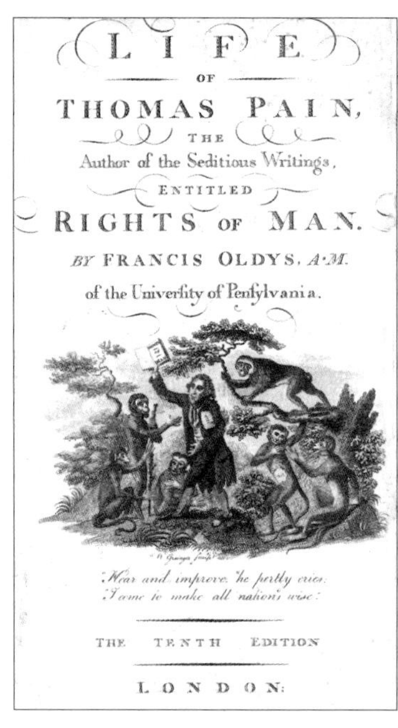
LIFE

OF

THOMAS PAIN,

THE

Author of the Seditious Writings,

ENTITLED

RIGHTS OF MAN.

BY FRANCIS OLDYS, *A·M.*

of the Univerſity of Penſylvania.

"Hear and improve, he pertly cries;
"I come to make all nations wise."

THE TENTH EDITION

LONDON:

TOM PAINE'S Nightly Pest.

islature; and judges were appointed by the executive and legislative branches. These opposing themes would play out across the nation's history, an argument at the heart of the American experiment that is still in debate today. If a republic exchanges the sovereignty of a monarch for that of its people, then which of its people should be sovereign? The Franklin-Paine-Jefferson camp, which over the next few years would be known as Republicans, wanted as inclusive a government as possible, while the Adams-Hamilton contingent, soon to take power as Federalists, believed in a state under the control of plutocrats. Adams (whose father was a cobbler) proclaimed that the United States should be governed "by the rich, the wellborn and the able," while Hamilton (who at the age of eleven was an illegitimate, pauperized orphan) would theorize:

> All communities divide themselves into the few and the many. The first are the rich and well born; the other the mass of the people. The voice of the people has been said to be the voice of God; and however generally this maxim has been quoted and believed, it is not true in fact. . . . Give therefore to the first class a distinct, permanent share in the government. . . . Nothing but a permanent body can check the imprudence of democracy.

Paine would argue in favor of the Adams-styled charter even though it fell far short of his dreams, insisting that regardless of its many faults, the new constitution was superior to none at all, and that it needed ratification for the country to continue, and prosper, and cohere as a nation for the difficulties that lay ahead, especially in terms of competition with the great European powers. When the U.S. Constitution was ultimately ratified, however, William V, the Prince of Orange, told Adams that "Sir, you have given yourselves a king under the title of president."

6. The Missionary Bereft of His Mission

BENJAMIN FRANKLIN may have negotiated a treaty with the French that would ultimately win the Revolution, but the decisive battles of the Anglo-American conflict were yet to be fought, and the civilian traumas attending the birth of the new country were yet to be eased. In 1779 the expression "not worth a continental" turned bitterly true when a colonial dollar sank below the buying power of a penny. Philadelphians created two ad hoc committees to investigate the city's painful wartime economy, one in the wake of rumors that financier Robert Morris was trying to corner the American flour market, and the second to consider colony-imposed price controls on various commodities, including flour and salt. Paine was appointed to both, but the committees dissolved without arriving at definitive solutions, and the prestige of these roles did nothing to solve the dilemma that, after turning down Gérard's offer to work as a propagandist for the Franco-American alliance, he was now both unemployed and broke.

From now until war's end was a time of flailing for Thomas Paine. He could not survive financially as a writer, and instead pursued one scheme after the next, hoping to create both a living and a life. The course of his biography, with its episodes of buoyant enthusiasm and mute withdrawal, as well as eyewitness accounts of his alternately overwhelmingly voluble and determinedly silent behavior, imply that Paine may have suffered from a form of bipolar disorder. His letters include reports of months spent alone and never leaving the house, while his life story repudiates that easy flow common to biographical narrative, instead changing course in leaps and jolts. The years 1779–87 will reveal a manic edge to an increasingly desperate Paine, pursuing one half-considered notion after the next. Even during these fallow times, however, he would write some of his most distinctive if least remembered essays, notably as one of the first ardent supporters of a vigorous national government.

Immediately after he left his clerkship, Paine's financial state became so precarious that he was forced to beg from such well-to-do friends as Henry Laurens:

> I have confined myself so much of late, taken so little exercise, and lived so very sparingly, that unless I alter my way of life it will alter me. I think I have a right to ride a horse of my own, but I cannot now even afford to hire one, which is a situation I never was in before, and I begin to know that a sedentary life cannot be supported without jolting exercise. . . . I intend this winter to collect all my publications, beginning with "Common Sense" and ending with the fisheries [a defense of the American claim to the Newfoundland Banks], and publishing them in two volumes Octavo, with notes. I have no doubt of a large subscription. . . . After that work is completed, I intend prosecuting a history of the Revolution by means of a subscription—but this undertaking will be attended with such an amazing expense, and will take such a length of time, that unless the States individually give some assistance therein, scarcely any man could afford to go through it. . . . Here lies the difficulty I alluded to in the beginning of this letter, and I would rather wish to borrow something of a friend or two in the interim than run the risk I have mentioned. . . . I have hitherto kept all my private matters a secret, but as I know your friendship and you a great deal of my situation, I can with more ease communicate them to you than to another.

Raw paper's wartime expense and scarcity would keep Paine from going forward with his publishing ventures; instead, he championed a new federalist cause. Congress was paralyzed by Maryland's refusal to ratify the Articles of Confederation until such states as Virginia renounced their charter claims to the wilderness of their western borders (in Virginia's case, a boundary at the Pacific Ocean). The answer seems plain, since, as Americans were not yet paying federal taxes, Congress was impoverished and needed the territories' revenue as the Articles would provide, but the issue was clouded by the fact that a number of Maryland's politicians were land speculators who would reap a windfall if Congress federalized the land instead of leaving it in the hands of the states.

With *Public Good, Being an Examination into the Claim of Virginia to the vacant western Territory, and of the Right of The United States to the Same; To which is added, Proposals for laying off a new State; To be applied as a Fund for carrying on the War, or redeeming the national Debt,* Paine sided with Maryland by arguing that since all the states had fought for independence, the income from the new lands should be shared by everyone. Many of Paine's Virginia friends and allies, such as Richard Henry Lee, James Madison, and Thomas Jefferson, were outraged that the greatly influential writer was taking a position in a quarrel with which he had no business. There were articles published at the time claiming that Paine was a covert speculator, having been surreptitiously hired by the Indiana Company to advance its Maryland-sided claims. Embarrassingly, a few months after *Public Good* was published, it was revealed that Paine was indeed a shareholder in the company. He insisted that he had written the article purely from virtuous principles of republicanism and had received his shares as a gift afterward.

Public Good would, however, go far beyond land disputes in its arguments elevating the national government's authority over states' rights. It was one of the first publications to criticize the Articles of Confederation (drafted in the wake of *Common Sense*) as being too weak for a country needing to defend itself and its commerce from a predatory Europe. In the end, after squabbling for three years, Virginia finally agreed to relinquish its immense frontier, and in March 1781 Maryland ratified the Articles of Confederation.

Paine's post-Deane era of bad luck and poverty had a temporary reprieve when Paine was appointed clerk of the Pennsylvania Assembly on November 2, 1779. Then, on March 1, 1780, his state was the first to achieve one of his longest-held Enlightenment dreams when it abolished slavery and emancipated six thousand men and women. On July 4, the University of Pennsylvania honored the man who never learned his Latin with a master of arts.

If things seemed to be looking up a bit for Paine, news from the front continued on a relentlessly grim course. By the end of 1779, the whole of Georgia was under British control, while Benedict Arnold had abandoned his West Point command to become a brigadier general for the English at New York City. Though the horrors of Valley Forge are legendary, the winter of 1779–80 was in fact a far more gruesome ordeal for the Continental

Army, battening down against the era's worst weather in Morristown, New Jersey. The federal treasury had run out of money, the troops were reduced to spending six weeks eating one-eighth rations, and over the course of that winter they would mutiny three times. Their clothing had become so threadbare that Baron von Steuben nicknamed them *sans-culottes* (no pants), while Nathanael Greene reported that his men were "more than half naked and two-thirds starved."

After four thousand Americans defending Charleston were forced to surrender on May 12, 1780, Washington sent a letter to every provincial legislature describing how the conditions of the Continental Army were now so parlous that further mutiny, abandonment, and collapse were inevitable. As part of his duties as clerk, Paine read the letter aloud to the Pennsylvania Assembly: "One state will comply with a requisition of Congress; another neglects to do it; a third executes it by halves; and all differ in the manner, the matter, or so much in point of time, that we are always working uphill, and ever shall be; and while such a system as the present one or rather want of one prevails, we shall ever be unable to apply our strength or resources to any advantage. . . . The crisis, in every point of view, is extraordinary."

Paine was so moved by this letter that he redoubled his support of Washington by donating his entire life's savings to the army and then politicked the wealthy of Philadelphia to join him in creating a subscription service, arguing that if the Continental Army failed, they would have the most to lose. Eventually, Philadelphians subscribed £300,000 to support Washington through the Bank of Pennsylvania, America's first true financial institution, established through Paine's efforts. On June 9 Paine released *American Crisis IX,* which tried using logic to sway other states to support the federal government by explaining what financial penalties they would face if they returned to being subjects of England: "Suppose Britain was to conquer America, and, as a conqueror, was to lay her under no other conditions than to pay the same proportion towards her annual revenue which the people of England pay: our share, in that case, would be six million pounds sterling yearly. Can it then be a question, whether it is best to raise two millions to defend the country, and govern it ourselves, and only three quarters of a million afterwards, or pay six millions to have it conquered, and let the enemy govern it?"

Paine was still obsessed by the notion that if the good people of Britain knew the full truth about the colonies, they would wholeheartedly support

American independence. He devised a scheme of traveling to London as an undercover agent to write propaganda for the cause, perhaps even to inspire English citizens to replace King George with their own republic. (The fact that he greatly missed his mother and father may have additionally had something to do with these plans.) Paine outlined the details—which he imagined Congress might subsidize through a novel cost-saving measure—to General Nathanael Greene on September 9, 1780:

> The manner in which I would bring such a publication out would be under the cover of an Englishman who had made the tour of America incognito. This will afford me all the foundation I wish for and enable me to place matters before them in a light in which they have never yet viewed them. . . . Now there is no other method to give this information a national currency but this—the channel of the press, which I have ever considered the tongue of the world, and which governs the sentiments of mankind more than anything else that ever did or can exist. . . . Having said thus much on the matter, I take the liberty of hinting to you a mode by which the expense may be defrayed without any new charge. Drop a delegate in Congress at the next election, and apply the pay to defray what I have proposed; and the point then will be, whether you can possibly put any man into Congress who could render as much service in that station as in the one I have pointed out.

The Pennsylvania Assembly refused to give him a year's leave for this secret mission, but Paine was so intent on pursuing it that he resigned his clerkship and made immediate arrangements to sail for Europe. Alarmed by the peril of this scheme and the author's bullheadedness, Greene visited Paine at his rooming house to talk him out of it. The general had personal reasons for his opinion, as he was at that moment overseeing the court-martial of British major John André, who had served as the negotiator between English officers and the American traitor Benedict Arnold. André was convicted of espionage and hanged. Greene plainly told his friend that if his identity was discovered by London authorities, his fate would be the same. Paine finally relented.

On August 16 two thousand redcoats under Lord Cornwallis defeated Horatio Gates and his four thousand men at Camden, South Carolina, in the worst American loss of the war, a military catastrophe that would finally silence those civilian congressmen promoting Gates at the expense of Washington. By year's end, the British had burned the Virginia capital of Richmond to the ground, nearly captured Virginia governor Thomas Jefferson, and triumphed decisively in battles against Lafayette and Steuben, while the majority of Washington's slaves joined the English to battle against him, and a quarter of his Continental Army—twenty-four hundred men—mutinied yet again.

Many of these failings had one simple cause—the poverty of the American national government. After consulting with his congressional allies, Paine drafted a letter to Vergennes, asking for the French to make a commitment of an annual grant or loan of one million pounds until the war was won. Congress, however, had more in mind than this polite correspondence. Contrary to Paine's assertions in his letters to Franklin, there were many leaders in Philadelphia—notably the Lee brothers—who believed that the country's minister to the court of Versailles was less than competent. The Lees even used the fact that Franklin's secretary (grandson Temple) was the son of a loyalist (estranged son William) to throw doubt on his patriotism, while the dismissed John Adams argued that Franklin was too old to endure the demands of his assignment. Beset by Franklin's enemies endlessly debating his value and his effectiveness, an impatient Congress reasoned that since the French were so notably enamored of George Washington (as they knew from Lafayette's testimony), an officer close to the commander might make a convincing argument for more (and quicker) aid.

The mission was accordingly offered to Alexander Hamilton, who declined, and then to Hamilton's closest friend, the twenty-six-year-old Colonel John Laurens, who, like his congressman father Henry, was a good friend of Paine's. Young Laurens accepted this assignment but requested that Congress hire Paine as his secretary to shore up his own lack of political experience. The congressional debate on that appointment grew so heated, however, that Paine had his nomination withdrawn and instead took the position gratis.

Laurens and Paine spent three days in briefings with George Washington, who plainly told them, "We are at the end of our tether, and now or never our deliverance must come." The two then sailed with the *Alliance* from Boston in the dead cold of that terrible winter on February 11, 1781. British warships were now so heavily patrolling the Atlantic that many American sailors, not without cause, feared being taken prisoner and refused to accept crew positions. The *Alliance*'s captain, John Barry, had to force-duty British POWs in their stead. Paine described one fearsome night aboard this wartime passage, his first voyage since he had nearly died on sailing to the New World:

> It was exceedingly dark and we were running eight or nine miles an hour till about nine at night, when from a sudden tremulous motion of the ship attended with a rushing noise, the general cry was that she had struck, and was either aground or on a rock. The noise and the motion increased fast, but our apprehensions were in a short time abated by finding ourselves surrounded with large floating bodies of ice against which the ship was beating. . . . The wind increased to a severe gale, and before we could take in the sails one of them was torn in two. Nothing could now be done but to lay the ship to and let her take her chance. The ice became every moment more formidable, and we began to apprehend as much danger from it as when we first supposed ourselves on ground. The sea, in whatever direction it could be seen, appeared a tumultuous assemblage of floating rolling rocks, which we could not avoid and against which there was no defence. The thundering attacks, that were every moment made by those massy bodies on the ship's sides, seemed as if they were breaking their way in. About eleven o'clock our starboard quarter gallery was torn away. Happily for Col. Laurens he had quitted it about a minute before, and the pleasure occasioned by his escape made us for a while the less attentive to the general danger. In this situation, dark, stormy, and plunging in an unguided ship to we knew not where, we remained from nine at night till four in the morning.

Paine arrived safely in Europe to find that *Common Sense* had made him internationally renowned and immensely admired—"I find myself no stranger in France, people know me almost as generally here as in America"—though not everyone was impressed. One expatriate, Philadelphian Elkanah Watson, hated Paine's writings and found him in person to be "coarse and uncouth in his manners, loathsome in his appearance, and a disgusting egotist, rejoicing most in talking of himself, and reading the effusions of his own mind. . . . He had been roasted alive on his arrival at L'Orient, for the scotch fiddle and well basted with brimstone [he had used sulfur to cure an itch], he was absolutely offensive, and perfumed the whole apartment." In Paris, Paine's Enlightenment passion for civil engineering was rekindled when he learned of M. de Montpetit's proposals for a single-span, pierless iron bridge. There were some North American rivers, notably one of Philadelphia's, the Schuylkill, so choked with winter ice floes that they could not be bridged by traditional means, and perhaps a variation on Montpetit's idea might offer a solution.

Laurens and Paine stayed in the town of Passy, just down the street from Franklin, and though the doctor was terribly insulted that Congress had sent this twenty-six-year-old to supplant him, he spent considerable hours consulting with Laurens, especially on the need to be tactful and moderate in wooing the courtly Europeans. Washington, however, had insisted that only belligerence would sway the French, which Laurens interpreted to mean making constant demands of Vergennes. When this approach did not produce results quickly enough for the American, he escalated with a threat to directly petition the king himself, and when the French minister called his bluff, Laurens, in a terrible breach of protocol, handed a letter of appeal to Louis XVI, outraging the court. French minister to America Lamartine reported that "the King loaded Paine with favors," instead of having to admit that the uncouth colonel's forthright demand had resulted in a gift from the French to the Americans of 4.8 million livres in money and matériel, topped by French guarantees for a loan from the Dutch of an additional 10 million livres. Though much of this bounty had been negotiated by Franklin before Laurens and Paine had even left Philadelphia—with Vergennes explicitly telling Congress exactly who was responsible for his magnanimity—and though the Dutch loans never came to fruition, Laurens, who unlike Franklin had fewer enemies to contend with, was acclaimed by almost every American leader for this achievement, with John Adams saying that the young colonel had done "more for the United States in the short time of his being in Europe than all the rest of their diplomatic corps put together." Franklin was so upset by the entire affair that he resigned—a resignation that Congress refused to accept—and when his good friend Robert Morris was appointed American superintendent of finance, he sent him a letter that warned, "The public is often niggardly even of its thanks, while you are sure of being censured by malevolent critics and bug writers, who will abuse you while you are serving them, and wound your character in nameless pamphlets, thereby resembling those little dirty stinking insects, that attack us only in the dark, disturb our repose, molesting and wounding us while our sweat and blood is contributing to their subsistence."

This episode is one of many where the lack of Paine documents is especially regrettable. What did the once impoverished staymaker and critic of aristocrats think while attending the Bourbon court and wandering the gardens of Versailles? What was his role in the emotionally complex transactions between Laurens and Franklin? We can be certain only that, perhaps between renewing his great friendship with the most famous American in France, enjoying his own acclaim, and seeing how authors were treated in civilized nations with copyright laws, Paine had such a remarkable time in Europe that he did not want to go home:

> I told Col. Laurens that though I had every wish it was possible a man could feel for the success of the cause which America was engaged in, yet such had been the treatment I had received, and such the hardships and difficulties I had experienced year after year, that I had no heart to return back, and was resolved not to do it. . . . As matters then stood, I could render her more service, by justifying her cause and explaining and clearing up her affairs in Europe, where they appeared to be but darkly understood, than by any thing I could do in America. But that it appeared an act of meanness to me, to return to a country where I had experienced so much thankless treatment. . . . But such was Col. Laurens's passionate attachment to me . . . that his importunities for my returning with him were pressing and excessive, and he carried them to such a height, that I felt I should not be very easy to myself do which I would; and as he would have had nobody with him on the passage if any misfortune had befallen him, I gave into his wishes and accompanied him back.

Protected by a fleet of gunships and brigantines headed by the French frigate *La Résolute,* their voyage back took a dreadful eighty-six days. As news arrived of British warships scouting the coast of Delaware, Laurens and Paine disembarked in Boston to safeguard their treasure—a million livres of supplies and two and a half million livres of silver—which required sixteen teams of oxen to carry to the bank in Philadelphia. Paine remembered this triumph with terribly mixed feelings: "After our return we parted company on the road soon after we left Providence, occasioned by the sulky I was in breaking down. We parted the money he had with him, of which I had six guineas, and he not much more, with which I had to bear my own expenses and that of a servant he left with me and two horses, for three hundred miles, and I was obliged to borrow a dollar at Bordentown to pass the ferry with. Perhaps two such travelers as Col. Laurens and myself on such a national business is a novelty."

The next year, John Laurens died in a skirmish with British forces. He was twenty-seven.

Over the course of the American Revolution France gave the United States twelve million livres and loaned it eighteen million more, while spending an additional two billion livres in sending sixty-three ships carrying 3,668 cannons and 47,000 troops in support of the rebel cause. It was during that summer of 1781, while Laurens and Paine were making their way home, that the greatest sailing of this armada, headed by French admiral François Joseph Paul, comte de Grasse, crossed the Atlantic with more than thirty warships and 3,200 troops.

Hearing this news, Washington told his French allies that now was the time for a direct strike on the British bastion of New York City, an attack to avenge the losses during his first years as Continental Army commander in chief, repair his professional reputation as a military leader, and ensure that the English were finally, categorically defeated. Well aware, however, of Henry Clinton's 14,500 troops in New York, and that his British fleet outnumbered the French, General Jean Baptiste Donatien de Vimeur, comte de Rochambeau, demurred. The French informed Washington that Admiral de Grasse's fleet could only travel as far north as the Chesapeake and then had to depart by October, giving the Americans a mere two months to use the French navy for an assault on Lord Cornwallis, 450 miles to the south of where Washington, Rochambeau, and their combined ground forces were stationed in Pennsylvania.

Washington's reaction was to have a tantrum that raged for half an hour. He was convinced that the French did not have the foresight to see the perils of this scheme, for if the English uncovered their strategy (and considering the success of British agents over the war's history, this was likely), Clinton could easily send his fleet south to defend Virginia, and Cornwallis could just as easily move his troops inland away from the firing power of French warships. But Washington then realized he could once again use the now signature feinting strategy that had been so successful in Brooklyn Heights and Princeton. While suspected British agents were leaked the news that de Grasse was moving north for an assault on Staten Island at the same time that a small number of American troops marched into New Jersey and toward New York as though on their way for just such an attack, the main body of the Continental Army began an interminable trek, at a grueling pace, due south toward Virginia and Cornwallis.

After hearing conflicting reports from their various spies, Tories, and turncoats, the English hedged, keeping a part of their fleet to defend New York and sending the rest south. On September 5 the latter force arrived at the outskirts of Chesapeake Bay, where a lookout reported many great ships, ten miles ahead, at anchor. From the ground Cornwallis estimated that "there are between thirty and forty sail within the capes, mostly ships of war and some of them very large," this last referring to the *Ville-de-Paris,* armed with 104 cannons.

The English fleet had the advantage, with the wind at its back and two thousand French sailors away and ashore, but de Grasse, pulling his ships of the line into attack formation with great speed and efficiency, struck first. British admiral Thomas Graves made two serious errors, one with his strategy and one with his signal flags. By nightfall, four British ships were sinking, and the next day de Grasse and his fleet had vanished. The British guessed the enemy's direction and made pursuit, only to now discover Graves's third error: another French armada, thought to be still in Newport, had slipped through the English patrols and joined de Grasse to fully control the Chesapeake Bay, with no room for the English to further engage. In defending Yorktown, Cornwallis had no navy to support him or to offer a quick means of retreat.

After Lafayette and his supporting troops arrived, trenches were dug and French siege cannons were dragged into position. On October 9, the 4,000 men of the Continental Army, reinforced by 2,000 state militia volunteers and 8,200 French troops, began their assault on the 5,800 men of the British regiments. A new flag called the Star-Spangled Banner was raised, and a new medal named the Purple Heart was awarded. Cornwallis had assured his troops that the enemy had no artillery worthy of the name, but in a mere eight days, by October 17, the fort had been so battered by the great French guns that the British were forced to raise the white colors.

Explaining that he was too ill to participate in the ceremonies, the Eton-educated Cornwallis had General Charles O'Hara surrender his sword to the French, but Rochambeau insisted that O'Hara offer it to Washington. In England, the humiliating defeat shocked even the most stalwart hawks out of their convictions. George III threatened to abdicate, announcing, "His Majesty therefore with much sorrow finds He can be of no further utility to His native country which drives Him to the painful step of quitting it for ever," but then changed his mind and never sent the letter of resignation to Parliament.

Between the Fabian evasions of George Washington and the diplomatic genius of Benjamin Franklin, the Americans had won their impossible-to-imagine victory. Congress named Franklin, Thomas Jefferson, John Jay, and Henry Laurens to augment John Adams as peace delegates to Paris. Adams regarded his newly shared duties as an offensive demotion and suffered a nervous breakdown, while Laurens, on being released from his captivity as a prisoner of war in the Tower of London, went to Paris as expected, but then sailed immediately home. Jefferson never sailed for Europe at all. British treaty delegate Richard Oswald thus arrived in Paris in April of 1782 to find only one American negotiator present, and Franklin began his treaty discussions with the point that, as the British had destroyed a great deal of American property in their pursuit of empire and lucre, an equitable and agreeable solution might be for England to give America some additional real estate—perhaps Canada? When Jay and Adams finally arrived and convinced Franklin to ignore Congress's direct instructions to negotiate a treaty only in consultation with the French, it was Franklin who had to apologize to Vergennes when the Anglo-American accord was prematurely announced, and it was Franklin who had to ask the French to loan America another six million livres. It was John Jay, however, who, after the treaty was completed, concluded that "if we are not a happy people, it will be our own fault."

Having returned from his own successful mission to France, surrounded by jubilant rebels crowding the streets of Philadelphia, screaming toasts into the night over the roar of fireworks, Paine found himself embittered, ignored by the country to which he felt he had given everything. While Deane supporters like Robert and Gouverneur Morris had gotten rich over the course of the Revolution, Paine was, as always, impoverished. That he had nothing to show for his work and for his devotion to the cause would gnaw at him over the coming years: "I had the mortification of knowing that all this arose from an anxiety to serve in, and promote the cause of a country, whose circumstances were then rising into prosperity, and who, though she owed something of that prosperity to me appeared every day careless of whatever related to my personal interest."

He asked General Nathanael Greene for help, and was immediately answered:

> I see you are determined to follow your genius and not your fortune. I have always been in hopes that Congress would have made some handsome acknowledgement to you for past services. I must confess that I think you have been shamefully neglected; and that America is indebted to few characters more than to you. But as your passion leads to fame, and not to wealth, your mortification will be the less. Your fame for your writings, will be immortal. At present my expenses are great; nevertheless, if you are not conveniently situated, I shall take a pride and pleasure in contributing all in my power to render your situation happy.

This was the last known letter that Paine received from Greene, who died of sunstroke in 1786 at the age of forty-four.

For a man so proud, asking friends for financial help must have been painfully difficult, and could only be a stopgap. Paine wanted both acknowledgment of his place in history and long-term financial security. If he had contributed the sort of services to a nation of Europe that he had to America, a monarch would have rewarded him substantially. With this in mind and believing a great favor was owed, he wrote to a man he had helped tremendously over the course of the war, George Washington:

> From an anxiety to support, as far as laid in my power, the reputation of the Cause of America, as well as the Cause itself, I declined the customary profits which authors are entitled to, and I have always continued to do so; yet I never thought (if I thought at all on the matter), but that as I dealt generously and honorably by America, she would deal the same by me. But I have experienced the contrary—and it gives me much concern, not only on account of the inconvenience it has occasioned to me, but because it unpleasantly lessens my opinion of the character of a country which once appeared so fair,

> and it hurts my mind to see her so cold and inattentive to matters which affect her reputation. . . . After all there is something peculiarly hard that the country which ought to have been to me a home has scarcely afforded me an asylum.

Washington acted immediately, raising the issue with Congress's new superintendent of finance, Robert Morris, who then held meetings with Paine and Gouverneur Morris to negotiate various possibilities. Two weeks later, in a secret contract signed by Washington, Morris, and Congress's secretary of foreign affairs, Robert Livingston, Paine was offered the position of writer for the American government at an annual salary of $800 ($65,000 today), working alongside the millionaire who had fought him so bitterly over the Deane affair, a man whose ethics he had once investigated as a war profiteer. Remarkably, Robert Morris and Thomas Paine would forget that history and, over the years, integrate as a fine match of blended sensibilities and complementary talents. For a fervid anti-aristocrat like Paine, the self-made son of an ironmonger would be about the only version of a patron he could tolerate besides state support. For Morris, Paine had the great talent and the broad popularity needed to convince the mass of American citizens of the validity of federal policy (in the immediate instance, of paying additional taxes to strengthen both the Continental Army and the national government). This unlikely pair had much in common; both were great admirers of the Locke-Addison-Smith theories that a boom in commerce would be a boon to all mankind at every level of society, that a thriving import-export trade might even be a method of ending war between nations. Morris and Paine were both committed urbanites, having no sympathy with the widespread certainty, shared by everyone from Jefferson to Cobbett, of the spiritual, economic, and patriotic superiority of farmers. Besides, and most important, Paine and Morris liked each other as men and enjoyed each other's company.

Even so, working as a government-paid writer included betrayals of Paine's convictions on political journalism. While repeatedly commenting that the American people, through their government, owed him for the great work he had done on their behalf, he simultaneously maintained that a political essayist should be beholden to no one but his fellow citizens, that reporters and essayists writing about the government must serve as an additional balance of power against the constant threat of state tyranny.

For almost any artist or writer living in a world without benevolent patrons, merely making a living demands compromise. But for a man who could be so preeningly self-righteous, this necessity is especially poignant, and the only way to reconcile what Paine must have regarded as a moral hypocrisy is to consider his great belief in a powerful national government—all of the writing he would do for Morris and Livingston would be as an ardent federalist—as well as his rapt devotion to George Washington, and of course, his desperate financial straits. In fact, little of the propaganda he wrote as a writer for hire was significantly different from what he would have written on his own, and the fact that he talked over his essays ahead of time with Morris was no different in technique from how he had written everything since *The Case of the Officers of Excise.*

Paine's first assignment as a federal author was March 5, 1782's "On the King of England's Speech," responding to the royal proclamations at Parliament's opening. It began with typical vigor—"The King of England is one of the readiest believers in the world. . . . The man has no doubt. Like Pharaoh on the edge of the Red Sea, he sees not the plunge he is making, and precipitately drives across the flood that is closing over his head"—but then became a treatise on the correctness of direct federal taxes instead of leaving Congress (and Washington) to the fiscal mercies of the states, with the novel and pleasant theory that taxes are something of a duty for the citizens of a democratic republic, and something of a gift. Using the inspirational language that had made him so famous and so popular, he urged Americans to imagine the future as he did, seeing a United States that would be the most powerful nation in the world, a power that originated in citizens devoted to their country as well as to their local town and state.

After Paine had Washington and Morris to his Philadelphia rooming house for dinner of "a few oysters or a crust of bread and cheese," he wrote *Crisis XI* on May 22, 1782, giving an extended rationale as to why the alliance between France and America was so strong in the face of grave British efforts to undermine it. In *Crisis XII,* Paine responded to an announcement by the Earl of Shelburne, Britain's next first minister, that England and the United States must reconcile, as American independence would "end in the ruin of Britain." Paine noted that as America had been free since 1776 and England had not yet been ruined, it was time for the country's leaders to end their public declamations of imperial melodrama and accept the United States as an independent nation. Besides, he explained, reunion was no longer possible for Americans, who "can look round and see the remains of burnt and destroyed houses. . . . We walk over the dead whom we loved. . . . There is scarcely a village but brings to life some melancholy thought, and reminds us of what we have suffered, and of those we have lost by the inhumanity of Britain."

In July he was one of the select ten thousand invited by minister La Luzerne to celebrate the birth of France's royal dauphin. Paine should have been in high spirits at this party of the decade—working at the center of American power again; a guest at the biggest celebration Americans had ever seen—but instead, as Benjamin Rush noted, he "appeared a solitary character walking among the artificial bowers in the gardens. . . . [He] retired frequently from company to analyze his thoughts and to enjoy the repast of his own original ideas."

Paine's most significant work from this period would turn out to be not his writing for Congress, but a book review. He had discovered in Morris's library an English translation pirated by his onetime *Common Sense* publisher, Robert Bell, of the Abbé Raynal's *Révolution d'Amérique*. He was incensed by Raynal's error-filled depiction of the American struggle as a minor matter involving tea and tariffs; a response would give him both an outlet for the research he had done on the history of the Revolution and an opportunity to make Europe (and especially the English) understand the American perspective. He additionally believed that the time had come for the success of the American Revolution to be exported back to the mother continent. *Letter to the Abbé Reynal, on the Affairs of North America in which the Mistakes in the Abbé's Account of the Revolution of America are Corrected and Cleared Up* included Paine's ideas for a global convention of delegates (not unlike a United Nations), a rumination on the philosophical ideals inherent in the Republic of Letters (including America's copyright-free iniquity), and a foreshadowing of his own destiny in an insistence that the world, liberated by science and commerce, would soon be inevitably following the American experiment of replacing feudal despots with republican democracies:

> In all countries where literature is protected, and it never can flourish where it is not, the works of an author are his legal property; and to treat letters in any other light than this, is to banish them from the country, or strangle them in the birth. . . . The state of literature

in America must one day become a subject of legislative consideration. Hitherto it has been a disinterested volunteer in the service of the Revolution, and no man thought of profits; but when peace shall give time and opportunity for study, the country will deprive itself of the honour and service of letters and the improvement of science, unless sufficient laws are made to prevent depredations on literary property. . . .

Letters, the tongue of the world, have in some measure brought all mankind acquainted, and by an extension of their uses are everyday promoting some new friendship. Through them, distant nations become capable of conversation, and losing by degrees the awkwardness of strangers, and the moroseness of suspicion, they learn to know and understand each other. Science, the partisan of no country, but the beneficent patroness of all, has liberally opened a temple where all may meet. Her influence on the mind, like the sun on the chilled earth, has long been preparing it for higher cultivation and further improvement. The philosopher of one country sees not an enemy in the philosopher of another; he takes his seat in the temple of science, and asks not who sits beside him. . . .

There is something exceedingly curious in the constitution and operation of prejudice . . . [which,] like the spider, makes every place its home. It has neither taste nor choice of situation, and all that it requires is room. Everywhere, except in fire or water, a spider will live. . . .

Perhaps no two events ever united so intimately and forcibly to combat and expel prejudice, as the Revolution of America and the alliance with France. . . . Our style and manner of thinking have undergone a revolution more extraordinary than the political revolution of the country. We see with other eyes; we hear with other ears; and think with other thoughts, than those we formerly used. We can look back on our own prejudices, as if they had been the prejudices of other people. We now see and know they were prejudices and nothing else; and relieved from their shackles, enjoy a freedom of mind, we felt not before.

Paine once again used his *Common Sense* marketing technique, giving away five hundred copies of this *Letter*, being especially generous with American foreign offices. The results were just as spectacular. One American reported from Europe, "I have lately traveled much, and find him everywhere. His letter to the Abbé Reynal has sealed his fame. . . . Even those who are jealous of, and envy him, acknowledge that the point of his pen has been as formidable in politics as the point of the sword in the field."

Paine and Washington would draw closer that year when the general took counsel from the writer over a disturbing incident. In March, loyalist raider Philip White had been captured by state militia troops and murdered by one of his guards. Soon after, New Jersey Militia captain Joshua Huddy was taken prisoner by the British, and New York's English commander, Sir Guy Carleton, assigned Huddy's case to the colony's Associated Loyalists, a civilian organization presided over by Ben Franklin's estranged son, William. One group of those loyalists, headed by a Captain Lippencott, had become so enraged over the unjust death of Philip White that they executed Joshua Huddy.

Washington demanded that Carleton relinquish Lippencott and his accomplices to face trial on charges of murder, but Carleton, claiming he had no responsibility for the civilians' actions, refused. As a threat, Washington then announced that a lottery would be held to determine a British POW to be executed in Lippencott's stead. A draw of straws resulted in the twenty-year-old Captain Charles Asgill, the only son of one of America's most prominent British Whig supporters, facing the gallows. While Carleton shipped the guilty loyalists to England so they could remain safely beyond the reach of American law, Congress gave Washington its approval to hang Asgill.

Paine immediately wrote to both Carleton and Washington, warning the former that he would be a murderer if he did not extradite Lippencott, and the latter that the execution of an innocent man would be an act of barbarism and a black mark on Washington's reputation. Washington then received letters from Vergennes and from Asgill's mother, who had written a direct appeal to Marie Antoinette. The general forwarded these documents to Congress, which resolved the imbroglio through the political expediency of releasing Asgill in honor of Louis and his queen.

On April 19, 1783, Paine celebrated the formal British assent to American independence and the eight-year anniversary of Lexington-Concord with a renewed plea for federalism (and a veiled threat of emigration) in *The Last Crisis:*

"The times that tried men's souls," are over—and the greatest and completest revolution the world ever knew, gloriously and happily accomplished. . . . Never, I say, had a country so many openings to happiness as this. Her setting out in life, like the rising of a fair morning, was unclouded and promising. Her cause was good. Her principles just and liberal. Her temper serene and firm. Her conduct regulated by the nicest steps, and everything about her wore the mark of honor. It is not every country (perhaps there is not another in the world) that can boast so fair an origin. Even the first settlement of America corresponds with the character of the revolution. . . .

As the scenes of war are closed, and every man preparing for home and happier times, I therefore take my leave of the subject. I have most sincerely followed it from beginning to end, and through all its turns and windings: and whatever country I may hereafter be in, I shall always feel an honest pride at the part I have taken and acted, and a gratitude to nature and providence for putting it in my power to be of some use to mankind.

Paine was then living at Hill Top, the Bordentown, New Jersey, home of his closest friend, Colonel Joseph Kirkbride. The two had fought together in the war, had similar religious training, loved to spend hours riding horses, and agreed on Enlightenment principles of reason and natural philosophy, Kirkbride having been a longtime member of the American Philosophical Society. On June 7, 1783, Congress finally released to Paine the $1,699 withheld from his salary over the Silas Deane affair. He immediately donated a third of it to the Continental Army, even though he was now in a parlous financial state, his work as government scribe having ended when Morris and Livingston had earlier that year resigned from Congress. While mulling over yet again his ill-treatment by the American government, he received an invitation from Washington, now living at a nearby estate provided by Congress outside Princeton, where a triumphant government was meeting to create a new nation:

ROCKY HILL,
Sept. 10, 1783.
DEAR SIR,

I have learned since I have been at this place, that you are at Bordentown. Whether for the sake of retirement or economy, I know not.

Be it for either, for both, or whatever it may, if you will come to this place, and partake with me, I shall be exceedingly happy to see you.

Your presence may remind Congress of your past services to this country; and if it is in my power to impress them, command my best services with freedom, as they will be rendered cheerfully by one who entertains a lively sense of the importance of your works, and who, with much pleasure, subscribes himself,

Your sincere friend,

G. WASHINGTON.

The invitation would dramatically lift Paine's spirits, and he would immediately reply:

BORDEN TOWN, Sept. 21.

SIR,

I am made exceedingly happy by the receipt of your friendly letter of the 10th. instant, which is this moment come to hand; . . . I most sincerely thank you for your good wishes and friendship to me, and the kind invitation you have honored me with, which I shall with much pleasure accept. . . .

By the advice of Mr. Morris I presented a letter to Congress expressing a request that they would be pleased to direct me to lay before them an account of what my services, such as they were, and situation, had been during the course of the war. This letter was referred to a committee, and their report is now before Congress, and contains, as I am informed, a recommendation that I be appointed historiographer to the continent [a recommendation originally made by Washington]. . . . I am now encouraged by your friendship to take your confidential advice upon it before I present it. For though I never was at a loss in writing on public matters, I feel exceedingly so in what respects myself.

I am hurt by the neglect of the collective ostensible body of America, in a way which it is probable they do not perceive my feelings. It has an effect in putting either my reputation or their generosity at stake; for it cannot fail of suggesting that either I (notwithstanding the appearance of service) have been undeserving their regard or that they are remiss towards me. Their silence is to me something like condemnation, and their neglect must be

> justified by my loss of reputation, or my reputation supported at their injury; either of which is alike painful to me. But as I have ever been dumb on everything which might touch national honor so I mean ever to continue so.
>
> Wishing you, Sir, the happy enjoyment of peace and every public and private felicity I remain &c.
>
> THOMAS PAINE.
>
> Col. Kirkbride at whose house I am, desires me to present you his respectful compliments.

Paine's trip to Rocky Hill was delayed when he came down with scarlet fever, but he recovered in time to spend most of October with Washington. While he was there, the legend that a creek on the estate's property could be enflamed caught their natural-philosophic attentions, and they decided to investigate. Some of Washington's aides had insisted that these fires were produced from bits of invisible "bituminous matter" rising to the surface, but Paine "supposed that a quantity of inflammable air was let loose, which ascended through the water and took fire above the surface."

In that era, the study of "airs"—inflammable, fixed, or dephlogisticated—was of great urgency, especially for one of Paine's political allies and significant influences, Joseph Priestley, who discovered oxygen, created carbon dioxide and nitrous oxide in his home laboratory, and invented seltzer by capturing the gas released by a Leeds brewery into water-filled bags. In 1774, Franklin wrote Priestley about the kind of American methane experiments that Paine and Washington would pursue at Rocky Hill: "When I passed through New Jersey in 1764, I heard it several times mentioned, that, by applying a lighted candle near the surface of some of their rivers, a sudden flame would catch and spread on the water, continuing to burn for near half a minute. But the accounts I received were so imperfect, that I could form no guess at the cause of such an effect, and rather doubted the truth of it."

Washington and Paine went to the mythic creek, and each tried holding a torch at various points and distances over the waters—but nothing happened. Then a group of visiting soldiers revealed that the secret was to first stir up the riverbank's mud. This was done, and Paine saw that "when the mud at the bottom was disturbed by the poles, the air bubbles rose fast, and I saw the fire take from General Washington's light and descend from thence to the surface of the water . . . demonstrative evidence that what was called setting the river on fire was setting on fire the inflammable air [methane] that arose out of the mud."

At Rocky Hill, Paine consulted with Washington about the letter he was drafting to Congress over being rewarded for his efforts supporting the American cause. Paine's belief that he deserved a substantial payment was justifiable in light of English law and history, in which printers and stationers kept the profits made through publishing, while authors were supported by patrons or the crown. A Congress facing massive debt, hordes of unpaid Continental Army soldiers, no consistent source of income, and decidedly mixed feelings about the value to history of one Thomas Paine, however, instead proposed hiring him as the official biographer of the Revolution ("Historiographer of the Continent"). Even though Paine had been working on just such a project for many years and was in grave financial need, instead of accepting this commission, he responded with a letter of singular political ineptitude. It is impossible to imagine that Washington had read this threatening and demanding jeremiad, for he could hardly have believed that it would be favorably received by a legislature that had, not so many years before, fired the writer for professional misconduct. No other document survives that so manifestly explains why a man as admired, popular, influential, and beloved as Paine had such difficulty making a way for himself in postwar America:

> Either I had been unworthy of the regard of America, notwithstanding the appearance of service, or that she had been remiss in her regard towards me. I was therefore desirous of placing matters in such an unambiguous light before Congress, that my departure from a country that did not afford me a home might, under any circumstance whatever, stand (should there be any occasion for it), as open and visible as every other part of my conduct had done. For to me who have often reflected upon it, it appears, that the continued neglect of the country towards me, has an effect in putting my reputation to stake; which as it has always been my principle, so it is now, more than ever my duty to preserve. . . .
>
> I cannot help viewing my situation as singularly inconvenient. Trade I do not understand. Land I have none, or what is equal to none. I have exiled myself from one country without making a home of another; and I cannot help sometimes asking myself, what am I better off than a refugee? and that of the most extraordinary

kind, a refugee from the country I have obliged and served, to that which can owe me no good will.

At the end of October, Paine joined Washington on a trip exactly mirroring the route along which the Continental Army had retreated so many years before. On November 25, 1783, as the very last of the British forces and their loyalist compatriots sailed from Long Island, Washington and Paine led an elated parade of thousands of soldiers and republicans down Broadway. Paine was also a guest at Washington's farewell dinner with the army's officers at Fraunces Tavern on Pearl Street, where the commander raised his glass of wine and said, "With a heart full of love and gratitude, I now take leave of you. I most devoutly wish that your latter days may be as prosperous and happy as your former ones have been glorious and honorable. . . . I cannot come to each of you, but I shall feel obliged if each of you come and take me by the hand." As each officer moved forward to kiss his general on the cheek, the room was filled with the plaintive sound of men openly weeping.

Leaving Paine behind in New York City, Washington rode on to Annapolis, Maryland, where at a meeting with Congress he relinquished his military command to civilian hands, and then retired to Mount Vernon. There he received an April 28 update from Paine:

> Mr. Duane and some other friends of yours and mine, who were persuaded that nothing [of a reward for Paine] would take place in Congress (as a single man when only nine states were present could stop the whole), proposed a new line which is to leave it to the States individually; and a unanimous resolution has passed the senate of this State [New York], which is generally expressive of their opinion and friendship. What they have proposed is worth at least a thousand guineas, and other States will act as they see proper. If I do but get enough to carry me decently thro' the world and independently thro' the History of the Revolution, I neither wish nor care for more; and that the States may very easily do if they are disposed to it. . . . Should the method succeed, I shall stand perfectly clear of Congress, which will be an agreeable circumstance to me; because whatever I may then say on the necessity of strengthening the union, and enlarging its powers, will come from me with a much better grace than if Congress had made the acknowledgment themselves.

Washington again took up his friend's cause, writing in turn to Richard Henry Lee, James Madison, and Patrick Henry to see what award could be made by the Virginia legislature:

> Unsolicited by, and unknown to Mr. Paine, I take the liberty of hinting the services and the distressed (for so I think it may be called) situation of that gentleman.
>
> That his Common Sense, and many of his Crisis, were well timed and had a happy effect upon the public mind, none, I believe, who will recur to the epochs at which they were published will deny. That his services hitherto have passed of[f] unnoticed is obvious to all; and that he is chagrined and necessitous I will undertake to aver. Does not common justice then point to some compensation?
>
> He is not in circumstances to refuse the bounty of the public. New York, not the least distressed nor most able State in the Union, has set the example. He prefers the benevolence of the States individually to an allowance from Congress, for reasons which are conclusive in his own mind, and such as I think may be approved by others. His views are moderate, a decent independency is, I believe, the height of his ambition, and if you view his services in the American cause in the same important light that I do, I am sure you will have pleasure in obtaining it for him.

Despite the support of four of the most prominent of America's founders, including the father of the nation, *Public Good* sabotaged any Virginia bequest for Thomas Paine, with Lee explaining to Washington, "I have been told that it miscarried from its being observed that he had shown enmity to this State by having written a pamphlet injurious to our claim of Western Territory. It has ever appeared to me that this pamphlet was the consequence of Mr. Paine's being himself imposed upon, and that it was rather the fault of the place than the man." It was eventually revealed that the key legislator rallying the Virginia assembly against Paine was none other than "the bilious" Arthur Lee. Madison was especially taken aback by this failure: "Should it finally appear that the merits of the man, whose writings have so much contributed to enforce and foster the spirit of independence in the people of America, are unable to inspire them with a just beneficence, the world, it is to be feared, will give us as little credit for our policy as for gratitude in this particular."

Paine was far from the only American suffering through these postwar years, as a great many fearful Tory predictions of the costs of leaving the British Empire had come true. American ships were no longer protected from pirates by the great English navy; settlers on the western frontiers had no British army to defend them from Indian attacks; plantation owners had lost their Welsh lines of credit; and fishermen no longer had ready markets in the British West Indies. Much of the South, notably the Carolinas, was in ruin, and the states' aggressive independence—with each colony maintaining its own currency, tariffs, customs, and border regulations—was triggering a collapse in the overall economy. Washington, however, persisted in trying to help his great friend and most significant public supporter. Finally, on October 3, 1785, Congress agreed to give Paine an honorarium of $3,000 ($250,000 today), while Pennsylvania offered £500 ($90,000). The largest bequest, strangely enough, was the one that came first, from New York, a colony that had spent the war years in British hands but whose new republican government included several Paine allies. The state honored him with a parcel of property abandoned by loyalist Frederick DaVoe when he fled to Canada—277 acres and a farmhouse outside New Rochelle. Paine was now a confirmed city dweller (though he would soon buy a small house in Bordentown, to be near Colonel Kirkbride), and New Rochelle was a full day's horse ride from New York City, so he quickly rented the house to a tenant farmer and arranged for the stable to quarter his beloved horse, Button.

Though they were no longer working together, Paine would come to Robert Morris's aid that year when the Bank of North America (begun with the silver livres brought from France by Paine and John Laurens) came under attack. The bank had refused to cooperate with the Pennsylvania Assembly, which had so overprinted its paper money that the state was being riven by inflation. The Assembly decided to take revenge by repealing the bank's charter, prompting a number of its more significant customers to pull their deposits. In *Dissertations on Government; the Affairs of the Bank; and Paper Money,* Paine again explained how money was an emblem of human labor, and he attacked the overprinting of paper currency as the equivalent of a profligate who leaves debt to be repaid by his children. He suggested that independent banks could serve as a form of checks and balances against state financial power, and critiqued the Assembly in what, for those who had not read much of Paine outside *Common Sense* and the various *American*

Crises, was a shocking argument. In this treatise, the ultimate eighteenth-century advocate of populist sovereignty said that the Assembly's revocation of the bank's charter was a form of democratic fascism. He explained that, from the most basic vigilante lynch mob to state-sanctioned discrimination against minorities, republics hold the potential of majority rule becoming voter-sanctioned totalitarianism, what Paine called "the despotism of numbers." He believed this could be countered by a free, vigorous press and an active federal judiciary. When it came to this one issue at least, Alexander Hamilton, John Adams, and Thomas Paine were all in perfect accord.

Some Paine historians have taken his changing views—in the years to come he would side, in turn, with Edmund Burke, Lafayette, and the Girondins, each a political enemy of the next—as a sign that he was some sort of overly impressionable philosophic chameleon, his principles depending on the beliefs held by his closest friends of the moment. Though the impact of his discussions with others about his ideas and writing cannot be underestimated—it may in fact have been that Paine the conversationalist was a greater artist than Paine the writer—the fundamental pragmatism of the Anglo-American Enlightenment grounded him and prevented him from turning into a fickle ideologue. He saw that the United Colonies were weak, and became one of the first and most vocal of the federalists. He saw that the nation's finances were pathetic, and fought for strong banks. He would, however, never accept, from his studies in natural philosophy, the logic of state executions and capital punishment, whether for a military captain or a French king.

In that same year of 1785 Paine was elected to the American Philosophical Society, and perhaps it was this honor that made him ultimately decide to forsake the vile and thankless career of a writer and return to his first love: Newton. It may seem odd that he changed course after finally receiving official government recognition for his work, but Paine did not consider this a sufficient reward, and he knew that times had changed. The *Common Sense*/Declaration of Independence era, with its glorious aspirational hopes and dizzying optimism, was over, replaced by the retrenchment period of war's end. Now was a time for the practical toil of creating a national government, instead of dreaming Enlightenment dreams. There had been a great era of utopians, but now the American Congress was by necessity a body of compromise, of down-and-dirty politics and expedient business negotiations. Though he had repeatedly championed the idea of revising the federal government through a constitutional convention, when that convention actually began to be assembled, Paine did not even try to become one of its deputies.

Though Paine's life had always included a sideline of natural philosophy, that interest now took center stage. He focused on useful discoveries that might increase the happiness of all mankind, such as a variant on the basis of the internal combustion engine: "When I consider the wisdom of nature I must think that she endowed matter with this extraordinary property for other purposes than that of destruction. Poisons are capable of other uses than that of killing. If the power which an ounce of gunpowder contains could be detailed out as steam or water can be it would be a most commodious natural power." By carving channels along its sides, he engineered a smokeless candle, while his "present arduous undertaking," as described by Ben Franklin, was the design of a new bridge, one inspired by models he had seen in France with John Laurens.

Paine had welcomed Franklin home to America from Europe in a letter of September 23, including the comment "so far as I have hitherto gone, I am not conscious of any circumstance in my conduct that should give you one repentant thought for being my patron and introducer to America." Franklin, urging Paine to reconsider his retirement from writing, replied on September 24, "Be assured, my dear friend, that instead of repenting that I was your introducer into America, I value myself on the share I had in procuring for it the acquisition of so useful and valuable a citizen. . . . I was sorry on my arrival to find you had left this city. Your present arduous undertaking, I easily conceive, demands retirement, and tho' we shall reap the fruits of it, I cannot help regretting the want of your abilities here where in the present moment they might, I think, be successfully employed. Parties still run very high—Common Sense would unite them. It is to be hoped therefore it has not abandoned us forever."

Today it would be strange for a famous writer to suddenly start engineering bridges, but in Paine's day such a breadth of interests was the hallmark of an Enlightened gentleman, not to mention that, at a time when waterborne traffic was a superior form of transportation, bridge design was considered an eighteenth-century lodestone for state-of-the-art technological innovation. Paine initially designed a 400- to 500-foot single-arch, pierless construction that he believed could be economically prefabricated by an ironworks.

Its lack of piers meant that such a bridge could solve the common problem of iced-over rivers in North America. He based his ideas on observations of the spider, since "when Nature enabled this insect to make a web, she taught it the best method."

Even though Ben Franklin believed that the quarreling, faction-ridden American nation needed Paine's thinking and advocacy to engineer a strong new government and society, as well as to serve as a bulwark against what he saw as an assault on democracy and representation in the government of elites proposed by Federalists Adams and Hamilton, when Paine asked for help in this new course of his life, Franklin gave it wholeheartedly. He hosted Paine's bridge model in the garden of his Philadelphia home on Market Street, and offered regular demonstrations to Philadelphia's civic leaders, who were impressed that it was strong enough to hold three of them at once.

With his bequest from the Pennsylvania Assembly, Paine hired as an engineering assistant one John Hall, a recent Leicester emigrant and carpenter experienced in the manufacture of steam engines, and a man who called inventions "saints" and inventors "saint makers." The only detailed account of Thomas Paine's extraordinary day-to-day life during this period survives in the pages of Hall's diaries:

> [Nov.] 22d. A remark of Mr. Paine's—not to give a deciding opinion between two persons you are in friendship with, lest you lose one by it; whilst doing that between two persons, your supposed enemies, may make one your friend.
>
> Sunday, Jan. 1st 1786. Mr. Paine went to dine with Dr. Franklin today; staid till after tea in the evening. They tried the burning of our candles by blowing a gentle current through them. It greatly improved the light. The draught of air is prevented by passing through a cold tube of tallow. The tin of the new lamp by internal reflections is heated and causes a constant current. This is the Doctor's conjecture.
>
> Feb. 25th. Mr. Paine not returned. We sent to all the places we could suppose him to be at and no tidings of him. We became very unhappy fearing his political enemies should have shown him foul play. Went to bed at 10 o.c., and about 2 o.c. a knocking at the door proves Mr. Paine.
>
> March 10th. Before 7 o.c., a brother saint-maker came with a model of machine to drive boats against stream. He had communicated

his scheme to H. who had made alterations and a company had taken it and refused saint-maker partnership. He would fain have given it to Mr. Paine or me, but I a stranger refused and Mr. Paine had enough hobbies of his own. Mr. Paine pointed out a mode to simplify his apparatus greatly. He gave him 5s. to send him one of his maps.

April 15th. Mr. Paine asked me to go and see Indian Chiefs of Sennaka Nation, I gladly assented. They have an interpreter. Mr. Paine wished to see him and made himself known to him by past remembrance as Common Sense, and was introduced into the room, addressed them as "brothers" and shook hands cordially. Mr. Paine treated them with 2s. bowl of punch.

Nov. 21st. . . . I put on Mr. Paine's hose yesterday. Last night he brought me in my room a pair of warm cloth overshoes as feel very comfortable this morning. Had a wooden pot stove stand betwixt my feet by Mr. Paine's desire and found it kept my feet warm.

December 14. This day employed in raising and putting on the [bridge model] abutments again and fitting them. The smith made the nuts of screws to go easier. Then set the ribs at proper distance, and after dinner I and Jackaway put on some temporary pieces on the frame of wood to hold it straight, and when Mr. Paine came they then tied it on its wooden frame with strong cords. I then saw that it had bulged full on one side and hollow on the other. I told him of it, and he said it was done by me—I denied that and words rose high. I at length swore by God that it was straight when I left it, he replied as positively the contrary, and I think myself ill used in this affair.

December 26. Went with Glentworth to see the Bridge at Dr. Franklin's. Coming from thence met Mr. Paine and Mr. Rittenhouse; returned with them and helped move it for all three to stand upon, and then turned it to examine. Mr. Rittenhouse has no doubt of its strength and sufficiency for the Schuylkill, but wished to know what quantity of iron [it used] as he seemed to think it too expensive.

March 15th [1787]. Mr. Paine called this evening; told me of his being with Dr. Franklin and about the chess player, or Automaton, and that the Dr. had no idea of the mode of communication.

April 20. Sitting in the house saw a chair pass down the street

> with a red coat on, and going out after it believed it to be Mr. Paine, so followed him up to Collins's. . . . He is now going for England by way of France in the French packet which sails the 25th instant. . . . He told me of the Committee's proceedings on Bridges and Sewers; anecdotes of Dr. Franklin, who had sent a letter by him to the president, or some person, to communicate to the Society of Civil Architects, who superintend solely over bridges in France. The model is packed up to go with him. The Doctor, though full of employ from the Vice President being ill, and the numerous visitors on State business, and others that his fame justly procures him, could hardly be supposed to pay great attention to trifles; but as he considers Mr. Paine his adopted political son he would endeavor to write by him to his friends, though Mr. Paine did not press, for reasons above.

When it became clear that no one in Philadelphia would actually construct this bridge, Franklin suggested the design be presented to the French Academy of Sciences, and Paine immediately seized on this idea, writing to Franklin on March 31:

> My father and mother are yet living, whom I am very anxious to see, and have informed them of my coming over the ensuing summer. . . . As I have taken a part in the Revolution and politics of this country, and am not an unknown character in the political world, I conceive it would be proper on my going to Paris, that I should pay my respects to Count Vergennes, to whom I am personally unknown; and I shall be very glad of a letter from you to him affording me that opportunity. . . . The Marquis La Fayette I am the most known to of any gentleman in France. Should he be absent from Paris there are none I am much acquainted with. I am on exceeding good terms with Mr. Jefferson which will necessarily be the first place I go to. As I had the honor of your introduction to America it will add to my happiness to have the same friendship continued to me on the present occasion.

Franklin replied with letters to the duc de la Rochefoucauld, the comte d'Estaing, and Jean-Baptiste Le Roy, just as he had done so many years before in dispatching a far different man off to the New World: "The bearer of this letter is Mr. Paine, the author of a famous piece entitled 'Common Sense,' published here with great effect on the minds of people at the beginning of the revolution. He is an ingenious, honest man; and as such I beg leave to recommend him to your civilities."

On April 26, 1787, the fifty-year-old Thomas Paine sailed for Europe. He had dinner with Thomas Jefferson on July 21 and, through Franklin, Jefferson, and the meetings of the Parisian abolitionist association La Société des Amis des Noirs, met such French luminaries as the philosophe marquis de Condorcet and publisher Jacques-Pierre Brissot. His bridge model was presented to the French Academy on July 21; five weeks later, the engineering committee reported that its design was solid and economical, novel in its use of iron, and worthy of manufacture, a report that thrilled its designer. While Paine went to visit his mother in England (his father having died from smallpox on November 14), Jefferson and Lafayette brought his designs before the French government as a new Seine crossing (simultaneously, none other than Beaumarchais was applying for a patent on his own somewhat similar bridge). The country was too much in debt, however, to even consider launching any grand engineering projects, save some crucial arches at the Pont de la Concorde, in traditional stone.

In Thetford Paine went to the grave of his father at St. Cuthbert's, and visited with his aunt, Miss Cocke, and with his ninety-year-old mother at her home on Heathenman Street. He bought his mother a weekly annuity of nine shillings—half his income as an excise officer, but sufficient for a retiree living in an English village. After hearing from Jefferson that the French seemed uninterested in building his bridge anytime soon, he decided to have his model shipped to Britain's Royal Society. Over the following years this peripatetic miniature would mirror Paine's own continental meandering as, released from economic worries for the first time in his life, he would migrate constantly between London and Paris, enjoying the company and admiration of some of Europe's most charismatic figures. Just as he had quickly come to know so many important Parisians, in London he was taken up as both political ally and companionable guest by the nation's most powerful Whigs, including the great party leader (and the man most hated by King George yet most loved by his heir, the Prince of Wales), Charles James Fox, as well as by playwright Richard Brinsley Sheridan, preacher Richard Price, educator William Godwin, and author Mary Wollstonecraft. Lewes friend Clio Rickman, now living in London, reported that Paine's "manners were easy and gracious, his knowledge was universal and boundless; in private company and among friends his conversation had every fascination that anecdote, novelty, and truth could give it," and that Godwin at one dinner became annoyed with Wollstonecraft's "talking so much that Paine, whose powers as a conversationalist he had looked forward to enjoying, lapsed into shyness and an unusual silence." A portrait of Paine during this period would also appear in Royall Taylor's novel *The Algerine Captive:*

> He was dressed in a snuff-colored coat, olive velvet vest, drab breeches, coarse hose. His shoe buckles of the size of a half dollar. A bob tailed wig covered that head which worked such mickle woe to courts and kings. If I should attempt to describe it, it would be in the same stile and principle with which the veteran soldier bepraiseth an old standard: the more tattered, the more glorious. It is probable that this was the same identical wig under the shadow of whose curls he wrote Common Sense, in America, many years before. He was a spare man, rather under size; subject to the extreme of low, and highly exhilarating spirits; often sat reserved in company; seldom mingled in common chit chat: But when a man of sense and elocution was present, and the company numerous, he delighted in advancing the most unaccountable, and often the most whimsical paradoxes; which he defended in his own plausible manner. If encouraged by success, or the applause of the company, his countenance was animated with an expression of feature which, on ordinary occasions one would look for in vain, in a man so much celebrated for acuteness of thought; but if interrupted by extraneous observation, by the inattention of his auditory, or in an irritable moment, even by the accidental fall of the poker, he would retire into himself, and no persuasion could induce him to proceed upon the most favorite topic.

Even surrounded by the great European luminaries of his day, however, Paine suffered from acutely mixed feelings on leaving America, as he wrote to a newly married friend, Kitty Nicholson Few:

> You touch me on a very tender part when you say my friends on your side of the water "cannot be reconciled to the idea of my

resigning my adopted America, even for my native England." They are right. Though I am in as elegant style of acquaintance here as any American that ever came over, my heart and myself are 3000 miles apart; and I had rather see my horse Button in his own stable, or eating the grass of Bordentown or Morrisania, than see all the pomp and show of Europe.

A thousand years hence (for I must indulge in a few thoughts) perhaps in less, America may be what England now is! The innocence of her character that won the hearts of all nations in her favor may sound like a romance, and her inimitable virtue as if it had never been. The ruins of that liberty which thousands bled for, or suffered to obtain, may just furnish materials for a village tale or extort a sigh from rustic sensibility, while the fashionable of that day, enveloped in dissipation, shall deride the principle and deny the fact.

When we contemplate the fall of empires and the extinction of nations of the ancient world, we see but little to excite our regret than the mouldering ruins of pompous palaces, magnificent monuments, lofty pyramids, and walls and towers of the most costly workmanship. But when the empire of America shall fall, the subject for contemplative sorrow will be infinitely greater than crumbling brass or marble can inspire. It will not then be said, here stood a temple of vast antiquity; here rose a Babel of invisible height, or there a palace of sumptuous extravagance; but here, ah painful thought! the noblest work of human wisdom, the grandest scene of human glory, the fair cause of freedom rose and fell!

Read this and then ask if I forget America . . . God bless you all! and send me safe back to my much loved America!

After Paine received an English patent for his bridge, he convinced Thomas Walker ironworks of Rotherham, Yorkshire, to construct an experimental ninety-foot version, which was erected over the Don River and visited by such dignitaries as Lord Fitz-William, the future Marquess of Rockingham, accompanied by the pale, stooped, and well-fed onetime colonial agent for New York, private secretary to the marquess's father, and now member of Parliament, Edmund Burke. If Beaumarchais was a great illustration of a sensibility at a historical turning point in France, Edmund Burke would be its British counterpart; Burke's volte-face would be so shocking, in fact, that Thomas Jefferson would note that "the revolution of

France does not astonish me so much as the revolution of Mr. Burke. I wish I could believe the latter proceeded from as pure motives as the former. . . . How mortifying that this evidence of the rottenness of his mind must oblige us now to ascribe to wicked motives those actions of his life which wore the mark of virtue and patriotism."

Known today as a patriarch of conservatism, Burke was in his own time no Tory, but a liberal Whig, and not even an Englishman, but an Irishman, born and raised in Dublin with a Catholic mother, an Anglican father, and an education at a Quaker boarding school. Friend to both conservative Samuel Johnson and progressive Joseph Priestley, author of the paean to sensibility *A Philosophical Enquiry into the Origin of Our Ideas of the Sublime and Beautiful,* an early opponent of slavery, and a harsh critic of Britain's egregious corruption in India, Burke was during the American Revolution one of the colonists' greatest supporters in Parliament, seeing in their treatment by the British an echo of the country's prejudice against Catholics. At the time, he insisted to his fellow legislators that if an entire citizenry was in revolt, it was the government that must be reformed.

Burke and Paine immediately struck up a friendship, and it is easy to imagine them spending countless hours together in animated conversation, agreeing on so many things and agreeing to disagree on smaller matters (such as the usefulness of aristocrats, and current events in France). Paine spent numerous weeks at Burke's Beaconsfield, Buckinghamshire, country house, at one time touring the nearby ironworks and England's other manufactories ("I have been to see the Cotton Mills—the Potteries—the Steel furnaces—Tin plate manufacture—White lead manufacture. All those things might be easily carried on in America," he reported back to Jefferson), and in London, Paine lived in the neighborhood of Fitzrovia at 154 New Cavendish, a mere five-minute stroll from Burke's home at 18 Charlotte. The beauty of the prose in one apparently never-before-published letter that Paine wrote to Burke reveals the great regard and sentiment he felt for his new English friend:

> Broad Street, Aug 7, 1788
>
> I begin this letter as we begin the world, without knowing whether it will be long or short, through what windings it may lead or where it will end. . . .
>
> I had been educated, as all under English government are, to look on France as a contentious nation striving at universal monarchy and

oppression: but experience, reflection and an intimacy with the political and personal character of that nation, removed those prejudices, and placed me in a situation to judge freely and impartially for myself.

Though I had closed my political career with the establishment of the independence of America, and had no other business in France than to execute the orders of the government of Pennsylvania with the Academy of Sciences respecting the model of the bridge, yet there appeared to me, at that moment, such a fair opportunity to bring England and France into a better understanding with each other than had formerly been the case, and as a man always feels a happy consolation in any attempt to do good, that I wrote to the Abbé Morellet on this subject, knowing that he was in the confidence of the Archbishop of Toulouse. . . .

But I am running into matters I have no business with and therefore I stop myself. . . . The quiet field of science has more amusement to my mind than politics and I had rather erect the largest arch on the world than be the greatest Emperor in it.

7. *Droits de l'Homme, ou Droits du Seigneur?*

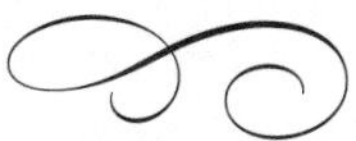

WHEN THOMAS PAINE first arrived in the Paris of 1787, he found himself engulfed once again in a nationwide jubilation over the American defeat of that belligerent despot, Britain. While the Philadelphia festivities had left him feeling ignored and unappreciated, for the Parisians he was a celebrated man of letters, a *philosophe républicain* representative of *le monde nouveau.* The French at that moment were entirely besotted with their victorious New World allies; the Ambigu-Comique's long-running vaudeville sensation, *L'héroine américaine,* was so popular that the troupe's great rival in the arts and sciences of burlesque, tightrope, clowns, mimes, acrobats, dancers, singers, and performing monkeys, Les Grands Danseurs du Roi, changed the name of its newest revue to *Le héros américain.* For the more refined arts lover, the Comédie Italienne was offering a *Ballet des Quakers,* while the great Parisian trend in home decorating featured newly etched prints of Ben Franklin, George Washington, New England whalers, and Chesapeake planters. In Marseille a club of thirteen (each associated with one state) picnicked on the thirteenth of every month and drank thirteen toasts to the future of the United States. Lafayette, now commander in chief of the King's Dragoons, would outdo everyone by naming his son George Washington and his daughter Virginie, and by having in his employ two Native Americans as houseboys.

Along with Jefferson, Franklin, and Adam Smith, Paine was a regular guest at the Hôtel de la Monnaie salon of the marquis de Condorcet and Sophie de Grouchie. If the Anglo-American Enlightenment was fueled to a great extent by the conversations of taverns and coffeehouses, the French Enlightenment followed a similar course, but in the salons of Paris. While the coffeehouses were ecumenical in class, the salons were almost wholly restricted to seigneurs, with some favored writers and philosophes ornamentally included. One of the latter characterized his subservient position as salon guest: "In England it was enough that Newton was the greatest mathematician of his century; in France he would have been expected to be agreeable, too." While the English and American taverns were exclusively male preserves, the French salons were hosted by women, and just as the culture of England had moved during the eighteenth century from court to coffeehouse, so did French society escape the inanity of Versailles for those salons, in what the main historian of this movement would call "the revenge of Paris." In the wake of the American Revolution, the minds of salon-going French aristocrats had become so intoxicated with visions of democracy that Condorcet admitted to Paine at one dinner that they "seized with joy the opportunity to avow publicly sentiments which prudence had prevented them from expressing."

At the same time that the French were becoming interested in a wide range of republican styles and notions, the billions of livres that their government had spent in losing the Seven Years War and winning the American Revolution were now wreaking domestic havoc. The nation was beginning to grasp that it is extremely difficult to lead the life of a Sun King while living within one's means. By 1788 France was using half of all its revenue solely to make interest payments on between three and four billion livres of state debt. It was, however, not the actual financial and agricultural difficulties of the state that would be critical factors in the long run—England at the same time was spending 70 percent of its revenue on interest payments with taxes set at three times per capita—but the public view of the French government as collapsing and inept. After all, it had become a nation that could not even feed itself.

France had been devastated by a series of excessively harsh winters, destructive hailstorms, and runs of drought, triggering famine and doubling the prices of bread and firewood. Traveling across the French countryside, English novelist Tobias Smollett would be shocked by the peasants he saw, reporting that they did not resemble human beings so much as "ravenous scarecrows." In that preindustrial era, drought not only precipitated agricultural woe, it also slowed or stopped the waterwheels of mills, leading to shortages of flour. The scarcity and cost of bread would be a central issue during the forthcoming revolution, as workers on average spent half their income to buy three pounds of it every day.

The French court would in time fall to revolution due to its inept efforts at public relations and its bad luck with agriculture—or was it real estate? The wisdom of the Hobbes-Locke-Paine notion that a nation's power rises from its citizens was briskly illustrated in the history of Versailles. Built as both a state-of-the-art residence and an intimidating display of absolute power, this château so removed the French monarch from his subjects that only an extremely commanding figure such as Louis XIV could maintain control of the axial powers of the nation. The dramatically less majestic XV and XVI would be undermined by this symbol in stone of God-anointed monarchs, so divorced and distant from their public that they eventually lost their way as sovereign leaders.

The current king, Louis XVI, had any number of admirable Enlightenment hobbies—cartography, locksmithing, and unstoppling the Versailles fountains to drench soigné toffs—but as a leader he was hapless and indecisive. While the English would continue to love and honor their King George III even in his madness, the French would come to consider their obtuse and distant monarch as less and less admirable, honorable, and respectable, beginning with that moment when he married one of the most loathsome of all foreigners, an *Austrian,* and a painful condition of his foreskin caused years of delay in producing a dauphin (Louis was known as the locksmith who couldn't find his keyhole). This was an especially difficult turn of events for a would-be absolute ruler who was known for admitting, "I would like to be loved."

The alliance between Seize and Marie Antoinette, arranged to guarantee peace and prosperity for both France and Austria, worked poorly at the diplomatic level and even worse with the French people, who referred to their queen as an *Autrichienne* (Austrian bitch) and passed around lewd illustrations portraying her as sexually promiscuous. So much has been written about this woman so typical of her class and era (undereducated, but opinionated; lacking in curiosity, but willful; firmly convinced of her ideas on government, no matter what catastrophes ensued), but perhaps the most telling is the notion that "Let them eat cake!" could not possibly have been true, as Marie Antoinette would not have noticed anything whatsoever about the diet of the French masses. Even her brother, Emperor Joseph II of Austria, would note of France's king and queen that "together they are a couple of awkward nincompoops."

By the late 1780s there were daily rumors—all untrue—that the French government would at any moment declare bankruptcy, and most Frenchmen believed that they had been reduced to this condition not by the costs of war but by outlandish royal profligacy—another nickname for Marie Antoinette being "Mme. Déficit." If the role of coffee cannot be overestimated in the history of the American Revolution, that of gossip holds similar pride of place for the French, as "inside information" would work hand in hand with what has been called the Great Fear—masses of the population, convinced of imminent catastrophe fueled by hair-raising stories, panicking themselves into action, which usually ended in looting, vigilantism, and heads on pikes. In fact, over time, the rumors of out-of-control spending by the royal family grew so pervasive that foreign bankers refused to grant the state further loans, and the French public, in turn, rioted. Like George III, Louis XVI would appoint one minister after the next to try to resolve his disastrous political quandaries, with all too predictable results.

To deal with the state's 1787 financial and public relations crises, Controller-General Charles-Alexandre de Calonne appointed various government functionaries, a baron, Lafayette, eight marshals, six marquises, nine counts, seven princes, seven archbishops, seven dukes, and the presidents of the *Parlements* (not a legislature, but the French judicial aristocrats known as *robins*) to meet at Versailles as an Assembly of Notables. Calonne was hoping to inspire the nation's aristocrats to start paying taxes (which they had never done); the Assembly of Notables' first act was to dismiss Calonne. Lafayette would tell Jefferson, in a variant on Paine's "nobility" equaling "no ability," that the "notables" were "not able."

Calonne's successor, the atheist cardinal Loménie de Brienne, dissolved the Assembly and, still unable to get further loans from Europe's moneylenders, turned to the *Parlement* of Paris to approve a vast new array of taxes. The Parisian *robins,* seizing the chance to engineer their own version of the Glorious Revolution and render monarchy in France quite a bit less than absolute, instead demanded that the king assemble the Estates-General (France's repesentative legislature, instituted in 1302 and dissolved in 1614, composed of 300 clergy, 291 aristocrats, and 610 property-owning commoners) to approve these new tariffs. Louis sent his army to shut down every *Parlement;* the French rioted once more.

On August 8, 1788, the king capitulated, publicly calling for elections and a collection of *cahiers de doléances*—any grievances that the French public might wish to make. Unless the nation could both right itself financially and resolve the various *doléances* in the eyes of its people, this capitulation would mark the beginning of the end of the divine right of kings in the country that, a mere two reigns earlier, had been ruled by the very manifestation of that notion.

Simultaneously with the king's agreeing to restore his country's legislature came the ten-year anniversary of the death of the man who would be to the French Revolution what John Locke had been to the American revolt. Always portrayed as half-smiling, twinkle-eyed, and wearing a humble fur cap (exactly the mien that Ben Franklin would adopt on arriving in Paris), Jean-Jacques Rousseau began his rise to prominence when he was contributing to Denis Diderot's *Encyclopédie,* and Diderot thought he might want to submit an essay for a newspaper's literary contest, the *Mercure de France*'s Dijon prize. Entrants were to compose a reflection on the topic "Has the revival of the arts and sciences done more to corrupt or purify morals?" and Diderot thought that if Rousseau argued in favor of *corrupt,* his essay would be noticed. He did and it did, winning the prize and launching the unique perspective that would guarantee his place as one of the most beloved of the philosophes. The coiner of the phrase *Liberté, Egalité, Fraternité,* who turned against all his friends; the highly admired theorist on parenting who abandoned all of his children; the deist who proclaimed that all other deists were infidels; and the playwright who consistently attacked the theater, Rousseau would begin his theories firmly in the Enlightenment tradition, and then take revenge on the Voltaire-Newton-Locke axis with such notions as "The man who thinks is a depraved animal."

Rousseau became an epochal figure for exactly this paradox: creating so many ideas that would become cornerstones of the French Enlightenment, and then proclaiming their very antitheses, embodying an era and the seeds of its destruction within one human form. Many echoes of Rousseau would appear in the sensational work that Thomas Paine would write next, especially the theses that government is a contract to provide security, liberty, and equality to its people, and that humans are born compassionate, but made cruel and selfish by a corrupt society—a notion promoted by both Rousseau and Montesquieu, and so doubly cherished in France.

Instead of the polite congeniality held with such high regard by Messrs. Locke and Spectator, Rousseau would insist on the free play of any and all emotion, a trend that became known as "sensibility," inspiring such foreign reactions as Greuze's *Girl Weeping over Her Dead Canary,* Gainsborough's portraits of English aristocrats gazing in melancholy contemplation to fully display the depth and breadth of their humane empathy, German *Sturm und Drang,* English Gothic horrors, and a good skewering by Jane Austen. Rousseau's championing of emotion would win such a following among the French, however, that the Roman sense of virtue that had so inspired Paine and the other American pragmatic utopians would be replaced by a virtue of the heart—not so pragmatic. If Enlightenment ideals under the American Revolution became a social and commercial theory of living and success, for the French they became a religion, a guide to morality, and a campaign of the human spirit. Instead of deploying the Newtonian series of deductions Paine used to express his formulas for government and society, French journalists and politicians would become masters of visceral oratory, always striving to leave their public weeping or enraged. The apex of virtuous sensibility would, over the coming years, appear in the form of a citizen army of Parisians, dressed in rags, their eyes brimming with tears, demanding to be fed, while armed with pikes and axes.

In so many ways Jean-Jacques Rousseau had a profound effect on French history, especially as he would inspire, in the closing years of the eighteenth century, an army of zealous acolytes, most notably a young lawyer of Artois noted for his meticulous appearance, for his carefully powdered wig and steel-framed eyeglasses, and for his two suits, one of velour and one of wool, an orphan who so worshipped the classics that as a teenager he was nicknamed "the Roman." In 1789, elected to the Estates-General, Maximilien François Marie Isidore de Robespierre arrived at Versailles to take his seat as a deputy representing the province of Arras.

On October 25, 1788, the king of England was riding in his enormous carriage through the Great Park of Windsor Castle when he was pleased and surprised to see his friend and relative, the king of Prussia, standing a short distance away. After he ordered his driver to halt, the two monarchs had a warm and lively conversation on that brisk autumn day, a conversation that greatly upset the royal servants in attendance, as George III was not in fact talking to another royal personage, but to an oak tree.

Today it is thought that the king suffered from porphyria, an inherited liver disease with symptoms of vomiting, paralysis, hysteria, delirium, and hallucinations, but in that era of Galen humors, it was only understood that the king had gone mad. Over the course of the next six months the English government would fall into crisis, with First Minister William Pitt and Whig leader Charles James Fox using the Prince of Wales's regency to fully exploit the king's (now visible to all) incompetence to rule. Just a month prior, Jefferson, from Paris, had written to Paine, who had returned to London, "I have great confidence in your communications, and since Mr. Adams's departure, I am in need of authentic information from that country." Paine would spend the next year regularly updating the U.S. government on the latest developments in British politics, especially on the condition of the monarch he would name "His Madjesty":

LONDON, Jan. 15 [1789]

. . . The King continues, I believe, as mad as ever. It appears that he has amassed several millions of money, a great part of which is in foreign funds. He had made a will, while he had his senses, and devised it among his children, but a second will has been produced, made since he was mad, dated the 25th of Oct., in which he gives his property to the Queen. This will probably produce much dispute, as it is attended with many suspicious circumstances. It came out in the examination of the physicians, that one of them, Dr. Warrens, on being asked the particular time of his observing the King's insanity, said the twenty-second of October, and some influence has been exerted to induce him to retract that declaration, or to say that the insanity was not so much as to prevent him making a will, which he has refused to do.

September 18.

The people of this country speak very differently on the affairs of France. The mass of them, so far as I can collect, say that France is a much freer country than England. The Peers, the Bishops, &c. say the National Assembly has gone too far. There are yet in this country, very considerable remains of the feudal system which people did not see till the revolution in France placed it before their eyes. While the multitude here could be terrified with the cry and apprehension of arbitrary power, wooden shoes, popery, and such like stuff, they thought themselves by comparison an extraordinary free people; but this bugbear now loses its force, and they appear to me to be turning their eyes towards the aristocrats of their own nation. This is a new mode of conquering, and I think it will have its effect.

Jefferson would reply to Paine's correspondence with continuing news of France's dramatic upheavals. As *doléances* were tallied and representatives for the Estates-General elected, questions about how this national legislature would actually conduct its business began to be raised, most notably by the Abbé Emmanuel-Joseph Sieyès in his essay *Qu'est-ce que le tiers état?* His answer was that the Third Estate was nothing less than the very nation of France itself, and, for equitable representation, must have as many votes as the First (clergy) and Second (seigneurial) estates combined. The abbé's notions turned out to be so widely popular that the king was forced to publicly renounce his proposal, but the representatives of the Third would not be dissuaded. On June 10 they invited the two other estates to join them in creating a new legislature, the National Assembly, and in nine days, eighty nobles and most of the clergy had agreed to go forward with a dramatically more representative and less feudal branch of government.

On July 12 the French public learned that the king had dismissed their beloved director-general, the Swiss Protestant Jacques Necker, whom many believed a financial genius and a counterforce against aristocrats conspiring to monopolize the prices of flour and bread. As more and more rumors spread, spontaneous riots began at the Palais-Royal, with rioters looting neighborhood shops of weapons, seizing rifles from the Hôtel des Invalides, convincing soldiers to join the patriot cause. Eventually, forty-eight thousand Parisians massed on July 14, looting twenty-eight thousand muskets and ten cannons from the armory of the Invalides and then marching to the Bastille, which they believed held the nation's largest store of gunpowder. The mob rushed the gates, releasing the prison's seven inmates and killing a soldier, and within four months the Bastille would be entirely dismantled. Beyond its value as a symbolic destruction of feudal despots, the great victory of Paris over the Bastille safeguarded the National Assembly, for Louis XVI realized he was now facing civil war and removed the vast garrisons he had assembled to menace the legislators into subservience. The king agreed to appear in public wearing the three-ribboned cockade of Paris (red and blue) and the Bourbons (white). At the same time, Marie Antoinette was burning incriminating documents and packing her jewels.

Also wearing the new *cocarde tricolore* was a citizens' militia, the National Guard, whose commander was the National Assembly's thirty-two-year-old vice president, the marquis de Lafayette, additionally charged with the negotiations of acceptable prices for flour and bread. On July 11 he presented to the Assembly the *Declaration of the Rights of Man and Citizen.* Combining the thoughts of Locke, Montesquieu, American state charters, Voltaire, and Rousseau to establish equality before the law, liberty of the press, and civilian control of the army, this declaration, which was drafted with Thomas Jefferson's assistance, so perfectly reflected modern French thinking that it would be included as part of the nation's various and conflicting constitutions of 1791, 1793, and 1795. One National Assembly deputy proclaimed, "In the new hemisphere, the brave inhabitants of Philadelphia have given the example of a people who reestablished their liberty. . . . France would give that example to the rest of the world." With its legislative approval, the *Declaration* immediately unleashed freedom of speech, transforming a country where print was forbidden into one where all was permitted.

In London, Paine was ecstatic to learn from Jefferson how firmly the American experiment was taking root in Paris. He began thinking a great deal less about the civil engineering of bridges, and a bit more about his very puzzling American feelings toward the struggles over mad King George in Westminster and constitutional monarchy in Versailles. He shared each of Jefferson's letters with Edmund Burke, expecting that the Whig deputy would also be pleased. Burke, however, was very much not pleased, a reaction that might seem churlish given that the National Assembly was at that moment transforming the absolute rule of the Sun King into a constitutional monarchy not all that different from England's. When Paine then wrote Burke that "there is no foreign court, not even Prussia that could now be fond of attacking France; they are afraid of their armies and their subjects catching the contagion. Here are reports of matters beginning to work in Bohemia, and in Rome. . . . Something is beginning in Poland, just enough to make the people begin to think," he could not imagine that Burke was in fact horrified at the news of democracy's potential spread across Europe. It was the beginning of the impasse that drove Burke and Paine into a public battle that galvanized world politics.

On August 4 in a grave and then joyous outburst of noblesse oblige, the members of the French National Assembly's onetime Second Estate voted to renounce their titles and their feudal aristocratic privileges. Over the next three years, Lafayette and his Fayettistes would draft a new government similar in many ways to Pennsylvania's, except that it was still bankrupt. Necker proposed a one-time assessment of 25 percent on every Frenchman earning more than four hundred livres, while the Second Estate's lead deputy, the bishop of Autun, Charles-Maurice de Talleyrand, countered by noting that "great dangers demanded equally drastic remedies," and suggested an immediate end to the country's financial crisis by seizing the local property of the Roman Catholic Church. As the church was not only immensely wealthy but also ran the nation's schools and its own judiciary, this was a shocking, radical idea. Talleyrand's measure was adopted.

The Lafayette government continued to be stymied by the costs of grain, flour, and bread. On October 5 a mob of between six and seven thousand women, led by *les poissardes* (muscular, knife-wielding fishmongers) and joined by fifteen thousand of the National Guard, marched from Paris to Versailles in a ceaseless rainstorm. On reaching the palace, the drenched and exhausted women were ready to give up and go home, but the militia had decided that the royal family must be brought to the capital city so that the king could see, firsthand, the suffering of his people. They believed that something would be done and the food crises would be ended, if only the king *knew*. A mob broke into the royal apartments, killed two guards, and chased Marie Antoinette from room to room. In a matter of hours, the royal family was packed and on its way in the middle of a parade, sixty thousand strong, of National Guardsmen, National Assembly deputies, and ministry employees.

At this point Paine could no longer tolerate living in England as a bystander to the great history being made across the Channel by his good friend and ally Lafayette. A month after writing to President George Washington on October 16, 1789, that "a share in two revolutions is living to some purpose," he sailed to Paris, filled with one overwhelming dream. For if France, with its history of absolute monarchy, could become a republic, then any country in Europe could be blessed by the light, and the modern principles of liberty, equality, and sociability would not begin and end in the New World but become manifest across the whole of civilization. By November 27 he was visiting the just-arrived Gouverneur Morris, who noted in his diary, "The people here are in general divided into those who know a great deal and those who know nothing, consequently they are not to be affected by those halfway arguments which form the excellence of Paine's writings. His conceptions and expressions are splendid and novel but not always clear and just." When the French government asked Morris to consult on reforming the *Parlements,* he remarked, "Today, at half-past three, I go to M. de Lafayette's. He tells me that he wishes to have a meeting of Mr. Short, Mr. Paine, and myself, to consider their judiciary, because his place imposes on him the necessity of being right. I tell him that Paine can do him no good, for that, although he has an excellent pen to write, he has but an indifferent head to think."

When Paine returned to London, he brought with him from Paris a souvenir to send on to the American president, a memento that today can be found at Washington's plantation, Mount Vernon. The cover letter explained:

> Our very good friend, the Marquis de Lafayette, has entrusted to my care the key of the Bastille, and a drawing handsomely framed, representing the demolition of that detestable prison, as a present to your Excellency, of which his letter will more particularly inform. I feel myself happy in being the person through whom the Marquis has conveyed this early trophy of the spoils of despotism, and the first ripe fruits of American principles transplanted into Europe, to his master and patron. . . . That the principles of America opened the Bastille is not to be doubted; and therefore the key comes to the right place.
>
> I beg leave to suggest to your Excellency the propriety of congratulating the King and Queen of France (for they have been our friends) and the National Assembly, on the happy example they are giving to Europe. You will see, by the King's speech, which I enclose, that he prides himself on being at the head of the revolution; and I am certain that such a congratulation will be well received, and have a good effect.

Inspired by all that he had seen in Paris, Paine began drafting on January 17 an essay on the principles embodied by the new France; Lafayette told Washington three days later that "Common Sense is writing for you a brochure in which you will see a portion of my adventures." But what overjoyed Paine—the Enlightenment fruits of the American Revolution returning home to dismantle feudal Europe—continued to horrify Edmund

Burke, who called it a "contagion," writing to a friend about the French that "I mean to set in full view their wicked principles and black hearts. I intend to state the true principles of our constitution in church and state, upon grounds opposite to theirs. I mean to do my best to expose them to the hatred, ridicule, and contempt of the whole world; as I shall always expose such calumniators, hypocrites, sowers of sedition, and approvers of murder and all its triumphs." Paine immediately learned of Burke's plans, as revealed in a letter to an unknown American:

> I went first to Debrets, bookseller, Piccadilly (he is the opposition bookseller). He informed me that Mr. Burke's pamphlet was in the press (he is not the publisher), that he believed Mr. Burke was much at a loss how to go on; that he had revised some of the sheets, six, seven, and one nine times! I then made an appointment with Lord Stanhope, and another with Mr. Fox. The former received me with saying "have I the pleasure of shaking hands with the author of Common Sense?" I told him of the condition of Mr. Burke's pamphlet, and that I had formed to myself the design of answering it, if it should come out at a time when I could devote myself to it. . . . But I am now inclined to think that after all this vaporing of Mr. B., he will not publish his pamphlet. I called yesterday at Debrets, who told me that he has stopped the work. (I had not called on Mr. Burke, and shall not, until his pamphlet comes out, or he gives it up.) I met Dr. Lawrence, an intimate friend of Mr. Burke, a few days ago, to whom I said, "I am exceedingly sorry to see a friend of ours so exceedingly wrong." "Time," says he, "will show if he is." He is, said I, already wrong with respect to time past.

At around this time Paine learned the terrible news that Benjamin Franklin had died on April 17, 1790. As would be the case with so many of the American founding fathers, the Doctor spent his final years in bitter disappointment. Though Congress had generously rewarded Arthur Lee and John Jay for their efforts in overseas diplomacy, they had endlessly delayed reimbursing Franklin for his own personal debts incurred in France, much less granting him any kind of honorarium. Instead, empowered Federalists heaped scorn on the dying man, calling him "one of our first Jacobins, the first to lay his head in the lap of French harlotry; and prostrate the Christianity and honour of his country to the deism and democracies of Paris."

Just after Washington's inauguration Franklin had written to the new administration to ask that son-in-law Richard Bache be appointed postmaster general, something of a morally just request, as Franklin had created the service, but his letters were ignored. Grandson Temple was hoping for a diplomatic assignment to France; Secretary of State Jefferson offered him nothing, though this might have been more a reflection of Temple's personal failings than any slight against his grandfather, as Jefferson would eventually make Franklin's grandnephew, Jonathan Williams, superintendent of West Point.

At Franklin's death, the French National Assembly mourned for three months and delivered a proclamation to his memory to the American government. The American Senate honored Franklin with nothing beyond a cold, perfunctory reading of that French tribute by Senate president John Adams.

On August 26, 1790, the Paris Commune (the city's municipal government) voted to grant honorary citizenship to seventeen foreigners, including James Madison, Alexander Hamilton, George Washington, and Thomas Paine, "who, by their writings and by their courage, have served the cause of liberty and prepared the freedom of the people." While Paine returned to France to enjoy this honor, Edmund Burke continued to revise the page proofs of his essay, which had begun as a letter to a deputy of the National Assembly, Charles Jean François Dupont, summarizing Burke's thoughts on recent events in France. The pamphlet that would in time become his most famous achievement found its greatest inspiration, however, from the sermon of an English minister, the Reverend Dr. Richard Price, considered in Britain the father of life insurance and retirement pensions, and called by Paine "one of the best-hearted men that lives." Dr. Price's November 4, 1789, sermon, "A Discourse on the Love of Our Country," was given in honor of the hundredth anniversary of the Glorious Revolution, tying together that revered moment in English history with what he knew would become another blessed memory: the fall of the Bastille. From the signing of the Magna Carta, Britons had considered theirs to be the finest government in all Christendom, commonly referring to it as "the envy and the admiration of the world." Learning of the upheavals in

France, however, many Englishmen now had second thoughts. Price made the shocking argument that the English deserved "the right to choose our own governors; to cashier them for misconduct; and to frame a government for ourselves. . . . Civil governors are properly the servants of the public and a king is no more than the first servant of the public, created by it, and responsible to it." His speech concluded by noting that he was overjoyed to have "lived to see thirty millions of people . . . demanding liberty with an irresistible voice, their king led in triumph, and an arbitrary monarch surrendering himself to his subjects."

Like the great majority of his noble betters, Burke was consumed with the idea that state reform would include a dose of Parisian-style mob rule. Many Londoners were particularly sensitive to English press accounts of rioting French masses, as they themselves had witnessed firsthand the terrifying and destructive power of democracy on June 2, 1780, when retired navy lieutenant Lord George Gordon, leading a crowd of fifty thousand, had stormed Parliament to petition against the Roman Catholic Relief Act. Memorialized by Dickens in *Barnaby Rudge,* the riots had a tremendous impact on British notions of representative democracy, especially among the noble and the propertied. A small reform movement that had started at the time, taking inspiration from America, was effectively quashed, and most important, a great chain of events was set in motion, beginning with the pamphlet that Paine would call "a tribute of fear."

Appearing at the stationers on November 1, 1790, *Reflections on the Revolution in France, and on the Proceedings in Certain Societies in London Relative to That Event: In a Letter Intended to Have Been Sent to a Gentleman in Paris* began with a citation of Dr. Price's Hobbes-Locke encomium that England's monarch "is almost the only lawful king in the world because he is the only one who owes his crown to the choice of his people." Burke called this idea "nonsense and therefore neither true nor false, or it affirms a most unfounded, dangerous, illegal, and unconstitutional position." According to *Reflections,* the power of English kings began instead with Parliament's oath to William of Orange in the Declaration of Right that "the Lords spiritual and temporal, and Commons, do, in the name of all the people aforesaid, most humbly and faithfully submit themselves, their heirs and posterities for ever . . . to the end of time." Burke would hold that this Glorious Revolution was in fact no revolution at all, but one mild step in the patient and gradual evolution that was Albion's great and noble political history:

> You will observe that from Magna Charta to the Declaration of Right it has been the uniform policy of our constitution to claim and assert our liberties as an entailed inheritance derived to us from our forefathers, and to be transmitted to our posterity—as an estate specially belonging to the people of this kingdom, without any reference whatever to any other more general or prior right. By this means our constitution preserves a unity in so great a diversity of its parts. We have an inheritable crown, an inheritable peerage, and a House of Commons and a people inheriting privileges, franchises, and liberties from a long line of ancestors. . . .
>
> The power of perpetuating our property in our families . . . makes our weakness subservient to our virtue, it grafts benevolence even upon avarice. The possessors of family wealth, and of the distinction which attends hereditary possession (as most concerned in it), are the natural securities for this transmission. . . . Let those large proprietors be what they will—and they have their chance of being amongst the best—they are, at the very worst, the ballast in the vessel of the commonwealth. . . . Some decent, regulated preeminence, some preference (not exclusive appropriation) given to birth is neither unnatural, nor unjust, nor impolitic. . . .
>
> Society is indeed a contract . . . [but] as the ends of such a partnership cannot be obtained in many generations, it becomes a partnership not only between those who are living, but between those who are living, those who are dead, and those who are to be born. Each contract of each particular state is but a clause in the great primaeval contract of eternal society, linking the lower with the higher natures, connecting the visible and invisible world. . . . Changing the state as often as there are floating fancies, . . . no one generation could link with the other. Men would be little better than the flies of a summer.

Burke explained that revolutions were entirely unnecessary for a country like the United Kingdom, which instead had followed centuries of clement political reform, unless those "revolutions have been conducted by persons who, whilst they attempted or affected changes in the commonwealth, sanctified their ambition by advancing the dignity of the people whose peace they troubled. They had long views. . . . Such was . . . our Cromwell." Burke considered the French Revolution, unlike the English civil wars, a chaotic and pointless annihilation of the great and noble Gallic society and civilization that had been created through centuries of wisdom and bravery, a catastrophic upheaval that could only end with its patriots destroyed and its government a military dictatorship: "In the weakness of one kind of authority, and in the fluctuation of all, the officers of an army will remain for some time mutinous and full of faction until some popular general . . . shall draw the eyes of all men upon him." In this prediction, Burke would be proved correct.

Opposing a tenet of modern Enlightenment beliefs, *Reflections* held that human reason was weak, and its dark passions strong. Tradition, custom, and religion were all bulwarks that countered the natural and depraved forces surging within each human animal, and without them, life had no meaning or purpose. Like Hamilton, Burke believed that only the nation's elite should be involved in the affairs of state, which in his mind meant not just the rich and the landed but chivalric nobles, and clearly not common tradesmen. He would say of France's Third Estate:

> The occupation of a hairdresser or of a working tallow-chandler cannot be a matter of honor to any person—to say nothing of a number of other more servile employments. Such descriptions of men ought not to suffer oppression from the state; but the state suffers oppression if such as they, either individually or collectively, are permitted to rule. . . . Whenever the supreme authority is vested in a body so composed, it must evidently produce the consequences of supreme authority placed in the hands of men not taught habitually to respect themselves, who had no previous fortune in character at stake, who could not be expected to bear with moderation, or to conduct with discretion, a power which they themselves, more than any others, must be surprised to find in their hands. Who could flatter himself that these men, suddenly and, as it were, by enchantment snatched from the humblest rank of subordination, would not be intoxicated with their unprepared greatness?

An immediate and immense sensation, *Reflections* found a natural readership among the carriage trade, who heartily agreed with Burke that the dreadful French reformers had inspired such "insolent irreligion in opinions" as "a king is but a man; a queen is but a woman." First resident of 10 Downing Street Horace Walpole wrote that he found it "far superior to what was expected even by his warmest admirers. I have read it twice, and though of 350 pages, I wish I could repeat every page by heart." It even received a nod from King George, who publicly recommended, "Read it, it will do you good! Do you good! Every gentleman should read it." An estimated thirty-five thousand copies were sold, and in less than two months seventeen essays would be published rallying to Burke's cause.

Burke's Whig colleagues, meanwhile, were shocked by his political reversal from liberal to conservative scion. The poet Samuel Taylor Coleridge would try to explain it by noting that Burke was "a great courtier," whose four decades of adult life had depended entirely on the generous patronage of the Marquess of Rockingham, to whom in turn Burke was a remarkably able protégé. If aristocrats were to be done away with, as Thomas Paine and his modern allies hoped, then the entire way of life that had been so good to Edmund Burke would come to an end. This did not mean that *Reflections* was written cynically or selfishly; regardless of such flaws as corrupt pocket boroughs and pension kickbacks, Burke sincerely believed that the English nobles' control of the government was far preferable to a tyrant on the throne or democratic mobs like Lord Gordon's rampaging through the streets. For the rest of his life, Burke would continually fear that the wise, selfless aristocrats he so admired might be democratically replaced by a government of "petty lawyers, constables, Jew brokers, keepers of hotels, taverns, and brothels, pert apprentices, clerks, shop boys, hairdressers, fiddlers and dancers."

By calling English workingmen a "swinish multitude," *Reflections* would additionally inspire a number of published attacks: *Pig's Meat, Hog's Wash,* and *Politics for the People: A Salmagundy for Swine* being just a few of the more memorable titles. The first rejoinder to appear in the shops, though, was *Vindication of the Rights of Man,* by the gray-haired, thirty-one-year-old daughter of a Spitalfields handkerchief weaver, Mary Wollstonecraft, who had been mentored by Richard Price and who worked for his publisher, Joseph Johnson. Wollstonecraft turned Burke's attacks on her friend back at Burke himself, explaining that the deputy was a basically decent man, brought down by the grotesque corruption that was English politics. His *Reflections* had little to offer philosophically, merely "that we are to reverence the rust of antiquity . . . and that, if we do discover some errors, our feelings should lead us to excuse, with blind love . . . the venerable vestiges of ancient days." To Burke's claim that government should be restricted to the rich and powerful, Wollstonecraft replied that "it is a palpable error to suppose, that men of every class are not equally susceptible of common improvement: if therefore it be the contrivance of any government, to preclude from a chance of improvement the greater part of the citizens of the state, it can be considered in no other light than as a monstrous tyranny. . . . From the respect paid to property flow, as from a poisoned fountain, most of the evils and vices which render this world such a dreary scene."

As Lafayette had mentioned to Washington a year before, Paine had already been at work drafting an essay extolling the history and principles of the marquis's new government. Even though in many respects this piece would be a revised edition of *Common Sense* for a European audience, Paine labored over his chains of logic as well as his prose (for as all writers know, a plain style paradoxically requires great effort). Part of the delay in its publication may also have been his shock at Burke's essay, which he took as a wounding betrayal. Though he would change his own mind about many key issues over the course of his life, Thomas Paine was at heart doggedly loyal, supporting with full-force devotion both key Enlightenment principles and his political allies working for the modern cause. When others did not respond in kind, he was deeply hurt, especially by what he felt were two brutal abandonments, the first by Edmund Burke and the second by George Washington. Paine and Burke would rupture so harshly that Burke would eventually say, "Paine was born in England, and lived under the protection of our laws; but, instigated by his evil genius, he conspired against the very country which gave him birth." Paine in turn would accuse Burke of having been bribed with a secret government pension, which would turn out to be mostly true.

Burke's *Reflections* nevertheless gave Paine a focus for the thrust of his argument, as well as new insights into the received notions of modern-day Britons. He would use this knowledge in an attempt to undermine their complacency about their unjust, costly government, just as he had inspired Americans in that nation's leap to independence. His new pamphlet's title originated with the folktale of Jack the Blaster, who, fed up with his treatment by a corrupt state, excavated a cave where he could live free of all government. One of his many admiring visitors was the poet Thomas Spence, who wrote with chalk on a wall:

> Ye landlords vile, whose man's peace mar,
> Come levy rents here if you can;
> Your stewards and lawyers I defy,
> And live with all the RIGHTS OF MAN.

Burke and Paine's disagreement would begin with each's concept of the state. On Dr. Price's assertion that English citizens have the right "to choose our own governors, to cashier them for misconduct [and] to frame a government for ourselves," Paine was astonished that Burke "denies that such a right exists in the nation, either in whole or in part, or that it exists anywhere; and, what is still more strange and marvelous, he says: 'that the people of England utterly disclaim such a right, and that they will resist the practical assertion of it with their lives and fortunes.' That men should take up arms and spend their lives and fortunes, not to maintain their rights, but to maintain they have not rights, is an entirely new species of discovery, and suited to the paradoxical genius of Mr. Burke."

While Burke claimed that Parliament's Declaration of Right at the Glorious Revolution established the throne for William and Mary and their descendants for eternity, Paine held that it is only the will of living citizens that empowers any ruler, with all governments that ever existed either rising from the will of the governed, or imposed upon them by force:

> Every age and generation must be as free to act for itself in all cases as the age and generations which preceded it. The vanity and presumption of governing beyond the grave is the most ridiculous and insolent of all tyrannies. Man has no property in man; neither has any generation a property in the generations which are to follow. . . . Every generation is, and must be, competent to all the purposes which its occasions require. It is the living, and not the dead, that are to be accommodated. . . .
>
> Although laws made in one generation often continue in force through succeeding generations, yet they continue to derive their force from the consent of the living. A law not repealed continues in force, not because it cannot be repealed, but because it is not

repealed; and the non-repealing passes for consent. . . . The circumstances of the world are continually changing, and the opinions of men change also; and as government is for the living, and not for the dead, it is the living only that has any right in it. That which may be thought right and found convenient in one age may be thought wrong and found inconvenient in another. In such cases, who is to decide, the living or the dead? . . . Only the living can exercise the rights of man.

In a letter sent after the publication of *Rights,* Thomas Jefferson expanded on this idea: "The earth belongs always to the living generation. . . . Every constitution then, and every law, naturally expires at the end of nineteen years. If it be enforced longer, it is an act of force, not of right."

One of the most egregious and offensive aspects of *Reflections* was its worship of an imperiled queen, while ignoring her regime's starving peasants and jailed political and religious dissenters. Paine used some of his greatest prose to attack Burke on this misplaced romantic foolishness:

Through the whole of Mr. Burke's book I do not observe that the Bastille is mentioned more than once, and that with a kind of implication as if he were sorry it was pulled down, and wished it were built up again. . . . Not one glance of compassion, not one commiserating reflection that I can find throughout his book, has he bestowed on those who lingered out the most wretched of lives, a life without hope in the most miserable of prisons. . . . [Burke] is not affected by the reality of distress touching his heart, but by the showy resemblance of it striking his imagination. He pities the plumage, but forgets the dying bird. Accustomed to kiss the aristocratical hand that hath purloined him from himself, he degenerates into a composition of art, and the genuine soul of nature forsakes him. His hero or his heroine must be a tragedy-victim expiring in show, and not the real prisoner of misery, sliding into death in the silence of a dungeon.

In portraying the terrors of unrestricted democracy, Burke prophesied that the mobs of the French Revolution were not merely replacing their own government, but were a force that could destroy all of European civilization. Paine replied that the only legitimate source of state power was a nation's citizens—in France's case, that very mob—and that the current English monarchical system was unjust, humiliating, and patently nonsensical:

> The error of those who reason by precedents drawn from antiquity, respecting the rights of man, is that they do not go far enough into antiquity. They do not go the whole way. They stop in some of the intermediate stages of an hundred or a thousand years, and produce what was then done, as a rule for the present day. This is no authority at all. If we travel still farther into antiquity, we shall find a direct contrary opinion and practice prevailing; and if antiquity is to be authority, a thousand such authorities may be produced, successively contradicting each other; but if we proceed on, we shall at last come out right; we shall come to the time when man came from the hand of his Maker. What was he then? Man. Man was his high and only title, and a higher cannot be given him. . . .
>
> It has been thought a considerable advance towards establishing the principles of freedom to say that government is a compact between those who govern and those who are governed; but this cannot be true, because it is putting the effect before the cause; for as man must have existed before governments existed, there necessarily was a time when governments did not exist, and consequently there could originally exist no governors to form such a compact with.
>
> The fact therefore must be that the individuals themselves, each in his own personal and sovereign right, entered into a compact with each other to produce a government: and this is the only mode in which governments have a right to arise, and the only principle on which they have a right to exist.

Dedicated to George Washington, and a rhapsody to France's new constitutional monarchy under the enlightened administration of his protégé, Lafayette, *Rights of Man* was first issued in London by Mary Wollstonecraft's publisher, Joseph Johnson of 72 St. Paul's Churchyard, on February 22, 1791, simultaneous with the opening of England's Parliament and Washington's birthday. After being repeatedly visited by government agents, however, Johnson feared he would be subject to a charge of sedition, and printed only a few copies. Because Paine needed to leave immediately for Paris to work directly with his longtime translator, François Xavier Lanthenas, on the French edition, in his stead a group of London friends, including Wollstonecraft's future husband, lapsed Presbyterian minister William Godwin, oversaw a new printing at J. S. Jordan's of 166 Fleet Street, paying him with forty pounds that Paine had borrowed from his old friend at the Excise, George Lewis Scott. Priced at a costly three shillings, *Rights of Man* was released to the shops on March 13. When, as Paine wrote Washington, "I shall then make a cheap edition, just sufficient to bring in the price of the printing and paper, as I did by *Common Sense*," the response was astounding.

At a time when the British population numbered ten million (with a 40 percent literacy rate) and most English novels sold 1,250 copies (while non-fiction averaged 750 copies), in its first three months of sale *Rights* sold 50,000 copies in its official edition, with anyone's guess as to the number of pirated, serialized, and excerpted versions. Just as with *Common Sense,* Paine was again slightly ahead of his time. One friend of Burke's, the Earl of Charlemont, summed up the ambivalence of liberal Whigs toward the piece: "I did, indeed, suppose that Paine's pamphlet, which is, by the way, a work of great genius, would be well received in [Belfast]; yet, in my opinion, it ought to be read with some degree of caution. He does, indeed, tear away the bandage from the public eye; but in tearing it off there may be some danger of injuring the organ." This fear of "injuring the organ" originated in the fact that, at a time when even the most reform-minded of British political activists were laboring for enhanced voting privileges and reduced political corruption, *Rights of Man* was advocating an entirely different form of government altogether.

Instead of Burke's gentlemanly agreements and history of chivalry, *Rights* called for importing all that was superior in the New World, including a written constitution, an elected chief of state, an elected legislature, voting for all adult males, the end of feudal benefits for aristocrats and clergy, and commerce unfettered by the intrusions of mercantile policy. At the same time *Rights* used Paine's pragmatic Newtonian logic to portray the absurdity of a people governed by monarchs and peers, his cool lines of reasoning acting as a lineament for ideas that, to the English mind, were violently shocking. Burke would sputter that Paine was hoping "to destroy in six or seven days" what "all the boasted wisdom of our ancestors has laboured to bring to perfection for six or seven centuries."

In the end Burke's *Reflections* accurately predicted that the French Revolution would finish in bloodshed and tyranny, while Paine's *Rights* just as brilliantly anticipated, two hundred years ahead of its time, the style of government for close to half the world's nations today. The great irony of this epic struggle in British political history is that, when it came to dear old Albion, both would be right. The English polity over the coming decades would glacially reform itself, just as Burke proposed, but into a structure not all that different from the one envisioned by *Rights of Man.*

When critics accused Paine of being nothing but a modern-day Leveller, he replied, "France has not leveled, it has exalted. It has put down the dwarf, to set up the man." It is the exaltation of the great mass of humankind that makes *Rights of Man* thrilling and distinctive, so much so that in the decades after its publication the very phrase "rights of man" would come to mean not just civil and natural rights, but a reengineering of government to provide for the greater good, a state designed for the happiness of the largest number of citizens instead of its elite ruling class. "As it is my design to make those that can scarcely read understand," Paine said, "I shall therefore avoid every literary ornament and put it in language as plain as the alphabet." Merchants and artisans responded with tremendous enthusiasm to the radical idea that they had as much a right as royals and aristocrats to be involved with the workings of their government. For the first time in the history of England, middle- and working-class citizens began to seriously discuss the architecture of the state and their role in it.

Whitehall attorneys carefully analyzed *Rights,* hoping to catch Paine in a chargeable offense, but could find nothing. Instead, the British government hired a Scots lawyer and onetime resident of Maryland, George Chalmers, to write, under the name Francis Oldys, a scurrilous attack, *The Life of Thomas Paine, Author of "The Rights of Man," with a Defence of his Writings.* Chalmers, an employee of the Board of Trade and biographer of Daniel Defoe, obviously did not enjoy his time in Maryland, as he was as anti-American as any Briton could possibly be. Ironically, as the documents of Paine's first thirty-seven years would vanish over the ensuing centuries, almost all that we know today of his childhood, buccaneering, staymaking, shopkeeping, tax collecting, and marriages has been derived or confirmed through the Chalmers/Oldys state-supported libel, a tabloid masquerade. The Pitt government did not rely on Chalmers alone, however; a counterfeit letter supposedly from Paine's mother was circulated, complaining of his debts, of the terrible treatment of his wife, and of his "undutiful behavior to the tenderest of parents." At the same time, one "Charles Harrington

Elliot" charged that Paine was known to engage in carnal relations with his "maiden wife," and a cat.

Rights of Man would eventually incite far-reaching government repression across Britain, but it first conjured a political scandal on the opposite side of the Atlantic. Simultaneously with its publication in London, a manuscript copy was carried by a Mr. Beckley to Thomas Jefferson for forwarding to a J. B. Smith, whose brother, S. H. Smith, had agreed to be its Philadelphia printer. At that moment just returning to America from Paris, Jefferson was stunned by what he had seen in Europe, and by the changes the Federalists had wrought in the United States. It was that period when the new American government fell from a united bliss of victory against Britain into an acid partisanship over the future of the nation, with Senate president Adams forced to cast thirty-one tiebreaking legislative votes, a still-historic record.

When the American edition of *Rights of Man* first appeared, released initially by Smith and then by Franklin's grandson Benjamin Franklin Bache (who had inherited his grandfather's printshop at the age of twenty-one), it contained not only a dedication to Washington, but a commendation from Jefferson:

> After some prefatory remarks the Secretary of State observes:
> "I am extremely pleased to find it will be reprinted, and that something is at length to be publicly said against the political heresies which have sprung up among us.
> "I have no doubt our citizens will rally a second time round the standard of Common Sense."

Everyone in the United States knew that by "political heresies," Jefferson meant the recently published essays and private comments of Vice President John Adams. Besides having become convinced that all should address him as "Your Majesty" (many whispered that "His Rotundity" would be more appropriate), Adams had written a series, "Discourse on Davila," for the Federalist *Gazette of the United States,* which included such comments as "Mankind has tried all possible experiment of elections of governors and senates . . . but they had almost unanimously been convinced that hereditary succession was attended with fewer evils than frequent elections. This is the true answer, and the only one, as I believe."

When attacks on Paine's *Rights of Man* then appeared in the *Massachusetts Centinel* under the name Publicola, it was assumed this was, again, the work of John Adams. In fact, Publicola was not the vice president but his son, John Quincy, though there was very little asserted with which his father would have disagreed.

James Madison, Jefferson's political right hand, immediately wrote Jefferson his agreement with those published comments on May 12:

> Mr. Adams can least of all complain. Under a mock defence of the Republican constitutions of his country [*Defence of the Constitutions*] he attacked them with all the force he possessed, and this in a book with his name to it, while he was the representative of his country at a foreign court. Since he has been the second magistrate in the new republic, his pen has constantly been at work in the same cause. . . . Surely if it be innocent and decent in one servant of the public thus to write attacks against its government, it cannot be very criminal or indecent in another to patronize a written defence of the principles on which that government is founded. . . . If offence could be justly taken [by the British], what would France have a right to say to Burke's pamphlet, and the countenance given to it and its author, particularly by the King himself? What, in fact, might not the United States say, when revolutions and democratic governments come in for a large charge of the scurrility lavished on those of France?

At a reception given by Martha Washington while her husband was away at Mount Vernon, an Englishman, Major Beckwith, approached the president's secretary, Tobias Lear, to complain that *Rights of Man* had been dedicated to Washington, which "could not but be offensive to the British government." When Lear replied that the president had not read the pamphlet and, in any case, was not responsible for the writings of Thomas Paine, Beckwith continued, "True, but I observe, in the American edition, that the Secretary of State has given a most unequivocal sanction to the book, as Secretary of State; it is not said as Mr. Jefferson." Lear insisted that it was not really his place to comment, "but I will venture to say that the Secretary of State has not done a thing which he would not justify." In a letter reporting this conversation to Washington, Lear would go on to note that Vice President Adams, with his hand to his chest, had said of *Rights of Man,* "I detest that book and its tendency, from the bottom of my heart."

After Attorney General Edmund Randolph talked with Beckwith and Jefferson, he wrote Washington that "Mr. Jefferson said that, so far from having authorized it, he was exceedingly sorry to see it there; not from a disavowal of the approbation which it gave the work, but because it had been sent to the printer, with the pamphlet for republication, without the most distant idea that he would think of publishing any part of it. And Mr. Jefferson further added that he wished it might be understood, that he did not authorize the publication of any part of his note." Jefferson then wrote to Washington directly: "I am afraid the indiscretion of a printer has committed me with my friend Mr. Adams, for whom, as one of the most honest and disinterested men alive, I have a cordial esteem, increased by long habits of concurrence in opinion in the days of his republicanism; and even since his apostasy to hereditary monarchy and nobility, though we differ, we differ as friends should do."

When Publicola asked of the secretary of state, "Does he consider this pamphlet of Mr. Paine's as the canonical book of political scripture?" Jefferson wrote to John Adams that "I thought so little of the note that I did not even keep a copy of it. . . . I was thunderstruck with seeing it come out at the head of the pamphlet. I hoped that it would not attract. But I found on my return from a journey of a month, that a writer came forward under the name of Publicola, attacking not only the author and principles of the pamphlet, but myself as its sponsor by name. Soon after came hosts of other writers, defending the pamphlet and attacking you by name as the writer of Publicola. Thus our names were thrown on the stage as public antagonists." At the same time, he explained to James Monroe that "Publicola, in attacking all Paine's principles, is very desirous of involving me in the same censure with the author. I certainly merit the same, for I profess the same principles; but it is equally certain I never meant to have entered as a volunteer in the cause. My occupations do not permit it." John Adams finally answered Jefferson with, "If you suppose that I have or ever had a design or desire of attempting to introduce a government of Kings, Lords, and Commons, or in other words a hereditary executive, or a hereditary senate, either into the government of the United States or that of any individual state in this country, you are wholly mistaken." When Jefferson resigned as secretary of state at the end of 1793, Adams would exult, "A good riddance of bad ware. . . . He is as ambitious as Oliver Cromwell. . . . His soul is poisoned with ambition."

Learning of the American controversy, Paine would tell William Short, "I had John Adams in mind when I wrote the pamphlet, and it has hit as I expected," and he would write the president:

> The same fate follows me here as I at first experienced in America, strong friends and violent enemies, but as I have got the ear of the country, I shall go on, and at least shew them, what is a novelty here, that there can be a person beyond the reach of corruption. . . . After the establishment of the American Revolution, it did not appear to me that any object could arise great enough to engage me a second time. I began to feel myself happy in being quiet; but I now experience that principle is not confined to time or place, and that the ardour of seventy-six is capable of renewing itself.

Washington would reply in language that perfectly illustrates how, while nearly the whole of his cabinet was at war, he would remain above the fray:

> The duties of my office, which at all times, especially during the session of Congress, require an unremitting attention, naturally become more pressing towards the close of it; and as that body have resolved to rise tomorrow, and as I have determined, in case they should, to set out for Mount Vernon on the next day, you will readily conclude that the present is a busy moment with me; and to that I am persuaded your goodness will impute my not entering into the several points touched upon in your letter. Let it suffice, therefore, at this time, to say, that I rejoice in the information of your personal prosperity, and, as no one can feel a greater interest in the happiness of mankind than I do, that it is the first wish of my heart, that the enlightened policy of the present age may diffuse to all men those blessings, to which they are entitled, and lay the foundation of happiness for future generations.

Despite the attacks by John Adams and his son, the American public responded to the first essay in eight years from Thomas Paine with an explosion of euphoria. Though written expressly for Englishmen, *Rights of Man* reminded Americans of the many glorious principles for which their nation was now a global symbol. French consul Louis Otto was pleased to report back to his government that the Philadelphia papers were overrun with articles praising *Rights of Man,* attacking "Discourses on Davila," and commenting favorably on events in revolutionary France. Jefferson wrote Paine,

> Indeed I am glad you did not come away till you had written your Rights of Man. A writer under the signature of Publicola has attacked it, and a host of champions has entered the arena immediately in your defence . . . contrary to the assertions of a sect here, high in name but small in numbers. . . . Would you believe it possible that in this country there should be high and important characters who need your lessons in republicanism, and who do not heed them? It is but too true that we have a sect preaching up and panting after an English constitution of King, lords, and commons and whose heads are itching for crowns, coronets and mitres. . . . [Even so,] our people, my good friend, are firm and unanimous in their principles of republicanism, and there is no better proof of it than that they love what you write and read it with delight. The printers season every newspaper with extracts from your last, as they did before. . . . Go on then in doing with your pen what in other times was done with the sword.

More than a hundred thousand copies were sold in North America, and the public acclaim grew so great that Jefferson, Madison, and Randolph attempted to bring Paine back to the United States as a political reinforcement with the offer of a cabinet position as postmaster general under Washington, as Randolph would write to Madison on July 21:

> I need not relate to you, that since the standard of republicanism has been erected, it has been resorted to by a numerous corps. The newspapers will tell you how much the crest of aristocracy has fallen. . . . But [Adams] is impotent, and something is due to past services. Mr. J. and myself have attempted to bring Paine forward as a successor to Osgood. It seems to be a fair opportunity for a declaration of certain sentiments. But all that I have heard has been that it would be too pointed to keep [that] vacancy unfilled until [Paine's] return from the other side of the water.

Instead of serving as the U.S. postmaster, Paine spent most of 1791 living at Lafayette's home in Paris while working on the French translation of *Rights*. The course of English politics was not progressing as he had hoped—those Whig reversals he had assured Jefferson were imminent due to the king's mental illness had not come to pass; instead, the recovered monarch and his Tory ministers had assumed even greater power than before. In France, meanwhile, Paine was at the very heart of the Revolution, close not only to Lafayette but also to many other key figures rising within the new government and its new society.

As France's centuries as a kingdom drew to a close, its leaders broke into factions, polarizing the nation even more dramatically than the Hamilton-Jefferson schism would in America. The most significant French political club began when the Estates-General were first meeting at Versailles and a group of Bretons, unhappy with the pace of reform, started gathering privately, eventually calling itself the Society of the Friends of the Constitution and meeting in Paris at a nationalized monastery on the rue Saint-Honoré. Since the monastery was originally owned by Dominican priests, the group was in time nicknamed after that order, which in French is Jacobin. Many neighborhoods, meanwhile, hosted their own local political groups, with one of the most influential being the Cordeliers, which championed the French Revolution mainstay that so terrified Burke, Adams, and Hamilton—direct democracy. The faubourg in which it was founded, populated almost entirely by artisans, merchants, and journalists, was home to an essayist as ready to test the limits of free speech in the new France as Paine was in England, a man in constant ache and paralysis from psoriatic arthritis and eternally enraged. Ophthalmologist Jean-Paul Marat had found his true calling as publisher of *L'Ami du Peuple;* when he began to believe that the Fayettistes had not gone far enough in reforming France, Marat began calling Lafayette and Necker "public enemies." A warrant was issued; three thousand troops marched into the Cordeliers on January 22, 1791, to arrest him, but the district's president, a lawyer named Georges-Jacques Danton, refused to cooperate, allowing Marat to escape.

The Cordeliers were not the only ones dissatisfied with Lafayette, for France was still suffering painful economic woes, and life for the majority of its people remained pitiful. A great number of patricians in Paine's circle (who were known as Brissotins in their time and Girondins in ours) complained publicly that the Fayettistes had not gone far enough in reforming the state and its finances. Manon Roland told the French translator of *Rights,* François Xavier Lanthenas, that she was "now convinced that liberty and the constitution will not belong to and do not belong to, the men who have given the most to the Revolution."

On April 18 the king, queen, and their children prepared to depart from the Tuileries for their summer estate at Saint-Cloud, a refuge from the constant stares of the Parisians and the vituperative attacks of the more militant newspapers. When the royal family emerged from their apartments that day, however, a large and hostile mob refused to let them leave. The king and queen at that moment came to understand that they were no longer the rulers of France but its captives, an acknowledgment that persuaded Louis to accept his wife's solution to their predicament, a plan developed through counsel from such émigré ministers as Calonne and Breteuil, and even from Edmund Burke, who urged his "delightful vision" to accept "no compromises with rebels! . . . Appeal to sovereign neighbors; above all trust to the support of foreign armies."

Before dawn on June 21, Paine was awakened by a frantic Lafayette with a shocking announcement: "The birds are flown!" Paine calmly replied, "It is well. I hope there will be no attempt to recall them." Disguised as servants, the royal family had made their escape at around midnight, heading for the closest border, just under two hundred miles from Paris at the Austrian Netherlands, ruled by the queen's brother, Emperor Leopold. But the royal entourage had been so delayed that news of their flight traveled faster than they did. At Varennes, just forty miles before the border, a local postmaster recognized the king from his profile on the fifty-livre bill, and the family was forced to spend the night upstairs, while the townspeople decided what to do with them. The next morning, National Assembly deputies accompanied by six thousand armed citizens escorted the Bourbons back to Paris, where they found notably somber crowds, as the legislature had posted everywhere the sign:

Anyone who applauds the King will be beaten;
Anyone who insults him will be hanged.

On hearing of this attempted abandonment by its royal family, France erupted with mass outrage, and every sign with the word "Louis" or the mark of the fleur-de-lis was immediately removed, reworded, and redesigned. A placard was hung from the gates of the Tuileries palace: *Maison à louer* ("For rent"). On the morning he learned that the king had vanished, Paine quickly dressed and accompanied Lafayette to the Hôtel de Ville, where a crowd accused the general of being a party to Louis's conspiracy. Paine fell into conversation with a friend, Thomas Christie, who remembered him saying, "You see the absurdity of monarchical governments; here will be a whole nation disturbed by the folly of one man."

Near the Tuileries Paine and Christie listened to a reading of the Assembly's proclamation that the government would continue working as well as it ever did, even without a king. When the speech ended and the audience put their hats back on, everyone was wearing that new symbol of patriotism, the *cocarde tricolore.* Paine, however, in his rush out the door that morning, had forgotten his hat ribbon, and to the revolutionary French this could mean only one thing. An accusing finger was pointed, and the shout was heard: "Aristocrat!" Every face turned to him; a fist boxed his cheek, and then a foot kicked him, hard. Too quickly, the chanting began: *"Aristocrat! A la lanterne! Aristocrat! A la lanterne!"*

It was mob rule at its sanguinary height: an accusation of villainy to be followed by the immediate justice of a hanging from the nearest lamppost. The results of "à la lanterne" could be seen everywhere at that moment in Paris; after an "aristocrat" had been hanged, his lynch mob would sever the head with a butcher's knife, disembowel the torso, and then thrust the heart, entrails, and head onto pikes for a tour of the neighborhoods the dead man had frequented while alive, as a lesson to his friends and neighbors.

As men grabbed Paine and dragged him to the curb, the chanting grew louder. Christie tried to intervene, but the crowd was too big and too overwhelmed with fury. Finally another Frenchman, perhaps a known legislator deserving respect, took control, explaining that this was no aristocrat deserving execution, but an American who had forgotten his hat ribbon. Paine was released.

The botched escape of the king who would now be known as Louis le Faux (Pas) also ended the reign of the Hero of Two Worlds. Mme. Roland said of the flight to Varennes that "it is virtually impossible that Lafayette is not involved," while Danton decided that he was either a traitor or an idiot to have allowed it to happen. At the same time, the king's fall from public grace inspired Paine and certain of his French colleagues to believe that this was the moment to push for a government more closely matching the American model; not Lafayette's constitutional monarchy, but a democratic republic, with no king required. They launched a new periodical, *Le Républicain,* which included an inaugural Paine salvo: "Being the citizen of a land that recognizes no majesty but that of the people, no government except that of its own representatives, and no sovereignty except that of the laws, I tender you my services in helping forward the success of those principles which honor a nation and contribute to the advancement of the entire world."

At that moment few French leaders were even entertaining the possibility of a democratic republic. Besides believing that their fellow citizens were not ready to forgo a monarch altogether, many in France worried that a dethronement would incite yet another brutal war with Marie Antoinette's Austrian relatives. Robespierre announced that no structure of government was superior to France's "republic with a monarch" currently in place, and Marat agreed, recommending in *L'Ami du Peuple* a French state composed of dictator combined with a legislature. Marat would even question Paine: "Is it possible that you believe in a republic? You are too enlightened to be the dupe of such a fantastic dream."

Lafayette's ideological colleague, the Abbé Sieyès, responded to Paine's proposal with a *Moniteur* article demanding proof that a republic is superior to a monarchy, for after all, "there is more liberty for the individual citizen under a monarchy than under a republic." Condorcet responded with a defense of Paine's notions. Five years later, deputy Joseph Lakanal would reveal that Condorcet had told him that this volley had been prearranged, with the abbé deliberately writing a mediocre tract in support of monarchy, and Paine and Condorcet then attacking it vigorously, all in order to encourage public interest in a democratic government. This does not seem entirely plausible considering the anti-abbé focus of *Rights of Man, Part the Second,* though Lakanal was so convinced of it that he would forever consider Condorcet, Sieyès, and Paine the true founders of the first French Republic.

On July 1 Paine's radical contingent launched another salvo when placards announcing "The Republican Proclamation" were overnight plastered on the public walls of the capital and tacked to the doors of the National Assembly's meetinghouse, the Manège. Announcing the formation of a new political club, the Société des Républicains, they declared, "The serene tranquility, the mutual confidence which prevailed amongst us, during the time of the late King's escape, the indifference with which we beheld him return, are unequivocal proofs that the absence of a King is more desirable than his presence, and that he is not only a political superfluity, but a grievous burden, pressing hard on the whole nation. . . . The reciprocal obligation which subsisted between us is dissolved. He holds no longer any authority. We owe him no longer obedience. We see in him no more than an indifferent person; we can regard him only as Louis Capet."

These concepts were so shocking at that moment that the Société des Républicains' membership roll was kept strictly anonymous, to the extent that even today the names are not reliably known, but are generally believed to include Paine, Achille François Duchâtelet (a young English-speaking aristocrat who became an immediate Paine disciple), Etiènne Chavière (soon to be named finance minister), Condorcet, and Brissot (both to become Legislative Assembly deputies). Etienne Dumont would recall the almost unanimous outrage that first greeted the Société des Républicains:

> Duchâtelet called on me, and after a little preface placed in my hand an English manuscript—a Proclamation to the French People. It was nothing less than an anti-royalist manifesto, and summoned the nation to seize the opportunity and establish a republic. Paine was its author. Duchâtelet had adopted and was resolved to sign, placard the walls of Paris with it, and take the consequences. He had come to request me to translate and develop it. I began discussing the strange proposal, and pointed out the danger of raising a republican standard without concurrence of the National Assembly, and nothing being as yet known of the king's intentions, resources, alliances, and possibilities of support by the army, and in the provinces. I asked if he had consulted any of the most influential leaders, Sieyès, Lafayette, etc. He had not: he and Paine had acted alone. An American and an impulsive nobleman had put themselves forward to change the whole governmental system of France. Resisting his entreaties, I refused to translate the Proclamation. Next day, The Republican Proclamation appeared on the walls in every part of Paris, and was denounced to the Assembly. The idea of a republic had previously presented itself to no one: this first intimation filled

> with consternation the Right and the moderates of the Left. Malouet, Cazales, and others proposed prosecution of the author, but Chapelier, and a numerous party, fearing to add fuel to the fire instead of extinguishing it, prevented this. But some of the seed sown by the audacious hand of Paine were now budding in leading minds.

When Gouverneur Morris had dinner with Paine on July 4 of that year, he remembered him "inflated to the eyes and big with a litter of revolutions." On the eighth Paine returned to London, *Rights of Man* having become so popular and its author so famous that the same day's *Oracle* would warn, "Paine is writing a new pamphlet to be entitled *Kingship* and its subject is to demonstrate the inutility of kings. It is to appear in November, in French, German, Spanish, Italian, and English at the same time, as persons are translating it into the four first languages as he advances in writing it. Such is the rage for disseminating democratic principles!" On July 14 a dinner held by Paine's Birmingham allies to celebrate the anniversary of the Bastille's fall, however, was met with two days of Tory-backed looting and rioting, which ended with the destruction of the home and laboratory of the great philosopher and religious leader Joseph Priestley.

If the vast majority of French legislators were not at that moment prepared to declare an end to the monarchy, many civilian Parisians were more than ready. On July 16 a group of political clubs released a petition that Louis XVI had, under French law, abdicated. On July 17 a group of fifty thousand led by the Cordeliers assembled at the Champ de Mars, demanding that the king relinquish his crown. When they refused to disband and were confronted by the National Guard, they threw stones. The troops opened fire, killing and wounding an estimated fifty unarmed men and women. This fiasco led to Lafayette's resignation from the militia. Two months later, the French National Assembly completed its constitution and dissolved itself, its deputies additionally voting to render themselves ineligible for positions in the new legislature. The resulting vacuum led to Lafayette and his allies slipping entirely from grace, while Paine's Société des Républicains—Brissot, Condorcet, and their associates—took control of both the new Assembly and the Jacobin Club.

Jacques-Pierre Brissot de Warville was an abolitionist, journalist, pamphleteer, founder of the Société Gallo-Américaine, and fervent believer in the modern spirit of American democracy—more or less the French counterpart to Thomas Paine. Besides his fellow English-speaking *républicains,* Brissot was politically allied with a group from the port cities, especially the southwest *département* of Gironde (known in British history as the Aquitaine). The Brissotins, or Girondins, had much in common with the American founding fathers. Most had either met Franklin, Jefferson, and Paine directly, or been inspired in their political thinking by reading *Common Sense,* the Declaration of Independence, *Rights of Man,* and the various constitutions of the American states. Like the American moderns, the Brissotins were comfortably prosperous (if not outright wealthy) lawyers and businessmen who believed fervently in the God-given power of human reason. Additionally, they were gifted with a talent for stirring oratory; like Paine had done with *Common Sense,* they would inspire their nation, especially their fellow deputies, to think of themselves not as ordinary citizens and petty bureaucrats but as global crusaders of liberty and freedom working for the greater good of all mankind. That crusade would be launched almost immediately, with a call to arms.

It was during those very first moments of being a republic under the *haute fraternité* Girondins that France, ignoring her financial traumas and internal combustions, fell into war. Every French leader, from Seize to Lafayette to Brissot, came to believe that combat would solve all their troubles, and the country's peasants became global crusaders working for the greater good as they were drafted by the millions into the *grande armée.* In regard to state finance, the nation's leaders would be proved right; in regard to France's germinating a European explosion of freedom and democracy in a continental struggle against malignant despots, they would be around six million dead wrong in a conflict that would last for twenty-three years.

In the fall of 1791, pressured by his sister Marie Antoinette, the enlightened, peaceable Austrian emperor Leopold and his longtime adversary, Prussian king Frederick William, jointly asked for the French to liberate their king and queen and threatened that if Louis and Marie Antoinette were harmed, all of the European powers would be forced to respond in some way. Brissot and his colleague Pierre-Victurnien Vergniaud convinced their legislature that this proclamation was a direct threat and that the French must strike with decisive first blows against their enemies. The king, the queen, and Lafayette all concurred, each for entirely different reasons. One of the few at that time arguing against war was Robespierre, who predicted it would lead to a military dictatorship and warned the Assembly,

"The most extravagant idea that can be born in the head of a political thinker is to believe that it suffices for people to enter, weapons in hand, among a foreign people and expect to have its laws and constitution embraced. No one loves armed missionaries."

As the French army of one hundred thousand volunteers marched to the frontiers, Paine waged ideological war in London. Burke and his fellow conservatives had published a number of attacks on *Rights of Man;* they would be answered with *Rights of Man, Part the Second,* which appeared in March 1792, and which had almost nothing in common with its predecessor. Though dedicated to Lafayette, *Part the Second* was in fact Paine's rebuke of the Fayettistes, especially the Abbé Sieyès, in favor of his fellow Brissotin *républicains.* It used economic reasoning to appeal to British burghers by claiming that, with no royal family, layabout aristocrats, or constant warmongering to support, a democratic republic was far more financially efficient than any kingdom with nobles and a throne. All England needed to do to solve the problem of her great mass of poor, in fact, was to emulate the government and economic model of America, which Paine described as an entire continent free of poverty (ignoring, for the sake of his argument, the New World's slaves and indentured servants):

> I presume that no man in his sober senses will compare the character of any of the kings of Europe with that of General Washington. Yet, in France, and also in England, the expense of the civil list only, for the support of one man, is eight times greater than the whole expense of the federal government in America. To assign a reason for this, appears almost impossible. The generality of people in America, especially the poor, are more able to pay taxes, than the generality of people either in France or England. . . . The presidency in America (or, as it is sometimes called, the executive) is the only office from which a foreigner is excluded, and in England it is the only one to which he is admitted. . . . In America, every department in the government is decently provided for; but no one is extravagantly paid. Every member of Congress, and of the Assemblies, is allowed a sufficiency for his expenses. Whereas in England, a most prodigal provision is made for the support of one part of the Government, and none for the other, the consequence of which is that the one is furnished with the means of corruption and the other is put into the condition of being corrupted. . . .

> What is called the House of Peers . . . amounts to a combination of persons in one common interest. No better reason can be given, why a house of legislation should be composed entirely of men whose occupation consists in letting landed property, than why it should be composed of those who hire, or of brewers, or bakers, or any other separate class of men. . . . The only use to be made of this power (and which it always has made), is to ward off taxes from itself, and throw the burthen upon those articles of consumption by which itself would be least affected. . . . The aristocracy are not the farmers who work the land, and raise the produce, but are the mere consumers of the rent; and when compared with the active world are the drones, a seraglio of males, who neither collect the honey nor form the hive, but exist only for lazy enjoyment.

While glossing over the history of civil disorder in the United States' early years, Paine would use one of Burke's own tenets against him in explaining why the American Revolution had been a relatively civil affair, while recent French history had been marked by violence:

> There is in all European countries a large class of people of that description which in England is called the mob. . . . How is it, that such vast classes of mankind as are distinguished by the appellation of the vulgar, or of the ignorant mob, are so numerous in old countries? . . . They arise, as an unavoidable consequence, out of the ill construction of all the old governments in Europe, England included with the rest. It is by distortedly exalting some men, that others are distortedly debased, till the whole is out of nature. A vast mass of mankind are degradedly thrown into the background of the human picture, to bring forward, with greater glare, the puppet-show of state and aristocracy. In the commencement of a revolution, those men [the mob] are rather the followers of the camp than of the standard of liberty, and have yet to be instructed how to reverence it. . . .
>
> If we look back to the riots and tumults which at various times have happened in England, we shall find that they did not proceed from the want of a government, but that government was itself the generating cause; instead of consolidating society it divided it. . . . Whatever the apparent cause of any riots may be, the real one is

> always want of happiness. It shows that something is wrong in the system of government that injures the felicity by which society is to be preserved.

Paine additionally used *Part the Second* to propose what one day would become the welfare state, including systems of health insurance; grants for the education of children and the first years of young adults; pensions for the elderly; and a graduated income tax: "When it shall be said in any country in the world, 'my poor are happy, neither ignorance nor distress is to be found among them; my jails are empty of prisoners, my streets of beggars; the aged are not in want; the taxes are not oppressive; the rational world is my friend, because I am the friend of its happiness'; when these things can be said, then may that country boast its constitution and its government."

No matter how harshly British conservatives would, over the next five decades, accuse Paine of radicalism, this vision of state support for its weakest citizens had long before entered the mainstream of Enlightenment thinking. Paine's observation "When in countries that are called civilized, we see age going to the work-house, and youth to the gallows, something must be wrong in the system of government" may have shocked English peers, but it was a sentiment that was accepted by moderns across all of Europe, echoed in such works as Jean-Jacques Rousseau's 1755 *Discourse on the Origin of Inequality* ("the spirit of society, and the inequality which society produces . . . is contrary to the law of nature . . . that the privileged few should gorge themselves with superfluities, while the starving multitude are in want of the basic necessities of life") and David Hume's 1752 *Of Commerce:* "A too great disproportion among the citizens weakens any state. Every person, if possible, ought to enjoy the fruits of his labour, in a full possession of all the necessaries, and many of the conveniences of life. No one can doubt, but such an equality is most suitable to human nature, and diminishes much less from the happiness of the rich than it adds to that of the poor." Even libertarian icon Adam Smith, who by "wealth of nations" meant not state treasuries but human capital, and not just economic but personal well-being, urged governments to help their needy: "They who feed, cloathe and lodge the whole body of the people, should have such a share of the produce of their own labour as to be themselves tolerably well fed, cloathed and lodged."

Paine used his experience as a tax man to show how inexpensive such a welfare system could be, and he brilliantly prefaced his proposals with an attempt to engender sympathy for the dispossessed among England's ruling class by pointing out that, due to primogeniture, scores of once noble but noninheriting descendants had been reduced to living decidedly lower-class lives. Every Whitehall patrician had or knew of such a relative, who might at some point be in need of state assistance.

Paine ended *Part the Second,* as always, with an uplifting message of hope, ennoblement, and inspiration:

> It is now towards the middle of February. Were I to take a turn into the country, the trees would present a leafless, wintry appearance. As people are apt to pluck twigs as they walk along, I perhaps might do the same, and by chance might observe, that a single bud on that twig had begun to swell. I should reason very unnaturally, or rather not reason at all, to suppose this was the only bud in England which had this appearance. Instead of deciding thus, I should instantly conclude, that the same appearance was beginning, or about to begin, every where; and though the vegetable sleep will continue longer on some trees and plants than on others, and though some of them may not blossom for two or three years, all will be in leaf in the summer, except those which are rotten. What pace the political summer may keep with the natural, no human foresight can determine. It is, however, not difficult to perceive that the spring is begun.

Instead of reaping a harvest of sensibility and constitutional reform, however, *Rights of Man, Part the Second* led to Paine's arrest on charges of sedition. The book's entire publishing history was shadowed in menace. After both Joseph Johnson and J. S. Jordan had refused it as too dangerous to print, a lifelong friend of Paine's, Thomas Christie, introduced him to one of his biggest English followers, Thomas Chapman, who was thrilled to serve as handmaiden to the great writer. Chapman had originally planned to issue *Part the Second* around Christmas, to coincide once again with the opening of Parliament. Paine, however, kept amending the last fifteen pages and failed to make his deadline, while simultaneously Chapman came to believe that he should own the copyright as all stationers had in times past. Between setting sheets of type, he began negotiations with the author, offering one hundred guineas, then five hundred guineas, and finally a shocking one thousand guineas (nearly $200,000 today). Paine assumed

Chapman wanted the copyright in order to rewrite the book in any way he imagined would make the most money, and refused; a more likely reason is that the government was attempting to buy the book in order to suppress it (which Paine eventually came to believe), or that the new publisher had no idea what he was doing. After Paine turned down his final offer, though, Chapman informed him that the book as written was too libelous to be published. That night, Paine came to the publisher's for dinner, and after drinking a good deal, Paine, Chapman, and Chapman's wife began arguing violently over religion. Paine stormed out, and the next morning Chapman returned the page proofs for the author to take elsewhere.

Paine once again was saved by Joseph Johnson and J. S. Jordan, but only after providing an explicit indemnity:

> February 16, 1792.
>
> SIR:
>
> Should any person, under the sanction of any kind of authority, enquire of you respecting the author and publisher of the *Rights of Man,* you will please to mention me as the author and publisher of that work, and show to such person this letter. I will, as soon as I am made acquainted with it, appear and answer for the work personally.
>
> Your humble servant,
>
> THOMAS PAINE.

In spite of its troubled history, *Part the Second* would outsell the original *Rights of Man,* becoming all over again the biggest bestseller in English history after the Bible. By the end of 1793, there were more than two hundred thousand copies of the two editions officially sold in the United Kingdom, outpacing Burke seven to one, and additionally finding immense audiences in the United States and France, not to mention German, Dutch, and Hungarian translations. In its first ten years, Paine estimated, *Rights* sold "between four and five hundred thousand"; by 1809, European sales exceeded one and a half million copies.

As with *Common Sense,* the author eventually made it clear that he was renouncing his copyrights, allowing anyone to print the whole of *Rights of Man.* The first results of this decision were revealed in a letter to his old employee, John Hall: "At present I am engaged on my political bridge. . . . I see the tide is yet the wrong way, but there is a change of sentiment beginning. I have so far got the ear of John Bull that he will read what I write which is more than ever was done before to the same extent. . . . I intend, after the next work has had its run among those who will have handsome printed books and fine paper, to print a hundred thousand copies of each work and distribute them at sixpence apiece; but this I do not at present talk of, because it will alarm the wise mad folks at St. James's."

In January of 1792 nine men met for pipes, cheese, bread, and port at London's Bell tavern on Exeter, near the Strand. Anyone wanting to attend had to pay a penny and agree to the proposition that "the welfare of these kingdoms requires that every adult person, in possession of his reason, and not incapacitated by crimes, should have a vote for a member of Parliament." The secretary-treasurer of what would be called the London Corresponding Society was a cobbler named Thomas Hardy, who used that first week's take to buy paper in order to announce the club's founding to the Society for Constitutional Information, the Revolutionary Society, and other English organizations that shared its political aims. Within six months, the LCS numbered two thousand members, a motley assemblage of tradesmen with one thing in common: none owned property, and so none according to English law was allowed the vote. Hardy explained that his club's popularity was due to its bible, *Rights of Man,* which the group printed as cheaply as possible for every member, and which "seemed to electrify the nation, and terrified the imbecile government of the day into the most desperate and unjustifiable measures."

The London Corresponding Society was hardly unique. Inspired by Paine and the news from France, dozens of other modern clubs rose to insist on English constitutional reform, joining a nationwide call for the country to form its own National Assembly to draft a written constitution. Edmund Burke, not surprisingly, called these clubs "loathsome insects that might, if they were allowed, grow into giant spiders as large as oxen," while the Shakespearean academic Edmund Malone wrote that "not less than four thousand per week of Paine's despicable and nonsensical pamphlet have been issued forth, for almost nothing, and dispersed all over the kingdom. At Manchester and Sheffield the innovators bribe the poor by drink to hear it read." One anonymous government minion recorded, "Reports came through of over a dozen clubs at Ipswich, to which the common ignorant people are invited, and a reader is elected in each, and explains Paine's pamphlet to those ignorant people who can neither write nor read."

The men of the Sheffield club replied that they "derived more true knowledge from the two works of Mr. Thomas Paine, entitled 'Rights of Man' . . . than from any other author on the subject."

The new political clubs were able to distribute such immense quantities of *Rights* across the country that the Society for Constitutional Information handed Paine the thousand pounds ($150,000 today) in royalties due from its edition, which he exuberantly donated back to their cause. Paine's success was now so enormous that his following surpassed even the glory years of *Common Sense* and *American Crisis*. There was no more celebrated man of letters in all of Europe; he was even able to commission a portrait by the great George Romney. His day-to-day existence—which had come to resemble that of a real-life Mr. Spectator—was vividly described by Lewes friend Clio Rickman, with whom he lived:

> Mr. Paine's life in London was a quiet round of philosophical leisure and enjoyment. It was occupied in writing, in a small epistolary correspondence, in walking about with me to visit different friends, occasionally lounging at coffee-houses and public places, or being visited by a select few. Lord Edward Fitzgerald, the French and American ambassadors, Mr. Sharp the engraver, Romney the painter, Mrs. Wollstonecraft, Joel Barlow, Mr. Hull, Mr. Christie, Dr. Priestley, Dr. Towers, Col. Oswald, the walking Stewart, Captain Sampson Perry, Mr. Tuffin, Mr. William Choppin, Captain De Stark, Mr. Horne Tooke, &c. &c. were among the number of his friends and acquaintance; and of course, as he was my inmate, the most of my associates were frequently his. At this time he read but little, took his nap after dinner, and played with my family at some game in the evening, as chess, dominos, and drafts, but never at cards; in recitations, singing, music, &c; or passed it in conversation: the part he took in the latter was always enlightened, full of information, entertainment, and anecdote. Occasionally we visited enlightened friends, indulged in domestic jaunts and recreations from home, frequently lounging at the White Bear, Piccadilly. . . .
>
> Mr. Paine in his person was about five feet ten inches high, and rather athletic; he was broad shouldered, and latterly stooped a little. His eye, of which the painter could not convey the exquisite meaning, was full, brilliant, and singularly piercing; it had in it the "muse of fire." In his dress and person he was generally very cleanly, and

> wore his hair cued [ponytailed], with side curls, and powdered, so that he looked altogether like a gentleman of the old French school. His manners were easy and gracious; his knowledge was universal and boundless; in private company and among his friends his conversation had every fascination that anecdote, novelty and truth could give it. In mixed company and among strangers he said little, and was no public speaker.

As *Rights Part the Second* was being read around the world, news arrived that President Washington had named Gouverneur Morris the American minister to Paris. Morris was in London at the time, working secretly on behalf of the president to lay the groundwork for commercial negotiations with Britain that would lead to the Jay Treaty, as well as encouraging a local group of French monarchists to rescue the royal family from the Parisians. During the Senate debate over his confirmation, James Monroe argued against Morris as being a "monarchy man . . . not suitable to be employed by this country, nor in France." Lafayette explicitly told Washington that appointing Morris was a terrible idea and urged him to reconsider, but the president refused. Paine wrote Jefferson that "I have just heard of Gouverneur Morris's appointment. It is a most unfortunate one; and, as I shall mention the same thing to him when I see him, I do not express it to you with the injunction of confidence. He is just now arrived in London, and this circumstance has served, as I see by the French papers, to increase the dislike and suspicion of some of that nation and the National Assembly against him."

Sanguine and serene as any buddha, Gouverneur Morris was peglegged from a phaeton accident, yet still pursued the life of an indefatigable epicurean in the full-blooded wine-women-and-song sense of that term. Morris imagined himself an aristocrat, even though due to primogeniture he had inherited little and was almost entirely self-made. At the same time, he was a great revolutionary patriot; James Madison would credit that "the finish given to the style and arrangement of the Constitution fairly belongs to the pen of Mr. Morris."

If the men who knew Thomas Paine either very much loved him or very much did not, Gouverneur Morris was the startling exception, the one who loved and loathed Paine in seemingly equal measure. His remarkable journals, as prolix as anything by diary prodigy John Adams, are filled, when it comes to Paine, with an extraordinary mix of admiration and contempt. While defending Silas Deane, the would-be seigneur had attacked Paine before Congress, helping to ensure his dismissal. When Deane was then revealed to be a loyalist, Morris contritely apologized to Paine that he had been correct all along and that Deane had made perfect fools of both him and Robert Morris—while confiding in others that it was apt justice for Paine to be fired from his clerkship due to his "impudence." While representing the United States in Paris, Morris complained that "Paine calls upon me and talks a great deal upon subjects of little moment," then agreed to make him a loan, "telling him at the same time that he is a troublesome fellow." Since he insisted that "there never was, and never will be a civilized society without an aristocracy," Morris was clearly in many ways as philosophically anti-Paine as John Adams.

In spite of their mutual ambivalence, in Philadelphia, London, and Paris, across nearly their entire lifetimes, Morris and Paine spent many nights drinking or dining together. Both were deists, abolitionists, and loyal supporters of George Washington. In fact, it appears from Morris's diary that Paine gave him either a manuscript or early proof copy of *Rights Part the Second,* since Chapman's change of heart meant the published edition did not reach the shops until March:

> February 22.
>
> I read Paine's new publication today, and tell him that I am really afraid he will be punished. He seems to laugh at this, and relies on the force he has in the nation. He seems to become every hour more drunk with self-conceit. It seems, however, that his work excites but little emotion, and rather raises indignation. I tell him that the disordered state of things in France works against all schemes of reformation both here and elsewhere. He declares that the riots and outrages in France are nothing at all. It is not worth while to contest such declarations. I tell him, therefore, that as I am sure he does not mean what he says, I shall not dispute it.

Morris later wrote that if Paine did not leave England immediately, "I think it quite as likely that he will be promoted to the pillory," a conclusion reached from such *Part the Second* comments as "I do not believe that monarchy and aristocracy will continue seven years longer in any of the enlightened countries in Europe." Burke would agree with Morris, saying of the arguments in *Part the Second* that "I will not attempt in the smallest degree to refute them. This will probably be done (if such writings shall be thought to deserve any other than the refutation of criminal justice) by others." Some would come to believe that Paine endangered himself not by fomenting revolt among a great part of the nation's working and middle class, but by exposing the financial corruption of the British crown in revealing that "forty-six millions of pound sterling had vanished in England since the commencement of the Hanover succession, with the Crown during this period being insolvent several times."

In time Whitehall took grave notice of Paine's growing fame and massive following. After the fall of Lord North over the loss of the United States, King George's government was led by First Minister William Pitt, called "the Younger" to distinguish him from his father, the great Earl of Chatham, winner of the Seven Years War and champion of the American colonists. A brilliant strategist, Pitt would hold the reins of Westminster for eighteen years and eleven months, and in that time achieve many admirable results, from introducing an income tax and uniting the parliaments of England and Ireland to surviving the madness of King George and controlling the national debt, which stood at £250 million—$42 billion today—when he took office. A known "three-bottle man" with a serious attachment to port, Pitt the Younger would die, according to his physician's diagnosis, "of old age" at forty-six.

Originally, Pitt, like most of the English government, did not consider *Rights of Man* and its horde of enthusiasts politically threatening, telling Lady Hester Stanhope that "Paine is quite right, but what am I to do? As things are, if I were to encourage Tom Paine's opinions I should have a bloody revolution." Within a year, however, the first minister came around to the Burkean position, believing that the French Revolution was "the severest trial which the visitation of providence has ever yet inflicted upon the nations of the earth," as it inspired utopians "to abandon the system which practice has explained and experience has confirmed, for the visionary advantages of a crude, untried theory." As the French Revolution escalated, this position would spread through every level of His Majesty's government and transform into a kind of paranoia. Eventually Britain would strike back to ensure no American- or French-styled reforms and revolts could gain momentum on her shores, with Thomas Paine the state's prime target. Considering the shocking news from Paris and the daily reports of more and more Britons demanding suffrage and civil rights, the overriding explanation for this excessive crackdown was a simple one: fear. The possibility of France's democratic "contagion" leaping the Channel and infecting the English masses, combined with the immense popularity and influence of Thomas Paine on those same masses, so terrified the government that it launched a public relations campaign and a series of feudal laws as draconian as if the country were imminently in danger of armed invasion, a campaign that would be called "Pitt's reign of terror."

This effort was so remarkably effective that today, in response to the phrase "French Revolution," a Briton or American will immediately conjure up a menacing guillotine. The French, however, remember their revolution in much the way that Americans do theirs, as the cradle of the Republic, a patriotic struggle that ended feudalism and tyranny and initiated equality for all before the law. An honest history of this period would spend as much time with Lafayette, Brissot, and Barras as it does with Robespierre, but in the Anglo-American world that seems impossible, thanks to Pitt's very astute campaign of hysteria, which was copied almost point for point by American Federalists during the presidency of John Adams.

The attacks began, on both sides of the Atlantic, with the governments and their presses. Almost every English newspaper of the period, either outright controlled by or directly loyal to the crown, regularly featured tragic yarns of dispossessed French émigrés, or humble, hardworking Parisians caught in political machinations and mercilessly guillotined, alongside editorials commenting on the questionable patriotism of English republican societies and workingmen's debating clubs, some hinting that these now sinister organizations were operating in tandem with French revolutionaries to bring down (or even murder) King George and the royal family. These reports were picked up by the American papers in due time, and used by Federalists against Thomas Jefferson's political allies as much as the Pitt ministry would use them against Thomas Paine and British constitutional reform.

The Pitt reign of terror then began in earnest when the secretary at war sent his deputy adjutant-general across the country to measure both the depth of revolutionary passions and the loyalty of British troops. The deputy reported back that civil war was brewing, as "the seditious doctrines of Paine and the factious people who are endeavoring to disturb the peace of the country had extended to a degree very much beyond my conception." After receiving further reports, with one London merchant testifying that *Rights of Man* "is now made as much a standard book in this country, as *Robinson Crusoe* and *The Pilgrims Progress,* and that if it has not its effect today, it will tomorrow," Home Secretary Henry Dundas informed Parliament that the revolutionary and inflammatory ideas of *Rights* were being "sedulously inculcated throughout the kingdom."

The government was not so much worried by Paine's ideas as it was by his readership. The attorney general noted that he could find no reason to prosecute the first *Rights,* as it had been limited to educated readers, but *Part the Second* was seditious since it was "ushered into the world in all shapes and sizes, thrust into the hands of subjects of every descriptions, even children's sweetmeats being wrapped in it." Paine himself believed this was the state's reasoning, saying that "while the work was at a price that precluded an extensive circulation, the government party, not able to controvert the plans, arguments, and principles it contained, had chosen to remain silent; but that I expected they would make an attempt to deprive the mass of the nation, and especially the poor, of the right of reading, by the pretense of prosecuting either the author or the publisher, or both."

At the start of May a royal proclamation against "wicked and seditious writings" was issued, specifically targeting Paine. It had of course the opposite effect; now everyone wanted to read this illicit pamphlet, and sales exploded all over again. Eventually, however, progressive publisher Richard Carlile would note that "one part of the community is afraid to sell, and another to purchase, under such conditions. It is not too much to say that, if 'Rights of Man' had obtained two or three years' free circulation in England and Scotland, it would have produced a similar effect to that which 'Common Sense' did in the United States."

On May 14 one of Paine's London publishers, J. S. Jordan, was ordered to appear at the Court of King's Bench. Paine offered to pay for his defense, but Jordan instead pled guilty. On May 21 a forty-one-page summons for Paine was left at Clio Rickman's house, charging him with seditious libel and "being a wicked, seditious, and ill-disposed person, and wickedly, seditiously, and maliciously intending to scandalize, traduce, and vilify the character of the said late Sovereign Lord, King William the Third, and the said late Happy [Glorious] Revolution, and the Parliament of England . . . and to bring the constitution, legislation, and government of this kingdom into hatred and contempt with his Majesty's subjects." When asked by Whig opposition leader Charles James Fox to explain the basis for these charges to Parliament, First Minister Pitt replied that "principles had been laid down by Mr. Paine which struck at hereditary nobility, and which went to the destruction of monarchy and religion, and the total subversion of the established form of government."

Paine was brought to court on June 8, 1792, but the trial was continued to the following December. Pitt's reign of terror, however, would not wait for the docket. Even though Paine removed the sentences that the government charged as being "wicked" in the new sixpence edition published in August, a reinvigorated book police continually harassed stationers offering any of Paine's works. Many would be arrested, fined, or sent to prison, suffering shockingly harsh penalties for minor infractions. For saying, "I am for equality. Why, no kings!" in a coffeehouse, the London Corresponding Society's barrister, John Frost, would spend eighteen months in jail, as would a bookseller from Leicester, Richard Phillips, for selling *Part the Second.* Pitt's attorneys additionally monitored every opposition society misstep. When Darwin's Derby Society published a manifesto demanding an expansion of the franchise in Birmingham's *Morning Chronicle,* the paper's editor was arrested. Government spies followed Paine everywhere and monitored gatherings of his followers. Progressive debating clubs were shut down. Barkeeps hosting *Rights* enthusiasts were so threatened that two hundred coffeehouse and tavern owners joined in declaring that they would not offer their rooms to clubs promoting "the destruction of this country."

Across England the government incited mass riots and public demonstrations through a national society, the Association for Preserving Liberty and Property Against Republicans and Levellers. Cambridge University gave its support to local mobs and their violent assaults on political discussions at public meetings. Effigies of Paine were hanged and then incinerated along with copies of his books to shouts of "God Save the King!" Local drinking songs included a new chorus: "Up with the cause of old England; And down with the tricks of Tom Paine!" (The origins of "Tom Paine" can in fact be traced to this tumultuous and partisan era in British politics, for Paine never referred to himself as "Tom" in any surviving document; it began as a monarchist slur, to signify his "commonness.") Another song of the time included:

Old Satan had a darling boy
Full equal he to Cain
Born peace and order to destroy
His name was—Thomas Paine.

Over the next few years, the Association for Preserving Liberty and Property Against Republicans and Levellers would sponsor riots in three hundred English towns against the villainous *Rights of Man*. One typical event was a parade in Leeds, which included "an image of Tom Paine upon a pole, with a rope round his neck which was held by a man behind, who continually lashed the effigy with a carter's whip. The effigy was at last burned in the market-place, the market-bell tolling slowly." Not every demonstration, however, sided with the government. A Sheffield mob of locals carried "a caricature painting representing Britannia—Burke riding on a swine ['the swinish multitude']—and a figure, the upper part of which was the likeness of [Home Secretary Henry Dundas] and the lower part that of an Ass . . . the pole of Liberty lying broken on the ground, inscribed 'Truth is Libel'—the Sun breaking from behind a Cloud, and the Angel of Peace, with one hand dropping the 'Rights of Man,' and extending the other to raise up Britannia." In one Suffolk village, after townspeople were paid by the parish rector to burn Paine in effigy, another resident paid them to burn the rector in effigy, which they did just as enthusiastically. When William Sharp created cheap gravure prints of a kindly-eyed Paine based on George Romney's portrait, they proved popular across the whole of the United Kingdom.

Government leaders knew all too well that a public trial would at the very least inspire even more Britons to read the illicit and alluring *Rights of Man*. When the Viennese government compiled a *Catalogue of Forbidden Books* in 1765, so many Austrians used it as a reading guide that the Hapsburg censors were forced to include the *Catalogue* itself as a forbidden book. Additionally, a judgment imprisoning or executing Paine might easily inflame the growing horde of his followers into open revolt. The London *Times* editorialized, "It is earnestly recommended to Mad Tom that he should embark for France and there be naturalized into the regular confusion of democracy," and documents would later reveal that this was in fact the state's ultimate goal, creating a relentless, nationwide harassment to convince the author to leave Britain for good. Then the whole problem would just quietly go away, in the proper English manner.

If the American Constitution had sided with the rich in positioning the fulcrum of state power, the first French Republic would take the opposite tack in favor of ordinary citizens, through a series of coincidences that drew to a peak over that summer of 1792, when a very large number of Parisian artisans and merchants started arming themselves, not just with pikes and muskets, but with artillery. Turning against the aristocratic men's fashion of fancy knee breeches and silk stockings, they wore full-length plain trousers and a floppy red cap, the *bonnet rouge,* and would be called *sans-culottes.* Their leaders were the bosses of the Cordeliers: Legendre, a butcher; Santerre, a brewer; and Varlet, a post office clerk.

The Cordeliers insisted that the government do something about food prices, and now they had a substantial armed force to back up their demands. On June 20, to protest the government's recent ineptitude, a group led by Santerre gathered to plant a symbolic liberty tree—a poplar, or cottonwood—on the grounds of the Tuileries. By mistake, the royal apartment gates were opened and the crowd rushed through, immediately finding the king and queen. For hours, the Parisians verbally assaulted the royals and their attendants, threatening them with raised guns and screaming out their many complaints. They insisted Louis be adorned with a *bonnet rouge,* which he wore, while giving a toast to the spirit of France. Finally at dusk, Mayor Pétion arrived and convinced everyone to go home.

On August 3 the Duke of Brunswick, commander of Prussian forces marching toward Paris, responded to the news of this incident with a proclamation that if the royal palace was ever again attacked, the city would be put to an "exemplary and unforgettable act of vengeance." Instead of cowing the Parisians, this only reminded them of the traitorous act of the royal family's abandonment. On August 9 an insurrectionary faction, including Robespierre and Danton, took control of the Parisian municipal government, the Commune, and the next day another mob of armed Parisians, enraged by the duke's proclamation and the Assembly's inaction, and accompanied by the city and provincial National Guard, attacked the Tuileries again. The royal family escaped by hiding with the legislature in its meetinghouse, the Manège, the royal riding school next to the palace. Six hundred of the one thousand Swiss guards defending the palace were slaughtered in a night of vigilante carnage.

A few days later, Lafayette, at the war's front lines, was told that his military commission had been revoked. Immediately understanding the dangers of returning to Paris, on August 19 he surrendered to the Austrians, and spent the next five years in the solitary confinement of an Olmütz prison. Hearing of Lafayette's fate, Gouverneur Morris, a man appreciative of moral denouements when it came to the lives of others, commented, "Thus, his circle is completed. He . . . is crushed by the wheel he put in motion. He lasted longer than I expected." Morris would, however, warn the Austrians that America would not respond well if the Hero of Two Worlds "should be in want," and loaned Mme. de Lafayette one hundred thousand livres from his private fortune.

Many of the country's legislators fled the city. The few remaining agreed that a new election should be held, to create a National Convention of 749 delegates, who would be responsible for writing a new republican constitution, as well as passing judgment on the future of the King of the Franks. This decision would lead to a remarkable turn of events for a man who could neither speak nor read French, as well as provide another illustration of the tremendous popular success of *Droits de l'homme,* with the arrival in 1792 of a letter from Paris to London:

> To Thomas Paine:
>
> France calls you, Sir, to its bosom, to perform one of the most useful and most honorable functions, that of contributing, by wise legislation, to the happiness of a people, whose destinies interest all who think and are united with the welfare of all who suffer in the world.
>
> It becomes the nation that has proclaimed the Rights of Man, to desire among her legislators him who first dared to estimate the consequences of those Rights, and who has developed their principles with that Common Sense, which is the only genius inwardly felt by all men, and the conception of which springs forth from nature and truth.
>
> The National Assembly gave you the title of Citizen, and had seen with pleasure that its decree was sanctioned by the only legitimate

> authority, that of the people, who had already claimed you, even before you were nominated. . . .
>
> The Electoral Assembly of the Department of Oise, anxious to be the first to elect you, has been so fortunate as to insure to itself that honour; and when many of my fellow citizens desired me to inform you of your election, I remembered, with infinite pleasure, having seen you at Mr. Jefferson's, and I congratulated myself on having had the pleasure of knowing you.
>
> Herault Séchelles,
> President, National Assembly

In fact, Oise was one of four *départements* nominating Paine to serve as its representative to the National Convention; Puy-de-Dôme, Somme, and Pas-de-Calais had also named him, as then Tory William Cobbett would later explain: "Thomas's having merited death, or at least transportation, in England, was a strong recommendation to him in France, whose newly enlightened inhabitants seem to have conceived a wonderful partiality for all that is vile. Several of the departments disputed with each other the *honour* of having a *convict* for their representative." Calais was the one *département* to send a district envoy, Achille Audibert, directly to London to convince Paine to accept its nomination, a strategy that made all the difference.

Paine was at first uninterested in helping the French draft their constitution, because instead of frightening him away, Whitehall's campaign of state-sanctioned mobs and gibbet threats only served to inflate his assessment of his status and political power. He imagined that the great mass of Englishmen had rallied to the cause of modern reform and at any moment the nation would begin its evolution into a modern republic. At the same time, even during his most conceited, self-absorbed moments, Paine suffered nagging doubts, and these worries and questions came to the fore in September 1792, finally to culminate one evening at a dinner hosted by publisher Joseph Johnson. There the painter, poet, mystic, and Paine ally William Blake, having heard rumor upon rumor of government plans and monarchist schemes, was stricken by a premonition. He turned to his friend and whispered, "You must not go home, or you are a dead man."

Blake's warning, coinciding with the praise and offers from France, triggered an immediate reversal in Paine's thinking. With the help of London Corresponding Society barrister John Frost and Calais's Achille Audibert, he quickly packed up his few possessions, and the three left that very night, September 13, 1792, for Dover and the Channel crossing to France. They took rooms at Dover's York Hotel, intending to rest until the next boat set sail, but that plan was thwarted, as Paine would report in a complaint to the home secretary, a complaint revealing something of the author's sterling nerve, coming as it does from a man charged with the hanging offense of seditious treason:

> We had taken our baggage out of the carriage, and put it into a room, into which we went. Mr. Frost, having occasion to go out, was stopped in the passage by a gentleman, who told him he must return into the room, which he did, and the gentleman came in with him, and shut the door. I had remained in the room; Mr. Audibert was gone to inquire when the packet was to sail. The gentleman then said that he was collector of the customs, and had an information against us, and must examine our baggage for prohibited articles. He produced his commission as collector. Mr. Frost demanded to see the information, which the collector refused to show, and continued to refuse, on every demand that we made. The collector then called in several other officers, and began first to search our pockets. He took from Mr. Audibert, who was then returned into the room, everything he found in his pocket, and laid it on the table. He then searched Mr. Frost in the same manner (who, among other things, had the keys of the trunks in his pocket), and then did the same by me.
>
> Mr. Frost wanting to go out, mentioned it, and was going toward the door; on which the collector placed himself against the door, and said, nobody should depart the room. After the keys had been taken from Mr. Frost (for I had given him the keys of my trunks beforehand, for the purpose of his attending the baggage to the customs, if it should be necessary), the collector asked us to open the trunks, presenting us the keys for that purpose; this we declined to do, unless he would produce his information, which he again refused. The collector then opened the trunks himself, and took out every paper and letter, sealed or unsealed.

One of the documents seized by the Dover customshouse, *Letter to the Addressers,* was Paine's response to the corrupt state's attempt to execute him: "If, to expose the fraud and imposition of monarchy, and every species of hereditary government—to lessen the oppression of taxes—to propose plans for the education of helpless infancy, and the comfortable support of the aged and distressed—to endeavor to conciliate nations to each other—to extirpate the horrid practise of war—to promote universal peace, civilization, and commerce—and to break the chains of political superstition, and raise degraded man to his proper rank—if these things be libellous, let me live the life of a libeller, and let the name of LIBELLER be engraved on my tomb."

The investigation took all night, and at sunrise the ferry began taking on passengers. The confrontation with the officials, however, had drawn a local crowd to the docks, where they learned that Thomas Paine was disgracing their town with his vile presence. As Audibert, Frost, and Paine carried their trunks to the ship, they were menaced by hisses and boos. Various Dovermen shouted out threats; one demanded a ducking, while another urged the crowd to take Paine away for an immediate tar and feathering. To escape the taunts Paine and his friends immediately went below deck, hoping the crowd would get bored and disperse. As the ferry set sail, however, the mob remained by the docks, shouting and waving their fists.

It was the last of England that Thomas Paine would ever see.

8. The Sovereigns Among Us

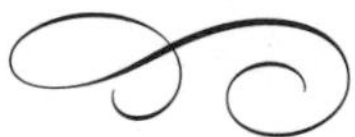

THE FIFTY-SEVEN-YEAR-OLD Paine left Britain assaulted by His Majesty's government and hounded by a taunting mob. He would arrive in France to a hero's embrace. News that he had docked at Calais to accept the *département*'s nomination to the National Convention traveled throughout the city with dramatic speed. John Frost, accompanying him, remembered that "all the soldiers on duty were drawn up; the officer of the guard embraced him on landing, and presented him with the national cockade, which a handsome young woman, who was standing by, begged the honour of fixing in his hat, and returned it to him, expressing a hope that he would continue his exertions in the behalf of liberty, France, and the Rights of Man. A salute was then fired from the battery to announce to the people of Calais the arrival of their new representative." Crowds lined the rue de l'Egalité in drenching rains to shout at his passing carriage: *"Vive Thomas Paine! Vive la nation!"* On the steps of city hall, he was publicly introduced by Achille Audibert, was greeted before an assembled crowd by the mayor, and formally accepted the honor of his appointment. That evening he attended the theater, with his box draped in a fabric lettered with the reservation "*pour l'auteur de* Droits de l'Homme." When he arrived in the city of Paris on September 19, 1792, to take his seat at the Convention, he was greeted all over again by the thrilling cheers of his fellow delegates: *"Vive Thomas Paine!"*

The majority of France's 749 new legislators were, like America's congressmen, lawyers, but also included were patricians and journalists. Many of the new French periodicals regularly employed the political shock tactics of unfounded, startling accusations and dramatic, wholesale attacks, a style some journalist-legislators brought with them to the humid and airless

Manège, which had been recently decorated with busts of such republican gods as Cincinnatus, Publicola, and Brutus, the last a man who killed a king but was forced to flee when his nation turned against him, and ended up with a republic lost to empire and himself to suicide. Their demagogic oratory, combined with the now ancient enmity of the 205 deputies returning from the Legislative Assembly, along with such fervid Jacobins as Robespierre and his comrade in arms, Louis Antoine Léon de Saint-Just, would permanently split the Convention into warring factions. Robespierre and his allies sat together in the very highest (and conspicuously separate) chairs against the wall to the left, and came to be nicknamed Montagnards, or the Mountain, while the Brissotins, or Girondins, sat opposite and to the right. In between, on the low chairs called the "Plain," were the uncommitted delegates whose votes swung back and forth. While the struggle of the Left (and their Parisian, Cordelier, *sans-culotte,* and antiwar allies) and the Right (with their every-*département*-but-Paris, bourgeois, and pro-military followers) took center stage in the nation's political life, it was the decisions of the uncommitted Plain that determined the course of the French Revolution.

Beyond such *républicain* Girondin allies as Jacques Brissot and Condorcet, Deputy Paine should have formed a natural friendship with the thirty-four-year-old Robespierre. They shared a profound range of philosophic and political tenets; both were known for, and proud of, being "incorruptible"; both were expressly sincere in their Enlightenment faith; both were (at that moment) stridently against the death penalty; both were concerned with the political power of "ordinary" people; and both were of similar spiritual beliefs. However, that Paine had met the Girondins in his first months in Europe through his ties to Franklin, Jefferson, and the abolition movement, and that so many of that faction spoke English while Paine never decently learned his French, kept a relationship with Robespierre from ever developing.

In traveling daily to the Convention, Paine rode through the Place du Carrousel in front of the Tuileries, a square now home to the latest Enlightenment innovation. Across the history of Europe, feudal despots had regularly used the gore of public execution to provide mass entertainment, establish their brutal authority, and terrorize their citizens into submissive obedience. After the noose, the most popular forms of state-sponsored death were burning at the stake; drawing (which included chopping off the genitals and disemboweling while the condemned was still conscious); quartering (tying each arm and leg to four different oxen and then beating the animals until the body was ripped apart); and beheading (where often the first blow of the axe was not wholly effective). As nobles could frequently pay or bargain their way into less painful executions while peasants could not, a method of equitable capital punishment became an Enlightenment goal, especially stirring the imaginations of French surgeon Antoine Louis, harpsichord mechanic Tobias Schmidt, and state executioner Charles-Henri Sanson. The three promoted a device that would be known by many names—in Yorkshire as "the Hallifax gibbet," in Scotland as "the Maiden," and in France as the *louisette,* the *louison,* and *le rasoir national,* as well as by such euphemisms as *jouer la main chaude* ("shaking the hot hand")—or as simply the *machine.* When in 1789 National Assembly deputy Dr. Joseph-Ignace Guillotin suggested a revision of standard practice so that, mercifully, "the criminal shall be decapitated; this will be done solely by means of a simple mechanism . . . a machine that beheads painlessly," Marat began referring to the *machine* as the guillotine.

The doctor proposed that state executions should be private and held in remote, out-of-the-way, honorable, and contemplative locations. The August before Paine's arrival, however, had brought with it an episode of horrifying anarchy inspired by Marat, who had publicly speculated on what might happen if the Austrians invaded Paris and opened the gates of every prison. In a fit of preemptive bloodlust, thousands of citizen vigilantes broke into the jails, held kangaroo courts, and butchered between eleven hundred and fourteen hundred men, women, and children—nearly half the city's inmates. This massacre forced the government to realize that it needed to visibly reestablish itself as the nation's fount of justice, as well as to offer the Parisian mob a taste of instructional fear. Contrary to the enlightened vision of Dr. Guillotin, French state beheadings would be as public as feasible, held in the city's greatest squares—the Carrousel, the Place St. Antoine, the Barrière Ranverse, and most prominently, the Place de la Révolution (today the Concorde), also adjoining the Tuileries and the newly-open-to-the-public museum, the Louvre. The French might not have bread, but they would have a circus; of the forty thousand killed during the Terror, fifteen thousand would meet the *machine.* In time, Parisians sharing their neighborhoods with it would complain of the stench and of their sewers being clogged with blood, and the state would keep moving it from place to place, while Dr. Guillotin's descendants would eventually petition the government to call the device something else. When that plea was ignored, *la famille en masse* changed its name.

One week after Paine's arrival the legislature announced Year One of French Liberty, unanimously voting on September 21 to blinding applause that "Royalty is from this day abolished in France." That evening, Gouverneur Morris commented in his diary, "History informs us that the passage of dethroned monarchs is short from the prison to the grave." The Brissotins who had been dismissed by the king were returned to their ministries, along with some new appointments: Cordelier brewer Santerre was now the commander of the Paris National Guard, while heading the Ministry of Justice was a decisive and commanding thirty-five-year-old with a taurine head gouged in pox scars, a lawyer son of a lawyer described by Mme. Roland as "repulsive and atrocious [with] brutal passions . . . half-concealed under the most jovial of manners, an affectation of frankness, and a sort of simple good-naturedness."

Georges-Jacques Danton had risen at dizzying speed through the ranks of the new government, joining the Cordeliers' citizen militia in July 1789, becoming the neighborhood's president three months later, and being elected to the Paris Commune three months after that. When, in the first week of the Convention, Danton proposed that judges be directly elected, Paine, not knowing the history of the aristocratic (and antirepublican) *robins,* argued instead that they should be appointed based on their education and training. Just as Paine's well-developed self-esteem and sanctimony had undermined his political bearings during the Deane affair, so now, in his first days as a representative, he would argue with the French over matters of local history and culture on which he was wholly uninformed. Danton's measure passed by a wide margin.

In October Brissot's name was stripped from the rolls of the Jacobin Club, a symbolic gesture, since he had left long before over his interminable disputes with Robespierre. On the eleventh, Paine was one of the nine delegates appointed to the committee to draft a new constitution; he basked in the honor of receiving the second highest number of votes. Like so much of the government in those years, the Girondins were able to stack this committee in their favor; very quickly, such abuse of majority power would carry the seeds of destruction through antagonizing the Plain. Of the members of Paine's constitutional committee, only three would survive the Terror.

In that fall of 1792, however, "bliss was it in that dawn to be alive, but to be young was very heaven," as William Wordsworth would remember. At the start of their constitutional committee's deliberations, Paine would tell Danton that the point of their enterprise was to transform the whole of Europe, as "France must speak for other nations who cannot yet speak for themselves . . . by showing the reason that has induced her to abolish the old system of monarchical government, and to establish the representative." Just as Jefferson had helped with Lafayette's constitution, so Paine assisted Condorcet in the drafting of language to be agreed on by the committee as a whole. The two became close friends, with deist Paine and atheist Condorcet arguing over religion, solving mathematical puzzles together, and sharing a relentless optimism in the faith of human progress.

Paine's reignited political enthusiasms resulted in a barrage of work, not just as a legislator but also as a writer, starting with "An Essay for the Use of New Republicans in Their Opposition to Monarchy" in Brissot's October 26, 1792, *Le Patriote Français,* which outlined what Paine viewed as a profound difference between the monarch and monarchy: "All Frenchmen have shuddered at the perjuries of the king, the plots of his court and the profligacy of his brothers; so that the race of Louis was deposed from the throne of their hearts long before it was deposed by legislative decree. We do not effect much, however, if we merely dethrone an idol; we must also break to pieces the pedestal upon which it rested. It is the office of royalty rather than the holder of the office that is fatal in its consequences."

Over the next two months, the Convention would be dominated by debate on the fate of its king. From the basics of procedure to the final outcome, no one had any experience or knowledge of legal precedent for conducting an inquiry and passing judgment on a monarch accused of sedition. There were those who felt one branch of the government was constitutionally incapable of passing judgment on another branch; there were those who believed that the National Convention was only empowered to draft a republican charter, not to assume the role of judge and jury. Saint-Just proposed, in his first speech before the deputies, a simple solution: as to be a king was now a crime in France, there was no need for the time or expense of a trial; Louis should just be immediately beheaded. Paine, accompanied by his translator, Bançal, rose to directly attack this suggestion; the most famous antimonarchist alive now found himself vigorously defending the king of France. Paine tried to calm the legislature's extravagant emotions on the subject by insisting that "Louis XVI, considered as an individual, is an object beneath the notice of the Republic." If monarchy was indeed a crime, he argued, then all who participated in it and benefited from it under the ancien régime should be considered criminals and, per Saint-Just, be subject to immediate execution.

Beheading the king, he concluded, would serve no purpose beyond making other countries condemn the French as uncivilized and barbaric: "France is now a republic; she has completed her revolution; but she cannot earn all its advantages so long as she is surrounded with despotic governments. Their armies and their marine oblige her also to keep troops and ships in readiness. It is therefore her immediate interest that all nations shall be as free as herself; that revolutions shall be universal; and since the trial of Louis XVI can serve to prove to the world the flagitiousness [brutality] of governments in general, and the necessity of revolutions, she ought not to let slip so precious an opportunity." The new nation, he explained, in its conduct of the trial of its king, was being given an enormous opportunity to inspire the world with its noble republican government, and needed to create, in tandem, an admirable and upstanding civil society firmly held accountable to the king of all democracies—the law.

As Paine and his translator stepped down, Robespierre hurried forward to respond. Defending Saint-Just's position, he pointedly ignored Paine's prudent call for reason and justice, instead decreeing that "Louis declared war on the Revolution, he has been defeated, and now it is the duty of the Convention to see that revolutionary justice is done. It must be done. Royalty must be abolished!"

On November 19 a locksmith from the town of Versailles by the name of Gamain asked to meet with French minister of the interior Jean-Marie Roland. The locksmith said that he had been hired to install a metal door over a secret cupboard under some wainscoting, and he wanted to report this suspicious enterprise to the proper authorities. The next day Roland announced to the Convention that a cache of royal documents had been seized from this cupboard, including pleas from Louis to the Austrians, asking them to invade the country and restore absolute monarchy, and a reference to the constitution as "absurd and detestable."

Paine worked on the French translation of *Rights of Man* while living at the Paris home of the marquis de Lafayette (LEFT), hero of the American Revolution and leader of the new French constitutional monarchy.

When the Lafayette government failed, it was replaced by a group known as Brissotins or Girondins, who were Paine's closest allies in the French legislature and who established a government on his American model. Their most significant leaders included the journalist Jacques-Pierre Brissot (ABOVE) and the philosophe the marquis de Condorcet (LEFT).

The fall of the Bourbons, as seen in a political cartoon . . .

in a depiction of the king's trial at the National Convention . . .

and in dinnerware celebrating his execution.

Rev. de Paris.
Le ci-devant roi à la Barre de la Convention Nationale.
Nº 179 P. 533.
Mardi XI décembre 1792. Louis capet dernier roi des français fut traduit de la tour du Temple à la barre de la Convention Nationale accompagné du Maire, du procureur de la commune, le Député Valazé qui lui passoit par derriere lui piece par piece pour lui faire reconnoitre.

One of Paine's French adversaries was the firebrand journalist and legislator Jean-Paul Marat, whose assassination turned him into a martyr.

BELOW: When the cost of living continued to skyrocket, eighty thousand Parisians attacked the legislature, purging the Brissotins and bringing to power a new government led by Maximilien Robespierre.

Georges-Jacques Danton tried to aid the Brissotins, but instead ended up in the same prison as Thomas Paine. Soon after, he would be guillotined.

Paine spent nearly a year of the Terror imprisoned at the Luxembourg, today the home of the French Senate.

Gouverneur Morris and Paine had a lifelong mutual love-hate relationship. While American minister to Paris, Morris refused to help Paine by claiming him as a citizen, for reasons that remain unclear.

After he published a series of articles outlining the conquest of England, Paine was visited by the greatest hero in France, Napoleon. Their relationship did not last long.

Over the course of his last years, Paine lived in a cottage on his New Rochelle property (TOP RIGHT) and at various New York City addresses, including this Herring Street (today, Bleecker Street) house in Greenwich Village (BELOW). At middle right, a view of the city in 1797.

One of Paine's New York roommates was artist John Wesley Jarvis, who created this late-in-life portrait and bust.

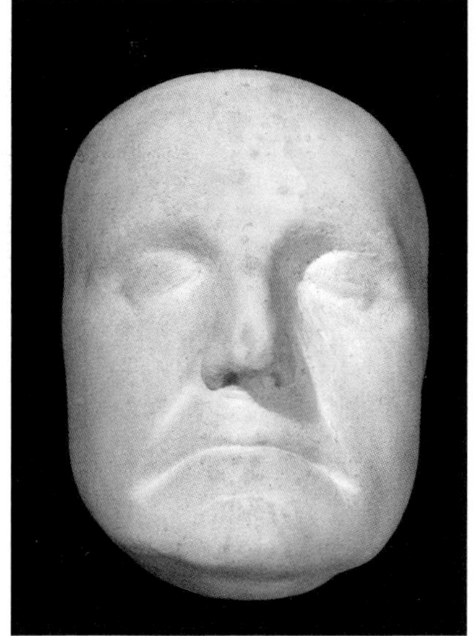

After Paine's death, Jarvis made one final mask of the writer, a technique then considered to be the most realistic one.

Napoleon told Paine that "a statue of gold should be erected to you in every city in the universe." Through the efforts of America's Thomas Paine National Historic Association, one was, in Paine's hometown, Thetford.

Men will learn to express all that is base, Malignant, Treacherous, Unatural & Blasphemous, by the single Monosyllable — Paine — written by me W. Cobbett. — I intend paying my Old Debts by raising a subscription on these Relics, must be doing something. Cursed World; Kicked out of France, driven from America & obliged to run awy from England.
Crusic. fecit
50 Piccadilly Pub^d by S W Fores Decr 1819
Dec. 1819
A RADICAL REFORMER.
Just arrived with his favorite, & precious Relics. The word Refom, according to Cobbetts Ideas, means a Conforming to existing circumstances purely, for ones own advantage, witness his Life and contrdictary Writing.

When William Cobbett brought Paine's remains to England in 1819, he expected to be greeted with honor and acclaim. Instead, he was universally ridiculed. This cartoon employed Cobbett's onetime anti-Paine rhetoric against him.

Everything that the gossips had feared was, in that moment, nakedly revealed as the truth. No one could now excuse Louis XVI; he had betrayed his own people.

On December 11 the man now called Louis Capet was brought before the Convention for a three-hour interrogation. Deputies presented evidence that, at every stage, the king had opposed liberal reform. In his defense a humbled Louis responded that all of his incriminating acts sprang not from treasonous monarchic counterrevolutionary principles but from fear.

On January 15, 1793, the French National Convention began deliberations over the king's perfidy, and Paine again rose to speak. He reminded everyone of Robespierre's address from two years before against capital punishment, and implied that summary execution was an act not of enlightened republicans but of despotic tyrants. The Convention should consider the solution that England had adopted for the Stuarts during its Glorious Revolution and send the royal family into exile, where in time they would be completely forgotten:

> It is to France alone, I know, that the United States of America owe that support which enabled them to shake off the unjust and tyrannical yoke of Britain. The ardour and zeal which she displayed to provide both men and money, were the natural consequence of a thirst for liberty. But as the nation at that time, restrained by the shackles of her own government, could only act by the means of a monarchical organ, this organ—whatever in other respects the object might be—certainly performed a good, a great action. Let then those United States be the safeguard and asylum of Louis Capet. There, hereafter, far removed from the miseries and crimes of royalty, he may learn, from the constant aspect of public prosperity, that the true system of government consists not in kings, but in fair, equal and honourable representation.

This was, as it turned out, a dream of reason offered to a nation of sensibility. Instead, Robespierre used his legal training to undermine Paine's proposal, arguing that under republican equality of law, if there should be an exception to execution for those found guilty of sedition, it should certainly not apply to an ex-monarch. Convention president Bertrand Barère then announced to the deputies, "It is for you to vote, before the statue of

Brutus, before your country, before the whole world. It is by judging the last king of the French that the National Convention will enter into the fields of fame." The legislature, by an overwhelming majority, answered: guilty.

The next day, January 16, debates over the king's sentence began; these would continue for the next twenty-four hours. After more rounds of voting on various alternatives, the final outcome was tallied: 387 to 334, in favor of death. Those voting yes included longtime court painter Jacques-Louis David and the king's own cousin, now named Philippe Egalité.

On the nineteenth, Paine tried to reverse this decision and save the life of Louis Seize. At the podium, Bançal translated his prepared speech: "The decision came to in the Convention yesterday in favor of death has filled me with genuine sorrow," for the guillotine rose "from a spirit of revenge rather than from a spirit of justice." Earlier, Condorcet had agreed with his position, insisting that "to nature belongs the right of death. Despotism has taken it from her; liberty will return it." Brissot, too, had given his support: "A cruel precipitation may alienate our friends in England, Ireland, America. Take care! The opinion of European peoples is worth to you armies!"

The Mountain, however, which had started to murmur in angry response by the end of Paine's first sentence, was now shouting its disapproval. Though Bançal at the tribune raised his voice again and again, he could barely be heard. An inflamed Marat then rushed forward to respond, insisting not only that every deputy should ignore Paine's argument, but that his ballot on the issue should be entirely revoked: "I submit that Thomas Paine is incompetent to vote on this question; being a Quaker, his religious principles are opposed to the death penalty." Paine, however, would not back down:

> I have the advantage of some experience; it is near twenty years that I have been engaged in the cause of liberty, having contributed something to it in the revolution of the United States of America. My language has always been that of liberty and humanity, and I know by experience that nothing so exalts a nation as the union of these two principles, under all circumstances. I know that the public mind of France, and particularly that of Paris, has been heated and irritated by the dangers to which they have been exposed; but could

> we carry our thoughts into the future, when the dangers are ended, and the irritations forgotten, what today seems an act of justice may then appear an act of vengeance. My anxiety for the cause of France has become for the moment concern for its honor. If, on my return to America, I should employ myself on a history of the French Revolution, I had rather record a thousand errors dictated by humanity, than one inspired by a justice too severe.

Marat strode to where Paine sat, questioned him in English, and then announced to the deputies, "I denounce the interpreter, and I maintain that such is not the opinion of Thomas Paine. It is a wicked and faithless translation." Deputy Jean-Philippe Garran took to the rostrum and countered that he had read Paine's original in English, and the translation was correct. Paine told Marat, "I voted against [the death penalty] both morally and politically." Against a deafening chorus of ridicule, Bançal struggled on with Paine's speech: "France has but one ally—the United States of America. . . . It happens, unfortunately, that the person now under discussion [Louis XVI] is regarded in America as a deliverer of their country. I can assure you that his execution will there spread universal sorrow, and it is in your power not thus to wound the feelings of your ally."

Though Paine may have held the moral high ground, his well-developed self-regard clearly colored these threats. He had at that moment spent less than four months as a French legislator; he needed an interpreter to understand both the written and the spoken language; he was uneducated in French history and culture; and yet he felt justified in repeatedly lecturing the other deputies on civic virtue. His attempts to save the king made lifelong foes of such men as Saint-Just and Marat, and the Convention as a whole voted against him once more.

With the first light on January 21, 1793, a dense mist covered the streets of Paris. On orders from the Commune, the city gates had been locked. Mary Wollstonecraft, vacationing with her lover, Captain Gilbert Imlay, wrote to publisher Joseph Johnson, "About nine o'clock this morning the king passed by my window, moving silently along, excepting now and then a few strokes of the drum, which rendered the stillness more awful, through empty streets, surrounded by the National Guards, who, clustering round the carriage, seemed to deserve their name. The inhabitants flocked to their windows, but the casements were all shut; not a voice was heard, nor did I see anything like an insulting gesture. . . . An association of ideas made the tears flow insensibly from my eyes, when I saw Louis sitting, with more dignity than I expected from his character, in a hackney-coach, going to meet death where so many of his race have triumphed."

Surrounded by a guard of twelve hundred in a procession that took two hours, the carriage—for even the Jacobins did not force their king to be humiliated with a tumbrel—made its way from the Temple prison holding the royal family to Sanson's platform at the Place de la Révolution, and an audience of twenty thousand. One of these was Lucy de la Tour du Pin, who, far from sharing Wollstonecraft's sentiments, said of Louis, "He looked like some peasant shambling along behind his plough; there was nothing proud or regal about him. His sword was a continual embarrassment to him, and he never knew what to do with his hat."

The king's hair was shorn to clearly expose the base of the neck, and his last words—"I die innocent of all the crimes of which I have been charged. I pardon those who have brought about my death and I pray that the blood you are about to shed may never be required of France. I hope that my blood may secure the happiness of the French people"—were inaudible to the crowd, as National Guard commander Santerre had ordered a staccato drum roll. Citizen Capet, his hands bound behind his back, was then tied face forward against a board. He was placed on the ground and slid until his neck slipped into the *machine*'s wooden collar. Over the citizens of the French Republic chanting as one, *"Vive la nation!"* the king's manservant, Jean-Baptiste Cléry, believed that he heard the king screaming because "his head did not fall at the first stroke, his neck being so fat."

After the executioner retrieved that head from the basket to deliver the proof of death, his staff began selling pieces of the king's clothing and locks of his hair to the crowd. Many dipped their handkerchiefs into the scaffold's pools of blood to make their own souvenirs. Within months, Sèvres would manufacture a white commemorative coffee cup, its face an illustration in gold of Sanson hoisting the dripping head of the last French king.

At the same time that Louis XVI stood trial for his life before his nation's legislature, Thomas Paine stood trial in absentia for his own life before a jury handpicked by the government of England at London's Guildhall.

Appearing for the defense was the brilliant and acidic Thomas Erskine, attorney general to the Prince of Wales, and the country's most successful criminal lawyer. The prince had sworn that he would dismiss Erskine from the royal sinecure if he took on Paine as a client, and not only was that promise kept, but throughout the proceedings the English papers assaulted Erskine as a Paine conspirator and an incorrigible Jacobin.

The trial began with prosecutor (and future prime minister) Spencer Perceval outlining the various ways in which *Rights of Man, Part the Second* was scurrilous and seditious. He then showed the jury a November 11 letter that the "wicked, malicious, seditious, and ill-disposed" Paine had written to the attorney general, Sir Archibald Macdonald, which said that judging him guilty made as much sense as attacking "the man in the moon," and demanding to know who was being put on trial, Thomas Paine, or "the rights of the people of England to investigate systems and principles of government." It is unlikely that Perceval read the letter in its entirety, as it described how "the government of England is as great if not the greatest perfection of fraud and corruption that ever took place since governments began . . . though you may not choose to see it, the people are seeing it very fast," and accused the crown of planning to stack the jury with Paine-haters. This is exactly what it did, selecting from among what had become a horde of prosperous Englishmen who believed they had much to lose if louche Paineites and Gallic revolutionaries overturned the king in favor of a republic of Levellers.

The prosecution then brought forward John Adams to press its case, with the government attorney testifying that "having the honor of [Mr. Adams's] acquaintance, I wrote to him relative to the prosecution, and in answer I was informed that it is the wish of Thomas Paine to convene the people of Great Britain to adopt a constitution similar to that of France and to establish a government proceeding directly from the sovereignty of the people." Adams's Publicola series and *Defence of the Constitutions* were entered as evidence, to illustrate "that the American government is not founded upon the absurd doctrine of the pretended rights of man, and that if it had been it could not have stood for a week."

One observer commented, "That vain fellow Erskine has been going about this month past, saying he would make a speech in defence of Paine's nonsensical and impudent libel on the English constitution, that would astonish the world, and make him to be remembered when Pitt and Fox and

Burke, etc., were all forgotten." Paine's lawyer needed four hours and an outburst of fainting (Adams being far from the only melodramatic attorney then in practice) to deliver a speech that should have resulted in a decisive acquittal, including that "government, in its own estimation, has been at all times a system of perfection; but a free press has examined and detected its errors, and the people have from time to time reformed them. This freedom has alone made our government what it is; this freedom alone can preserve it; and therefore, under the banners of that freedom, today I stand up to defend Thomas Paine." When the prosecution stood to reply, foreman Campbell interrupted, telling the judge, "My Lord, I am authorized by the jury here to inform the Attorney-General that a reply is not necessary for them, unless the Attorney-General wishes to make it, or your Lordship."

One eyewitness who was a friend of John Hall's wrote, "Mr. Paine's trial is this instant over. Erskine shone like the morning-star. Johnson was there. The instant Erskine closed his speech the venal jury . . . without waiting for any answer, or any summing up by the Judge, pronounced him guilty. Such an instance of infernal corruption is scarcely upon record. I have not time to express my indignant feelings on this occasion. At this moment, while I write, the mob is drawing Erskine's carriage home, he riding in triumph—his horses led by another party. Riots at Cambridge, Manchester, Bridport Dorset &c. &c. O England, how art thou fallen!"

That trial would expose the country's immense political schism. As publisher James Ridgeway (who will also be jailed for author William Cobbett) was taken off to prison in chains, Erskine's horses were released from their harnesses and his carriage was pulled through the streets by a cheering mob. As the attorney, traveling home, was met with shouts of "God bless you, my dear Erskine" and "Paine and the Liberty of the Press!" Thomas Paine was forever made an exile from the nation of his birth. If he ever set foot on British soil, or was captured by English forces while traveling by sail, he would be summarily imprisoned and hanged.

Within days, commemorative medallions were being sold in the streets of London, one for a halfpenny with the motto "End of Pain," and another illustrated with the author bound and swinging from the hangman's noose: "We Dance, Paine Swings." English aristocrats particularly enjoyed wearing shoe nails inscribed with "T.P." in order to trample on Paine and his ideas with every step they took. An earthenware manufactory in Leeds produced a water pitcher with Paine's head on the body of a snake and the rousing anthem:

God save the King, and all his subjects too,
Likewise his forces and commanders true,
May he their rights forever hence maintain
Against all strife occasioned by Tom Paine.
Prithee Tom Paine why wilt thou meddling be
In others' business which concerns not thee;
For while thereon thou dost extend thy cares
Thou dost at home neglect thine own affairs.
God save the King!
Observe the wicked and malicious man
Projecting all the mischief that he can.

This court victory did not satisfy the frightened heads of the British state, however, for Paine's conviction and exile turned out to be merely the start of Pitt's crackdown, which now escalated at full force. Government spies were sent to infiltrate republican clubs. Informants were encouraged with cash awards to give testimony against the better-known progressives. One letter of the period said, "The prosecutions that are commenced all over England against printers, publishers, etc., would astonish you; and most of these are for offences committed many months ago. The printer of the *Manchester Herald* has had seven different indictments preferred against him for paragraphs in his paper; and six different indictments for selling or disposing of six different copies of Paine—all previous to the trial of Paine. The man was opulent, supposed worth £20,000; but these different actions will ruin him, as they were intended to do." When the London Corresponding Society's secretary-treasurer, cobbler Thomas Hardy, was arrested for treason, he was able to hire Thomas Erskine for his own defense. Over the next two years Hardy would be imprisoned at the Tower of London and at Newgate until his case came to trial, where he was, remarkably, acquitted. The case was so controversial that the jury foreman was barely able to announce the verdict before fainting. During Hardy's arrest and imprisonment, his wife, pregnant, died of shock.

Like every other issue in the Paine-Burke war, the state's campaign did not meet with universal British approval. When Thomas Muir was sentenced to fourteen years of transportation (overseas exile) for merely suggesting that others might want to read *Rights of Man,* the courtroom erupted in boos and hissing. The judge ordered that all those disrespecting the majesty of the court be arrested, but his sergeant replied, "My lord, they're all hissing."

In many respects the Pitt reign of terror would be far more successful than its French counterpart. The widespread English clamor for constitutional reform, equality, and social justice that had grown alongside the broadening audience for *Rights of Man* was brought to an immediate (if temporary) halt when war between England and France reignited on February 1, 1793. Britons responded with an upsurge of nationalism, love for King George and his newly aggressive first minister, and a concomitant hatred of the French. Now it was widely known that enemy spies lurked throughout the country, working behind the scenes to prepare for a French invasion, after which England would be forced to renounce its beloved king and be ruled by a Gallic democracy, including parades of bloody heads waving about. If the deputies of the National Convention imagined their army on a crusade for liberty, British citizens could equally imagine theirs as a bulwark against a grotesque and lawless anarchy.

Before leaving England to join the French National Assembly, Paine had promised a friend that "if the French kill their King, it will be a signal for my departure, for I will not abide among such sanguinary men." Now, however, he was trapped. He could not return to England, while a passage to America was perilous, as the Atlantic shipping lanes were patrolled by a British navy that stood in wartime readiness to board French or American vessels. If they discovered a famous criminal such as Paine among a ship's passengers, he would immediately be brought in chains to London for a prompt execution.

Beyond the ongoing drama of the legislative factions and the turmoil of the Parisian *sans-culottes,* however, Paine was living at what remained the very center of modern European society. Besides attending the regular soirees of the marquis de Condorcet, Mme. Roland, and the other Girondin hosts and enjoying the pleasures of being both a national legislator and a famous, popular author, Paine spent many glorious evenings at White's (or Philadelphie) Hotel surrounded by such like-minded expatriates as Mary Wollstonecraft, English lawyer John Frost, Clio Rickman (who had fled England after being convicted of selling *Rights of Man*), and American poet Joel Barlow (who was importing black-market goods with Gilbert Imlay). At one of their dinners, Lord Edward Fitzgerald and Sir Robert Smyth, enraptured with the spirit of the new France, publicly renounced their titles, with Fitzgerald writing to his mother on October 30 that "I lodge with my friend Paine—we breakfast, dine, and sup together. The more I see of his interior, the more I like and respect him. I cannot express how kind he is to me; there is a simplicity of manner, a goodness of heart, and a strength of mind in him, that I never knew a man before possess."

In addition to socializing with this remarkable coterie of friends and allies, Paine lived at the time with six colleagues in a magnificent home that was once owned by Mme. de Pompadour in the faubourg St. Denis, which he described as a dream of rural living:

> In Paris, in 1793, I had lodgings in the Rue Faubourg St. Denis, Na. 63. They were the most agreeable . . . of any I ever had in Paris, except that they were too remote from the Convention of which I was then a member. But this was recompensed by their being also remote from the alarms and confusions into which the interior of Paris was then often thrown. The news of those things used to arrive to us, as if we were in a state of tranquility in the country.
>
> The house, which was enclosed by a wall and gateway from the street, was a good deal like an old mansion farmhouse, and the courtyard was like a farmyard; stocked with fowls, ducks, turkeys and geese; which, for amusement, we used to feed out of the parlor window on the ground floor. There were some hutches for rabbits, and a sty with two pigs. Beyond was a garden of more than an acre of ground, well laid out, and stocked with excellent fruit trees. The orange, apricot, and green-gage plum were the best I ever tasted; and it is the only place where I saw the wild cucumber. The place had formerly been occupied by some curious person.
>
> My apartments consisted of three rooms; the first for wood, water, etc., with an old fashioned closet chest, high enough to hang up clothes in; the next was the bedroom; and beyond it the sitting room, which looked into the garden through a glass door; and on the outside there was a small landing place railed in, and a flight of narrow stairs almost hidden by the vines that grew over it, by which I could descend into the garden without going down stairs through the house. . . . As it was summer we spent most of our time in the garden, and passed it away in those childish amusements that serve to keep reflection from the mind, such as marbles, scotch-hops, battledores, etc., at which we were all pretty expert.

. . .

What is it in human nature that, when a great foe is defeated, causes the winners to turn on each other? With the king dead, the French government began to self-destruct, its factions eventually becoming so unsatisfied with mere political victories that they sought one another's annihilation. In March 1793 the war with Austria, Prussia, and England was joined by a civil war involving tens of thousands in the Vendée, Marseille, Nantes, Lyon, Bordeaux, and Brittany *départements* battling federal authorities in protest against the economy and the draft. Simultaneously, the French commander in Belgium, General Charles Dumouriez, followed Lafayette and defected to the Austrians, while inflation in league with currency collapse again struck Paris, with soap doubling and sugar tripling in price. The Convention tried to address these economic woes by searching for treasonous agricultural conspirators through a Committee of Public Safety and a Revolutionary Tribunal, with the committee's head, Danton, announcing, "Let us be terrible so that the people will not have to be." Being terrible did not solve the crises; instead, Parisians set off on looting sprees.

On February 15, Paine and his Girondin-dominated committee released their eighty-five-page constitutional draft to a general vote. It was roundly defeated, and an entirely new committee, stacked with Robespierristes, began work on revisions, which would be adopted on June 24. By April, Paine knew that he had made an enemy of Marat, who found in the Anglo-American's relationships with Gouverneur Morris and General Dumouriez suspicions of treason, telling a good friend of Paine's, General Thomas Ward, that "Frenchmen are mad to allow foreigners to live among them. They should cut off their ears, let them bleed a few days, and then cut off their heads." Ward pointed out that Marat, having been born in Switzerland of a Sardinian father and a Swiss mother, was himself a foreigner.

When the Jacobin Club elected Marat its president, the Girondins seized an opportunity to strike at their opponents. Citing passages from his newspaper urging attacks on legislators, Marat was impeached from the Convention and brought before the Revolutionary Tribunal. One of Paine's housemates in the St. Denis farmhouse was a wealthy English doctor, William Johnson, who was so devoted to Paine that he had followed him from London to Paris. Johnson had heard numerous times of Marat's threats against his friend, the latest having been made at a meeting of the Friends of Liberty and Equality Club, when Marat demanded the recall from the Convention "of all of those faithless members who had betrayed their duties in trying to save a tyrant's life." Johnson made a will leaving everything he owned to Paine, and then started knifing himself, but was stopped before he could finish committing suicide.

At Marat's trial the Brissotins introduced William Johnson's odd tale as moral evidence. When the Revolutionary Tribunal called Paine to testify, he said, "I would observe to the tribunal that Johnson gave himself two blows with the knife after he had understood that Marat would denounce him." To this, Marat surged from his chair and shouted, "Not because I would denounce the youth who stabbed himself, but because I wanted to denounce Thomas Paine!"

After Dr. Johnson himself testified that "the friendship I had for Thomas Paine led me to want to kill myself," the Brissotins' case began to collapse. Marat's oratory in defense of his freedom as a journalist so overwhelmed the prosecution that he had to ask the gallery twice to not disrupt the court with their outbursts of supporting applause. An acquitted Marat was then lofted through the streets of Paris by a jubilant mob, his head crowned with roses and leaves of oak. Later that month, a despondent Paine would write Jefferson, "Had this revolution been conducted consistently with its principles, there was once a good prospect of extending liberty through the greatest part of Europe; but I now relinquish that hope. . . . As the prospect of a general freedom is now much shortened, I begin to contemplate returning home. . . . I just now received a letter from General Lewis Morris, who tells me that the house and barn on my farm at N. Rochelle are burnt down [from a lightning strike]. I assure you I shall not bring money enough to build another." Even amid this great sense of disheartenment, however, Paine would plead with Danton in a May 6, 1793, letter to end the partisan war and repair the legislature to its original mandate:

> I am exceedingly disturbed at the distractions, jealousies, discontents and uneasiness that reign among us, and which, if they continue, will bring ruin and disgrace on the Republic. When I left America in the year 1787, it was my intention to return the year following, but the French Revolution, and the prospect it afforded of extending the principles of liberty and fraternity through the greater

part of Europe, have induced me to prolong my stay upwards of six years. I now despair of seeing the great object of European liberty accomplished, and my despair arises not from the combined foreign powers, not from the intrigues of aristocracy and priestcraft, but from the tumultuous misconduct with which the internal affairs of the present Revolution are conducted. . . .

The danger every day increases of a rupture between Paris and the departments. The departments did not send their deputies to Paris to be insulted, and every insult shown to them is an insult to the departments that elected and sent them. I see but one effectual plan to prevent this rupture taking place, and that is to fix the residence of the Convention, and of the future assemblies, at a distance from Paris.

I saw, during the American Revolution, the exceeding inconvenience that arose by having the government of Congress within the limits of any municipal jurisdiction. . . . In any one of the places where Congress resided, the municipal authority privately or openly opposed itself to the authority of Congress, and the people of each of these places expected more attention from Congress than their equal share with the other states amounted to. The same thing now takes place in France, but in a far greater excess. . . .

There ought to be some regulation with respect to the spirit of denunciation that now prevails. If every individual is to indulge his private malignancy or his private ambition, to denounce at random and without any kind of proof, all confidence will be undermined and all authority be destroyed. Calumny is a species of treachery that ought to be punished as well as any other kind of treachery. It is a private vice productive of public evils; because it is possible to irritate men into disaffection by continual calumny who never intended to be disaffected.

This attempt at mediation found no audience. In the wake of Marat's exultant victory, the Brissotins' enemies knew their time had come, and Robespierre called the *sans-culottes* on May 26 "to rise in moral insurrection." Five days later, armed citizens stormed the offices of the Paris Commune to demand that all government officials who had shown sympathy for the ancien régime, as well as those with the potential of manipulating the food supply, be immediately taken into custody. The Commune was forced to accede. On June 2, while the mayor of Paris petitioned for the arrest of twenty-two legislators, including many Paine *républicain* allies, eighty thousand armed Parisians surrounded the National Convention, with cannons directly pointed at the Manège. Paine tried to enter the building but was refused. He found Danton, who warned him to be prudent, as he could so easily be included on the list of "enemies of the revolution." When the American commented that Vergniaud had been right in saying the French state had become a Saturn, a god who eats his children, the Frenchman supposedly replied, "Revolutions cannot be made with rosewater."

The Convention deputies agreed that, now that they represented the will of a republic, they must follow the wishes of the people. To the mob's shouts of *"Purgez la convention! Tirez le mauvais sang!"* ("Purge the Convention! Leech the bad blood!"), the Jacobins indicted thirty-one of their fellow deputies as traitors and dismissed their legislative credentials, Saint-Just explaining that "those who make revolutions by halves dig their own grave." When a group of 120 other legislators protested, their credentials were suspended as well.

A number of the accused escaped to the provinces, where they tried to rally support against the Parisians. Instead, almost all were captured and executed, or committed suicide. Condorcet (who was not a Girondin, but who had denounced the Jacobins) hid from the authorities at the home of Mme. Vernet. Believing his presence was endangering her, he instead tried to live in the woods near the Clamart stone quarries. After three days of starving, he went to the village tavern for an omelet, aroused suspicion, could not produce identity papers, was taken into custody, and the following morning was found in his cell, dead, for reasons that have never been explained. The Girondins who did not flee were taken to the Conciergerie, Philip the Fair's thirteenth-century palace, converted into France's Revolutionary Tribunal and worst prison, site of twelve hundred *oubliettes* (forgotten places) where prisoners who could not afford the fees for a bed slept atop piles of hay in their own excrement like farm animals.

Later that month, a Caen priest who had refused to support the new government was guillotined. One of his parishioners, a Mlle. d'Armont, rode to Paris on July 9, bought a kitchen knife at the Palais-Royal, and went to the Convention. She was disappointed to learn that Marat was not there, but at home in the bath, his psoriatic arthritis inflamed by that summer's heat wave. When she went to his house, Marat's fiancée, Simone, turned her away, but d'Armont shouted that she had come with crucial information about the Girondin traitors of Normandy, and Marat called out from his tub, "Let her in." When Simone left for a few minutes, Mlle. d'Armont—Charlotte Corday—stabbed Marat with her kitchen knife, striking the base of his neck, severing the carotid, and killing him. Rumor among the *sans-culottes* turned this assassination into a Girondin conspiracy, and Corday would join the purged deputies at the Conciergerie. At her trial, she said, "Now that he's dead, peace will return to my country," and at her execution, Vergniaud announced that "she taught us how to die." Instead of saving the Republic, however, Corday became the emissary of future horror, as Marat was transformed into the Revolution's greatest martyr, with deputy Jacques-Louis David painting his death in the pose of a sacred pietà, and the great mass of Parisians unsatisfied until those responsible—the Girondins—were punished for their conspiring in his murder. Surrounded by the rest of the world's invading armies, by provincial Frenchmen preparing for civil war, and by the constant Parisian mob that had brought down every prior government in short order, the Jacobins responded with totalitarian panic, with both the Committee of Public Safety and the National Convention now believing *"que la Terreur soit à l'ordre du jour"*—"that terror is the order of the day"—while pursuing a full-fisted control and strengthening of the state with what Robespierre would name *"une volonté une"* ("a single will"), colored by the black-eyed sanctimony of Saint-Just that "the republic consists in the extermination of everything that opposes it. . . . Those who want to do good in this world must sleep only in the tomb."

The Jacobin constitution, approved by the Convention in June, was suspended in light of the national crisis, withholding every civil right promised by Lafayette's and Jefferson's *Declaration* that had been fought for from the first of the Revolution. Instead, the Law of Suspects, passed in the first week of September, allowed magistrates to arrest "those who by their conduct, relations or language spoken or written, have shown themselves partisans of tyranny or federalism and enemies of liberty." More than two hundred thousand people were incarcerated, with the majority never going to trial, and of those forced to suffer under the indefinite limbo of an uncharged and indeterminate prison term, nearly ten thousand died. On December 4, the National Convention was changed from a temporary body whose main purpose was to draft a constitution into a permanent legislature headed by the Committee of Public Safety, which now controlled the military, local government officials, and judicial tribunals, while officially anointing Jacobin Club members as agents of the French state.

The signature feature that had made the French Revolution so different from its American counterpart—the large percentage of state power held by plebeian (but armed) Parisians, whose mass uprisings frequently directed the course of government—would now meet its greatest challenge. No form of French government had succeeded in either channeling the *sans-culottes* into a civil political process or in curbing and punishing self-appointed vigilantes through the judicial system. The Reign of Terror, however, would not even try to direct or channel the masses; instead, the influence that had been held by Parisian newspapers, *sans-culottes,* and Commune officials over the monarchy, the Estates-General, Lafayette, and the Girondins was now to be quashed.

Thomas Paine responded to the Terror by withdrawing entirely from public life. He could not bear to make alliance with the Jacobins determined to guillotine his friends; neither could he publicly oppose them without becoming one more target. On June 21, 1793, delegates from Arras arrived in Paris to "declare in the name of the citizens of the Commune of that city, that Donoux, Personne, Maignan, Vailet, and Thomas Paine, deputies to the Convention from the Department of Pas-de-Calais, have lost their confidence," the first step in the revocation of Paine's legislative credentials. Two months later, however, Bertrand Barère, a onetime moderate of the Plain but now president of the Committee of Public Safety, contacted Paine for help in getting American flour to Paris, and in the drafting of a new constitution. Paine would use this entrée to negotiate a diplomatic issue that had been ignored by American minister Gouverneur Morris, and this small favor would turn out to be one more of Paine's dangerously impolitic acts.

Over the course of their years together in Paris, Thomas Paine was a far more important figure than Gouverneur Morris could ever be, a dreadful slight in the mind of the very grand Morris. One typical incident occurred when the French appointed a new minister to America, and Morris would have to write Washington that "I have not yet seen M. [Edmond] Genêt, but Mr. Paine is to introduce him to me." Soon after, at Genêt's insistence, the French government once again asked Washington to recall Morris, and Morris suspected that Paine was involved. In the great diplomatic tradition of indirect communication, Morris wrote President Washington's close friend, Robert Morris, "I suspected that Paine was intriguing against me, although he put on a face of attachment. Since that period I am confirmed in the idea, for he came to my house with Col. Oswald [an American journalist who irritated Washington], and being a little more drunk than usual, behaved extremely ill, and through his insolence I discovered clearly his vain ambition." To his cabinet superior and known Paine friend, Secretary of State Jefferson, Morris would remark that Paine's ambition was "so contemptible that I shall draw over the veil of oblivion."

On September 5 Paine sent Barère notes from his constitutional drafts, along with a letter that, among other things, attempted to help a group of American ships that had been detained over the war with England: "Mr. Jefferson . . . is an ardent defender of the interests of France. Gouverneur Morris, who is here now, is badly disposed towards you. I believe he has expressed the wish to be recalled. The reports which he will make on his arrival will not be to the advantage of France. This event necessitates the sending direct of commissioners from the Convention. Morris is not popular in America. He has set the Americans who are here against him, as also the Captains of that nation who have come from Bordeaux, by his negligence with regard to the affair they had to treat about with the Convention. Between us he told them: 'That they had thrown themselves into the lion's mouth, and it was for them to get out of it as best they could.' "

During this period Gouverneur Morris met frequently with the minister of foreign affairs, François Deforgues, about issues of diplomacy between France and its only ally, the United States. Morris described one meeting in an October 18, 1793, letter, not to his direct superior, Jefferson, but over his head once again, to Washington: "I told the minister that I had observed an overruling influence in their affairs which seemed to come from the other side of the channel, and at the same time had traced the intention to excite a seditious spirit in America; that it was impossible to be on a friendly footing with such persons, but that at present a different spirit seemed to prevail, etc. This declaration produced the effect I intended."

"Such persons" meant Thomas Paine; "the other side of the channel" referred to his being born in a country with which France was at war; and "the effect I intended" referred to a name included in André Amar's October 3 denunciation of seventy-three deputies for voting against the Convention's purge of traitors: "The Englishman Thomas Paine, called by the [Brissotins] to the honor of representing the French nation, dishonored himself by supporting the opinion of Brissot, and by promising us in his fable the dissatisfaction of the United States of America, our natural allies, which he did not blush to depict for us as full of veneration and gratitude for the tyrant of France."

Robespierre stopped Amar's move for additional arrests, saying that "the Convention must not multiply the guilty." Danton tried to encourage this moderate stance, urging his fellow legislators to vote in favor of clemency for the surviving members of the royal family and the Girondins. For this he was attacked for treasonous indulgence, or *modératisme,* by the most radical of the Jacobins, Jacques-René Hébert, whose faction demanded a never-ending white heat of revolt, war, and purgings. At the beginning of October, Danton had to tell a Girondin ally, "I shall not be able to save them," and broke down, sobbing.

On October 15 the Girondin mass trials began with a series of witnesses offering accusation, hearsay, and rumor to prove that the defendants had been a faction conspiring against the Revolution. This vague charge would mean that no individual need be proved personally and directly liable; anyone could be judged traitorously seditious, purely by association. On October 30, after a mere six days of testimony, every one of the accused was unanimously found guilty and sentenced to death.

Almost all of Paine's closest friends in Paris were now either imprisoned and scheduled for the guillotine, or desperate to flee the country. His dream of bringing Enlightenment ideals back across the Atlantic to launch a renaissance of European republican democracy was shattered. It is no surprise that the fifty-seven-year-old fell into another great trough of depression and took comfort in brandy; he admitted later to Clio Rickman, "Borne down by public and private affliction, [I was] driven to excesses in Paris." Along with a period in his final years when he would self-medicate and more with liquor, this behavior would tarnish Paine with a centuries-long reputation as a drunkard. The truth is that he enjoyed carousing (as did many of the men of his time), and took an occasional bender (especially when hit by a plague of depression), but there is no serious evidence of chronic alcoholism.

While helping everyone he could flee the Terror, Paine himself remained behind. Like so many others in history who become engulfed in an immense horror, he did not grasp his own vulnerability. The following year, he would write of this terrible period, and of the philosophical discoveries of a changed man:

> Memory, like a beauty that is always present to hear itself flattered, is flattered by everyone. But the absent and silent goddess, Forgetfulness, has no votaries, and is never thought of; yet we owe her much. She is the goddess of ease, though not of pleasure. When the mind is like a room hung with black, and every corner of it crowded with the most horrid images imagination can create, this kind, speechless goddess of a maid, Forgetfulness, is following us night and day with her opium wand, and gently touching first one and then another, benumbs them into rest, and at last glides them away with the silence of a departing shadow. It is thus the tortured mind is restored to the calm condition of ease, and fitted for happiness. . . .
>
> As to myself, I used to find some relief by walking alone in the garden after dark, and cursing with hearty good will the authors of that terrible system that had turned the character of the Revolution I had been proud to defend.
>
> I went but little to the Convention, and then only to make my appearance; because I found it impossible to join in their tremendous decrees, and useless and dangerous to oppose them. My having voted and spoke extensively, more so than any other member, against the execution of the King, had already fixed a mark upon me: neither dared any of my associates in the Convention to translate and speak in French for me, anything I might have dared to have written.
>
> Pen and ink were then of no use to me: no good could be done by writing, and no printer dared to print; and whatever I might have written for my private amusement, as anecdotes of the times, would have been continually exposed to be examined, and tortured into any meaning that the rage of party might fix upon it; and as to softer subjects, my heart was in distress at the fate of my friends, and my harp hung upon the weeping willows.

The Jacobins had by now succeeded in jailing, exiling, or executing their political foes, with the exception of Thomas Paine. That his pamphlets were still widely admired across France, and that he was a citizen of the new republic's sole ally, the United States, likely inspired Paine to consider himself invincible. There were, however, various men with urgent reasons for wanting him rendered quiet and invisible. The most determined and vengeful of these, as it would be discovered after both of their deaths, would turn out to be Paine's lifelong colleague, Gouverneur Morris.

9. The Religion of Science

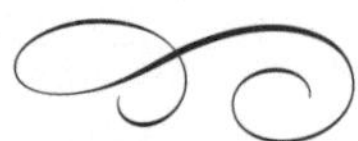

As Thomas Paine descended, a victim of the Terror, into the second great abyss of his life, he did not become paralyzed by brandy and despair, but instead wrote the last of his great works, the background of which he described to Samuel Adams:

> My friends were falling as fast as the guillotine could cut their heads off, and as I expected, every day, the same fate, I resolved to begin my work. I appeared to myself to be on my death bed, for death was on every side of me, and I had no time to lose. This accounts for my writing at the time I did, and so nicely did the time and intention meet, that I had not finished the first part of the work more than six hours before I was arrested and taken to prison. The people of France were running headlong into atheism, and I had the work translated in their own language, to stop them in that career, and fix them to the first article of every man's creed, who has any creed at all—believe in God.

This pamphlet for the greater good would all but destroy Paine's American reputation, and its drafting would offer a profound insight into the author's very character. If there is any moment in his life that reveals Paine as the Enlightenment's most adamantine evangelist, it is this. For exactly what kind of man, with dozens of friends either imprisoned or dead by guillotine or by their own hand, with his own life directly imperiled, and expecting at any moment the knock at the door and the presentation of the warrant—just what kind of human being would write a book under such conditions, and call it *The Age of Reason*?

Before the Terror, in fact, Paine had not seemed particularly interested in spiritual matters. He led a life congruent with his ideas of Roman virtue by relinquishing a fortune in copyrights, and he set a Christian (and Quaker) example by habitually turning the other cheek, one example being when he refused to press charges against an English Tory who had punched him in the face at a dinner party, an offense that, because Paine was a French legislator, would have meant immediate execution; later Paine even helped the man to escape France. Now, however, Paine's essays and correspondence would focus on God, morality, scriptural analysis, and the afterlife, almost to the exclusion of all other topics.

Beyond its worship of God-given human reason, the Enlightenment fostered a religion—deism—that combined Aristotle, Epicurus, Cicero, and Newton, and was widely embraced by such luminaries as Smith, Gibbon, Wollstonecraft, Franklin, Washington, Hancock, Jefferson, Madison, both Morrises, Hamilton, Montesquieu, Rousseau, Diderot, Lafayette, Robespierre, and Bonaparte. It was a faith with many fathers, the first being Lord Herbert of Cherbury, whose *De religione gentilium errorumque apud eos causis* (1645) argued that deism's key doctrines—the belief in a supreme being, the worship of that being through a life of virtue and goodness, the repenting of sin, and the hope for a benevolent afterlife—were the underpinnings of all worthy religions, and were so innate that they must have originated with the first thinking human creatures. The turning point in deist influence began with Newton, who uncharacteristically struck up a correspondence with theologian Richard Bentley to demonstrate how his theories of physics could in fact be taken as proofs for the existence of God. Bentley transformed Newton's letters into sermons and books, most popularly *The Folly and Unreasonableness of Atheism,* which inspired a round of like-minded titles that would become the deism library, including Matthew Tindal's *Christianity as Old as the Creation, or the Gospel a Republication of the Religion of Nature* (1730) and Lord Shaftesbury's *Letter Concerning Enthusiasm* (1798), which held that any religion of fanatics or hysterics was a perversion of humankind's innate spirituality, just as any faith that portrayed God as destructive, petty, jealous, childish, angry, or vengeful was blasphemy. Besides identifying the deist principles that underlay all faiths, deists suggested that Socrates, Jesus, the Buddha, and Mohammed were each attempting to return his society's corrupt religion back to its natural state—the state of deism.

Almost all of these concepts would be echoed in *The Age of Reason.* Many who never read *Age* would unjustly brand Paine an atheist, when in fact he relentlessly attacked godlessness in this essay. Like most deists, Paine believed that losing faith in God could extinguish human compassion, selflessness, morality, ethics, virtue, and grace, turning society into nothing but a gathering of beasts. Paine would make these beliefs as explicit as possible by framing them, after some prefatory remarks, at the very start of *Age:*

> I believe in one God, and no more; and I hope for happiness beyond this life.
>
> I believe [in] the equality of man, and I believe that religious duties consist in doing justice, loving mercy, and endeavoring to make our fellow-creatures happy.
>
> But, lest it should be supposed that I believe many other things in addition to these, I shall, in the progress of this work, declare the things I do not believe, and my reasons for not believing them.
>
> I do not believe in the creed professed by the Jewish church, by the Roman church, by the Greek church, by the Turkish church, by the Protestant church, nor by any church that I know of. My own mind is my own church.
>
> All national institutions of churches, whether Jewish, Christian, or Turkish, appear to me no other than human inventions set up to terrify and enslave mankind, and monopolize power and profit. . . .
>
> Every national church or religion has established itself by pretending some special mission from God, communicated to certain individuals. The Jews have their Moses; the Christians their Jesus Christ, their apostles and saints; and the Turks their Mahomet; as if the way to God was not open to every man alike.
>
> Each of those churches shows certain books, which they call revelation, or the Word of God. The Jews say that their Word of God was given by God to Moses face to face; the Christians say, that their Word of God came by divine inspiration; and the Turks say, that their Word of God (the Koran) was brought by an angel from heaven. Each of those churches accuses the other of unbelief; and, for my own part, I disbelieve them all.

While Paine was drafting *The Age of Reason* in the autumn of 1793, France was undergoing a state-sponsored process of dechristianization.

Robespierre would be historically identified with this movement as, draped in a Roman toga, flanked by choruses of old men and blind children and accompanied by Convention deputies waving sheaves of wheat in the Tuileries gardens, he served as lead celebrant at the Festival of the Supreme Being, setting fire to an effigy of atheism while announcing, "The true priest of the Supreme Being is Nature itself; its temple is the universe; its religion virtue; its festivals the joy of a great people assembled under its eyes to tie the sweet knot of universal fraternity." The extreme anti-Christian faction in France was in fact led by Danton's great enemy, Hébert, under whose fanaticism cathedrals and cemeteries were looted and vandalized; priests were slaughtered; forges were constructed at the Luxembourg, Tuileries, and Invalides gardens to melt church bells into artillery; the length of a week was changed from seven days to ten; the calendar was dated not from the death of Christ but from the founding of the Republic; and the new three-week months were renamed with such evocations of natural splendor as Germinal, Floreal, and Fructidor. Under Hébert, the Cathedral of Notre Dame became the Temple of Reason.

With *The Age of Reason* Paine offered a new faith for those French citizens who felt abandoned by these cataclysmic changes, giving them a spiritual ballast for when Christianity ultimately collapsed: "The circumstance that has now taken place in France, of the total abolition of the whole national order of priesthood, and of everything appertaining to compulsive systems of religion, and compulsive articles of faith, has not only precipitated my intention, but rendered a work of this kind exceedingly necessary, lest, in the general wreck of superstition, of false systems of government, and false theology, we lose sight of morality, of humanity, and of the theology that is true." Additionally, in the wake of Pitt's reign of terror, Paine was disheartened by England's cowed obedience to a corrupt judiciary, a Parliament of oligarchs, and a mad ruler; with *Age,* he hoped to promote the great benefits of deism to the masses of the world. Though Paine believed in an afterlife, he did not approve of organized religion's use of it to control its adherents, and if ordinary citizens could be convinced that ultimate justice and equality were not to be found in heaven and hell but in daily life, perhaps they would more fully support progressive efforts to make society and the state more just and more equal.

Today considered a "radical" work, *The Age of Reason* was in fact a fairly accurate reflection of contemporary mainstream Anglo-American religious discourse in its own time. The Christian faith had appeared in that era less given to worshipping the Prince of Peace than to engaging in near-constant warfare. Beyond the three hundred years of battles originating in religious disputes between England and Spain, Spain and Holland, and England and France, there were the English civil wars of Catholic kings and Protestant parliaments, of Gordon riots against Catholics, of Catholic Queen Mary burning Protestants at stakes, of Catholic Guy Fawkes trying to blow up the Westminster of Protestant James I. The children of Puritan Massachusetts learned to read with *The New England Primer,* which featured a frontispiece illustration of the pope being struck with darts, while English Protestants so often referred to the Roman Catholic Church as "the Scarlet Whore of Babylon" that William Cobbett remembered, "I firmly believed when I was a boy, that the Pope was a prodigious woman, dressed in a dreadful robe, which had been made red by being dipped in the blood of Protestants." John Locke, surrounded by England's religious tumult, would come to believe that "truly the Christian religion is the worst of all religions, and ought neither to be embraced by any particular person, nor tolerated by any commonwealth."

Early American settlers wanted to remove their country as far as possible from Europe's religious wars. Rhode Island founder and clergyman Roger Williams, banished from the Calvinist Bible Commonwealth, wrote in 1643 that there needed to be "a wall of separation between the garden of the church and the wilderness of the world," and by "world" he meant government. James Madison explained why the great majority of devout Americans agreed with Williams on the need for that wall: "The people feared one sect might obtain a pre-eminence, or two combine together, and establish a religion to which they would compel others to conform." In the first years of the American Republic, five states categorically refused clergymen the right to run for elective office.

John Adams was the most openly Christian of the first American presidents; he also was certain that, without the restraint of civil law, Puritan fundamentalists would unreservedly "whip and crop, and pillory and roast," while privately noting that the Bible was full of "whole cartloads of trumpery." As a young man, he had chosen to become a lawyer instead of a clergyman because lawyers had a history of "noble and gallant achievements," while ministers were tainted with the "pretended sanctity of some absolute dunces." As president, Adams signed the 1797 Treaty of Peace and Friendship between the United States of America and the Bey and Subjects of Tripoli, or Barbary, unanimously ratified by the Senate after negotiations by Paine's friend Joel Barlow, which included the statement "As the government of the United States of America is not in any sense founded on the Christian religion . . . it is declared by the parties that no pretext arising from religious opinions shall ever produce an interruption of the harmony existing between the two countries."

With the exception of Adams, the first five American presidents took great care never to refer publicly to a specific deity or to any one religion in particular. The most politically astute of that generation—Franklin, Washington, and Jefferson—avoided discussing religion, either publicly or in correspondence, to a remarkable extent. Washington almost never even used the word "God," preferring "Almighty Being" or "Invisible Hand"; as Joseph Ellis described his faith: "The historical evidence suggests that Washington did not think much about heaven or angels: the only place he knew his body was going was into the ground, and as for his soul, its ultimate location was unknowable. He died as a Roman stoic rather than a Christian saint." When Alexander Hamilton was asked why the U.S. Constitution made no mention of God, he said the country did not require "foreign aid"; when his mother insisted on a serious reply, he explained, "We forgot." James Madison would ask, meanwhile, "During almost fifteen centuries has the legal establishment of Christianity been on trial. What have been its fruits? More or less in all places, pride and indolence in the clergy, ignorance and servility in the laity, in both, superstition, bigotry, and persecution. . . . Religious bondage shackles and debilitates the mind and unfits it for every noble enterprise."

Besides their perception of Christianity as having a tendency to inspire prejudice and violence in its most vigorous believers, its historical use as a tool for despots and corrupt priests to enslave the lower classes, and the fact that they considered the religion barbaric, vulgar, and intolerant, many eighteenth-century moderns also held Christians accountable for helping to destroy the greatest civilization of human history: Rome. Edward Gibbon's 1776 *Decline and Fall of the Roman Empire* would conclude that Christianity was "vile . . . debased . . . servile and pusillanimous," and he would become so disgusted from his research on the early years of the Christian church that, when on vacation in France, as his party approached Chartres Cathedral, Gibbon noted, "Pausing only to dart a look of contempt at the stately pile of superstition, we passed on." At the same time that the moderns considered the church reprehensible, however, they worried that if children were not Sunday schooled in notions of good and evil, of striving for the rewards of heaven and fearing the punishments of hell, they would become as immoral as apes. For this and many other reasons, a number of deists did not believe in sharing their faith with the middle and lower classes—who made up the principal readership of Thomas Paine. The majority of critics of *The Age of Reason* in its own time attacked it not for its content but for appealing to a mass audience—the same criticism that had been leveled by the English government against *Rights of Man.*

Like many of his fellow eighteenth-century critics of Christianity, Thomas Paine praised the teachings of Jesus. While offering scathing proofs that the Bible was not the word of God but a "history of wickedness that has served to corrupt and brutalize mankind" and that effectively supported the rich and the powerful over the poor and the dispossessed, *The Age of Reason* considered Christ "a virtuous and amiable man. The morality that he preached and practiced was of the most benevolent kind." Joseph Priestley arrived at similar conclusions in *Socrates and Jesus Compared,* which inspired Thomas Jefferson to think that the teachings of Christ had been corrupted over the centuries, and to create his own four-language version of the New Testament, with all the supernatural elements removed: *The Life and Morals of Jesus of Nazareth Extracted Textually from the Gospels in Greek, Latin, French and English.*

Instead of being based on faith in scripture, deism rose from mankind's manifold awe in the face of the universe, the ultimate expression of the era's passion for natural philosophy. Since nature is such a cornucopia of gifts, logic insists that the God who made it must be beneficent, though not necessarily concerned with the day-to-day lives of human beings, and so cannot be prayed to. The God of the deists can best be worshipped through studying his work, and through treating other living creatures with the same benevolence as shown by the life-giving natural world. Deism could be said to be the ultimate creation of the pragmatic utopians, a religion based on science:

> The word of God is the creation we behold: And it is in this word, which no human invention can counterfeit or alter, that God speaketh universally to man. . . . It cannot be forged; it cannot be counterfeited; it cannot be lost; it cannot be altered; it cannot be suppressed.

> It does not depend upon the will of man whether it shall be published or not; it publishes itself from one end of the earth to the other. It preaches to all nations and to all worlds; and this word of God reveals to man all that is necessary for man to know of God.
>
> Do we want to contemplate his power? We see it in the immensity of the creation. Do we want to contemplate his wisdom? We see it in the unchangeable order by which the incomprehensible Whole is governed. Do we want to contemplate his munificence? We see it in the abundance with which he fills the earth. Do we want to contemplate his mercy? We see it in his not withholding that abundance even from the unthankful. In fine, do we want to know what God is? Search not the book called the scripture, which any human hand might make, but the scripture called the Creation.
>
> The only idea man can affix to the name of God, is that of a first cause, the cause of all things. And, incomprehensibly difficult as it is for a man to conceive what a first cause is, he arrives at the belief of it, from the tenfold greater difficulty of disbelieving it. It is difficult beyond description to conceive that space can have no end; but it is more difficult to conceive an end. It is difficult beyond the power of man to conceive an eternal duration of what we call time; but it is more impossible to conceive a time when there shall be no time.

The Age of Reason first appeared in both France and England in 1794, in printings arranged through Paine's friend Joel Barlow and his French translator, François Xavier Lanthenas. Once again, its sales exceeded those of Paine's previous works. In the United States alone seventeen editions would be printed, and the book was especially popular at American colleges, even among divinity students. *Age* caused such a ruckus at Harvard that the college felt obliged to give every student a free copy of Bishop Watson's critique, *Apology for the Bible,* to counter its appeal.

The Age of Reason was an immense sensation in England; within four years, more than thirty replies were published. Some of the first and most urgent came from Unitarian theologians, and a telling sign of how mainstream *Reason*'s ideology was at the time was the fact that these ministers considered Paine's work a form of plagiarism. Notably in Gilbert Wakefield's 1794 *An Examination of The Age of Reason* and Joseph Priestley's 1795 *An Answer to Mr. Paine's Age of Reason, being a Continuation of Letters to the Philosophers and Politicians of France, on the Subject of Religion; and of the Letters to a Philosophical Unbeliever,* Paine was attacked for his poor biblical scholarship (Wakefield commenting that he was "not acquainted with such a compound of vanity and ignorance as Thomas Paine in all the records of literature"); for his lack of understanding of the more forward-thinking Christian philosophers; for offering nothing but variants on ideas they had been writing about and discussing for decades; for the foolishness of deism's nature-as-beneficent-God's-handiwork theodicy (their prime example being the "natural" Lisbon earthquake of 1755, which killed more than one hundred thousand); and for the fact that deism, in the end, fails to supplant what religion has to offer, as it does not address such crucial human needs as justice, succor, ritual, and moral uplift.

The more advanced mainstream church leaders echoed these complaints, most notably the bishop of Llandaff, Richard Watson, as did the most popular of all British essayists following in Paine's wake, Hannah More. More's *Cheap Repository Tracts* had refuted *Rights of Man* by describing the indecency of radicalism, and the need for politics to be practiced solely by an educated few. Now, under the pseudonym "Will Chip, Carpenter, in Somersetshire," and for a cover price of a halfpenny, More would attack *The Age of Reason* by insisting that, though the Bible may be filled with astonishments and miracles, that did not mean it was not true. She would sell millions of copies in bulk to English churches.

At the same time, it was not enough for Whitehall that Paine the man had been driven from the United Kingdom; his work would have to be wholly expunged as well. By the end of 1796 the British government declared *Age* blasphemous and confiscated every copy its book police could uncover. As late as 1811 Daniel Eaton was arrested and sentenced to eighteen months' incarceration for selling a Paine *Age* sequel, *Examination of the Prophecies,* while Richard Carlile was imprisoned for three years and fined fifteen hundred pounds for publishing an 1819 edition of *Age;* the following year, his wife Mary Ann was sentenced to two years of prison for continuing her husband's business. In absentia the Carliles tried to evade the law's restrictions on bookselling with an "invisible shopman," a vending machine that dispensed illicit writings seemingly without the use of human agency. The authorities confiscated it, and over the three years of Carlile's imprisonment, 150 Britons would be arrested for selling printed contraband. The government was so thorough in suppressing Paine, in fact, that the Thetford

Library would not carry his work until 1908. In the underground British market, however, *Age* sold briskly for many years.

In the United States *The Age of Reason* would be another immense Paine success for publisher Benjamin Franklin Bache, selling 100,000 copies in 1797 alone. And as it had in Britain, it received withering criticism. Initially, Parson Weems (the future hagiographer of George Washington) supported the book, as long as the rejoinder from his "Immortal Mentor" Richard Watson was included as an addendum, and even worked to distribute the pamphlet for publisher Matthew Carey in Virginia. Weems then changed his mind (perhaps in reaction to Paine's rancorous *Age of Reason, Part II*), saying in 1800 that the author has "no other church but the alehouse, and [his] palsied legs can scarce bear him to that sink of vomiting and filth."

A number of Paine's revolutionary Christian brothers, including Samuel Adams, Benjamin Rush, John Dickinson, Patrick Henry, and John Jay, were repulsed by what they had heard of *The Age of Reason*. Benjamin Rush wrote in 1800 to Thomas Jefferson that "I have always considered Christianity as the *strong ground* of republicanism. . . . It is only necessary for republicanism to ally itself to the Christian religion to overturn all the corrupted political and religious institutions in the world." *Age* would end his friendship with Paine. John Adams said, "The Christian religion is, above all the religions that ever prevailed or existed in ancient or modern times, the religion of wisdom, virtue, equity and humanity, let the Blackguard Paine say what he will." As was true of many other of its critics, however, it does not seem likely that Adams read *The Age of Reason,* for, though he referred to himself as a "church going animal," his Unitarian beliefs were not all that different from Paine's deism, so much so that it became commonplace for some Unitarian ministers to use *The Age of Reason,* stripped of its harsher criticisms and strident language, as a sermon.

The criticism of *Reason* that deeply hurt Paine came from the eighty-year-old Samuel Adams, with whom Paine had shared so much during their years waging revolution and common cause. Their letters would be published in Philadelphia's *National Intelligencer,* with Paine's serving as the introduction to *The Age of Reason* that he should have written originally, describing religion's tribal tendency to insist that each faith is the sole, infallible answer, rendering all else infidel, unclean, and unsaved, with contempt, prejudice, bigotry, and persecution immediately to follow. Unfortunately, their dialogue did not extend beyond Adams's original letter and Paine's response:

SIR:

I have frequently with pleasure reflected on your services to my native and your adopted country. Your "Common Sense" and your "Crisis" unquestionably awakened the public mind, and led the people loudly to call for a Declaration of our national Independence. I therefore esteemed you as a warm friend to the liberty and lasting welfare of the human race. But when I heard that you had turned your mind to a defence of infidelity, I felt myself much astonished and more grieved that you had attempted a measure so injurious to the feelings and so repugnant to the true interest of so great a part of the citizens of the United States. . . . Do you think that your pen, or the pen of any other man, can unchristianize the mass of our citizens, or have you hopes of converting a few of them to assist you in so bad a cause?

SAMUEL ADAMS

MY DEAR AND VENERABLE FRIEND SAMUEL ADAMS:

I received with great pleasure your friendly and affectionate letter of November 30, and I thank you also for the frankness of it. Between men in pursuit of truth, and whose object is the happiness of man both here and hereafter, there ought to be no reserve. Even error has a claim to indulgence, if not to respect, when it is believed to be truth. . . .

With respect to "The Age of Reason," which you so much condemn, and that I believe without having read it, for you say only that you "heard" of it, I will inform you of a circumstance, because you cannot know it by other means. . . .

I endangered my own life, in the first place by opposing in the Convention the execution of the king, and by laboring to shew they were trying the monarchy and not the man, and that the crimes imputed to him were the crimes of the monarchical system; and I endangered it a second time by opposing atheism; and yet some of your priests, for I do not believe that all are perverse, cry out, in the

> war-whoop of monarchical priestcraft, What an Infidel, what a wicked Man, is Thomas Paine! They might as well add, for he believes in God and is against shedding blood. . . .
>
> Our relation to each other in this world is as men, and the man who is a friend to man and to his rights, let his religious opinions be what they may, is a good citizen, to whom I can give, as I ought to do, and as every other ought, the right hand of fellowship, and to none with more hearty goodwill, my dear friend, than to you.

If it is clear that the politics of Thomas Paine live on to present times, it is just as commonly thought that his faith has become nothing but an artifact of history. Though few today call themselves deists, in fact the religion of science has continued, most visibly with scientists themselves, those men and women whose knowledge of the latest discoveries in physics, cosmology, or biology directly augments their faith in God. Albert Einstein described this modern deism in an essay that was nothing less than a point-by-point echo of *The Age of Reason:*

> There is a third stage of religious experience which belongs to all of them, even though it is rarely found in a pure form: I shall call it cosmic religious feeling. It is very difficult to elucidate this feeling to anyone who is entirely without it, especially as there is no anthropomorphic conception of God corresponding to it. The individual feels the futility of human desires and aims and the sublimity and marvelous order which reveal themselves both in nature and in the world of thought. . . .
>
> The religious geniuses of all ages have been distinguished by this kind of religious feeling, which knows no dogma and no God conceived in man's image; so that there can be no church whose central teachings are based on it. Hence it is precisely among the heretics of every age that we find men who were filled with this highest kind of religious feeling and were in many cases regarded by their contemporaries as atheists, sometimes also as saints. Looked at in this light, men like Democritus, Francis of Assisi, and Spinoza are closely akin to one another. How can cosmic religious feeling be communicated from one person to another, if it can give rise to no definite notion of a God and no theology? In my view, it is the most important

function of art and science to awaken this feeling and keep it alive in those who are receptive to it. We thus arrive at a conception of the relation of science to religion very different from the usual one. . . . A contemporary has said, not unjustly, that in this materialistic age of ours the serious scientific workers are the only profoundly religious people.

10. The Perfidious Mr. Morris

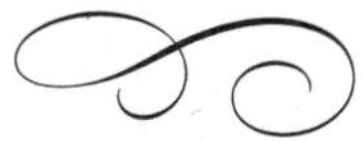

On October 16, 1793, a year before *The Age of Reason* appeared, a wholly unremarkable thirty-seven-year-old woman, dramatically aged before her time, was forced to grasp her hands behind her back so that her wrists could be bound together. Her collar was then torn in half, to fully expose the base of her neck. Her hair, thin, wispy, and the color of ash, was chopped tight, with the executioner's son saving the cuttings to sell later that afternoon. Her complexion, once the envy of a continent, was now sallow and wan. In a white bonnet, black stockings, and red high-heeled shoes, the widow Capet, Marie Antoinette, was then led to Sanson's platform and guillotined. On the thirty-first, sixty Girondin deputies of the French National Convention, convicted of treason before the Revolutionary Tribunal, followed her passage across the Salle des Perdus (Room of the Lost) on their way to the tumbrels. On November 7 Philippe Egalité, duc d'Orléans, joined them, and on the eighth, Mme. Roland arrived at the Place de la Révolution to bow to the statue of Liberty and say, *"O Liberté, que de crimes on commet en ton nom!"* ("O Liberty, what crimes are committed in your name!")

On Christmas Day in the Manège, Convention president Barère criticized Robespierre for forgetting to mention in his Committee of Public Safety report that there was a clear danger to the nation posed by aliens working for the state. Bourdon de l'Oise echoed this sentiment, complaining, "They have boasted of the patriotism of Thomas Paine. *(Ridiculous!)* Since the Brissotins disappeared from the bosom of this Convention he has not set foot in it. And I know that he has intrigued with a former agent of the bureau of Foreign Affairs." The legislature accordingly passed a law decreeing the "exclusion of foreigners from every public function during the war," which, following Marat's death, meant the stripping of immunity from two remaining deputies. These revoked credentials led to an immediate order issued by the Committee of General Surety and Surveillance:

> On the 7th Nivose [December 27] of the 2d year of the French Republic, one and indivisible.
>
> TO THE DEPUTIES:
>
> The Committee resolves, that the persons named Thomas Paine and Anacharsis Clootz, formerly Deputies to the National Convention, be arrested and imprisoned, as a measure of General Surety; that an examination be made of their papers, and those found suspicious put under seal and brought to the Committee of General Surety.
>
> Citizens Jean Baptiste Martin and Lamy, bearers of the present decree, are empowered to execute it—for which they ask the help of the civil authorities and, if need be, of the army.

Sometime between three and four in the morning of December 28, 1793, Paine was awakened by five policemen and two CGS agents pounding at the door of his room at the Hôtel de Philadelphie. They ransacked his quarters looking for suspicious documents and finally discovered the manuscript of *The Age of Reason*. Reading it briskly, one CSG agent said to the author, "It is an interesting work; it will do much good." The other informed the accused that his private papers needed to be inspected. Paine led the agents to Joel Barlow's so he could give his friend *Age* for safekeeping and publication; admitting the ruse, he was taken to the St. Denis mansion for his documents to be collected. He was then incarcerated at the Luxembourg prison.

Originally built between 1615 and 1627 as a Florentine-styled palais for Louis XIII's mother, Marie de Médicis, the Luxembourg was, of the dozen prisons used during the Revolution, by far the least onerous, especially when compared to the medieval horrors of the Conciergerie or the grossly overcrowded Marie and Force. Besides its decent construction, it had as its superintendent a M. Benoît, who became famous for his conscientious and humane treatment of prisoners, the majority of whom were not criminals but English expatriates caught during the war, various other foreigners in the wrong place at the wrong time, and better-regarded political victims of the Terror.

Paine's eight-by-ten cell was on the ground floor, with brick pavement and a boarded-over window, a straw-stuffed mattress, a chair, and a box for personal items. All those incarcerated in French prisons at this time were required to clean their cells and the public areas, and to pay for their food and anything else they might want, such as candles.

On January 20 Joel Barlow assembled eighteen Americans to petition the Committee of General Surety for Paine's release. Two U.S. citizens previously jailed by the French had been freed after receiving such petitions a few months before, and Barlow was certain they would prevail once again. Instead, the petition was rejected, as National Convention president Marc Vadier explained: "Thomas Payne is a native of England; this is undoubtedly enough to apply to him the measures of security prescribed by the revolutionary laws. It may be added, citizens, that if Thomas Payne has been the apostle of liberty, if he has powerfully co-operated with the American Revolution, his genius has not understood that which has regenerated France; he has regarded the system only in accordance with the illusions with which the false friends of our revolution have invested it. You must with us deplore an error little reconcilable with the principles admired in the justly esteemed works of this republican author."

At the same time that Barlow directly approached the legislature, Paine asked American minister Morris to intervene. Unaware that Jefferson had retired from his cabinet post and returned to Monticello, Morris wrote him that "lest I should forget it, I must mention that Thomas Paine is in prison, where he amuses himself with publishing a pamphlet against Jesus Christ. I do not recollect whether I mentioned to you that he would have been executed along with the rest of the Brissotins if the [Robespierristes] had not viewed him with contempt. I incline to think that if he is quiet in prison he may have the good luck to be forgotten, whereas, should he be brought much into notice, the long suspended axe might fall on him. I believe he thinks that I ought to claim him as an American citizen; but considering his birth, his naturalization in this country, and the place he filled, I doubt much the right, and I am sure that the claim would be, for the present at least, inexpedient and ineffectual."

It is true that Paine asked Morris to claim him as an American citizen; it is untrue, as Morris would assert to both Washington and Jefferson, that

Morris made much effort to comply with that request, as is clear in his correspondence with Foreign Minister Deforgues of February 14 and 19:

> SIR,
>
> Thomas Paine has just applied to me to claim him as a Citizen of the United States. These (I believe) are the facts which relate to him. He was born in England. Having become a citizen of the United States, he acquired great celebrity there through his revolutionary writings. In consequence he was adopted as [a] French citizen, and then elected [a] member of the Convention. His behaviour since that epoch is out of my jurisdiction. I am ignorant of the reason for his present detention in the Luxembourg prison, but I beg you, Sir, if there be reasons which prevent his liberation, and which are unknown to me, be so good as to inform me of them, so that I may communicate them to the Government of the United States.
>
> I have the honour to be, Sir, Your very humble servant,
>
> Gouv. MORRIS.

Deforgues's reply:

> In your letter of the 26th of last month you reclaim the liberty of Thomas Payne as an American citizen. Born in England, this ex-deputy has become successively an American and a French citizen. In accepting this last title, and in occupying a place in the Legislative Corps, he submitted himself to the laws of the Republic, and has *de fait* renounced the protection which the right of the people and treaties concluded with the United States could have assured him.
>
> I am ignorant of the motives of his detention, but I must presume they are well founded. I shall nevertheless submit the demand you have addressed me to the Committee of Public Safety, and I shall lose no time in letting you know its decision.

This exchange seems utterly reasonable; but in fact, given that Paine was arrested on the charge of being a foreigner, he could not at the same time be considered a French citizen, as Morris and Foreign Minister Deforgues agreed to agree. Learning of Deforgues's rejection, Paine was forced to beg Morris to save him:

> I received your letter enclosing a copy of a letter from the Minister of Foreign Affairs. You must not leave me in the situation in which this letter places me. You know I do not deserve it, and you see the unpleasant situation in which I am thrown. I have made an essay in answer to the Minister's letter, which I wish you to make ground of a reply to him. They have nothing against me—except that they do not choose I should be in a state of freedom to write my mind freely upon things I have seen. Though you and I are not on terms of the best harmony, I apply to you as the Minister of America, and you may add to that service whatever you think my integrity deserves. At any rate I expect you to make Congress acquainted with my situation, and to send to them copies of the letters that have passed on the subject. A reply to the Minister's letter is absolutely necessary, were it only to continue the reclamation. Otherwise your silence will be a sort of consent to his observations.

Immediately after this letter was received, the French government closed off all communication between Luxembourg inmates and the outside world "by an order of the police," as Paine would tell Washington. "I neither saw, nor heard from, anybody for six months." Morris wrote Jefferson on March 6:

> Mr. Paine wrote me a note desiring I would claim him as an American, which I accordingly did, though contrary to my judgment, for reasons mentioned in my last. The Minister's letter to me of the 1st Ventose, of which I enclose a copy [note that Morris does not include his original], contains the answer to my reclamation. I sent a copy to Mr. Paine, who prepared a long answer, and sent it to me by an Englishman, whom I did not know. I told him, as Mr. Paine's friend, that my present opinion was similar to that of the Minister, but I might, perhaps, see occasion to change it, and in that case, if Mr. Paine wished it, I would go on with the claim, but that it would be well for him to consider the result; that, if the government meant to release him, they had already a sufficient ground; but if not, I could only push them to bring on his trial for the crimes imputed to him; seeing that whether he be considered as a Frenchman, or as an American, he must be amenable to the tribunals of France for his conduct while he was a Frenchman, and he may see in the fate of the

> Brissotins, that to which he is exposed. I have heard no more of the affair since; but it is not impossible that he may force on a decision, which, as far as I can judge, would be fatal to him: for in the best of times he had a larger share of every other sense than common sense, and lately the intemperate use of ardent spirits has, I am told, considerably impaired the small stock he originally possessed.

These dispatches would be handled eventually by the new secretary of state, Edmund Randolph, who wrote Washington at Mount Vernon on June 25 a redaction, including "that he has demanded Paine as an American citizen, but that the Minister holds him to be amenable to the French laws." To the American government, it appeared that Morris had done everything he should on Thomas Paine's behalf.

Over the years, historians have offered various theories as to Morris's duplicity. Paine himself at first thought his imprisonment was the work of Robespierre, writing that "among the papers of Robespierre that were examined and reported upon to the Convention by a Committee of Deputies, is a note in the handwriting of Robespierre, in the following words: *'Demander que Thomas Paine soit décréte d'accusation, pour l'intérêt de l'Amérique autant que de la France'* ['Demand that Thomas Paine be decreed of accusation, for the interests of America, as well as of France']. From what cause it was that the intention was not put in execution, I know not." As Robespierre had said that "America has not clearly pronounced her opinion concerning the French Revolution," he may have wanted to prevent Paine's possible negative influence on France's only ally, but there is nothing in the documentary record to show that Robespierre had any personal animosity toward him beyond the *"demander"* note (and it has been suggested that this might have been Robespierre's comment on someone else's demand).

Paine would later come to believe that there had been collusion, or at least an intersection of interests, between Morris and the Committee of Public Safety, telling James Monroe that "however discordant the late American Minister Gouverneur Morris and the late French Committee of Public Safety were, it suited the purposes of both that I should be continued in arrestation. The former wished to prevent my return to America, that I should not expose his misconduct; and the latter lest I should publish to the world the history of its wickedness."

There is a third motive to consider. Morris may have been acting in consideration of Washington's great aim at this time, the negotiations of the Treaty of Amity, Commerce and Navigation, between His Britannic Majesty and the United States of America, by their President, more commonly known in honor of its American representative as the Jay Treaty. Washington was intent on removing English forts from the American northwest frontier, reopening U.S. trade to the British West Indies, ensuring peace with the belligerent mother country, and ending the British seizures of American ships and impressment of American sailors. John Jay had been able to secure a temporary peace, an abandonment of the forts, and an opening of West Indies harbors to American ships below seventy tons.

Though the treaty is considered favorably today by historians, more than a few Americans at the time, including Jefferson and Paine, believed Jay's capitulation was nothing less than a return to British vassal status, as if the American Revolution had never been won. When Benjamin Franklin Bache printed the treaty's terms in his *Aurora* (considered the first press scoop in American history), New Yorkers and Bostonians rioted, while mobs in Philadelphia labeled Jay a traitor and burned his effigy. Jefferson was so enraged that he wrote an April 1796 letter to Philip Mazzei that complained, "In place of that noble love of liberty & republican government which carried us triumphantly thro' the war, an Anglican monarchical & aristocratical party has sprung up whose avowed object is to draw over us the substance, as they already have the forms, of the British government. . . . It would give you a fever were I to name to you the apostates who have gone over to these heresies, men who were Samsons in the field and Solomons in the council, but who have had their head shaved by the harlot England." This letter was printed in the January 25, 1797, *Moniteur*, and it was widely understood that "Samson" was George Washington; the incident terminated Jefferson's and Washington's personal and professional relationship. The Jay Treaty also meant that the military and commercial agreements negotiated between Franklin and Vergennes that had helped win the American Revolution were now wholly abrogated. As Gouverneur Morris regularly worked overseas for Washington on a confidential basis, including opening preliminary discussions with British officials long before Jay's arrival, it is plausible that keeping the American most hated by the Pitt government quietly sidelined was politically expedient.

Morris had another reason not to intervene in the matter of Paine's imprisonment, as the Washington administration was doing all it could to maintain American neutrality in European affairs. The U.S. president had taken no action on behalf of Mme. Lafayette, the wife of one of Washington's dearest friends, or even extended himself over the case of Lafayette's imprisonment in Austria. Additionally, if Morris believed jail a form of moral justice in the case of Lafayette, then he clearly would have appreciated Paine's confinement, as punishment for his impudence and as justice for his championing of revolution. Finally, Morris may have been sincere in his explanation that a voluble Paine, kept out of the way and silent, would escape the worst of the Terror.

The final answer can never be known, for even in his otherwise explicit diary, Gouverneur Morris would never confess or explain the worst of his behavior.

If the French had no valid reason for jailing Thomas Paine, his plight was hardly exceptional. Joining him at the Luxembourg was the same General O'Hara who had tried to insult Washington at Yorktown by surrendering the sword of Cornwallis to French commander Rochambeau. Paine gave him two hundred pounds to be able to return home to England, while Rochambeau himself was being held at the Conciergerie and would barely survive the Terror. Another Luxembourg inmate was the very man who had helped canonize Jean-Paul Marat, the great painter Jacques-Louis David, who sketched his famous *Sabine Women* while there. Paine's fellow foreign deputy Anacharsis Clootz, arrested on the same warrant, did not last long in prison, as Robespierre considered him an unsavory lunatic. He rode to the guillotine on March 24, 1794, alongside the militant anti-Christian Jacques-René Hébert and his *hébertistes,* accused by Robespierre of counterrevolutionary atheism. Foreign Minister Deforgues, whose connivance with Gouverneur Morris kept Paine jailed, spent a few days at the Luxembourg before he was executed on April 2.

As prepared by Saint-Just and edited by Robespierre, Danton's arrest warrant indicted him for trying to rescue Brissot from revolutionary justice, plotting to restore monarchy with the duc d'Orléans, and laughing at the word "virtue." At the Luxembourg, Danton maintained this relentless bonhomie, telling Paine, "That which you did for the happiness and liberty of your country, I tried in vain to do for mine. I have been less fortunate, but not less innocent. They will send me to the scaffold; very well, my friends,

I shall go gaily." Turning to the crowd of watching prisoners, he continued: "I hoped soon to have got you all out of this; but here I am myself; and one sees not where it will end." Accompanied in the stream of tumbrels by Cordelier publisher Camille Desmoulins, as well as by the very man who had originally invited Paine to join the French government so long before—Marie de Séchelles, now convicted of being an aristocrat—Danton was guillotined on April 5.

Many Luxembourg detainees remembered Paine's warm companionship over the course of their last days, one writing that he "found a refuge from evil in the charms of his society." Paine himself bitterly described this period: "I was one of the nine members that composed the first Committee of Constitution. Six of them have been destroyed. Sieyès and myself have survived—he by bending with the times, and I by not bending. The other survivor [Barère] joined Robespierre; he was seized and imprisoned in his turn, and sentenced to transportation. He has since apologized to me for having signed the warrant, by saying he felt himself in danger and was obliged to do it."

By June, eighty thousand French citizens had been incarcerated. After a young girl named Cécile Renault was found carrying a pair of knives while attempting to meet Robespierre to learn "what a tyrant looks like," the Convention on June 10 passed the Law of the 22nd Prairial, granting the *tribunal criminel-révolutionnaire* absolute power, disallowing defense lawyers or witnesses, and giving its judges one of two verdicts: acquittal, or death. For the next forty-seven days, nearly 30 Frenchmen were guillotined every twenty-four hours, with 161 executed in one night of frenzy. In the six weeks from June 10 to July 27, the French government executed 1,376 people, and Paine knew his own death could come at any moment, as he wrote George Washington:

> The state of things in the prisons was a continued scene of horror. No man could count upon life for 24 hours. To such a pitch of rage and suspicion were Robespierre and his committee arrived, that it seemed as if they feared to leave a man living. Scarcely a night passed in which ten, twenty, thirty, forty, fifty or more were not taken out of the prison, carried before a pretended tribunal in the morning and guillotined before night. . . . Many a man whom I have passed an hour with in conversation I have seen marching to

> his destruction the next hour, or heard of it the next morning; for what rendered the scene more horrible was that they were generally taken away at midnight, so that every man went to bed with the apprehension of never seeing his friends or the world again.

Despite its pleasant architecture, the Luxembourg still offered the same medical threat as any prison, sailing ship, or other eighteenth-century confined space, and just as had happened on his passage to America, Paine became deathly ill with typhus. In June 1794, he was moved to a larger cell with three Belgians—Charles Bastini and Michael Robyns of Louvain, and Joseph Vanhuele of Bruges—who cared for him when his temperature spiked for months on end. At his worst, Paine could not remain conscious for more than a few minutes at a time: "My illness rendered me incapable of knowing anything that passed either in the prison or elsewhere; and my comrades also made it a point all the time that my recovery continued doubtful not to inform me of anything that was passing."

On July 24 Public Prosecutor Antoine-Quentin Fouquier-Tinville presented to the governing committees the daily lists of the accused, the recently executed, and those scheduled to be executed on the following day. Paine's name appeared on this final list. That morning a prison employee walked through the halls of the Luxembourg, chalking a mark on the door of each of the condemned. On Paine's, he scrawled a "4" to indicate that all four inside were to be guillotined. The Belgians, however, had gotten permission to leave the door open to let in some air to relieve Paine's suffering and fevers. The trusty dutifully marked the inside frame of the door.

That night his cellmates told a guard that Paine had recovered, and permission was granted to close the door. At 11 p.m. the death squad cart rolled through, already filled with chained prisoners. The "4," however, was now hidden, and the four lives were temporarily spared. Paine noted the irony of this miracle: "A violent fever which had nearly terminated my existence was, I believe, the circumstance that preserved it. I was not in a condition to be removed, or to know of what was passing, or of what had passed, for more than a month. It makes a blank in my remembrance of life."

The bureaucratic misstep—perhaps engineered by someone highly placed, or a bribe in the right hands—that saved Paine and his cellmates took place just as Robespierre and Saint-Just were being overwhelmed by political hubris. Although the crises that had led to the cancellation of the French constitution and given rise to the totalitarian committees had passed—the army had recently won a significant victory against the Austrians, the civil tumult in the Vendée had been brought under control, the Parisian newspapers were cowed, and the *sans-culottes* obedient—Robespierre on July 26 announced that he had uncovered another group plotting "a conspiracy against liberty," whose names he would not release. Between deputies who had grown weary of the excesses of the Terror and those who feared their names might be on this new list, he and Saint-Just were now outnumbered, and warrants were issued for their own arrests. Beginning on July 28, Robespierre and 108 of his allies were guillotined. The *machine* was then destroyed, and the Terror was over.

Paine justifiably thought that this state upheaval would lead to his release, yet he remained incarcerated. On August 5 and 6 he wrote to the deputies of the Convention and the members of the Committee of Public Safety, asking to be judged and freed. He received no answer. Two weeks later, he found reason for hope when the French government for the third time asked that Gouverneur Morris be recalled, and Washington finally agreed. When Morris's replacement, Virginia senator James Monroe, arrived and presented his documents, however, he was not officially recognized at first, for Morris's allies on the Committee of Public Safety delayed rescinding the former's credentials (and diplomatic immunity) until he was fully prepared to depart France.

Paine remembered, "As soon as I was able to write a note legible enough to be read, I found a way to convey one to [Monroe] by means of the man who lighted the lamps in the prison, and whose unabated friendship to me, from whom he never received any service, and with difficulty accepted any recompense, puts the character of Mr. Washington to shame." This smuggled note to the new American minister pleaded:

> I have now no expectation of delivery but by your means—Morris has been my inveterate enemy, and I think he has permitted something of the national character of America to suffer by quietly letting a citizen of that country remain almost eight months in prison, without making every official exertion to procure him justice. . . . [The United States] has had the services of my best days, she has my allegiance, she receives my portion of taxes for my house in Bordentown and

> my farm at New Rochelle, and she owes me protection both at home and through her ministers abroad, yet I remain in prison, in the face of her minister, at the arbitrary will of a committee.

This was only the beginning of their correspondence, as Paine reported:

> In a few days I received a message from Mr. Monroe, conveyed in a note from an intermediate person, with assurance of his friendship, and expressing a desire that I should rest the case in his hands. After a fortnight or more had passed, and hearing nothing farther, I wrote to a friend, a citizen of Philadelphia, requesting him to inform me what was the true situation of things with respect to me. I was sure that something was the matter; I began to have hard thoughts of Mr. Washington, but I was unwilling to encourage them. In about ten days I received an answer to my letter, in which the writer says: "from what I learn from the Americans lately arrived in Paris, you are not considered, either by the American government or by individuals, as an American citizen."

Paine, enraged, spent the next ten days composing a forty-three-page treatise on the meaning of republican citizenship for Monroe's edification.

As would be expected from the Morris-Jefferson-Randolph trail of letters, Monroe was startled to arrive in France and find the author in jail. When he discussed the case with French foreign minister Bouchot, Bouchot asked what instructions he had brought with him concerning Paine. Of course, he had none, and while waiting for a decision from Secretary Randolph, Monroe (described by Jefferson as "so honest that if you turned his soul inside out, there would not be a spot on it") wrote Paine on September 18, assuring him that he would be working to gain his release, and concluding:

> It is unnecessary for me to tell you how much all your countrymen, I speak of the great mass of the people, are interested in your welfare. . . . The crime of ingratitude has not yet stained, and I trust never will stain, our national character. You are considered by them, as not only having rendered important services in our own revolution, but as being on a more extensive scale, the friend of human rights, and a distinguished and able advocate in favor of public liberty. To

> the welfare of Thomas Paine the Americans are not and cannot be indifferent. Of the sense which the President has always entertained of your merits, and of his friendly disposition towards you, you are too well assured to require any declaration of it from me.

After finally receiving a letter from Randolph that stated, "We have heard with regret that several of our citizens have been thrown into prison in France, from a suspicion of criminal attempts against the government. If they are guilty we are extremely sorry for it; if innocent we must protect them," Monroe wrote to the Committee of General Surety on November 2, explaining that all Americans from the revolutionary generation shared Paine's status as citizens of Great Britain before the United States was formed. He claimed Paine fully as an American, and asked that either he be brought to trial and his guilt proven, or he be immediately released. Monroe then related the outcome in a November 7 letter to Randolph: "After some time had elapsed, without producing any change in his favor, I finally resolved to address the Committee of General Surety in his behalf, resting my application on the above principle. . . . On the morning of the day after, which was yesterday, I was presented by the Secretary of the Committee of General Surety with an order for his enlargement. I forwarded it immediately to the Luxembourg, and had it carried into effect; and have the pleasure now to add that he is not only released to the enjoyment of liberty, but is in good spirits." On November 6, 1794, after ten months and nine days in prison, Paine was freed.

The questions of both why he remained incarcerated for so long and how he escaped execution, though, remain unanswered. The questionable story of the hidden chalk mark does not explain why he and his cellmates were not immediately rescheduled for the guillotine as soon as the error was discovered. That the French government quickly released Paine on Monroe's insistence speaks to the power of the American minister's office; perhaps Morris had been the key instigator all along. Another explanation might be Paine's lifelong nemesis—politics—in that he did not have enough allies among the deputies surviving the Girondin purge to argue for his release, while at the same time his enemies were not strong enough to send him off to the Salle des Perdus. Finally, the French Revolution has a remarkable and underwritten history of those whom the Robespierristes could not bring themselves to execute quickly. Their solution was to leave the victims confined and ignored until nature took its course. Paris's Fifth arrondissement had its notorious *caveau des oubliettes* (cave of the forgotten), a prison for such abandoned souls, and there is no better-known case than that of the dauphin himself. After both of his parents were guillotined, the child who was to have been Louis XVII was left incarcerated until 1795, when he died of tuberculosis at the age of ten. It is easy to imagine that, when Paine escaped his writ of execution, he was commuted to a similar sentence of (not exactly benign) neglect.

His release and his freedom, which should have been among the happiest moments of Paine's life, were not a time of great celebration. He was now severely ill, with neurological disorders, a gout that paralyzed his hands, recurrent fevers, and an open wound on his abdomen that would not heal. A year after the Monroe family took him in to recuperate, the American minister wrote that "for some time the prospect of his recovery was good; his malady being an abscess in his side, the consequence of a severe fever in the Luxembourg. Latterly his symptoms have become worse, and the prospect now is that he will not be able to hold out more than a month or two at the furthest. I shall certainly pay the utmost attention to this gentleman, as he is one of those whose merits in our Revolution were most distinguished." Two months later, that prospect was revised, and Monroe commented to James Madison that Paine needed to remain under his care "till his death or departure for America, however remote either the one or the other event may be."

Beyond his profound physical deterioration, ten months of confinement had undermined Paine's spirit. Even after he was recalled to the Convention by a unanimous vote, given eighteen hundred livres in back pay, and nominated to be rewarded for his literary efforts on behalf of the nation, he failed to recover either mentally or emotionally. His bountiful Enlightenment optimism and his boyish good-naturedness were now all but extinguished into bitterness and parsimony, and to medicate his physical and emotional suffering he started drinking again. Perhaps it was that his manic energy had finally collapsed and a depressive grip now held long sway. In many respects, the great Thomas Paine of *Common Sense* and *Rights of Man* had been done away with as effectively as if he had been guillotined. Paine's onetime English roommate, Henry Redhead Yorke, visited with the author in Paris, and described this changed man:

Time seemed to have made dreadful ravages over his whole frame, and a settled melancholy was visible on his countenance. He desired me to be seated, and although he did not recollect me for a considerable time, he conversed with his usual affability. I confess I felt extremely surprised that he should have forgotten me; but I resolved not to make myself known to him, as long as it could be avoided with propriety. In order to try his memory, I referred to a number of circumstances which had occurred while we were in company, but carefully abstained from hinting that we had ever lived together. He would frequently put his hand to his forehead, and exclaim, "Ah! I know that voice, but my recollection fails!" At length I thought it time to remove his suspense, and stated an incident which instantly recalled me to his mind. It is impossible to describe the sudden change which this effected; his countenance brightened, he pressed me by the hand, and a silent tear stole down his cheek. Nor was I less affected than himself.

For some time we sat without a word escaping from our lips. "Thus are we met once more, Mr. Paine," I resumed, "after a long separation of ten years, and after having been both of us severely weather-beaten." "Aye," he replied, "and who would have thought that we should meet in Paris?" He then enquired what motive had bought me here, and on my explaining myself, he observed with a smile of contempt, "They have shed blood enough for liberty; and now they have it in perfection. This is not a country for an honest man to live in; they do not understand anything at all of the principles of free government, and the best way is to leave them to themselves. You see, they have conquered all Europe, only to make it more miserable than it was before." Upon this, I remarked that I was surprised to hear him speak in such desponding language of the fortune of mankind, and that I thought much might yet be done for the Republic. "Republic!" he exclaimed, "do you call this a Republic? Why they are worse off than the slaves of Constantinople; for there, they expect to be bashaws in heaven by submitting to be slaves below, but here they believe neither in heaven nor hell, and yet are slaves by choice. I know of no Republic in the world except America, which is the only country for such men as you and I. It is my intention to get away from this place as soon as possible, and I hope to be off in the autumn; you are a young man

> and may see better times, but I have done with Europe, and its slavish politics."
>
> I have often been in company with Mr. Paine, since my arrival here, and I was not a little surprised to find him wholly indifferent about the public spirit in England, or the remaining influence of his doctrines among its people. . . . This gave rise to an observation respecting his "Age of Reason," the publication of which I said had lost him the good opinion of numbers of his English advocates. He became uncommonly warm at this remark, and in a tone of singular energy declared that he would not have published it if he had not thought it calculated to "inspire mankind with a more exalted idea of the Supreme Architect of the Universe, and to put an end to villainous imposture." He then broke out with the most violent invectives against our received opinions, accompanying them at the same time with some of the most grand and sublime conceptions of an Omnipotent Being, that I ever heard or read of.

Other evidence from this period confirms Yorke's assessment. When Convention deputies honored Paine's great friend Condorcet by interring his remains in the Panthéon, it seemed not to have registered with Paine in any meaningful way. He likewise made no mention of the great irony of the French legislature's new meeting hall being situated in the Luxembourg, or the fact that when in England it was reported that he had been guillotined, his last speech supposedly began, "I am determined to speak the truth in these my last moments, although I have written nothing but lies all my life."

Though the Monroe family in time grew weary of their guest who would not leave, Paine was remarkably helpful to the new American minister, being a source of detailed knowledge on recent French political history and the personalities of the government's most powerful figures. He additionally continued working as adjunct American minister (which Monroe may have appreciated more than Morris), notably in helping one of the American Revolution's most beloved figures. Immediately after his release, Paine received a letter from the marquis de Lafayette's wife, Adrienne: "The news of your being set at liberty, which I this morning learnt from General Kilmaine, who arrived here at the same time with me, has given me a moment's consolation in the midst of this abyss of misery, where I shall all my life remain plunged. Gen. Kilmaine has told me that you recollected me, and have taken great interest in my situation; for which I am exceedingly grateful." Paine was able to work with Monroe to help Lafayette's wife and his daughters, Anastasie and Virginie (his son, George Washington, had safely spent the Terror living in Virginia with his namesake and godfather), to escape from France and to be reunited with Lafayette in Austria. For his efforts on behalf of Paine and Lafayette, Monroe would hear from Secretary Randolph on March 8, 1795, that "your observations on our commercial relations to France, and your conduct as to Mr. Gardoqui's letter, prove your judgment and assiduity. Nor are your measures as to Mr. Paine, and the lady of our friend, less approved."

Though the new French government seemed solidly aligned with his politics, Paine understandably avoided the legislature. In July 1795, however, he broke his self-imposed exile and appeared at the Convention with an attack on aristocracy and a plea to restore universal suffrage, the *Dissertation on First Principles of Government:* "The right of voting for representatives is the primary right by which other rights are protected. To take away this right is to reduce a man to slavery, for slavery consists in being subject to the will of another, and he that has not a vote in the election of representatives is in this case." Paine was received honorably and politely, but his proposals were ignored.

Considering his deteriorated medical and spiritual condition, it is not surprising that this period saw the appearance of the worst of his major works. Lacking the style, humor, and personality of everything that made his other essays so expressly Paineite, *The Age of Reason, Part II* would respond to the critics of the original through an analysis of the credibility of the Bible, which Paine found wanting. The great majority of *Age II* is a snide, sneering, and obsessive rant, with none of the first *Reason*'s lyrical evocation of the spiritual to be found in natural philosophy. If there is a reason for Paine's reputation to be sullied beyond Englishmen wanting monarchy and Americans Christianity, it is the catastrophic rancor of *Age II,* another example of the Terror's devastation of Paine's psyche.

In typically paradoxical fashion, however, Paine would go on to compose one final great essay, a coda to *Rights of Man, Part the Second*'s blueprint for a government that offered more than policemen and tax collectors. Inspired by the bishop of Llandaff's comment on "the wisdom and goodness of God in having made both rich and poor," and originally drafted as a proposal for French government at the end of 1795, *Agrarian Justice, opposed to Agrarian Law, and to Agrarian Monopoly* explored the origins of poverty just as *Common Sense* had the origins of monarchy. It held that the dramatically inequitable distribution of land was a violation of humankind's natural rights, and proposed rectifying this through an estate tax to be used in assisting young adults and the elderly.

Many have interpreted *Agrarian Justice* as a precursor to socialism. Paine was, however, too great a supporter of Adam Smith–styled commerce to be so quickly ushered into that church; he intended that the monies generated by his proposal be paid to all, regardless of their financial means. *Agrarian Justice* was, however, shocking to those who defined a citizen by whether or not he owned property, as it questioned the very origins of "landed," and urged nations to be vigilant with all the rights of their people, including their economic welfare: "Whether that state that is proudly, perhaps erroneously, called civilization, has most promoted or most injured the general happiness of man, is a question that may be strongly contested. On one side, the spectator is dazzled by splendid appearances; on the other, he is shocked by extremes of wretchedness; both of which it has erected. The most affluent and the most miserable of the human race are to be found in the countries that are called civilized." Jefferson expressed the same ideas in a February 1787 letter to the Reverend James Madison: "Whenever there are in a country uncultivated lands and unemployed poor, it is clear that the laws of property have been so far extended as to violate the natural right. The earth is given as a common stock for man to labor and live on. If for the encouragement of industry we allow it to be appropriated, we must take care that other employment be provided for those excluded from the appropriation."

Paine continued his economic theorizing with an essay that would, many years later, so affect William Cobbett—*The Decline and Fall of the English System of Finance,* published in April 1796. Noting that England owed its lenders four hundred million pounds, while having in its bank a mere one million pounds, with the country's national debt always rising from its eternal warmongering, he predicted that the Bank of England would suspend cash outlay. After Paine distributed gratis copies of *Decline and Fall* to the French legislature, various deputies in the Council of Elders agreed that it could become a powerful propaganda weapon; the government had it translated into German and then distributed throughout the moneylending centers of Europe. *Decline and Fall* was additionally issued by a dozen London printers, in Italy, and in America. Paine would be proved right when on May 3, 1797, Pitt was forced to counter a run on the bank with a bill from Parliament ceasing all cash outlays in excess of one pound, a stopple that would remain in effect until 1819.

Though Paine had returned to writing and to something of a public life, he was still not well. More serious than his physical suffering and emotional depression was his inability to bring himself to forgive the injustice he had suffered. This bitterness was not directed against Morris or the Robespierristes intoxicated by revolutionary zeal, but instead against those Americans who had ignored his plight, especially a man who had once been Paine's dear friend, a friend who Paine now believed had turned into as much of a Judas to him as Edmund Burke. Over time, these feelings of abandonment and betrayal became a seething obsession.

On February 22, 1795, Paine sent George Washington, on his birthday, a *j'accuse* of endless grievance. At the last minute, Monroe discovered his intentions and informed Paine that he could not send such a missive while living at the residence of the American minister in Paris; that in fact he could not write anything about American politics whatsoever while a guest of the Monroes. Paine argued back, saying that he needed to speak out, and that no one in the United States would ever imagine Monroe's taking a hand in his work. He did, however, recall the letter, and then repeatedly tried to evade Monroe's stricture. He wrote an attack on the Jay Treaty to be published by a London paper, but Monroe was able to intervene and keep it from being issued; he arranged to print an analysis of the British-American relationship in both England and Philadelphia, but Monroe stopped that as well.

Finally, after eighteen months of hospitality, the Monroes suggested to Paine that it was time for him to live elsewhere. Worried over the repercussions, Monroe preemptively wrote Jefferson's right hand, James Madison, that Paine "thinks that the President winked at his imprisonment, and wished he might die in gaol, and bears him resentment for it; also he is preparing an attack upon him of the virulent kind. Through a third person I have endeavoured to divert him from it without effect. It may be said I have instigated him but the above is the truth." Monroe also told Madison that he was shocked by Paine's lack of both discretion and gratitude, and he was right to be cautious, for immediately after Paine moved out, he drafted a new letter to Washington. When the American president did not respond, Paine's anger was ignited to even greater heights. He decided to craft an exposé, and sent *Letter to George Washington* to his longtime American publisher (and Washington critic), Benny Bache. When Franklin had bequeathed his Philadelphia printshop to his grandson, he most likely imagined he was in turn passing down his commercially astute tradition of evenhanded reporting, light bawdy humor, and moneymaking *Poor Richard.* Bache, who had apprenticed under the greatest printer in all of France, François Didot, started his business with the very pleasant, very Franklin-like *General Advertiser.* In time, however, he became convinced that the Washington administration was turning its back on the democratic principles of the Revolution to become a corrupt variant of British monarchy, and the business-friendly *General Advertiser* was replaced by the political attack-dog *Aurora.* If the ruling Federalists had treated the elder Franklin with contempt in his dying years, his grandson now returned the favor.

Reversing his original puffing of the general in the various numbers of *Crisis,* Paine's *Letter to George Washington* asserted that the commander in chief deserved no credit whatsoever for winning the American Revolution; being Fabian was not such a noble or admirable strategy after all. An examination of the original manuscript of this document reveals just how personally Paine took his friend's betrayal. While his normal handwriting is fluid and elegant, a fine French intaglio script, the penmanship here is tight and cramped. But Paine did not attack only Washington in this *Letter;* he also assaulted John Adams, John Jay, Gouverneur Morris, and the whole of the Federalist Party. It was a period when many founding fathers were turning against one another, but doing so privately, such as in Jefferson's January 8, 1797, letter to Madison: "[Washington] is fortunate to get off just as the bubble is bursting, leaving others to hold the bag. Yet, as his departure will mark the moment when the difficulties begin to work, you will see, that they will be ascribed to the new administration, and that he will have his usual good fortune of reaping credit from the good acts of others, and leaving to them that of his errors." Just as no other American modern had publicly criticized traditional religion, however, no one from the revolutionary generation had made an express, public attack on George Washington, except Thomas Paine:

> Had it not been for the aid received from France, in men, money and ships . . . your cold and unmilitary conduct (as I shall show in the course of this letter) would in all probability have lost America; at least she would not have been the independent nation she now is. You slept away your time in the field, till the finances of the country were completely exhausted, and you have but little share in the glory of the final event. . . .
>
> John Adams is one of those men who never contemplated the origin of government or comprehended anything of first principles. If he had, he might have seen that the right to set up and establish hereditary government . . . is of a degree beyond common treason. It is a sin against nature. . . . John Adams would himself deny the right that any former deceased generation could have to decree authoritatively a succession of governors over him, or over his children; and yet he assumes the pretended right, treasonable as it is, of acting it himself. His ignorance is his best excuse. . . . John Jay . . . always the sycophant of everything in power . . . has said that the Senate should have been appointed for life. He would then have been sure of never wanting a lucrative appointment for himself, and have had no fears about impeachment. These are the disguised traitors that call themselves Federalists. . . .
>
> It has been some time known by those who know [Washington], that he has no friendships; that he is incapable of forming any; he can serve or desert a man, or a cause, with constitutional indifference; and it is this cold, hermaphrodite faculty that imposed itself upon the world. . . .
>
> It is laughable to hear Mr. Washington talk of his sympathetic feelings, who has always been remarked, even among his friends, for not having any. He has, however, given no proofs of any to me. . . . When we speak of military character, something more is to be understood than constancy; and something more ought to be understood than the Fabian system of doing nothing. The nothing part can be done by anybody. . . .
>
> As to you, Sir, treacherous in private friendship (for so you have

> been to me, and that in the day of danger) and a hypocrite in public life, the world will be puzzled to decide whether you are an apostate or an impostor; whether you have abandoned good principles, or whether you ever had any.

Benny Bache published *Letter to George Washington* on October 17, 1796, perfectly timed to coincide with the presidential elections, and the result was an uproar. For many in the United States, *The Age of Reason* and *Letter to George Washington* permanently destroyed Paine's reputation; the attacks on Christianity in the first and a great American hero in the second would only reinforce the opinion of those who already thought of Paine as deserting the noble American experiment for the sanguinary barbarism of the French. Washington himself wrote (referring to himself in the third person), "Although he is soon to become a private citizen, his opinions are to be knocked down, and his character reduced as low as they are capable of sinking it, even by resorting to absolute falsehoods. As an evidence whereof, and of the plan they are pursuing, I send you a letter of Mr. Paine to me, printed in this city [Philadelphia], and disseminated with great industry."

At the same time, however, many Americans welcomed Paine's forthright criticism. The year following *Letter*'s publication, his U.S. foes could enjoy the Francis Oldys attack biography originally subsidized by the British government and reissued in Philadelphia by William Cobbett, while Paine enthusiasts could purchase the author's first collected works, published in two volumes by Thomas Carey.

The election of 1796 resulted in Adams winning the presidency by three votes, with runner-up Jefferson becoming vice president and Senate chair. At first, Adams offered Jefferson a cabinet position (from his own experience, he considered the vice presidency worthless), but his secretaries of war, treasury, and state, High Federalists inherited from Washington and more loyal to Alexander Hamilton than to their own chief, threatened to resign en masse if he pursued this course. After an inaugural dinner together in March 1797, Jefferson would complain that Adams "never after that said one word to me on the subject or ever consulted me as to any measure of the government," perhaps because, as Adams had observed at the time of his vice president, "His patronage of Paine and [anti-Federalist *National Gazette* editor Philip] Freneau and his entanglements with characters and politics which have been pernicious are and have been a source of inquietude and anxiety to me."

The United States was now fully rent by political factions, with Federalists promoting a government of plutocrats and seeking alignment with Britain, while Republicans wanted one more broadly democratic and championed alliance with France. Each side was equally fearful and angry, the Federalists certain that their opponents wanted guillotines imported from Paris, while the Republicans were convinced that their foes would transform the nation into one based on class, with patronage and hereditary succession leading to a new form of corrupt and despotic aristocracy. There was no middle ground.

Even with his long-standing philosophical opponent installed as president alongside a majority party wholly antagonistic to the ideas of *Rights of Man,* Thomas Paine yearned to come home to America for his last years. He traveled to Le Havre, expecting to book passage for a transatlantic crossing, but gave up after hearing that the English were still boarding French and American vessels. From that port city he wrote a letter to Jefferson that again illustrates the depth of his Luxembourg spiritual collapse: "You can have but little conc[eption] how low the character of the American government is sunk in Europe. The neutral powers despise her for her meanness, and her desertion of a common interest; England laughs at her imbecility, and France is enraged at her ingratitude and sly treachery. Such is the condition into which Washington's administration has brought America, and, what makes it worse is that John Adams has not character to do any good."

Paine was now staying at the home of the thirty-seven-year-old French publisher of *Rights of Man, Part the Second* and *The Age of Reason,* Nicolas de Bonneville, who himself had barely survived incarceration during the Terror, and had named his second son Thomas in honor of the writer. Paine would live with this family for the next five years, and during that sojourn show some signs of recovery, as Bonneville's wife, Marguerite, recalled:

> Our house was at No. 4 Rue du Théâtre Français. All the first floor was occupied as a printing office. The whole house was pretty well filled; and Mr. Bonneville gave up his study, which was not a large one, and a bedchamber to Thomas Paine. He was always in his apartments excepting at meal times. He rose late. He then used to read the newspapers, from which, though he understood but little of the French language when spoken, he did not fail to collect all the

> material information relating to politics, in which subject he took most delight. When he had his morning's reading, he used to carry back the journals to Mr. Bonneville, and they had a chat upon the topics of the day.
>
> If he had a short jaunt to take, as for instance, to Puteaux just by the bridge of Neuilly, where Mr. Skipwith lived, he always went on foot, after suitable preparations for the journey in that way. I do not believe he ever hired a coach to go out on pleasure during the whole of his stay in Paris. He laughed at those who, depriving themselves of a wholesome exercise, could make no other excuse for the want of it than that they were able to take it whenever they pleased. He was never idle in the house. If not writing he was busily employed on some mechanical invention, or else entertaining his visitors. Not a day escaped without his receiving many visits. . . . Many travelers also called on him; and, often, having no other affair, talked to him only of his great reputation and their admiration of his works. He treated such visitors with civility, but with little ceremony, and, when their conversation was mere chit-chat, and he found they had nothing particular to say to him, he used to retire to his own pursuits, leaving them to entertain themselves with their own ideas.

Although some of his later critics have made much of Paine's lifelong discinclination to pay rent, it is perhaps more charitable to attribute his staying with his hosts far longer than anticipated to the fact that he had no family of his own. For the Bonnevilles, the author's extraordinary social draw may have compensated somewhat for his five years in residence. One visitor at this time was the leader of the republican revolution in Poland, Tadeusz Kościuszko, who so charmed Paine that he considered forgetting about trying to return to America and instead applying for Polish citizenship. Also paying court was the inventor Robert Fulton, who looked over Paine's bridge sketches and made many admiring comments. Paine in turn declared Fulton's paddlewheel steamboat design a folly, reasoning that "the weight of the apparatus necessary to produce steam is greater than the power of the steam to remove that weight." Famed Irish rebel Theobald Wolf Tone did not enjoy his Anglo-American counterpart, reporting after a 1797 visit that Paine was

> vain beyond all belief. . . . He converses extremely well, and I find him wittier in discourse than in his writings, where his humour is

> clumsy enough. . . . He seems to plume himself more on his theology than his politics, in which I do not agree with him. I mentioned that I had known Burke in England, and spoke of the shattered state of his mind, in consequence of the death of his only son Richard. Paine immediately said that it was the *Rights of Man* which had broken his heart, and that the death of his son gave him occasion to develop the chagrin which had preyed upon him ever since the appearance of that work. I am sure the *Rights of Man* have tormented Burke exceedingly, but I have seen myself the working of a father's grief on his spirit, and I could not be deceived. *Paine has no children!* . . . He drinks like a fish, a misfortune which I have known to befall other celebrated patriots. I am told, that the true time to see him to advantage is about ten at night, with a bottle of brandy and water before him, which I can very well conceive.

Another visitor from Ireland, Catherine Wilmot, was kinder: "In spite of his surprising ugliness, the expression of his countenance is luminous, his manners easy and benevolent, and his conversation remarkably entertaining. . . . Altogether his style of manner is guileless and good-natured, and I was agreeably disappointed in him, considering the odiously disagreeable things I was led to expect." Such extreme mixed reactions to the man were the rule. German hermetic philosopher Georg Foster would describe how "his blazing-red face dotted with purple blotches make him ugly," while a ship's captain from Cape Cod, Massachusetts, R. R. Crocker, would recall Paine as "a well-dressed and most gentlemanly man, of sound and orthodox republican principles, of a good heart, a strong intellect, and a fascinating address."

From 1797 to 1798 Paine wrote a series for Bonneville's newspaper, *Le Bien Informé,* discussing various strategies by which France could invade England. As well as drawing analogies with classical warfare gleaned from Edward Gibbon, he used his personal knowledge of the North Sea coastline from his days as an excise rider—a coastline easily accessible to gunboats sailing from the shores of France's newest military ally, Holland—and calculated how quickly a public subscription could finance the construction of a fleet of one thousand gunboats for just this purpose. The series caused such a stir of excitement and interest among the leaders of the new French government that it brought Paine to the attention of the most famous man in the world.

. . .

Just after the adoption of the 1795 constitution, a powerful group of French royalists organized a mob to attack the legislature in order to *tirez le mauvais sang* yet again, and restore the Bourbon crown. National Convention president Barras came to believe that his Parisian commander of the army might side with the monarchists, and he looked to replace him with an officer unquestionably loyal to the government. Barras eventually chose a brilliant and ambitious Corsican who so loved snuff that his shoulders and lapels were forever shaded in it, a twenty-six-year-old brigadier general who had successfully used artillery strategy to end civil insurrection at Toulon. On October 5, 1795, Napoleon Bonaparte successfully led the army of the interior in defending the Convention from an attack by thousands of counterrevolutionary troops, saving the legislature and preserving the Republic.

Edmund Burke and John Adams were correct in predicting that the French Revolution would end in dictatorship—by 1804, Napoleon as the emperor would have powers far beyond the dreams of the Sun King—but they could not have imagined that this dictator would at the same time be capable of inspiring a miraculous renaissance of his nation. France's economic maladies, which had paralyzed, tormented, and destroyed one government after the next, would finally be cured with the profits of Napoleon's military victories. Once surrounded by invading enemies, the French Republic would by 1797 defeat Belgium and Holland, and force Austria, Prussia, and Spain to accept peace. With triumph came tribute—in 1796 alone, fifteen million livres from the Vatican and twenty million from Milan—until the 750,000-man army became, truly, the financial engine of the nation, a strategy that another European dictator with a country in severe financial distress would employ 135 years later.

It is hardly surprising that the majority of these troops would turn their allegiance to a heroic general rather than to one more in a series of ministers, and that the nation as a whole would in due course follow. With dictatorship came ballast, stability, and equanimity; a trusted banking system with a working currency; a nationwide pyramid of lower and higher education; the return of the church, and peace with the Vatican; the creation of a meritocratic class with the Legion of Honor; and modern codes of commercial, criminal, and civil law, all of which would last for centuries. The new federal government even had a new (not particularly revolutionary) motto: *Authority from Above, Confidence from Below.*

After reading Paine's articles on the invasion of England, Napoleon himself arrived at the Bonneville home in the spring of 1800, seeking the Englishman's military advice, as well as offering to bring him along on that invasion for a position in Britain's new republican government. Paine assured Napoleon that the great majority of Englishmen would welcome French liberation from their oppressive monarch and parasitic aristocrats, at the same time writing to Jefferson that "the intention of the expedition was to give the people of England an opportunity of forming a government for themselves, and thereby bring about peace." At dinner Napoleon unleashed his charisma, telling Paine that he slept every night with a copy of *Rights of Man* under his pillow, and that "a statue of gold should be erected to you in every city in the universe." At the general's invitation, Paine spoke to a military council, advising that "if the expedition should escape the fleet I think the army would be cut to pieces. The only way to kill England is to annihilate her commerce."

After Bonaparte had inspected the troops assembled for the invasion of Great Britain, however, he reported to the legislature that they were insufficient, but that he had in the meantime devised a superior strategy—to strike at the treasure route of British India by taking control of Egypt. Napoleon's subsequent catastrophic defeat in North Africa, with his army abandoned and almost the whole of the French navy lost to Nelson at Aboukir, would inspire Turkey, Russia, Austria, and Britain to reassemble their coalition against France. Yet afterward, when he appeared in Marseille, he still held the whole of France in his arms.

Although Napoleon became more and more powerful, he never invaded Britain, and Paine explained to Jefferson that it had all been "only a feint to cover the expedition to Egypt, which was then preparing." In time, Paine turned wholly against the emperor, telling friends that he was "the completest charlatan that ever existed," that "the whole nation may be made as enthusiastic about a salad as about a constitution; about the color of a cockade as about a consul or a king. You will shortly see the real strength and figure of Bonaparte. He is willful, headstrong, proud, morose, presumptuous; he will be guided no longer; he has pulled the pad from his forehead, and will break his nose or bruise his cranium against every table, chair, and brick in the room; until at last he must be sent to the hospital. . . . Tyrants in general shed blood upon plan or from passion; he seems to have shed it only because he could not be quiet."

Paine's opinions did not go unnoticed. At a dinner celebrating Napoleon's homecoming from North Africa, he stared directly at Paine while saying in a voice loud enough to be heard by many, "The English are all alike; in every country, they are rascals." As the hostilities with Britain continued, Paine's constant stream of English visitors was not looked upon with favor by the government; one state bureaucrat stopped by to tell him that "the police are informed that he is behaving irregularly and that at the first complaint against him he will be sent back to America, his country." At around this time Bonneville published an article in *Le Bien Informé* making light of Director Sieyès, and the Directory shut down the paper. Paine was able to intervene as a deputy to get the ban repealed. When *Le Bien Informé* then carried an article comparing Bonaparte to Cromwell, Bonneville was arrested and imprisoned. In time he was released but was no longer allowed to publish, and the family was driven to the edge of bankruptcy.

The nation's relationship with the United States was equally abysmal. An incensed French government responded to the Jay Treaty by nullifying the 1778 Franco-American agreements, refusing to accept the credentials of Monroe's replacement as U.S. ambassador, and seizing any American vessel that might be harboring British goods for the war effort. President John Adams sent a peace delegation to Paris in 1797; they reported on their negotiations that French foreign minister Talleyrand had demanded a loan of thirty-two million Dutch guilders for his government and a cash gift of $150,000 for himself, that the American Congress assume all costs associated with the seized vessels, and that Adams apologize to the nation of France. Enraged American Federalists urged war; Republicans, equally insulted by the Jay Treaty, urged a renegotiation of Franklin's original agreements.

These partisan battles were openly conducted in the pages of the press with what would today be called smear campaigns. Republicans made regular pseudonymous appearances in Benjamin Franklin Bache's *Aurora,* while Federalists held court in John Fenno's *Gazette of the United States* and William Cobbett's *Porcupine's Gazette.* First Lady Abigail Adams became so incensed by Bache's attacks on her husband that she wrote her sister on May 10, 1798, "Bache is cursing and abusing daily. If that fellow . . . is not suppressed, we shall come to a civil war." Three weeks later, Vice President Jefferson would write a similar note to John Taylor, saying of the Adams administration, "A little patience, and we shall see the reign of witches pass over, their spells dissolved, and the people recovering their true sight, restoring their government to its true principles. . . . It is hardly necessary to caution you to let nothing of mine get before the public; a single sentence got hold of by the Porcupines will suffice to abuse and persecute me in their papers for months." When on May 16 Adams warned his citizens that anyone supporting the French Revolution was a danger to the nation, a Philadelphia mob stoned the windows of Benny Bache's offices. The next time a mob roused by Federalist demagogues showed up to attack Bache, however, it was met with an equally threatening mob of Republicans, organized by his brother.

Between American hysteria over the French "quasi-war" and Federalist anger at the ever more vituperative Republican press, Adams and his majority-held Congress legislated the Alien and Sedition Acts. The first allowed the president to exile (with no need for hearing, trial, or justification) anyone foreign-born whom he judged "dangerous." The second stated that "if any person shall write, print, utter, or publish . . . any false, scandalous, and malicious writing or writings against the Government of the United States, or either House of the Congress of the United States, or the President of the United States with intent to defame . . . or bring them, or either of them, into contempt or disrepute; or to excite against them, or either or any of them, the hatred of the good people of the United States . . . then such persons . . . shall be punished by a fine not exceeding two thousand dollars [today $150,000] and by imprisonment not exceeding two years." It was remarkable that the Federalists felt they had the power to enact such patently unconstitutional legislation in the wake of Adams's winning the presidency by such a slim margin, and it was even more remarkable that the Sedition Act was pursued with such despotic vigor. The editors of Boston's *Independent Chronicle,* Connecticut's *New London Bee,* and New York's *Argus, Mount Pleasant Register,* and *Time Piece* were all immediately arrested and their papers shut down. But this proved to be a law that could also be used against any Federalist enemy. When Vermont representative Matthew Lyon was heard stating that Adams had "an unbounded thirst for ridiculous pomp, foolish adulation, or selfish avarice," he was sentenced to four months of prison and a fine of a thousand dollars. Even so, Vermont reelected him to another term.

On June 26, 1798, Benjamin Franklin Bache was charged with "libeling the President and the Executive Government in a manner tending to excite sedition and opposition to the laws." At the time of Bache's arrest, a yellow fever epidemic swept through Philadelphia, forcing forty thousand to evacuate. Three who would not survive included the city's mayor, *Gazette of the United States* publisher John Fenno, and Benjamin Franklin Bache, who died three months later, on September 10, 1798, at the age of twenty-nine. A thrilled Adams wrote Benjamin Rush that "the yellow fever arrested [Bache] in his detestable career and sent him to his grandfather from whom he inherited a dirty, envious, jealous, and revengeful spite against me for no other cause under heaven than because I was too honest a man to favor or connive at his selfish schemes of ambition and avarice."

Just as jailing and executing a king did not end despotism in France, however, the imprisonment of newspaper editors did not stop press attacks on an American government gone awry. In one of history's small ironies, the Pitt reign of terror, triggered by the enormous public following for Paine's *Rights of Man,* incited a mass exodus from Britain to America of republican moderns. The great majority of these were journalists and printers fleeing indictments for sedition; arriving in the United States, many would continue publishing, wholly to the detriment of the Federalists. On his deathbed, Benny Bache had asked that one of these British exiles, William Duane, be named editor of the *Aurora.* On July 30, 1799, Duane too was jailed on charges of sedition. At his trial for claiming that John Adams had insisted Washington had British influences in his administration, Duane produced a letter proving that Adams had said exactly that, and his case was dismissed. President Adams eventually lamented, "Is there no pride in American bosoms? Can their hearts endure that Callendar, Duane, Cooper and Lyon should be the most influential men in the country, all foreigners and degraded characters?"

The efforts of the Pitt expatriates were not in vain. At the polls of 1800, Jefferson and his Republicans won a national landslide, taking the presidency, both houses of Congress, and the majority of state offices. Jefferson would fully credit the press with this victory in what he called the "Revolution of

1800," saying the Republican newspapers had created a "revolution . . . on the public mind, which arrested the rapid march of our government toward monarchy." If it had not been for Britain's overreaction to Paine's *Rights of Man,* John Adams and his party might have at least enjoyed a second term.

When on March 4, 1801, Jefferson became president of the United States, the Alien and Sedition Acts expired, and the new government pardoned all those who remained imprisoned or accused. With none of the ceremonial pomp of the inaugurations of Washington or Adams, Jefferson's swearing in was a plain affair, his speech a plea for conciliation and unity. Adams did not hear it, as he refused to attend the ceremony, having left for Massachusetts as early as possible. He and Jefferson would not speak or exchange letters for the next dozen years.

With the Republicans in power, the stage was set for a glorious homecoming for Thomas Paine. Two weeks later, on March 18, Jefferson wrote Paine that he had arranged for the U.S. warship *Maryland* to bring his old friend safely home across the Atlantic: "I am in hopes you will find us returned generally to sentiments worthy of former times. In these it will be your glory to have steadily labored, and with as much effect as any man living. That you may long live to continue your useful labors and to reap the reward in the thankfulness of nations, is my sincere prayer. Accept assurances of my high esteem and affectionate attachment." Paine dithered, and *Maryland* sailed without him, but the Federalist enemies of the new administration were able to exploit the fact that the president was using the navy to bring to American shores an atheist advocate of violent revolution. It would be only the first of many political assaults employing Paine against Jefferson.

Within a year, on March 27, 1802, France and England signed the Treaty of Amiens, which included terms that allowed Paine to finally sail without fear of capture. The political climate in Paris had become so oppressive for republicans, meanwhile, that the Bonneville family decided that they too would emigrate, imagining that Jeffersonian America held a much brighter future for their three sons than did Napoleonic France. Nicolas, however, had to take care of various matters before he could leave, so it was arranged for Marguerite and the boys to sail first, with the father to join them shortly after. They could not, however, make arrangements in time to join their future benefactor, and so it was that on September 1, 1802, at the invitation of the president of the United States, and following a bon voyage arranged by lifelong friend Clio Rickman, the sixty-five-year-old Thomas Paine sailed off and alone from Le Havre, for yet one more try at another life in the New World.

11. Utopian Dissolves

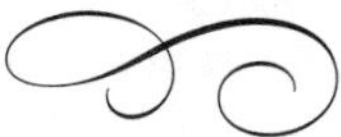

Paine's last great voyage, from the most glorious capital in all of Europe to the New World's faltering imitation of same, is painful to contemplate. If he left Paris with any nostalgic reverie for the brotherhood of '76, or with any hopeful imaginings of his status in the new American society, these would quickly be shattered when he arrived in Federal City. Authorized by Congress in 1790 and overseen by Washington and Jefferson, the American capital was suffering from debilitating growing pains. Its designer, Continental Army engineering major Pierre-Charles L'Enfant—an eccentric hothead with no civic experience—had argued with the president over creative control; Washington fired him, but retained his design of avenues radiating into traffic circles decorated with monuments and fountains, which had originated in L'Enfant's edenic childhood as the son of a court painter and his fond remembrance of the garden designs of his youth. The grid of the capital of the first modern democratic republic was therefore based on that triumphant symbol of absolute monarchy, Versailles.

When Paine arrived twelve years later on November 7, 1802, little progress had been made. Many visitors to the city during this period asked the locals where the capital of the United States was, only to be told that they were already in it. Federal City housed a population of 291 souls, but 152 of these were congressmen, only in town for the six months of the year when the legislature was in session. During those meetings, deputies were forced to shout to be heard over the constant explosion of musket fire, as nearby was a fine wood for hunting quail and turkey. Much of the city-to-be was still planted in corn, while its swamps had yet to be drained, and the nights were filled with the whine of attacking mosquitoes and the raucous wooing of bullfrogs. L'Enfant's monumental circles, meanwhile, were already in active use—as garbage dumps. Abigail Adams described the town to her sister Mary as "nothing but a forest and woods on the way, for sixteen and eighteen miles not a village. Here and there a thatched cottage without a single pane of glass, inhabited by Blacks."

Paine had returned to America for his retirement, clearly expecting a life of quiet ease; he was instead met with fierce partisan rage. He wrote Clio Rickman, "I arrived at Baltimore on the 30th October, and you can have no idea of the agitation which my arrival occasioned. From New Hampshire to Georgia (an extent of 1500 miles), every newspaper was filled with applause or abuse." The Federalist press attacked him with unbridled fury, its *General Advertiser* calling him "that living opprobrium of humanity . . . the infamous scavenger of all the filth which could be raked from the dirty paths which have been hitherto trodden by all the revilers of Christianity." The *Baltimore Republican; or The Anti-Democrat* referred to him as "this loathsome reptile," the Philadelphia *Port Folio* said he was "a drunken atheist, and the scavenger of faction," and Boston's *Mercury and New-England Palladium* called him a "lying, drunken brutal infidel, who rejoiced in the opportunity of basking and wallowing in the confusion, devastation, bloodshed, rapine, and murder, in which his soul delights." At the same time, the Republican press was guarded in its welcome, with the *National Intelligencer* commenting on November 3 and 10, "Be his religious sentiments what they may, it must be [our] wish that he may live in the undisturbed possession of our common blessings, and enjoy them the more from his active participation in their attainment. . . . [He] has received a cordial reception from the Whigs of Seventy-six, and the republicans of 1800 who have the independence to feel and avow a sentiment of gratitude for his eminent revolutionary services."

When Paine's boat from France first docked in Baltimore, however, he was in fact greeted by a large and friendly crowd. Yet so notorious was his reputation that he then needed an alias and help from a presidential aide in order to secure a room at Lovell's, Federal City's only hotel. When his whereabouts were revealed, one Federalist wrote that "he dines at the public table, and, as a show, is as profitable to Lovell as an *Ourang Outang,* for many strangers who come to the city feel a curiosity to see the creature." A Republican paper finally felt compelled to rise to his defense: "Mr. Paine is not now, whatever he might have been, inclined to inebriety, but is as abstemious as the *Tories* would wish him otherwise."

However controversial, Paine was frequently invited to dinner at the President's Palace, Jefferson educating his pious daughters that the writer "is too well entitled to the hospitality of every American, not to cheerfully receive mine." One guest at the executive mansion recalled, "Thomas Paine entered, seated himself by the side of the President, and conversed and behaved towards him with the familiarity of an intimate and an equal!" Just as he had abjured the pomp of Adams's inauguration, Jefferson decorated the executive mansion in a neoclassical style that pared away flourishing embellishments in favor of a simplicity of line congruent with Roman and Enlightenment ideals. He opened the residence to the public for morning visits, and served dinner at four on a regular basis for around a dozen guests. After the food was brought to the table—soup, roasts, spiced vegetables in butter, sugar pastries, fruit, cheese, various puddings, and America's first vanilla ice cream, made from Jefferson's own recipe—the servants were dismissed and dumbwaiters employed so that everyone could feel free to speak openly. Jefferson must have been in an exultant mood during that autumn of 1802, for his immense popularity had led to another triumph at the polls, with Republicans now controlling fourteen of seventeen American states.

The "two Toms" were often seen strolling the capital roads in the cool of the evening, in visibly animated conversation. Apart from his close friendship with the president, however, Paine never became a fixture in the social life of Federal City; as the French attaché's December 21 report to Foreign Minister Talleyrand observed, the Washington elite wanted nothing to do with him. Not surprisingly, Paine did himself no favors when it came to *fraternité*. Lingering bouts of Luxembourg pains and fevers, along with a profound reservoir of bitterness, seemed to exaggerate the least attractive elements of his personality—his egotism, sanctimony, vanity, and parsimony—making him a disagreeable party guest. It may be that these same qualities kept Paine from being employed by the new government, where he likely hoped to find a net of financial security. That this never happened may be due to Jefferson's decision that, no matter how strong their friendship, having Paine as part of his administration was a political risk he could not afford.

Though the Federalist press regularly featured stories about a drunken Paine denouncing Christianity and causing brouhahas at various grand Washington fêtes, he was in fact almost never invited to such affairs. What makes this rebuff by the capital's gentry so poignant is the fact that the new American generation was entirely Paine's offspring. The Smith-Franklin-Paine faith, that the right form of democratic republic would unleash political and economic opportunity and equality across the entire class spectrum of society, had come, in unforeseen ways, entirely true in the young United States, particularly in the dramatic rise in social prominence of the "self-made man." That *Age of Reason, Letter to Washington,* and his own peccadilloes kept Paine from reconnecting with an American public wholly in tune with his *Common Sense* and *Rights of Man* revolution in thinking is a sad and puzzling biographical finale. Though a lifelong hound for the latest information—Paine, on meeting a friend, never said, "Hello," but always, "What news?"—he seemed on his return to America to have lost both his impeccable sense of timing and his common touch, no longer being attuned to the pulse of his country or grasping the key issues affecting the great majority of its people.

As Ben Franklin had predicted, America at that moment crucially needed the renewal of values and the inspiration to virtue that had always been a Paine hallmark. If Paine himself was no longer capable of writing a *Common Sense, American Crisis,* or *Rights of Man* for the United States of the 1800s, he tried, with a series of ten articles on modern American politics, *To the Citizens of the United States and Particularly to the Leaders of the Federal Faction,* published November 15, 22, and 29 and December 6, 1802, and April 21, 1803, in the *National Intelligencer,* the *Aurora,* and the Trenton *True American.* In this series, Paine said that the Federalists relentlessly attacked him because "the faction was in the agony of death," and so acted much like a rabid animal. He announced that he would be spending the rest of his life in the United States, as he had his salad years in the United Colonies, sharing his political thoughts gratis: "I must be in everything what I have been, a disinterested volunteer. My proper sphere of action is on the common floor of citizenship, and to honest men I give my hand and my heart freely."

Besides attacking the Federalists and supporting the Jeffersonians during this period, Paine continued writing essays on deism, though it was clear that few Americans were interested, while religious leaders and local authorities considered these not merely blasphemous but dangerous, as a writer with such an immense readership might easily create a nation of infidels. On November 27 *Aurora* editor William Duane told Jefferson that he had advised Paine not to publish any more attacks on Christianity as these views were so loathed "by the only party that respects or does not hate him, that all his political writings will be rendered useless, and even his fame destroyed." It seems that many others warned Paine similarly, but he would ignore them all, and then, just before his death, admit that "an author might lose the credit he had acquired by writing too much."

In the final days of 1802 Paine would have one last moment in the sun, when he became involved with Jefferson's finest achievement as the nation's chief executive. In 1795 Spain had signed a treaty permitting American commercial access to the port of New Orleans and its warehouses for transiting goods between river craft and oceangoing ships, only the latest in an interminable round of negotiations between British Americans and the various European owners of Mississippi ports and piers, dealings so endless and painful that onetime negotiator John Jay proclaimed, "Would that the world had no Mississippi!" In 1801 European treaty negotiations ended with a Louisiana held by Bonaparte, and on October 16, 1802, Juan Ventura Morales, the territory's acting intendant, cancelled the American agreement and closed the port to all foreign traffic, a catastrophe for the Western Territories' residents. Alexander Hamilton wrote that the only answer was to immediately seize New Orleans and the Floridas by force, and then negotiate a new arrangement with France; other Federalists insisted that the United States declare an immediate war against Bonaparte.

Paine discussed the matter with one of his fellow boarders at Lovell's, a Pennsylvania congressman. Knowing something of France's eternal financial woes, he suggested there might be another answer, and the congressman urged him to write Jefferson immediately with this idea, which he did on Christmas Day of 1802: "Suppose then the [American] government begins by making a proposal to France to repurchase the cession made to her by Spain, of Louisiana, provided it be with the consent of the people of Louisiana, or a majority thereof. . . . The French treasury is not only empty, but the government has consumed by anticipation a great part of the next year's revenue. A monied proposal will, I believe, be attended to."

The next day at the mansion, Jefferson told Paine that "measures were already taken in that business," but would not reveal anything else to his voluble friend, who took this as an insult. In Paris American ambassador Robert Livingston had approached Napoleon with an offer to purchase New Orleans, threatening that if a fair bid was refused, the United States might join the British in the next battle against France, forcing the country to wage war on opposite sides of the globe. Eager to have a New World empire to complement his conquests in Europe, Bonaparte ignored the American offer; Livingston reported that "there never was a government in which less could be done by negotiation than here. There is no people, no legislature, no counselors. One man is everything. He seldom asks advice, and never hears it unasked." Jefferson then sent James Monroe to Paris to supplement Livingston's efforts, while two thousand Americans in the Western Territories prepared to battle the French over control of the river. Immediately after came the resumption of war between Britain and France, and astonishing news from the Caribbean.

Held by France since 1697, the colony of Saint-Domingue (today's Haiti) would by the 1780s become so wealthy through its exports of sugar, cotton, indigo, cacao, and coffee that seven hundred ships sailed through its port every year, its population boomed to 556,000 (500,000 of whom were slaves), and it amassed nearly 65 percent of France's overseas investment capital. It was also home to a class consciousness that would put Britain to shame, a society divided into *grands blancs* (the local aristocrats), *petits blancs* (the working class), *blancs menants* (poor, but white), *affranchis* (black or mixed, but free), slaves (of West African origin), and *maroons* (slaves who had escaped to the mountains and who waged guerrilla warfare against the *blancs*). In May of 1791, the French government under Lafayette granted citizenship to the more affluent of the *affranchis,* but Domingue *blancs* refused to accept this decree. Tens of thousands of slaves joined the *affranchis* in revolt against the completely outnumbered *blancs,* until all *affranchis* were granted citizenship and the slaves were freed.

Believing that the restoration of slavery would make his Caribbean holdings more profitable, Napoleon in January 1802 sent an attack force under Revolutionary War hero Rochambeau to reconquer the island; the French were defeated by a black army with the help of violent tropical fevers. When the news reached Europe that twenty-four thousand Frenchmen had lost their lives, Bonaparte declared, "Damn sugar, damn coffee, damn colonies!" On April 11 French foreign minister Talleyrand asked Livingston, "What would the U.S. give for the whole?" and on May 3, 1803, the Franco-American agreement to sell the Louisiana Territory for three cents an acre was sealed, more than doubling the nation's size. Natural philosopher Jefferson then initiated the apogee of New World Enlightenment by dispatching a mission to catalog, exactly, what he had bought, through the Lewis and Clark Corps of Discovery, whose journals of weather, geology, geography, indigenous American human culture, and the plant and animal life of the Western Territories epically advanced the state of science in the United States.

Even though he knew his nation needed to control the Mississippi (and did not need a neighbor with the enthusiasms of a Bonaparte), Jefferson worried over the constitutional ramifications of what he had done. It could be said, in fact, that the Louisiana Purchase was an act more egregiously federalist than anything the Federalists had ever imagined. The president asked Paine for his thoughts, and Paine—a great enthusiast of what would come to be known as Manifest Destiny—replied, "The Constitution could not foresee that Spain would cede Louisiana to France or to England, and therefore it could not determine what our conduct should be in consequence of such an event. The cession makes no alteration in the Constitution; it only extends the principles of it over a larger territory, and this certainly is within the morality of the Constitution. . . . The English Government is but in a tottering condition and if Bonaparte succeeds, that Government will break up. In that case it is not improbable we may obtain Canada, and I think that Bermuda ought to belong to the United States."

If the Louisiana Purchase and its Corps of Discovery were highlights of the Jefferson administration, one decided travesty was the nation's response to its new republican neighbor. Just as English Tories feared that a contagion of the French Revolution might jump the Channel and infest England, so did American slave owners imagine that Haitian independence might infect the minds of their own human property. Haiti was not formally recognized by the United States until 1862, after the southern states had seceded to form the Confederacy. On New Year's Day 1805, Paine wrote Jefferson the outlines of an American policy for the Republic of Hayti that foreshadowed in detail what would be known two decades later as the Monroe Doctrine, a policy drafted by Monroe's secretary of state (and *Rights of Man* critic), John Quincy Adams: "The United States is . . . now the parent of the Western world, and her knowledge of the local circumstances of it gives her an advantage in a matter of this kind superior to any European nation. She is enabled by situation, and grow[ing] importance, to become a guarantee, and to see, as far as her advice and influence can operate, that the conditions on the part of Domingo be fulfilled. It is also a measure that accords with the humanity of her principles, with her policy, and her commercial interest."

On February 21, 1803, Paine rode to Philadelphia for a visit, stopping by Independence Hall to see the display of his bridge models at Charles Willson Peale's museum. Benjamin Rush refused to have anything to do with him, saying that "his principles avowed in his 'Age of Reason,' were so offensive to me that I did not wish to renew my intercourse with him." During this visit a Reverend Mr. Hargrove told Paine that members of his Swedenborgian congregation had discovered a four-thousand-year-old key to interpreting the Bible, which had been lost to humankind for centuries. Paine replied that the key "must have been very rusty."

A few months later, Paine traveled to Bordentown, where his old mechanical engineering assistant John Hall reported he "never saw him jollier," and E. M. Woodward remembered his visits to the local tavern, Washington House: "Mr. Paine was too much occupied in literary pursuits and writing to spend a great deal of his time here, but he generally paid several visits during the day. His drink was invariably brandy. In walking he was generally absorbed in deep thought, seldom noticed anyone as he passed, unless spoken to. . . . He was by the mass of the people held in odium." When Paine went with Colonel Kirkbride to visit his friend's brother-in-law, the man refused to shake his hand. In time, posters appeared throughout Bordentown picturing the devil dragging off to hell the diabolical author of *The Age of Reason.*

In March Paine arranged to visit James Monroe in New York City just before Monroe was to sail to France to aid Livingston in negotiating the purchase of New Orleans. Kirkbride accompanied his old friend to Trenton, where he asked for a seat on the express coach. Voorhis, the owner, refused to take Paine, saying, "I'll be damned if he shall go in my stage," as did another driver, explaining, "My stage and horses were once struck by lightning, and I don't want them to suffer again." Paine was accepted in the third carriage, but news of his presence had traveled throughout Federalist Trenton. A mob of locals gathered and started throwing rocks at the cab's windows. One man menacingly beat a drum to scare its horses. Paine came out of the carriage to put a stop to this, with the Trenton *True American* reporting that he "discovered not the least emotion of fear or anger, but calmly observed that such conduct had no tendency to hurt his feelings or injure his fame."

In New York City Paine was the guest of honor at a dinner for s served at Lovett's City Hotel on March 18. Unlike Bordentown, Trenton, Washington, D.C., New York City was filled with republican deists, including one of Paine's biggest admirers, Mayor DeWitt Clinton. After meeting extensively with Monroe to discuss various strategies that might be successful in negotiating with the French (for which he had prepared extensive notes in advance), a citywide epidemic of yellow fever made Paine decide to leave quickly for his farm in New Rochelle. As the main house had been burned to the ground, he restored a small cottage, the "Thomas Paine Cottage" that can be seen in New Rochelle today.

Mme. Bonneville and her three sons, Benjamin, Louis, and Thomas, arrived in August of 1803 and moved in with the Kirkbrides in Bordentown. Paine now had a family to worry about, a particular concern as Mme. Bonneville greatly enjoyed spending far beyond her, her husband's, and Paine's collective means. Like many born in poverty, Paine had become almost eccentrically frugal with age, a tendency that only became exaggerated by the burden of the high-living Mme. Bonneville. After a lifetime of depending on the kindness of friends, he now realized how few American friends he had left, and for the rest of his life he would worry about there being enough money to support himself and the Bonnevilles, as well as to leave the boys a birthright.

He first tried setting up an agricultural export business, writing Jefferson that "I shall be employed the ensuing winter in cutting two or three thousand cords of wood on my farm at New Rochelle for the New York market distant twenty miles by water. The wood is worth 3½ dollars per load as it stands. This will furnish me with ready money, and I shall then be ready for whatever may present itself of most importance next spring." When he returned to New Rochelle, however, he was once again afflicted with the gout he had suffered just after being released from the Luxembourg. With his hands paralyzed, and in so much pain he could not walk, he had to abandon the cottage for nursing care and an apartment in town. For two months he lived on tea, toast, brandy, and snuff, with the woman who nursed him, a Mrs. Staple, reporting that "though careless in his dress and prodigal of his snuff, he was always clean and well-clothed." During this convalescence news arrived that his dear friend Colonel Kirkbride had died. Even so, he did not return to drinking, as Mrs. Staple would notice; instead he was "really abstemious, and when pressed to drink by those on he called during his ride, he usually refused with great firmness but politely."

Paine recovered sufficiently to spend much of the winter in New York City, but returned to New Rochelle in the spring of 1803 to discover that his tenant of seventeen years had not only decided not to pay rent, but was insisting that Paine owed *him* money for fence work done on the property. Paine took the man to court, lost, and was required to pay the debt and both parties' legal expenses, forcing him to sell sixty acres. At the same time, Mme. Bonneville, aghast at finding herself in Bordentown, announced that she must live in New York City. Paine agreed, and moved south to be with his adopted French family, as well as to find work for Marguerite as a French tutor, an effort that failed. While Paine was doing everything he could to make sure the Bonneville boys were properly cared for, their mother lived with no such considerations, running up an extra tab of $35 ($2,700 today) at their hotel. Paine then decided it might be best to remove her from the constant temptations of New York to a life on the New Rochelle farm, where she could at least cook, clean, and take care of the house. Paine soon learned, however, that Mme. Bonneville's domestic skills were seriously underdeveloped.

As he had once constantly sailed between London and Paris, the elderly Paine spent his last years migrating between New Rochelle and New York City, living as much as possible in his rent-free cottage, but returning to town when forced by winter weather or physical incapacity. During that period New York was undergoing an astounding transformation, becoming the most cosmopolitan of American towns, perhaps due to its port being able to remain open longer than either Boston's (with its ice) or Philadelphia's (with its fevers). Though New York's fifty thousand souls still had very English tastes when it came to furniture, fashion, decorating, and food, the city's temper had turned modern and progressive, hungry for new inventions, new ideas, and new businesses, such as the municipal pipeworks carrying water to every building on the island, and avant-garde regulations like a law forcing residents to keep their hogs from wandering at will through the streets. In fact, New York was so progressive that its suburb of Greenwich would name one of her lanes "Reason" (today Barrow Street) in honor of the Enlightenment muse.

Though some detractors still occasionally shouted invective at him on the streets, in New York Paine was commonly surrounded by boisterous supporters of every class and distinction. He would at times return to drinking, heartily welcomed at taverns by immigrant enthusiasts of *Rights of Man*. Much of the city's political power was concentrated in a society named for Delaware chief Tamenend, who in legend was as friendly and hospitable to newcomer William Penn as the society aimed to be to recent European immigrants. The Columbian Order of New York City (or Tammany Society), controlled in Paine's time by Aaron Burr, gave strong backing to every Republican candidate from Jefferson to Jackson, by offering social services to recent immigrants not supplied by the city or state, helping them find employment, housing, and naturalization, and then assisting them with their votes. Against Federalist attacks on Paine as a chronic drunkard, Burr defended his sometime political ally: "I always considered Mr. Paine a gentleman, a pleasant companion, and a good-natured and intelligent man; decidedly temperate, with a proper regard for his personal appearance, whenever I have seen him."

Paine tried to solicit subscriptions for an authorized *Complete Works,* both to raise money and to remind the United States of its incendiary origins, but this plan fell through. In 1804 he became a regular contributor to *The Prospect; or, View of the Moral World,* published by Elihu Palmer, a lapsed Presbyterian minister blinded by yellow fever. Palmer had converted to deism after reading *The Age of Reason;* he called Paine "probably the most useful man that ever existed on the face of the earth." A great orator and much-loved friend, Palmer quickly brought his philosopher hero into his New York social orbit, a great help in years to come to the elderly Thomas Paine.

A new tenant farmer, Christopher Derrick, rented the New Rochelle property that year. When Paine and the Bonnevilles returned upstate, Paine gave Derrick various jobs around the farm that the family could not manage. Throughout this time Paine and Derrick quarreled over matters large and small, until finally Paine announced he wanted nothing more to do with him. On Christmas Eve, 1804, Derrick drank himself near-comatose with rum, borrowed a musket, and decided it would be a fine night to kill his ex-landlord, as Paine would describe to another émigré from Lewes, farrier William Carver:

> What you heard of a gun being fired into the room is true.... Christmas Eve and about eight o'clock at night the gun were fired.

> I ran immediately out, . . . but the person that had done it was gone. I directly suspected who it was, and I halloed to him by name; that he was discovered. I did this that the party who fired might know I was on the watch. I cannot find any ball, but whatever the gun was charged with passed through about three or four inches below the window making a hole large enough [for] a finger to go through. The muzzle must have been very near as the place is black with the powder, and the glass of the window is shattered to pieces.

Even though the would-be assassin owed Paine forty-eight dollars and had cheated him over purchases from the general store, Paine had the charges against Derrick dropped. At the same time, Marguerite Bonneville insisted she could no longer tolerate the interminable boredom of living in New Rochelle and needed to return immediately to New York. It was not a moment too soon for Paine, as he would write to longtime friend and manager of New York City's waterworks, John Fellows:

> I enclose the fifty dollars for Mr. Lewis and the five for yourself. It is the last money Mrs. Bonneville will ever put me to the expense of paying. When the house was hired she was to have gone among the French dry good merchants and seen upon what terms she could have got credit. But this was what she did not want to do. She wanted to get hold of 800 or a 1000 dollars ready money. I shall take care of the poor children as well for their own sakes as for their father's, but with respect to herself, I wish her to do well, and this is all I have to say. . . . It is certainly best that Mrs. Bonneville go into some family as a teacher, for she has not the least talent of managing affairs for herself. . . .
>
> I am master of an empty house, or nearly so. I have six chairs and a table, a straw-bed, a featherbed, and a bag of straw for [Bonneville godson] Thomas, a tea kettle, an iron pot, an iron baking pan, a frying pan, a gridiron, cups, saucers, plates and dishes, knives and forks, two candlesticks and a pair of snuffers. I have a pair of fine oxen and an ox-cart, a good horse, a chair, and a one-horse cart; a cow, and a sow and 9 pigs. When you come you must take such fare as you meet with, for I live upon tea, milk, fruit-pies, plain dumplings, and a piece of meat when I get it; but I live with that retirement and quiet that suit me. Mrs. Bonneville was an encumbrance upon me all the while

> she was here, for she would not do anything, not even make an apple dumpling for her own children. If you cannot make yourself up a straw bed, I can let you have blankets, and you will have no occasion to go over to the tavern to sleep.

When the weather turned unbearably cold Paine moved to 36 Cedar Street in New York with that Lewes farrier, William Carver. Consumed with worry over money, however, he then returned as quickly as possible to New Rochelle. The sixty-nine-year-old man was now too physically infirm to care for himself properly, as his mental capacities were beginning to fail. He wrote Jefferson to ask if the government might consider further reward to him for his services to the Revolution; Jefferson did not respond. Paine wrote again, demanding an answer; Jefferson again did not reply. Paine finally asked instead to be appointed special envoy to Napoleon, now that a French invasion of England was imminent. At long last Jefferson answered, thanking Paine for his thoughts and his offer, and explaining that America already had a sufficient number of European envoys.

Early in the spring of 1806 William Carver rode upstate to check on his friend. When he found Paine's cottage empty, he searched through New Rochelle, eventually finding Paine at a tavern, as he later told him, in a shirt

> nearly the color of tanned leather, and you had the most disagreeable smell possible, just like that of our poor beggars in England. Do you recollect the pains I took to clean you? That I got a tub of warm water and soap, and washed you from head to foot, and this I had to do three times, before I could get you clean. I likewise shaved you and cut your nails, that were like birds' claws. . . . Many of your toenails . . . had grown round your toes.

Carver took the derelict and disheveled man back home with him to the city, where, on July 25, Paine, reported that

> [I] was struck with a fit of an apoplexy that deprived me of all sense and motion. I had neither pulse nor breathing, and the people about me supposed me dead. I had felt exceedingly well that day, and had just taken a slice of bread and butter for supper, and was going to bed. The fit took me on the stairs, as suddenly as if I had been shot

> through the head; and I got so very much hurt by the fall that I have not been able to get in and out of bed since that day, otherwise than being lifted out in a blanket, by two persons; yet all this while my mental faculties have remained as perfect as I ever enjoyed them. I consider the scene I have passed through as an experiment on dying, and I find that death has no terrors for me.

After recovering, Paine published his theory that yellow fever arose from the noxious airs sometimes produced by the stirring of underwater soils—the same methane he and Washington had uncovered in another lifetime at Rocky Hill. This article was widely admired and reprinted across the nation. Paine's health then rapidly declined again, which may explain the confused tale of his feud with the Carvers. While still living at Cedar Street, Paine often and bitterly complained to friends in common that William and his wife mistreated him, leaving him locked in a closet for days at a time with nothing to eat or drink. When informed of this, the Carvers explained that Paine had become filthy and miserly, that he could not be trusted to use the facilities, and that he was so much trouble the family was forced to hire a nurse, Elihu Palmer's widow. After about six months of such domestic squabbles, William Carver insisted that Paine leave, and he returned to New Rochelle.

In the autumn of 1806 Paine went to vote and his ballot was refused. He described the details of this outrage to DeWitt Clinton's uncle, the vice president of the United States:

> Elisha Ward and three or four other Tories who lived within the British lines in the Revolutionary war, got in to be inspectors of the election last year at New Rochelle. Ward was supervisor. These men refused my vote at the election, saying to me: "You are not an American; our minister at Paris, Gouverneur Morris, would not reclaim you when you were imprisoned in the Luxembourg prison at Paris, and General Washington refused to do it." Upon my telling him that the two cases he stated were falsehoods, and that if he did me injustice I would prosecute him, he got up, and calling for a constable, said to me, "I will commit you to prison." He chose, however, to sit down and go no farther with it.
>
> I have written to Mr. Madison for an attested copy of Mr. Monroe's letter to the then Secretary of State Randolph, in which

> Mr. Monroe gives the government an account of his reclaiming me and my liberation in consequence of it; and also for an attested copy of Mr. Randolph's answer, in which he says: "The President approves what you have done in the case of Mr. Paine." The matter I believe is, that, as I had not been guillotined, Washington thought best to say what he did. As to Gouverneur Morris, the case is that he did reclaim me; but his reclamation did me no good, and the probability is, he did not intend it should.

Paine sued Elisha Ward in New Rochelle over his mistreatment, but, as always in the courts of New Rochelle, he lost.

Over the winter of 1806–7 Paine moved in with the thirty-year-old painter John Wesley Jarvis at 85 Church Street. Jarvis later wrote, "I have had Tom Paine living with me for these five months; he is one of the most pleasant companions I have met with for an old man. . . . [Contrary to rumor, he] did not and could not drink much." As Jarvis daily paraded through Manhattan's streets in a fur-dappled greatcoat bookended by a leashed pair of immense hounds, Paine's own eccentricities may not have made any real impression.

Soon after, Paine received a bill from the Carvers demanding $150 payment for Mrs. Palmer's nursing salary, along with the months of room and board spent under their care. When Paine insisted that he would reimburse these costs only after seeing a detailed invoice, Carver replied with a pained letter of attacks and accusations. Paine still refused to pay, and continued to remain so adamant in disputing the bill that a friend to both men, John Fellows, decided to end the squabble and pay the debt himself. Thomas Haynes, who also knew both parties, blamed Paine entirely: "Mr. Paine's extreme parsimony, which disposes him to live on his friends' [money] while he has plenty of his own, together with his intemperance, has alienated a great many of his friends who were firmly attached to him for the good he had done for mankind."

During this period, Paine would finish "My Private Thoughts on a Future State," which would be published across the United States: "My own opinion is, that those whose lives have been spent in doing good, and endeavoring to make their fellow-mortals happy, for this is the only way in which we can serve God, will be happy hereafter and that the very wicked will meet with some punishment. But those who are neither good nor bad, or are too insignificant for notice, will be dropped entirely." He then wrote five articles for Jacob Frank's *Public Advertiser,* one notably urging that the U.S. Constitution be revised so that federal judges would be elected instead of appointed (a reversal of the position he had held against Danton in his first week as a French legislator). Writing for Frank was a dramatic change, as previously in New York Paine had solely contributed to British expatriate James Cheetham. In Manchester, Cheetham had been a haberdasher and a radical United Englishman noted for running "from tavern to tavern and from brothel to brothel with *Rights of Man* in one hand and *Age of Reason* in the other." He became so notorious that to escape the Pitt crackdown he had to be smuggled out of Liverpool in a crate marked "dry goods." In New York, Cheetham's *American Citizen* became the city's preeminent Republican paper, and its publisher was a promoter of the City Hotel dinner honoring Paine on his first arrival.

According to William Carver, Paine and Cheetham ended their personal friendship and professional relationship when Cheetham decided to secretly edit his celebrity author. When Paine saw the published copy, he rebuked the publisher: "I, sir, never permit anyone to alter anything that I write. You have spoiled the whole sense that it was meant to convey on the subject." Cheetham replied that the style was "too harsh to appear in print," and Paine retorted, "That was not your business to determine; why, sir, did not you return it to me?" The fight grew so heated that Paine began referring to Cheetham as "Cheat 'Em"; the publisher in turn attacked one of Paine's *Public Advertiser* essays as being completely derivative from the ideas of John Locke; Paine counterstruck that Cheetham "is an ugly tempered man, and he carries the evidence of it in the vulgarity and forbiddingness of his countenance—God has set a mark upon Cain. . . . I never read Locke nor ever had the work in my hand, and by what I have heard of it from Horne Tooke, I had no inducement to read it. It is a speculative, not a practical work, as all Locke's writings are." Paine then attacked Cheetham as now publishing a "Tory paper" and being too British to be bothered with: "As a John Bull, it is impertinence in him to come here to spew out his venom against France." In time, his health would not allow Paine to maintain these volleys, but insisting on the last word, a Cheetham fueled by rage and sorrow would spend two years creating the ultimate salvo, a vicious biography that would help destroy at least temporarily the writer's place in history.

. . .

The last years of Thomas Paine's life were especially unkind. He tried selling the whole of his New Rochelle farm for $10,000, but just days before the final paperwork was to be signed, the buyer died, and the widow could not go forward. He left Jarvis's for an apartment on Broome Street, but when the landlord, Baker Hitt, then raised the rent, Paine decided he could not afford it, and found a small room over a dive near the Bear Market on 63 Partition (now Fulton) Street. Visiting friends were so horrified by these squalid quarters that they arranged for Cornelius Ryder, a Paine supporter, to give the dying man a room at his house on Herring Street a mile and a half to the north of the city in Greenwich. An Englishman by the name of Adams visited at this time and commented, "His blue eyes were full, lucid, and indicated his true character. His conversation was calm and gentleman-like, except when religion or party politics were mentioned. In this case he became irascible, and the deformity of his face, rendered so by intemperance, was then disgusting." A still hostile William Carver, meanwhile, spent the last of Paine's years trying to extort the dying man. When that failed, he threatened Mme. Bonneville with blackmail, and when she refused to be victimized, he found common cause with James Cheetham, providing him with materials for his biography.

Over the course of his last two years, Paine spent months at a time as a bedridden invalid. After suffering through repeated fevers and episodes of dropsy (edema), he knew that he was dying. On July 6, 1808, he sold his beloved seven-and-one-fifth-acre property in Bordentown to John Oliver for $800. He wrote a new will on January 18, 1809, leaving $100 (about $8,000 today) to Elihu Palmer's widow, $1,500 ($125,000) to Marguerite de Bonneville "for her own sole and separate use," a quarter of his New Rochelle estate to Clio Rickman, another quarter to Nicolas de Bonneville, and the remaining half to the Bonneville sons. His will included the request that "I know not if the Society of people called Quakers, admit a person to be buried in their burying ground, who does not belong to their Society, but if they do, or will admit me, I would prefer being buried there; my father belonged to that profession, and I was partly brought up in it. But if it is not consistent with their rules to do this, I desire to be buried on my own farm at New Rochelle. The place where I am to be buried, to be a square of twelve feet, to be enclosed with rows of trees, and a stone or post and rail fence, with a headstone with my name and age engraved upon it, author of 'Common Sense.'" Worried that the design of his monument would not be in keeping with their plain style, that Paine's reputation as an infidel would color their own public image, and that his disciples would interfere with the sanctity of their burial ground, the Quakers refused his grave.

Eventually Paine needed more constant care than even the devoted Mrs. Ryder could offer, and he and Mme. Bonneville moved to rooms at 59 Grove Street, then the country home of Aaron Burr's law partner, William A. Thompson, and his wife, Maria Holdron, Elihu Palmer's niece. A woman named Hedden was hired to help with his care, and she brought to the house a Dr. Manly, who later contributed to Cheetham's libels.

In his last weeks, everything Paine ate triggered episodes of vomiting, so he gave up food entirely. Even as he lay on his deathbed, visitors came to torment him. An admirer of *Rights of Man,* Presbyterian seed merchant Grant Thorburn, snidely commented that "you, who were once the companion of Washington, Jay, and Hamilton, are now deserted by every good man," to which Paine replied, "I care not a straw for the opinions of the world." William Carver, at least, returned to make amends, and Captain Daniel Pelton, owner of New Rochelle's general store, rode down to make his farewells. As a tribute, Jacob Frank reprinted *The American Crisis XIII* in his *Public Advertiser,* and brought by a copy to cheer up the old man.

In his last month Paine was both physically and mentally enfeebled. If he awoke alone in the room, he would become frightened and begin to scream. When Dr. Manly saw that Paine's bedsores threatened to become gangrenous, he realized that his chance had arrived. Manly leaned forward and carefully enunciated, syllable by syllable, "Do you wish to believe that Jesus Christ is the son of God?" Paine weakly replied, "I have no wish to believe on that subject."

Mme. Bonneville remembered her benefactor's final moments:

> He was now become extremely weak. His strength and appetite daily departed from him. . . . In a conversation between him and [Albert] Gallatin, about this time, I recollect his using these words: "I am very sorry that I ever returned to this country." . . . The swelling, which had commenced at his feet, had now reached his body, and someone had been so officious as to tell him that he ought to be tapped. He asked me if this was necessary. I told him, that

I did not know; but, that, unless he was likely to derive great good from it, it should not be done. The next [day] Doctor Romaine came and brought a physician with him, and they resolved that the tapping need not take place.

He now grew weaker and weaker very fast. A very few days before his death, Dr. Romaine said to me, "I don't think he can live till night." Paine, hearing some one speak, opens his eyes, and said: " 'Tis you Doctor: what news?" "Mr. such an one is gone to France on such business." "He will do nothing there," said Paine. "Your belly diminishes," said the Doctor. "And yours augments," said Paine.

When he was near his end, two American clergymen came to see him, and to talk with him on religious matters. "Let me alone," said he; "good morning." He desired they should be admitted no more. One of his friends came to New York; a person for whom he had a great esteem, and whom he had not seen for a long while. He was overjoyed at seeing him; but, this person began to speak upon religion, and Paine turned his head on the other side, and remained silent, even to the adieu of the person.

Seeing his end fast approaching, I asked him, in presence of a friend, if he felt satisfied with the treatment he had received at our house, upon which he could only exclaim, "O! yes!" He added other words, but they were incoherent. It was impossible for me not to exert myself to the utmost in taking care of a person to whom I and my children owed so much. He now appeared to have lost all kind of feeling. He spent the night in tranquillity, and expired in the morning at eight o'clock [on June 8, 1809], after a short oppression. . . . Mr. Jarvis, a painter, who had formerly made a portrait of him, moulded his head in plaster, from which a bust was executed. . . .

He was, according to the American custom, deposited in a mahogany coffin, with his name and age engraved on a silverplate, put on the coffin. His corpse was dressed in a shirt, a muslin gown tied at neck and wrists with black ribbon, stockings, drawers; and a cap was put under his head as a pillow. (He never slept in a night-cap.) Before the coffin was placed on the carriage, I went to see him; and having a rose in my bosom, I took it out, and placed on his breast. Death had not disfigured him. Though very thin, his bones were not protuberant. He was not wrinkled, and had lost very little hair.

His voice was very strong even to his last moments. He often exclaimed, "Oh, Lord help me!," an exclamation the involuntary effect of pain. He groaned deeply, and when a question was put to him, calling him by his name, he opened his eyes, as if waking from a dream. He never answered the question, but asked one himself; as, what is it o'clock, &c.

On the ninth of June my son and I, and a few of Thomas Paine's friends, set off with the corpse to New Rochelle, a place 22 miles from New York. It was my intention to have him buried in the orchard of his own farm; but the farmer who lived there at that time said, that Thomas Paine, walking with him one day, said, pointing to another part of the land, he was desirous of being buried there. "Then," said I, "that shall be the place of his burial." And, my instructions were accordingly put in execution.

The headstone was put up about a week afterwards with the following inscription: "Thomas Paine, Author of 'Common Sense,' died the eighth of June, 1809, aged 74 years." According to his will, a wall twelve feet square was erected round his tomb. Four trees have been planted outside the wall, two weeping willows and two cypresses. Many persons have taken away pieces of the tombstone and of the trees, in memory of the deceased; foreigners especially have been eager to obtain these memorials, some of which have been sent to England. They have been put in frames and preserved. Verses in honor of Paine have been written on the head stone. The grave is situated at the angle of the farm, by the entrance to it.

This interment was a scene to affect and to wound any sensible heart. Contemplating who it was, what man it was, that we were committing to an obscure grave on an open and disregarded bit of land, I could not help feeling most acutely. Before the earth was thrown down upon the coffin, I, placing myself at the east end of the grave, said to my son Benjamin, "stand you there, at the other end, as a witness for grateful America." Looking round me, and beholding the small group of spectators, I exclaimed, as the earth was tumbled into the grave, "Oh! Mr. Paine! My son stands here as testimony of the gratitude of America, and I, for France!" This was the funeral ceremony of this great politician and philosopher!

After Paine was refused a plot in New York City's Quaker cemetery, Mme. Bonneville confirmed with him personally that he wanted to be buried at New Rochelle, and he replied, "I have no objection to that. The farm will be sold, and they will dig my bones up before they be half rotten." Mme. Bonneville insisted that this would never happen: "I have confidence in your friends. I assure you, that the place where you will be buried, shall never be sold." When her sons' share of one-half the property was sold in 1818 at a price of $3,625, she paid $50 to keep her word, with the forty-five-foot-square gravesite withheld from the transaction.

One year later, Mr. William Cobbett, his son, and his hired hand appeared with their bags and shovels.

12. Provenance

IN THE FALL OF 1809 James Cheetham exacted his revenge, and *Life of Thomas Paine* helped to challenge its subject's place in history by attempting to establish that the author of *Common Sense* and *Rights of Man* was nothing but a perverse, squalid drunk. Cheetham had spent two full years in researching this scabrous work, writing to such onetime Paine friends and acquaintances as Benjamin Rush that

> Since Mr. Paine's arrival in this city from Washington, when on his way you very properly avoided him, his life, keeping the lowest company, has been an uninterrupted scene of filth, vulgarity, and drunkenness. As to the reports, that on his deathbed he had something like compunctious visitings of conscience with regard to his deistical writings and opinions, they are altogether groundless. He resisted very angrily, and with a sort of triumphant and obstinate pride, all attempts to draw him from those doctrines. Much as you must have seen in the course of your professional practice of everything that is offensive in the poorest and most depraved of the species, perhaps you have met with nothing excelling the miserable condition of Mr. Paine. He had scarcely any visitants. It may indeed be said that he was totally neglected and forgotten. Even Mrs. Bournville [*sic*], a woman, I cannot say a Lady, whom he brought with him from Paris, the wife of a Parisian of that name, seemed desirous of hastening his death. . . . An ill-natured epitaph, written on him in 1796, when it was supposed he was dead, very correctly describes the latter end of his life. He
>
> Blasphemes the Almighty, lives in filth like a hog,
> Is abandoned in death and interr'd like a dog.

In his book, Cheetham cited William Carver as the source of the report that "Paine brought with him from Paris, and from her husband in whose house he had lived, Marguerite Brazier Bonneville, and her three sons. Thomas has the features, countenance, and temper of Paine." Mme. Bonneville immediately filed suit for libel, one of ten libel suits that the author would have to defend simultaneously. When Carver took the stand supposedly in Cheetham's favor, however, the witness instead announced that "he had never seen the slightest indication of any meretricious or illicit commerce between Paine and Mrs. Bonneville, that they never were alone together, and that all the three children were alike the objects of Paine's care." The jury returned quickly with a verdict of guilty, but the Federalist judge praised Cheetham's book for serving "the cause of religion," and fined him a mere $150. Paine's first great biographer, Moncure Daniel Conway, would in time discover William Carver's copy of *Life of Thomas Paine* in the Concord, Massachusetts, public library, and have its elaborate and illiterate marginal notes transcribed: "Cheetham was a hypocrite turned Tory . . . [who] knew that he told a lie saying Paine was drunk."

While the legendarily impoverished Paine left behind an estate of about one million dollars in today's money, William Cobbett died, in 1835, a bankrupt, and all of his property had to be submitted to public auction to satisfy his creditors. When Pigott the auctioneer refused to include Paine's corpse in the proceedings, Cobbett's eldest son and executor, J.P., petitioned the lord chancellor for relief. This was denied. Afterward, besides editing and republishing his father's work, J.P. authenticated the bones by marking them with inscriptions and indexing them in a journal.

J.P. eventually sold the bones to a neighboring Hampshire day laborer, or they fell into the receivership of farmer George West, along with the rest of Cobbett's unsold estate, when J.P. was himself incarcerated for debt. Either the laborer or the farmer then sold Mr. Paine to London furniture salesman and onetime Cobbett secretary Benjamin Tilly, of no. 13 Bedford Square East, who in turn sold at least part of the skeleton to the orthodox Reverend Robert Ainslie, who insisted in 1854 that he owned the skull and the right hand, but refused to allow anyone to see them. When Conway in his research pursued this lead, Ainslie's daughter told him that the bones had been lost, but in fact they had been taken by her brother, Oliver, to be examined by Royal College of Surgeons anatomist John Marshall, who determined that "the head was . . . small for a man, and of the Celtic type, I should say, and somewhat conical in shape, and with more cerebellum than frontal development." Others have claimed they have buttons carved from Paine bone, and there were constant rumors of a rib cage's surfacing in France. In the 1930s, a letter from an anonymous Brighton housewife was published in the *Daily Telegraph:*

> My grandmother's first husband, Mr Wilkinson, was a Custom House Officer in Liverpool at the time that William Cobbett brought over Thomas Paine's bones for burial in England. Mr Cobbett gave Mr Wilkinson Thomas Paine's "jawbone." My grandmother thought so much of it that she took it with her to her new home when she became the wife of Richard Beverley, a schoolmaster of Eglwysbach, North Wales. My mother used to play with it when a child, but after her marriage and when on a visit to her old home she thought that it should have a decent burial. Her father gave his consent, and she placed it in an open grave in the village churchyard. It must therefore have had a Christian burial.

Coinciding with this chain of ownership is a note from Cobbett's archives: "On Tuesday, January 27, 1833, I went to 11 Bolt Court, Fleet Street, and there, in company with Mr. Antsell and Mr. Dean, I saw at the house of Mr. Cobbett the remains of Mr. Thomas Paine, when I procured some of his hair, and from his skull I took a portion of his brain, which has become hard, and is almost black.—B Tilly." When Benjamin Tilly himself then died a bankrupt, this relic ended up in the hands of his landlords, the Ginn family. Baptist minister George Reynolds visited the Ginns, and asked to see the Tilly Paine items; Mr. Ginn said he did not know their whereabouts, as his wife was away, and when the wife returned, she explained that the keepsakes had been tossed out with the other rubbish left behind by Tilly when he died. Over time, Reynolds was able to unearth the hair and brain, which he eventually sold to herbalist Louis Breeze, who in turn sold them to Paine biographer Conway, who gave them to Dr. Edward Bliss Foote, who interred them in the obelisk marking the Thomas Paine National Historical Association in New Rochelle in 1905.

So it is that one of the first great proponents of civil rights has been bought, sold, and inherited across history . . . one of the church's harshest critics has had his bones treated in the fashion of the reliquaries of the most pious of Catholic saints . . . one of the greatest proponents of Diogenes' "citizen of the world" has his remains scattered across a global network of attics and basements. The desecration of Paine's grave was not the only humiliation visited upon the Enlightenment generation. After the Bourbons returned to power in 1814, royalist fanatics stormed the Panthéon, tore open its lead coffins, gathered the corpses of Voltaire and Rousseau into cloth bags, and rode out to the Barrière de la Gare, where a pit of quicklime had been prepared. Into this pit, the bones of the philosophes were cast, and dissolved.

While the Paine bones have been swept, in parts and pieces, across the globe, his original documents have been treated by history in an equally desultory fashion. In 1802, Redman York visited Paine in France and reported that the author showed him two volumes of memoirs and correspondence; three years later, Paine wrote Jefferson that he had assembled more than two thousand pages of his annotated complete works. If these survived Paine's return to and final years in the United States, they were all inherited by Marguerite de Bonneville, who in turn passed them over to her son, U.S. Army brigadier general Benjamin Bonneville of St. Louis. When biographer Conway tried to examine them, however, he was informed by the general's widow, Sue, that "the papers you speak of regarding Thomas Paine are all destroyed—at least all which the General had in his possession. On his leaving St. Louis for an indefinite time all his effects—a handsome library and valuable papers included were stored away, and during his absence the storehouse burned down, and all that the General stored away [was] burned."

The great treasure of surviving Paine manuscripts is today held by Philadelphia's Library of the American Philosophical Society, the same organization founded by Benjamin Franklin in 1763 and still glowing with Enlightenment decor: squared Corinthian columns, antique ivory walls, crimson cotton chairs, and heavy oak tables. Here is where noted Paine collector Colonel Richard Gimbel bequeathed his plain white cardboard boxes of sixty-three letters and documents, returning Paine home to his beloved political father.

In the magnificent neoclassical home of the New-York Historical Society overlooking Manhattan's Central Park, behind the security of doubled

Plexiglas and surrounded by the crowded heads of generic American Indians, Benjamin Franklins, and a toga-clad George Washington, rests a sulfur-yellow Paine death mask. The profile of the English, American, and French prodigal father is immediately recognizable from his aquiline nose, prognathous chin, and enormous forehead. From time to time the society has had to withdraw its Paine holdings from public view to keep them from being destroyed by fervid vigilantes. The Thomas Paine National Historical Association, meanwhile, owns a Paine "grave mask," made from the Cobbett-snatched skull, but not Paine's New Rochelle cottage, which was bought by the Huguenot and New Rochelle Historical Association. Living in that house today is John Wright, who introduces children to the clothing and the quill pens of the eighteenth century, and who said that "if I had been alive during the Revolution, I would have been on the side of the British, and had Tom Paine hanged for treason."

In the 1960s the TPNHA's Joseph Lewis decided that Napoleon's "statue of gold" pronouncement about Paine should actually be pursued, starting with the hometown of Thetford. After a group of Americans arranged for such a statue to be sculpted and cast by Charles Wheeler and shipped to England, however, a group of Thetford's more conservative citizens rallied to send it back to New Rochelle, with the chairman of the Women's Section of the British Legion explaining that "Tom Paine, the philanderer and an unmitigated scamp, is the last man Thetford should honour." These reactionaries stirred up such a public and national protest that in 1963 a group of advocates, including politician Michael Foot and historian E. P. Thompson, created the Thomas Paine Society to promote the author's legacy in the United Kingdom. In the end Thetford decided to accept the statue. When the town's conservative deputy mayor insisted that Paine's trial and conviction for traitorous sedition should be engraved on its base, enough residents were able to rally behind the public relations of the society to prevent this.

If for much of their lives Thomas Paine and William Cobbett were political blood foes, in death they would be united in philosophic common cause and share a historical legacy. This transformation would begin as the world once more turned upside down over the course of the eighteenth century's one final revolution, when the independent home workshops of artisan mechanics were replaced by the factory behemoths of the Industrial Age. James Watt's condensing-and-reciprocating steam engine and its descendants would, by the mid-1800s, take the place of waterwheels as the dominant motor of British manufacture, while the spinning jenny and its offspring would drive skilled mechanics into debtors' prison. A new workday of fourteen hours arose, as did a new employee, the machine attendant, whose job was so mindless that even a child could do it, and often did. The pace of work was no longer set by humans, but by machines; one nineteenth-century foreman awarded a weekly garland of flowers to his most productive apparatus (but not to its operator).

Over the course of the Industrial Revolution thousands of working people had their way of life annihilated, and at the same time suffered unbearable civil and economic oppressions. After repealing habeas corpus and the right of assembly under Pitt the Younger, a Parliament controlled by landlords and factory owners additionally made unionizing illegal through the Combination Acts. Workers responded with the only organizations they had left: the organizations, inspired by *Rights of Man,* that had been driven underground by the Seditious Societies Act of 1799. These various constitutional reform groups had remade themselves into "friendly" associations of workingmen, but their social views had not changed; when the government and factory owners cracked down on these men and women, the writings of Thomas Paine and William Cobbett inspired them to fight back.

In Leeds, a building used by independent weavers to try to forestall the growth of factory oligarchs was known as "Tom Paine Hall"; in Merthyr, "a few who thought highly of his *Rights of Man* and *Age of Reason* would assemble in secret places on the mountains, and taking the works from concealed places under a large boulder or so, read them with great unction"; in London, "if anybody bought a book and would pay . . . three times as much as was marked, [a bookseller would] give the 'Age of Reason.' " In Sheffield, secret meetings would chant a new drinking song, "God Save Great Thomas Paine":

> Facts are seditious things
> When they touch courts and Kings.
> Armies are rais'd.
> Barracks and bastilles built.
> Innocence charged with guilt,

Blood most unjustly spilt,
Gods stand amaz'd.

Since the reigns of Edward VI, Elizabeth I, and Philip and Mary, various nationwide British statutes were in effect that should have allowed for a slow, Burkean evolution from artisan to industry. Instead, in 1809, Parliament revoked every piece of legislation protecting woolens artisans in order to permit the overnight industrialization of the textile business. The reaction was immediate. Gangs of men, numbering into the thousands, stormed into Lancashire spinner, Nottinghamshire loom, and Yorkshire shearing mills in the middle of the night, smashing machines and torching supplies. These rioters, who would be called Luddites, published anonymous newspaper essays, distributed manifestos, and were so widely popular that by 1812, frame-breaking was rewritten as a capital offense, and more than fourteen thousand British troops marched into the Midlands to quell their protests. Twenty-four of the movement's leaders were hanged, another two dozen imprisoned, and thirty-seven exiled to Botany Bay.

"At this time the writings of William Cobbett suddenly became of great authority," one mill worker remembered. "They were read on nearly every cottage hearth in the manufacturing districts of South Lancashire, in those of Leicester, Derby, and Nottingham; also in many of the Scottish manufacturing towns. . . . He directed his readers to the true cause of their sufferings—misgovernment; and to its proper corrective—parliamentary reform." With similar goals, moderate London Whigs created the Hampden Club, whose Major John Cartwright lectured the working poor on the hopelessness of the vigilante rage of the Luddites and the great promise of joining the middle class to support state reform. By 1816 the Hampden Club had over one million signatures on its reform petition, which was sent to the Commons in a barrel; the Peers responded by announcing that "a traitorous conspiracy has been formed in the metropolis for the purpose of overthrowing, by means of a general insurrection, the established government." Parliament suspended habeas corpus once again and enhanced the Seditious Societies Act, driving William Cobbett back to America.

The government's crackdowns did not work, with Luddites and Hampden Clubs quickly succeeded by waves of workers demanding change, notably the Pentridge Rising, the Owenites, and the Ten Hours Movement.

In 1831–32 more than one hundred thousand demonstrators massed across Birmingham, London, Bristol, Derby, and Nottingham, insisting on reform and frightening the government into believing it faced imminent civil war. The vote was granted to middle-class merchants, who elected to Parliament a returned Cobbett, now a confirmed Paineite who informed the English gentry that "God gave [the rural poor] life upon this land; they have as much right to be upon it as you have; they have a clear right to a maintenance out of the land, in exchange for their labour; and, if you cannot so manage your lands yourselves as to take labour from them, in exchange for a living, give the land up to them."

The working class, however, was still shut out from any role in government. In 1838, London cabinetmaker William Lovett, Irish landlord Feargus O'Connor, Leicestershire preacher Thomas Cooper, Newport tailor John Frost, and hand-loom weaver Ben Rushton began a religious and political movement that included a People's Charter for reform. These Chartists demanded a Leveller/Paine slate of universal suffrage, annual elections, ballot voting, legislator salaries, and equality of electoral gerrymandering; their charter included as its appendix a copy of *Rights of Man*. When the Chartist East London Democratic Association was formed, its manifesto announced a support of the working class "by disseminating the principles propagated by that great philosopher and redeemer of mankind, the Immortal Thomas Paine," and when at a Cheltenham meeting one delegate mentioned Tom Paine, the chairman brusquely replied, "I will not sit in the chair and hear that great man reviled. Bear in mind he was not a prizefighter. There is no such person as Tom Paine. Mister Thomas Paine, if you please."

The Chartists petitioned the government in 1839, 1842, and 1848, and were rejected each time, but they set the stage for the next twenty years of struggle, and in 1867 the franchise was finally extended to the working class, doubling the electorate. In 1884 the number of British voters was tripled when all property restrictions were abolished and rural laborers were included. Parliamentary reform was not the end of Paine's influence in England, however, for the Labour Party's history and its ideas at many points seem so directly inspired by Paine that onetime leader of the party Michael Foot would say, "International arbitration, family allowances, maternity benefits, free education, prison reform, full employment; much of the future later offered by the British Labour Party was previously on offer, in better English, from Thomas Paine."

Forswearing the immediate convulsions of the American and French revolutions, the British had spread their constitutional reform over one hundred years—a Burkean evolution leading to a government closely resembling the one outlined by *Rights of Man.* Yet this transformation shared with the American and French revolutions what could be seen as a John Adams–Thomas Paine joint effort, in that all three required the cooperation of working- and middle-class masses with aristocratic noblesse oblige. Before the war, the United Colonies' founding-father elite did nothing that affected British policy as powerfully as the masses' continent-wide consumer boycotts; French *sans-culottes* would never have achieved their niche of power without the seigneurs' relinquishments at the founding of the Estates-General; the British working class may have forced the state's hand, but it took Lords and Commons to actually enact reform. Paine was the Enlightenment Mercury who sparked political common cause between men who worked for a living and empowered aristocrats across all three nations.

In at least the United States today, however, that coalition seems to have come to an end, with the Adams-Hamilton style of government triumphant, as even American news anchor Walter Cronkite admitted in 2005: "The ruling class is the rich, who really command our industry, our commerce, and our finance. And those people are so able to manipulate our democracy that they really control the democracy." While Franklin, Paine, and Jefferson would be crestfallen that the modern-day American federal government is the reserve of a new aristocracy—multimillionaire plutocrats and their corporate sponsors—Adams and Hamilton would be just as shocked to learn that their admired ruling elite no longer even pretends to lives of virtue.

Ultimately Paine did achieve the great Enlightenment dream of a global fame lasting for centuries. Instead of the Roman version of heaven, however, his reputation has drifted through something of a limbo, the dead man alternately repudiated and honored just as the living one had been befriended and reviled. The biographies by James Cheetham and Francis Oldys marked him as a filthy, dissolute, and drunken atheist for the next two hundred years, while his religious writings and his political convictions were used by his enemies to brand him a crazed radical. His image was so tarnished, in fact, that almost one hundred years would pass before the first serious Paine biography appeared.

As Thomas Jefferson and his political heirs controlled the American government for a great part of the nineteenth century, Paine's reputation was ascendant in the immediate decades after his death. During that time many in the United States forgave and forgot *The Age of Reason* and *Letter to Washington* while remembering and celebrating *Common Sense* and *Rights of Man*. Paine birthday dinners were widely popular, with the 1830s including galas in New York, Albany, Cincinnati, Philadelphia, and Boston; New York's 1834 celebration drew seven hundred. Like their English counterparts, American working-class organizations passed out copies of *Rights of Man* to new members, and many union leaders could recite by heart great swaths of Paine. His American stature reached a peak under the presidency of Andrew Jackson, who said that *Rights of Man* would be "more enduring than all the piles of marble and granite that man can erect. . . . Thomas Paine needs no monument by hands; he has erected a monument in the hearts of all who love liberty."

The writer's public persona was so elevated in this period that the first patient committed to the New York State Lunatic Asylum in 1843 was convinced that he was Thomas Paine; Paine also became the most popular voice from beyond the grave heard by nineteenth-century American spiritualists. The founder of the modern Republican Party, Abraham Lincoln, converted to a life of deism after repeatedly studying *The Age of Reason;* as a young man, Lincoln wrote a pamphlet extolling Paine's faith, which his friends, fearing for his political life, tossed into the stove.

Each progressive historic force in America, from the Populists to the civil rights movement and beyond, is in some way indebted to Paine's utopian dream, which inspired such leaders as Susan B. Anthony, Eugene V. Debs, and Franklin Roosevelt. There are a number of surprises among Paine admirers, though; General George Patton used "Tyranny, like hell, is not easily conquered" as a motto to inspire his men as they fought their way across Europe, while Ronald Reagan accepted the Republican Party's nomination for president with "We have it in our power to begin the world over again." At least Reagan accurately cited *Common Sense,* for almost every other modern reference instead quotes "to begin the world anew," which seems to have started with Paine's own final *To the Citizens of the United States* essay: "It was the opportunity of *beginning the world anew,* as it were; and of bringing forward a *new system* of government in which the rights of *all men* should be preserved that gave *value* to [American] independence." This variant has so fully replaced the original that it is the Paine citation inscribed on the stone floor of Philadelphia's National Constitution Center.

Many historians have commented on the poignancy of Paine's last years, quick to find particular relevance in his funeral's sparse attendance. The truth is that, just as he had once shared an animating philosophy with a host of modern colleagues, so he would share with them final years of bitter disappointment and brokenhearted failure, most notably with the other American founding fathers. That band of patriot rebels who had united in the heady spirit of 1776 would, by the end of their days, find their bond almost wholly destroyed. In time (to give five examples), Benjamin Rush would have nothing to do with Thomas Paine, as would Paine with Washington, Washington with Jefferson, Jefferson with Adams (for a dozen years), and Adams with Hamilton. During this same period, these men lived to see their greatest dreams come true in the United States, falter in Europe, and then crumble in America. The U.S. generation that followed the revolutionaries, though so clearly the offspring of Franklin, Washington, Paine, and Jefferson, fully turned its back on the founders in forming a society that had little to do with either Roman virtues or British parliamentary history. In 1834, Ralph Waldo Emerson described this new American era as "the age of severance, of dissociation, of freedom, of analysis, of detachment. Every man for himself. The public speaker disclaims speaking for any other; he answers only for himself. The social sentiments are weak; the sentiment of patriotism is weak; veneration is low; the natural affections feebler than they were."

Since aristocracy by birth had been devalued, a new arbiter of social hierarchy had to be invented for this new land, and the chosen paragon was the self-made millionaire. When it was said, at the time, that a South Carolina politician "had no relations or friends, but what his money made for him," it was considered a compliment. The rich were believed to be morally superior, with hard work exalted as never before, and the unrestricted market implied by Adam Smith becoming nothing less than a birthright. When Andrew Jackson's presidency begat the spoils system of patronage for the political faithful, few bothered to remember that it was exactly this behavior by the Hanoverian court that had proved a key inspiration for the American Revolution. Gordon S. Wood described the transformation:

> A new generation of democratic Americans was no longer interested in the revolutionaries' dream of building a classical republic of elitist virtue out of the inherited materials of the Old World. America, they said, would find its greatness . . . by creating a prosperous free society belonging to obscure people with their workaday concerns and their pecuniary pursuits of happiness—common people with their common interests in making money and getting ahead. No doubt the cost that America paid for this democracy was high—with its vulgarity, its materialism, its rootlessness, its anti-intellectualism. But there is no denying the wonder of it and the real earthly benefits it brought to the hitherto neglected and despised masses of common laboring people.

The Enlightenment moderns who lived long enough to see these changes in their Republic were devastated. In his last years, George Washington lost all faith in the future of democracy; Alexander Hamilton sadly declared, "This American world was not made for me"; John Adams wondered, "Where is now, the progress of the human mind?" Benjamin Rush spent his last decade so filled with regret over a revolution that had changed the "principles and morals" of its citizens for the worse and a government that had fallen "into the hands of the young and ignorant and needy part of the community" that he took every paper he had gathered and every draft he had written for his history of America, and burned them. In his last years Thomas Jefferson wrote, "All, all dead, and ourselves left alone amidst a new generation whom we know not, and who knows not us. . . . I regret that I am now to die in the belief that the useless sacrifice of themselves by the generation of 1776 . . . is to be thrown away by the unwise and unworthy passions of their sons, and that my only consolation is to be, that I live not to weep over it. . . . I have sometimes asked myself whether my country is the better for my having lived at all."

American moderns were not the only ones suffering through tarnished golden years. After his home, library, and laboratory in Birmingham were destroyed in 1791 by a reactionary mob, Joseph Priestley emigrated to Pennsylvania. When he realized that he could not afford the life of Philadelphia, the philosopher-chemist-divine made his way to the rural town of Northumberland. There in 1797 he would document the kind of New World refuge he had found with the heartbreaking *Case for Poor Emigrants,* which included such pleadings from the Old Testament as "Love ye, therefore, the stranger. For ye were strangers in the land of Egypt." After he wrote a newspaper article that appeared mildly sympathetic to the French Revolution, local magistrates had Priestley investigated for imprisonment or expulsion under John Adams's Alien and Sedition Acts. Meanwhile, the feudal and despotic Europe that all moderns had hoped would be transformed into republican democracies had instead been strengthened by Pitt's civil crackdowns and the ever-growing powers of France's dictator. Samuel Taylor Coleridge wrote William Wordsworth in 1799 that "I wish you would write a poem in blank verse addressed to those who, in consequence of the complete failure of the French Revolution, have thrown up all hopes for the amelioration of mankind, and are sinking into an almost epicurean selfishness, disguising the same under the soft titles of domestic attachment and contempt for visionary *philosophes*."

Almost all of Thomas Paine's Enlightenment colleagues spent their last years as he did, believing that their revolutionary programs had failed, that the philosophy of the light had been proved a pipe dream, that their life's work had been entirely for naught and the great dreams of their youth would go forever unrealized. Instead, of course, it would be the shared, hopeless despair of their last years that would in time be proven almost categorically wrong, with "almost categorically" the modern paradox of the world they made. According to the annual survey conducted by human rights organization Freedom House, slightly less than half of the world in 2004 lives in eighty-nine countries that regularly conduct democratic elections and have "freedom of expression, assembly, association, education, and religion"—almost everything the revolutionary generation hoped to establish. If this is not 100 percent, it is still an astounding achievement, especially considering how extravagantly radical the Enlightenment program once was, and how overwhelmingly powerful were its enemies. In fact, it could be said that the most significant reason to read the works of Thomas Paine today is as an act of fealty, for anyone living in a modern nation will already know by heart every one of his ideas and innovations, as they have been so completely adopted by modern government and society as to seem as though never needing invention, as sui generis as Newton's gravity or Priestley's oxygen. Yet, for anyone needing to be reminded of core Enlightenment beliefs—that government can only be empowered by its citizens; that such citizens are born with certain natural rights; that none are born superior to any other; that all will be treated equally before the law; and that the state has a duty to help the neediest of its people—reading Paine offers a political and spiritual inspiration, one that has driven men and women to achieve greatness across history. Of Paine's many reasons for daring to publish work for which he could have been hanged or guillotined in the United Colonies, the United Kingdom, or France, this legacy is his glory.

On June 24, 1826, the dying Thomas Jefferson wrote his final letter. Declining the mayor of Washington's request to attend the city's Fourth of July celebration, he set aside his terrible disappointment at the recent course of world history in order to offer one last bravura manifesto combining the ideas of the Enlightenment, the American and French revolutions, and Thomas Paine:

> May it be to the world, what I believe it will be (to some parts sooner, to others later, but finally to all), the signal of arousing men to burst the chains under which monkish ignorance and superstition had persuaded them to bind themselves, and to assume the blessings and security of self-government. . . . All eyes are opened or opening to the rights of man. The general spread of the light of science has already laid open to every view the palpable truth, that [alluding to a speech given by Leveller Richard Rumbold as he was to be hanged] the mass of mankind has not been born with saddles on their backs, nor a favored few, booted and spurred, ready to ride them legitimately by the grace of God. These are the grounds of hope for others; for ourselves, let the annual return to this day forever refresh our recollection of these rights, and an undiminished devotion to them.

Notes

All citations of Paine are from Philip S. Foner's *Complete Writings,* unless otherwise specified.

1. The Mission of Atonement

2 **"I knew that my road lay through a hamlet called Churt":** Cobbett, *Rural Rides,* Sunday, November 24, 1822.

2 **"exactly the contrary of what I expected":** Cobbett to Rachel Smither, July 7, 1794. Wilson, 3, citing Melville, ed., *Life and Letters of William Cobbett,* 1:87; *Cobbett's Weekly Political Register,* October 12, 1805.

3 **"a despotism of the many over the few":** Cobbett, *Porcupine's Gazette,* August 19, 1797.

3 **"a whore-master, a hypocrite and an infidel":** Cobbett, *Porcupine's Gazette,* September 18, 1797.

3 **"Doctor Sangrado":** Cobbett, *Porcupine's Gazette,* September 19, 1797.

4 **"At his expiring flambeau":** Spater, 2:387.

4 **natural philosophy** meant almost anything you wanted it to mean in the eighteenth century, from exhuming corpses to collecting twigs to gardening bulbs, but it would most commonly be used to describe the act of studying the natural world to further understand God. Chemist Robert Boyle would describe what today we call scientists as "priests of nature" who read the world instead of the Bible. The word "scientist" wouldn't be coined until 1833 and would not become generally used until the very end of the nineteenth century; even Charles Darwin never called himself a scientist.

5 **"humanity, like that of all the reforming philosophers of the present enlightened day":** Cobbett, *Antidote,* 10.

5 **"How Tom gets a living now":** Cobbett, *Cobbett's Review.*

5 **"Any man may fall into error":** Linton, citing *Cobbett's Weekly Political Register,* vol. 35, 382.

6 **"Paine lies in a little hole under the grass":** Foot and Kramnick, 29.

6 **"These bones will effect the reformation":** Wilson, 3, citing *Cobbett's Weekly Political Register,* 88 volumes, May 1, 1819, September 18, 1819, and November 13, 1819.

7 **"There, gentlemen, are the mortal remains of the immortal Thomas Paine":** *Times* (London), November 28, 1819.

7 **"Since October 1819":** *The Truth-Seeker,* August 8, 1909.

8 **"In digging up your bones":** Lord Byron, *Occasional Pieces 19, 1807–1824.*

8 **nearly a million dollars in today's money:** Besides his enemies' propaganda and his late-in-life hysterical parsimony, the third reason for Paine's reputation as impoverished stems from a widespread lack of interest in economic research among eighteenth-century historians. The source for my calculations is Robert Twigger, who estimated that one 1776 pound sterling was equivalent to eighty-seven 1998 British pounds, or $150 U.S., while a 1776 shilling today would be worth $7.50. Picard, 55, 294, offers Joseph Massie's 1759 statistics of English annual family income versus London prices:

Seamen, alesellers, paupers, vagrants, husbandmen, farmers, laborers (i.e., half the country's population): £23 or less;
Tradesmen, builders, mechanics: £40;
Clergy, army and navy officers: £50–100;
Barristers, extraordinarily successful tradesmen, builders, mechanics: £200;
top ten noble families: £27,000
costs:
one shilling—dinner in a steakhouse of beef, beer, and bread;
between four and six shillings—a pound of coffee;
nine shillings—a dozen chickens;
one pound—a good beaver hat;
five pounds: a sword with a hilt of silver;
six pounds: a bagnio evening of supper, bath, and courtesan;
eight pounds: a man's suit;
thirty-two pounds: price for a boy slave in 1771.

9 **"the equal of Washington in making American liberty possible":** Edison.

9 **"a dirty little atheist":** Edison.

9 **"history is to ascribe the American Revolution to Thomas Paine":** Del Veccio, 45.

9 **"a disastrous meteor":** Foot and Kramnick, citing L. H. Butterfield, ed., *Adams Diary and Autobiography,* 3:330.

9 **"I am willing you should call this":** Adams to Benjamin Waterhouse, October 29, 1805, in Worthington Chauncey Ford, ed., *Statesman and Friend: Correspondence of John Adams with Benjamin Waterhouse, 1784–1822,* Boston, 1927, 31.

10 **"If this piece of biography should analyze his literary labors":** Vale, 135–37, citing Joel Barlow to James Cheetham, August 11, 1809.

11 **"The name is enough":** Katz, "Age of Paine."

2. Begotten by a Wild Boar on a Bitch Wolf

12 **"ink, paper, account books":** McCullough, *John Adams,* 177.

19 **"I heard the bullets whistle":** George Washington to John Washington, June 3, 1754, Papers of George Washington, Library of Congress.

20 **"To cruise against the French":** *London Advertiser,* October 16, 1756.

22 **"If I would drink water":** Smollett, *Humphry Clinker* (1771).

23 **"A rich man can sup, bathe and sleep with a fashionable courtesan":** Picard, 208.

23 **"learned pig, dancing dogs":** McCullough, *John Adams,* 343.

23 **"Do you Englishmen then pretend":** Uglow, 167, citing Franklin Papers 17:341–42.

23 **"the whole appears as a vast wood":** Fielding.

24 **The city's 1758 Bill of Mortality:** Picard, 106ff.

25 **"the last great act of the Renaissance":** J. G. A. Pocock, reviewing Gordon S. Wood's *Creation of the American Republic* (1969), in "Virtue and Commerce in the Eighteenth Century," *Journal of Interdisciplinary History* 3:1 (1972): 124: "An effect of the recent research has been to display the American Revolution less as the first political act of revolutionary enlightenment than as the last great act of the Renaissance."

26 **"Enlightenment is man's leaving his self-caused immaturity":** "An Answer to the Question: 'What Is Enlightenment?'" Hans Reiss, ed., *Kant: Political Writings,* Cambridge, MA: Harvard University Press, 1970.

27 **"the book was so different":** Spater, 74.

27 **"What a revelation it was to me":** Rose.

28 **"no longer depend on the great for subsistence":** Porter, *Creation,* 85. In the years before his death, Porter's *Creation of the Modern World* led the overhaul of Anglo-American Enlightenment history, which is why I've used "moderns" to describe that generation instead of Gay's salon-begotten philosophes, or "enlighteneds" (which reads confusingly Buddhist to modern eyes). His hints on the crucial role of mechanics in that era, supported by the work of Eric Foner, give Paine the rich, vigorous background he deserves.

28 **"to collect all knowledge scattered over the face of the earth":** Kramnick, *Portable.*

29 **"not only for the inspection and entertainment of the learned and the curious":** the 1753 Act of Parliament establishing the British Museum.

29 **Originating in Constantinople:** What is believed to be Europe's first coffeehouse is still extant (but serving dinner): Le Procope, 13 rue de l'Ancienne Comédie, St-Germain-des-Prés.

31 **"a person of imagination and feeling":** Porter, *Creation,* 72.

31 **"I will faithfully pursue":** Porter, *Creation,* 263.

34 **"a close, naked, natural way of speaking":** Boorstin, 387.

38 **"a hateful tax levied":** Powell, 29.

40 **"eye, of which the painter could not convey the exquisite meaning":** Rickman, n.p.

42 **"Do not ask me, for I am so ignorant":** Williamson offers the finest treatment of Wilkes's influence on Paine.

42 **"Tobacco, Snuff, Cheese":** *Sussex Weekly Advertiser; or, Lewes Journal,* September 11, 1769.

43 **"in 1772 the excise officers throughout the kingdom":** Rickman, 40–41.

45 **"trade I do not understand":** Paine, *To a Committee of the Continental Congress,* October 1783. Philip S. Foner, *Complete Writings,* 2:1228.

45 **"To be sold . . . all the Household Furniture":** *Sussex Weekly Advertiser; or, Lewes Journal,* April 11, 1774.

45 **"not at any time thereafter":** Conway, *Life,* 1:33. Newton may have been coy with his "if I have seen further, it is by standing on the shoulders of giants," but in my own case, I may not have seen much further, but I do owe greatly to those giants and their shoulders. Of the many Paine biographies, Conway's is the first serious effort and still perhaps the finest, being especially rich in uncovering primary documents. I am especially grateful to the Thomas Paine National Historical Association for digitizing his work, dramatically easing the research of this book. Keane's, meanwhile, is the very essence of today's definitive, scholarly biography, and his efforts were a crucial aid to my own. Aldridge is my true predecessor in trying to craft a Paine biography that can be appreciated by those outside academia, and Williamson provided an English perspective that was invaluable.

46 **"Thomas Paine did not like to be questioned":** Conway, *Life,* 2:456.

46 **"As ecstasy abates, coolness succeeds":** Paine, "Reflections on Unhappy Marriages," *Pennsylvania Magazine,* June 1775.

47 **"A little thing sometimes produces a great effect":** Conway, *Life,* 2:58.

48 **"the happiness of mankind":** Adam Smith, *Theory of Moral Sentiments,* 1759.

48 **Sometime between December 7 and 12:** Paine in the *Pennsylvania Evening Post* of April 30, 1776, said he was "a cabin passenger in Jeremiah Warder's ship, the London Packet, last Christmas twelvemonth." Historian Albert Matthews found "Ship London Packet, J. Cooke, Lewes, on Delaware," in the Inward Entries of the *Pennsylvania Gazette* and the *Pennsylvania Journal* of December 14, 1774, and fixed the date of Paine's entry as between December 7 and December 12, 1774.

49 **"adopted political son":** Paine employee John Hall, a mechanic and recent émigré from Leicester, in a letter from Trenton dated April 20, 1787, reported that Franklin "considers Mr. Paine his adopted political son." Conway, *Life,* 2:461.

50 **"so convenient a thing it is to be a reasonable creature":** Brands, 32.

3. Pragmatic Utopians

51 **"A little thing sometimes produces a great effect":** Conway, *Life,* 2:58.

53 **"particular design was to establish an academy":** Paine, *To the Citizens of the United States,* 1805.

53 **"it is a great and terrible spectacle to see one-half of the globe":** Caesar.

54 **"that golden age of which men talk so much":** Bailyn, *Ideological Origins,* 82. For anyone working in this era, Bailyn and Wood are the gods who stride among us.

55 **"prizes, stage plays, cards, dice":** Fischer, *Albion's Seed,* 552. One issue of crucial importance in Paine's life is its revelations of the struggles that begat modern statehood, and the origins of those struggles are brilliantly revealed in David Hackett Fischer's masterpiece.

55 **"For three centuries, New England families gave thanks":** Fischer, *Albion's Seed,* 135.

58 **"no men nor number of men upon earth hath power":** Bailyn, *Ideological Origins,* 188, the primary source for this survey of the American Revolution's history of New Whig ideas.

58 **"The appointed governors soon discovered":** Rahe, 547. Paine and his colleagues' rapture with the classical world is beautifully explored by Rahe and Richard, while American religious history is brilliantly developed by Noll.

62 **"On one of the occasions, when Paine had neglected":** Thomas, 2:346.

62 **"one kind of life I am fit for":** Paine to John Hall, November 25, 1791.

63 **"You will say that in this classification of citizens":** Paine to Henry Laurens, spring 1778.

64 **It was long believed:** Frank Smith is the scholar responsible for removing Paine's credit from "An Occasional Letter on the Female Sex"; his research proves the magazine's publisher's central role in presenting modern topics.

65 **"I met him accidentally in Mr. Aitkin's bookstore":** Conway, *Life,* 1:40.

66 **"taxation without representation is tyranny!":** Leckie, 11.

69 **"Because monarchs are prey to delusions of grandeur":** Locke, *An Essay Concerning Human Understanding,* 2, xxi, 55.

69 **"What lay behind every political scene":** Bailyn, *Ideological Origins,* 55. This is the primary source for the American Revolution's history of New Whig ideas.

71 **"Nations, as well as individuals, had their different ages":** Mossner, 554.

72 **"Be a King, George!":** Ayling, *George,* 104.

75 **"The die is now cast":** Ayling, *George,* 247–48.

75 **"We have not men fit for the times":** Langguth, 208.

75 **"a kind of lawsuit":** Paine, *American Crisis VII.*

75 **"When your lordships look at the papers transmitted from America":** Langguth, 216.

76 **"We are told":** Samuel Johnson, *Taxation No Tyranny: An Answer to the Resolutions and Address of the American Congress,* 1774. *Works,* 14:93–144.

76 **"an object of nearly universal scorn and detestation":** McCullough, *John Adams,* 96.

77 **"when the country, into which I had just set my foot":** Paine, *American Crisis VII.*

79 **"I suggested to him":** Aldridge, *Man of Reason,* 34.

79 **"there were two words which [I had warned him] to avoid":** Eric Foner, *Tom Paine,* 61.

79 **"It cannot at this time a day be forgotten":** Paine, *To a Committee of the Continental Congress,* October 1783.

80 **"In October, 1775":** Conway, *Life,* 1:67.

81 **(There is new evidence . . .):** See Fliegelman for details.

81 **"a one-man show":** Bailyn, *Ideological Origins,* 77.

83 **"a work of genius—slapdash as it is":** Bailyn, *Faces of Revolution,* 67.

83 **Real Whig James Harrington's:** A revealing history of *Common Sense's* sources can be found in Robert Ferguson.

89 **"attachment to Britain was obstinate":** Paine, *American Crisis VII.*

89 **"from any person drunk or sober":** Conway, *Life,* 1:56.

89 **"when the work was at a stand for want of a courageous typographer":** Conway, *Life,* 1:67.

90 **"As my wish was to serve an oppressed people":** Paine, *To a Committee of the Continental Congress,* October 1783.

90 **"in figure and utility as much as a British shilling":** Powell, 73.

90 **"received in France and in all of Europe with rapture":** Charles Francis Adams, 3:189.

91 **"Understanding that Congress has it in contemplation":** Archives of the New-York Historical Society.

92 **"I thank God there are no free schools nor printing":** Sir William Berkeley, *Report to the Commissioners of Plantations,* 1671.

92 **"you have declared the sentiments of millions":** Anonymous, *Connecticut Gazette,* March 22, 1776.

92–93 **"I believe no pages was ever more eagerly read":** Hawke, *Paine,* 47.

92 **"independence a year ago":** Keane, 145.

93 **"Have you seen the pamphlet *Common Sense*?":** Del Veccio, 45.

93 **"the sound doctrine and unanswerable reasoning":** Eric Foner, *Tom Paine,* 86.

93 **"a tolerable summary of the arguments which I had been repeating":** Eric Foner, *Tom Paine,* 61.

93 **"every post and every day rolls upon us independence like a torrent":** Del Veccio, 45.

93 **"no writer has exceeded Paine in ease and familiarity of style":** Lipscomb and Bergh, 7:198.

94 **"unites the violence and rage of a republican with all the enthusiasm and folly of the fanatic":** Paine, *To a Committee of the Continental Congress,* October 1783.

95 **"In the course of this winter appeared":** Butterfield, *Diary and Autobiography,* 3:333.

96 **"throbbing, intricately constructed, and obssessive":** Grant, 166.

96 **"you are afraid of the one, I, the few":** McCullough, *John Adams,* 380.

96 **"democratic tyranny":** Butterfield, *Diary and Autobiography,* 3:333.

96 **"a few of the most wise and good":** Butterfield, *Diary and Autobiography,* 3:333.

96 **"Mr. Thomas Paine was so highly offended":** Butterfield, *Diary and Autobiography,* 2:198.

97 **"above six feet high, of an ample long frame":** "Descriptions of Thomas Jefferson," *American Memory,* Library of Congress, http://memory.loc.gov/ammem/collections/jefferson_papers/mtjquote.html.

98 **"he remained throughout his long career":** Bailyn, "Jefferson and the Ambiguities of Freedom."

99 **"the people seem to recognize this resolution":** Langguth, 363.

99 **"*Common Sense* has been translated":** Deane papers, Archives of the New-York Historical Society.

4. Hell Is Not Easily Conquered

102 **"the Hessians and our brave Highlanders gave no quarter":** McCullough, *John Adams,* 152.

103 **"so much martial dignity in his deportment":** McCullough, *1776,* 43.

103 **"could see no possible advantage":** Paine, *Crisis V.*

103 **"Common Sense and Colonel Snarl":** Conway, *Life,* 1:83.

104 **"the celebrated Thomas Paine":** Aldridge, *Man of Reason,* 45.

104 **"He was not given the title Monsieur":** Brands, 520.

104 **"Nothing was more astonishing":** Powell, 88.

106 **"This retreat was censured":** Paine, *Retreat Across the Delaware.*

106 **"I tremble for Philadelphia":** Conway, *Life,* 1:84.

106 **"Your imagination can scarce extend":** Conway, *Life,* 1:84.

107 **"Christmas Day at night":** Langguth, 408.

107 **"the deplorable and melancholy condition":** Paine to Henry Laurens, January 14, 1779.

107 **"the very blackest of times":** Paine to Benjamin Franklin, June 20, 1777.

107 **"bring reason to your ears":** Paine, *The American Crisis.*

111 **"your country is at stake":** McCullough, *1776,* 285.

111 **"in the mouths of everyone going to join the army":** Aldridge, *Man of Reason,* 49.

111 **"the achievements of Washington and his little band of compatriots":** Lossing, 212.

113 **"The King of England is like a fish":** Paine, *On the Question, Will There Be War?*

113 **"I've beat them, I've beat all the Americans!":** Powell, 97.

116 **"You mistake the matter":** Larabee, 25:236n.

117 **"All these barbarians have the law of wild asses"** and **"valued themselves above anything that you can imagine":** Mann.

118 **"I feel a much greater interest":** Richard, 32.

119 **"as pious as Numa":** Richard, 65. Richard and Rahe are the key sources for this overview of the Anglo-American religion of Rome.

119 **"call no man happy until he is dead":** McMahon.

121 **"How strangely is antiquity treated!":** Paine, *Rights of Man.*

122 **"the people of America have been guilty of idolatry":** Powell, 99.

122 **"Washington got the reputation of being a great man":** Rosenfeld, 475.

122 **"I am sick of Fabian systems":** John Adams to Abigail Adams, September 2, 1777, Massachusetts Historical Society.

122 **"actors, accommodators, candle snuffers":** Fiske, 2:39.

123 **"Paine would walk of a morning until 12 o'clock":** Aldridge, *Man of Reason,* 56.

123 **"When a party was forming":** Paine, *To the Citizens of the United States and Particularly to the Leaders of the Federal Faction.*

5. The Silas Deane Affair

126 **"all sensible people in England":** Powell, 82.

126 **"the bilious Arthur Lee":** Brands, 535.

127 **"revolution already in action":** Lefebvre, 1:211.

128 **"if the colonies are determined":** Powell, 91.

128 **"sacrifice a million to put England to the expense":** Conway, *Life,* 2:119.

129 **"I am persuaded that the human race was created to be free":** Bernier, *Lafayette,* 212.

129 **"the United States is the most marvelous land on earth":** Bernier, *Lafayette,* 214.

129 **"We must be embarassed to show ourselves" . . . "I am here to learn":** Bernier, *Lafayette.*

130 **"the destruction of the army of Burgoyne":** Rosenfeld, 245.

130 **"May these brave Americans":** Gay, 2:557.

131 **"You have lost by this mad war":** Leckie, 452.

132 **"The French naturally had a great many questions":** Charles Francis Adams, 3:189.

132 **"Franklin was beneath contempt":** McCullough, *John Adams,* 195.

132 **"If I have often received and borne your magisterial snubbings":** Langguth, 545.

133 **"I can have no dependence on his word":** Langguth, 545.

133 **"those who feel pain at seeing others enjoy pleasure":** Rosenfeld, 260.

133 **"having placed my papers and yours in safety":** Philip S. Foner, *Complete Writings,* 2:96.

133 **"no repayment will ever be required":** Conway, *Life,* 1:119.

134 **"the single publication of the libel":** Aldridge, *Man of Reason,* 60.

134 **"It appeared to me like a dissolution of the constitution":** Butterfield, *Diary and Autobiography,* 2:353.

134 **"If Mr. Deane or any other gentleman will procure":** *Pennsylvania Packet,* January 2, 1779.

135 **"measures suitable to the circumstances":** Hawke, *Paine,* 88.

135 **"What would be the idea of a gentleman in Europe of Mr. Paine?":** Del Veccio, 151.

136 **"So you, great Common Sense":** Keane, 184.

136 **"When I had denounced to Congress the assertions of M. Payne":** Conway, *Life,* 133, begins the most thorough documentation of the Silas Deane affair yet assembled.

137 **"Mr. Gérard through the medium of another gentleman":** Conway, *Life,* 1:139.

137 **"From the manner in which I was called before the House yesterday":** Conway, *Life,* 1:144.

137 **"did not preface his alliance with any supplies whatever sent to America":** Conway, *Life,* 1:144.

138 **"Thin skin, after all, is what a writer is in business to have":** James, "The Good of a Bad Review."

139 **"Your former friend Silas Deane has run his last length":** Conway, *Life,* 1:175.

140 **"Dr. Franklin is taciturn, deliberate, and cautious":** Conway, *Life,* 1:144.

140 **"I conjecture it must be money advanced":** Brands, 659.

140 **"there never was a man less beloved":** Williamson, 92.

141 **"the most malicious enemy I ever had":** Conway, *Life,* 1:90.

142 **"The Congress have not taken the least notice of me":** John Adams to Abigail Adams, February 28, 1779, Massachusetts Historical Society.

142 **"I congratulate you on your accession":** Paine to Benjamin Franklin, October 24, 1778.

142 **"Paine's wrath was excited":** Charles Francis Adams, 2:347–52.

143 **"did not even make the constitution of Pennsylvania":** Charles Francis Adams, 2:347–52.

143 **"owed their final and fatal catastrophe":** Conway, *Life,* 1:290, citing Adams to S. Perley, June 19, 1809.

143 **"The fate of America is already decided":** Rosenfeld, 453, which includes an extensive description of the controversy surrounding Adams's *Defence.*

144 **"Can anyone read Mr. Adams' defense":** Rosenfeld, 464.

144 **"has diffused such excellent principles":** Rosenfeld, 470.

145 **"by the rich, the wellborn":** Powell, 143.

145 **"All communities divide themselves":** Brands, 675.

145 **"Sir, you have given yourselves a king under the title of president":** Rosenfeld, 478.

6. The Missionary Bereft of His Mission

149 **"more than half naked and two-thirds starved":** Langguth, 562.

149 **"One state will comply":** Philip S. Foner, *Complete Writings,* 1:171.

151 **"We are at the end of our tether":** Leckie, 632.

152 **"It was exceedingly dark":** Paine to James Hutchinson, March 1781.

152 **"I find myself no stranger in France":** Paine to James Hutchinson, March 1781.

152 **"coarse and uncouth in his manners, loathsome in his appearance":** Aldridge, *Man of Reason,* 87.

153 **"the King loaded Paine with favors":** Conway, *Life,* 1:173.

153 **"more for the United States in the short time of his being in Europe":** Schiff, *Improvisation,* 275, citing Franklin to Jackson, July 6, 1781.

153 **"The public is often niggardly even of its thanks":** Schiff, *Improvisation,* 277, citing Franklin to Robert Morris, July 26, 1781.

154 **"I told Col. Laurens":** Paine, *To a Committee of the Continental Congress,* October 1783.

154–55 **"After our return we parted company on the road":** Paine, *To a Committee of the Continental Congress,* October 1783.

156 **"there are between thirty and forty sail":** Langguth, 526.

157 **"His Majesty therefore with much sorrow":** Powell, 125.

157 **"If we are not a happy people, it will be our own fault":** Langguth, 551.

158 **"I had the mortification":** Paine, *To a Committee of the Continental Congress,* October 1783.

158 **"I see you are determined to follow your genius":** Conway, *Life,* "The Cobbett Papers," citing November 18, 1782 (unfolioed).

158 **"From an anxiety to support":** Paine to George Washington, November 30, 1781.

160 **"a few oysters or a crust of bread and cheese":** Paine to Washington, March 17, 1782.

160 **"end in the ruin of Britain":** Aldridge, *Man of Reason,* 96.

161 **"appeared a solitary character walking among the artificial bowers":** Keane, 229, citing Benjamin Rush to Elizabeth Graeme Ferguson, July 16, 1782, in Butterfield, *Letters of Benjamin Rush,* 1:278–82.

163 **"I have lately traveled much, and find him everywhere":** Smith, *Tom Paine, Liberator,* 100.

164 **"I have learned since I have been at this place":** Papers of George Washington, Manuscript Division, Library of Congress, http://memory.loc.gov/ammen/gwhome.html.

166 **"supposed that a quantity of inflammable air was let loose":** Paine, *The Cause of the Yellow Fever,* June 27, 1806.

166 **"When I passed through New Jersey in 1764":** Franklin to Joseph Priestley, April 10, 1774; http://www.historycarper.com/resources/twobf3/letter13.htm.

166 **"when the mud at the bottom was disturbed by the poles":** Paine, *The Cause of the Yellow Fever,* June 27, 1806.

168 **"With a heart full of love and gratitude":** Langguth, 561.

169 **"Unsolicited by, and unknown to Mr. Paine":** Washington to Patrick Henry, Richard Henry Lee, and James Madison, Mount Vernon, June 12, 1784, Papers of George Washington, Library of Congress.

169 **"I have been told that it miscarried":** Papers of George Washington, Library of Congress.

169 **"Should it finally appear that the merits of the man":** Conway, *Life,* 1:204.

172 **"When I consider the wisdom of nature":** Conway, *Life,* 1:240.

172 **"Be assured, my dear friend":** Powell, 189.

173 **"when Nature enabled this insect to make a web":** Conway, *Life,* 1:243.

173 **"A remark of Mr. Paine's":** Conway, *Life,* "The Hall Manuscripts," 2:461.

175–76 **"The bearer of this letter is Mr. Paine":** Larabee, 9:565.

177 **"manners were easy and gracious":** Conway, *Life,* 1:321.

177 **"talking so much that Paine":** Williamson, 125.

177 **"He was dressed in a snuff-colored coat":** Taylor, 202.

177 **"You touch me on a very tender part":** Paine to Kitty Nicholson Few, January 6, 1789.

178–79 **"the revolution of France does not astonish me so much":** Hitchens, "Reactionary Prophet."

179 **"I have been to see the Cotton Mills":** Paine to Thomas Jefferson, June 17, 1789.

179 **"I begin this letter as we begin the world":** Library of the American Philosophical Society. I mention this letter as "apparently never before published" since in researching documentary evidence of Burke's and Paine's deep friendship before their separation, I did not find it in any of the literature. It is, however, sitting in plain sight in the finest collection of Paine documents.

7. *Droits de l'Homme, ou Droits du Seigneur?*

182 **"In England it was enough that Newton was the greatest mathematician":** Craveri, 111. Craveri is the key source on the history of French salons.

182 **"seized with joy the opportunity":** Powell, 145.

183 **"I would like to be loved":** Hitchens, *Days,* 28.

183 **"together they are a couple of awkward nincompoops":** Hitchens, *Days,* 22.

184 **the "notables" were "not able":** Ellis, *American Sphinx,* 125.

185 **"The man who thinks is a depraved animal":** Barash offers a nice overview of the pleasures of Rousseau.

187 **"I have great confidence in your communications":** Conway, *Life,* 1:255.

189 **"In the new hemisphere, the brave inhabitants of Philadelphia":** Lefebvre, 1:414.

189 **"there is no foreign court":** Paine to Edmund Burke, January 17, 1790.

190 **"great dangers demanded equally drastic remedies":** Schama, *Citizens,* 483. Despite Schama's humorous obsession with the "sanguinary" French, *Citizens* is the best English-language history of the French Revolution. While there is a great deal of fascinating recent scholarship on the Anglo-American Enlightenment and the American Revolution, there is a remarkable paucity for the French sequel in the English-language journals. A great shame, and a great mystery.

190 **"a share in two revolutions is living to some purpose":** Paine to George Washington, October 16, 1789.

190 **"The people here are in general divided":** Gouverneur Morris, November 27, 1789.

191 **"Today, at half-past three, I go to M. de Lafayette's":** Gouverneur Morris, January 26, 1790.

191 **"Our very good friend, the Marquis de Lafayette":** Paine to Washington, May 1, 1790.

191 **"Common Sense is writing for you a brochure":** Aldridge, *Man of Reason,* 126, citing Lafayette to Washington, January 12, 1790.

192 **"I mean to set in full view their wicked principles and black hearts":** Powell, 178, citing Burke to Sir Philip Francis, February 20, 1790.

192 **"I went first to Debrets":** Paine to Anonymous, April 16, 1790.

192 **"one of our first Jacobins":** Wood, *Americanization,* 204.

193 **"who, by their writings and by their courage":** Keane, 244.

193 **"one of the best-hearted men that lives":** Paine, *Rights of Man.*

194 **"a tribute of fear":** Hawke, 200.

197 **"far superior to what was expected":** Keane, 289, citing W. S. Lewis, ed., *Horace Walpole's Correspondence,* vol. 11, New Haven, CT: 1944, 131–32.

197 **"Read it, it will do you good!":** Frank L. Lucas, *The Art of Living,* London, 1959.

197 **"a great courtier":** Kramnick, *Rage,* 32.

197 **"petty lawyers, constables, Jew brokers, keepers of hotels":** Kramnick, *Rage,* 144.

198 **"Paine was born in England":** Conway, *Life,* 2:373n.

200 **"The earth belongs always to the living generation":** Jefferson to Madison, September 6, 1789. Lipscomb and Bergh, 396.

202 **"I shall then make a cheap edition":** Paine to Washington, July 21, 1791; Papers of George Washington, Library of Congress.

202 **"I did, indeed, suppose that Paine's pamphlet":** Conway, *Writings,* 313.

202 **"to destroy in six or seven days":** Foot and Kramnick, 18, citing "Letters on a Regicide Peace," Bohn, ed., *Burke's Works,* London, 1855, 5:395.

203 **"France has not leveled":** Paine, *Rights of Man.*

203 **"As it is my design":** Eric Foner, *Tom Paine,* 82–83.

203 **"undutiful behavior to the tenderest of parents":** Keane, 330.

204 **"maiden wife":** Wilson, 84.

204 **"Mankind has tried all possible experiment":** For John Adams's monarchical tendencies, see Adams to Benjamin Rush, June 19, 1789: "You seem determined not to allow a limited monarchy to be a republican system, which it certainly is, and the best that has ever been tryed" and a July 28, 1807, letter to John Adams from Mercy Warren:

> Do you not recollect, sir, that in the course of conversation on the way you replied thus to something that I had observed? "It does not signify, Mrs. Warren, to talk much of the virtue of Americans. We are like all other people, and shall do like other nations, where all well-regulated governments are monarchic." I well remember my own reply, "That a limited monarchy might be the best government, but that it would be long before Americans would be reconciled to the idea of a king." . . . In the morning, at breakfast

at Mercy your own table, the conversation on the subject of monarchy was resumed. Your ideas appeared to be favorable to monarchy, and to an order of nobility in your own country. Mr. Warren replied, "I am thankful that I am a plebeian." You answered: "No, sir, you are one of the nobles. There has been a national aristocracy here ever since the country was settled, your family at Plymouth, Mrs. Warren's at Barnstable, and many others in very many places that have kept up a distinction similar to nobility." This conversation subsided by a little mirth. Do you not remember that, after breakfast, you and Mr. Warren stood up by the window, and conversed on the situation of the country, on the Southern States, and some principal characters there? You, with a degree of passion, exclaimed, "They must have a master"; and added, by a stamp with your foot, "By God, they shall have a master." In the course of the same evening you observed that you "wished to see a monarchy in this country and an hereditary one too."

205–6 **"Mr. Adams can least of all complain," "could not but be," "True, but I observe," "But I will venture to say," "I detest that book," "Mr. Jefferson said that," "Does he consider," "I thought so little of the note," "Publicola, in attacking all Paine's principles,"** and **"If you suppose":** Conway, *Life,* 1:295, et seq.

206 **"A good riddance of bad ware":** McCullough, *John Adams,* 435.

207 **"I had John Adams in mind":** Rosenfeld, 511.

207 **"The same fate follows me here":** Paine to George Washington, July 21, 1791.

207 **"The duties of my office":** Washington to Paine, May 6, 1792, Papers of George Washington, Library of Congress.

208 **"Indeed I am glad you did not come away":** Jefferson to Paine, July 29, 1791; Lipscomb and Bergh, 3:212.

208 **"I need not relate to you":** Conway, *Life,* 1:295.

210 **"now convinced that liberty and the constitution":** Kates.

210 **"no compromises with rebels!":** Lefebvre, 3:212.

210 **"The birds are flown!":** Conway, *Life,* 1:308.

211 **"You see the absurdity of monarchical governments":** Conway, *Life,* 1:308.

211 **"it is virtually impossible that Lafayette":** Perroud, 2:240.

212 **"republic with a monarch":** Schama, *Citizens,* 560.

212 **"Is it possible that you believe in a republic?":** Conway, *Life,* 2:5.

212 **"there is more liberty for the individual citizen under a monarchy":** Conway, *Life,* 1:312.

213 **"Duchâtelet called on me":** Conway, *Writings,* 3:vi–vii.

214 **"inflated to the eyes and big with a litter of revolutions":** Powell, 195.

214 **"Paine is writing a new pamphlet":** Keane, 319.

216 **"The most extravagant idea":** "La plus extravagante idée qui puisse naître dans la tête d'un politique est de croire qu'il suffise à un peuple d'entrer à main armée chez un peuple étranger, pour lui faire adopter ses lois et sa constitution.

Personne n'aime les missionnaires armés; et le premier conseil que donnent la nature et la prudence, c'est de les repousser comme des ennemis." *Sur la guerre (1ère intervention),* Jacobin Club speech, January 2, 1792.

216 **had almost nothing in common with its predecessor:** See Kates for the many distinctions between Parts 1 and 2 of *Rights of Man.*

217 **"There is in all European countries":** For more on the difference between French and American revolutionary mobs, see Rudolph.

220 **"At present I am engaged on my political bridge":** Paine to John Hall, November 25, 1791.

221 **"the welfare of these kingdoms requires":** E. P. Thompson, 17.

221 **"seemed to electrify the nation":** Wilson, 83.

221 **"loathsome insects that might, if they were allowed":** Wollstonecraft, vi.

221 **"not less than four thousand per week":** Conway, *Writings,* 2:108.

221 **"Reports came through of over a dozen clubs at Ipswich":** Wilson, 83.

222 **"derived more true knowledge from the two works of Mr. Thomas Paine":** Aldridge, *Man of Reason,* 162.

222 **"Mr. Paine's life in London was a quiet round of philosophical leisure":** Rickman.

223 **"monarchy man . . . not suitable to be employed by this country":** Brookhiser, 128.

223 **"the finish given to the style and arrangement of the Constitution":** Sparks, 1:284.

224 **"Paine calls upon me and talks a great deal":** Brookhiser, 102.

224 **"I read Paine's new publication today":** Gouverneur Morris, February 22, 1792.

224 **"I think it quite as likely that he will be promoted to the pillory":** Keane, 244.

225 **"I will not attempt in the smallest degree to refute them":** Edmund Burke, *An Appeal from the New to the Old Whigs, in consequence of some late discussions in Parliament, relative to the Reflections on the French Revolution,* 1791.

225 **"of old age" at forty-six:** Hague, 5.

225 **"Paine is quite right, but what am I to do?":** Powell, 189.

225 **"the severest trial which the visitation of providence":** Hague, 212.

226–27 **"the seditious doctrines of Paine":** Keane, 330.

227 **"is now made as much a standard book in this country":** Jones, citing Rogers, *Crowds, Culture and Politics in Georgian Britain,* Oxford: Clarendon Press, 1998, 203.

227 **"ushered into the world in all shapes and sizes":** Aldridge, *Man of Reason,* 169.

227 **"while the work was at a price":** Paine, *Letter to the Addressers.*

227 **"one part of the community is afraid to sell":** Conway, *Life,* 2:346.

228 **"principles had been laid down by Mr. Paine":** Keane, 329.

229 **"an image of Tom Paine upon a pole":** E. P. Thompson, 104.

229 **"a caricature painting representing Britannia":** E. P. Thompson, 108.

229 **"It is earnestly recommended to Mad Tom":** *Times* (London), May 21, 1792.

231 **"Thus, his circle is completed":** Brookhiser, 133.

231 **"France calls you, Sir, to its bosom":** Conway, *Life,* 2:349.

232 **"Thomas's having merited death, or at least transportation":** Cobbett, *Cobbett's Review.*

232 **"You must not go home, or you are a dead man":** Conway, *Life,* 2:352, citing Alexander Gilchrist, *Life of William Blake,* 94.

233 **"We had taken our baggage":** Paine to Mr. Secretary Dundas, Calais, September 15, 1792.

234 **"If, to expose the fraud and imposition of monarchy":** Paine, *Letter to the Addressers.*

8. The Sovereigns Among Us

235 **"all the soldiers on duty were drawn up":** Carlile, citing John Frost to Horne Tooke, September 20, 1792.

237 **"the criminal shall be decapitated":** Blom, 212.

238 **"History informs us that the passage of dethroned monarchs":** Gouverneur Morris, 2:555.

238 **"repulsive and atrocious [with] brutal passions":** Williamson, 176.

239 **"bliss was it in that dawn to be alive":** William Wordsworth, "French Revolution—As It Appeared to Enthusiasts at Its Beginning," 1805. *The Complete Poetical Works,* London: Macmillan and Co., 1888.

239 **"France must speak for other nations":** Williamson, 180.

239 **Paine assisted Condorcet:** See Jones for details on their collaborative efforts.

240 **"Louis XVI, considered as an individual":** Paine, *To the National Convention,* November 21, 1792.

240 **"Louis declared war on the Revolution":** Keane, 381.

240 **"absurd and detestable":** Schama, *Citizens,* 660.

241 **"It is to France alone":** Paine, *To the National Convention,* January 15, 1793.

241 **"It is for you to vote":** J. M. Thompson, 449.

242 **"The decision came to in the Convention yesterday":** Paine, *To the National Convention,* January 19, 1793.

242 **"to nature belongs the right of death":** Conway, *Life,* 2:15.

242 **"A cruel precipitation":** Conway, *Life,* 2:8.

242 **"I submit that Thomas Paine is incompetent":** Conway, *Life,* 2:6.

242 **"I have the advantage of some experience":** Paine, *To the National Convention,* January 19, 1793.

243 **"I denounce the interpreter":** Conway, *Life,* 2:6.

243 **"I voted against [the death penalty]":** To James Monroe, Prison of the Luxembourg, Sept. 10th, 1794.

243 **"France has but one ally":** Conway, *Life,* 2:9

243 **"About nine o'clock this morning the king passed by my window":** Williamson, 192.

244 **"He looked like some peasant shambling along behind his plough":** Williamson, 196.

244 **"I die innocent of all the crimes of which I have been charged":** Schama, *Citizens,* 666.

244 **"his head did not fall at the first stroke":** Hitchens, *Days,* 188.

245 **"wicked, malicious, seditious":** Conway, *Life,* 1:342.

245 **"the man in the moon":** Paine to Attorney-General Sir Archibald Macdonald, Paris, 11th of November, 1st year of the Republic.

245 **"having the honor of [Mr. Adams's] acquaintance":** Rosenfeld, 516, citing James Thomson Callendar, *The American Annual Register, or, Historical Memoirs of the United States, for the year 1796,* Philadelphia: Bloren and Madan, 1797, 230–31.

245 **"That vain fellow Erskine":** Conway, *Writings,* 313.

246 **"government, in its own estimation":** Williamson, 185.

246 **"My Lord, I am authorized by the jury":** Conway, *Life,* 2:55; *Howell's State Trials,* 22:357.

246 **"Mr. Paine's trial is this instant over":** J. Redman, London, Tuesday December 18, 5 p.m., to John Hall, Leicester, England; Library of the American Philosophical Society.

247 **"The prosecutions that are commenced all over England":** Conway, *Life,* 2:29.

248 **"My lord, they're all hissing":** Conway, *Life,* 2:29.

248 **"if the French kill their King":** Paine to John King, January 3, 1793.

249 **"I lodge with my friend Paine":** Conway, *Life,* 2:357.

249 **"In Paris, in 1793, I had lodgings in the Rue Faubourg St. Denis":** *From the Castle in the Air to the Little Corner of the World* [Paine to Lady Robert Smyth], undated, est. 1794.

250 **"Let us be terrible so that the people will not have to be":** Schama, *Citizens,* 707.

250 **"Frenchmen are mad to allow foreigners to live among them":** Conway, *Life,* 2:46.

251 **"of all of those faithless members":** Conway, *Life,* 2:50.

251 **"I would observe to the tribunal"** and **"Not because I would denounce the youth":** Conway, *Life,* 2:48.

251 **"the friendship I had for Thomas Paine":** Conway, *Life,* 2:48.

251 **"Had this revolution been conducted consistently":** Paine to Thomas Jefferson, April 20, 1793.

252 **"to rise in moral insurrection":** Schama, *Citizens,* 680.

253 **"those who make revolutions by halves":** Keane, 390.

254 **"Now that he's dead, peace will return to my country":** Schama, *Citizens,* 696.

254 **"she taught us how to die":** Schama, *Citizens,* 696.

254 **"the republic consists in the extermination of everything that opposes it":** Schama, *Citizens,* 758.

255 **"declare in the name of the citizens of the Commune":** *Le Moniteur,* June 21, 1793.

255 **"I have not yet seen M. [Edmond] Genêt":** Anne Cary Morris, citing Gouverneur Morris to George Washington, December 28, 1792.

256 **"I suspected that Paine was intriguing against me":** Anne Cary Morris, citing Gouverneur Morris to Robert Morris, June 25, 1793.

256 **"so contemptible that I shall draw over the veil of oblivion":** Anne Cary Morris, citing Gouverneur Morris to Thomas Jefferson, October 18, 1793.

256 **"I told the minister that I had observed":** Anne Cary Morris, citing Gouverneur Morris to George Washington, October 18, 1793.

257 **"The Englishman Thomas Paine," "the Convention must not multiply the guilty,"** and **"I shall not be able to save them":** See Michelet, 2:184, for the details of this period.

257 **"Borne down by public and private affliction":** Rickman.

258 **"Memory, like a beauty that is always present to hear itself flattered":** *From the Castle in the Air to the Little Corner of the World* [Lady Robert Smyth], undated, est. 1794.

9. The Religion of Science

260 **"My friends were falling as fast as the guillotine could cut their heads off":** Paine to Samuel Adams, Federal City, January 1, 1803.

263 **"The true priest of the Supreme Being is Nature itself":** Schama, *Citizens,* 831.

264 **"I firmly believed when I was a boy":** *Cobbett's Weekly Political Register,* January 13, 1821.

264 **"truly the Christian religion is the worst of all religions":** Locke, *Two Treatises.*

264 **"a wall of separation":** "Mr. Cotton's Letter Lately Printed, Examined and Answered," in *The Complete Writings of Roger Williams,* 1:108, 1644.

264 **"The people feared one sect might obtain a pre-eminence":** Rahe, 550. Rahe and Noll are the key sources for this history.

264 **"whip and crop, and pillory and roast":** Allen.

264 **"noble and gallant achievements":** Charles Francis Adams, John Adams to Charles Cushing, October 19, 1756.

265 **"As the government of the United States of America":** Rahe, 753.

265 **"The historical evidence suggests":** Ellis, *His Excellency,* 388.

265 **"foreign aid" . . . "We forgot":** Allen.

265 **"During almost fifteen centuries":** Joseph Gardner, ed., *James Madison, A Biography in His Own Words,* New York: Newsweek Books, 1974, citing James Madison to William Bradford, April 1, 1774.

265 **"vile . . . debased . . . servile and pusillanimous":** Richard, 189.

265 **"Pausing only to dart a look of contempt":** Blackburn, "Ethics of Belief."

268 **"not acquainted with such a compound of vanity and ignorance":** Prochaska.

269 **"no other church but the alehouse":** Keane, 393.

269 **"I have always considered Christianity":** Noll, 64.

269 **"The Christian religion is, above all the religions that ever prevailed":** John Adams, diary entry for July 26, 1796; Charles Francis Adams, 3:421.

269 **"church going animal":** "Religion and the Founding of the American Republic," Library of Congress, http://www.loc.gov/exhibits/religion/religion.html.

271 **"There is a third stage of religious experience":** Einstein.

10. The Perfidious Mr. Morris

273 **"O Liberty, what crimes are committed in your name!":** Perroud, 2:519.

273 **"They have boasted of the patriotism of Thomas Paine":** Conway, *Life,* 2:102.

274 **"On the 7th Nivose [December 27] of the 2d year":** Bibliothèque Nationale, Paris.

274 **"It is an interesting work; it will do much good":** Keane, 395.

275 **"Thomas Payne is a native of England":** Bibliothèque Nationale, Paris.

275 **"lest I should forget it":** Conway, *Life,* is the original source for all of this underlying material, beginning 2:115, citing Gouverneur Morris to Thomas Jefferson, January 21, 1794.

276 **"Thomas Paine has just applied to me":** Conway, *Life,* 2:120, citing Gouverneur Morris to Deforgues, Paris, 14th February (26 Pluviose) 1794.

276 **"In your letter of the 26th of last month":** Paris, 1st Ventose, 2nd year of the Republic [February 19, 1794]. The Minister of Foreign Affairs to the Minister of the United States.

277 "**Mr. Paine wrote me a note":** Conway, *Life,* 2:115, citing Gouverneur Morris to Thomas Jefferson, March 6, 1794.

278 **"that he has demanded Paine as an American citizen":** Conway, *Life,* 2:119, citing Edmund Randolph to George Washington, June 25, 1794.

278 **"among the papers of Robespierre":** Paine, *The Age of Reason.*

278 **"America has not clearly pronounced her opinion":** Hawke, *Paine,* 294.

278 **"however discordant the late American Minister Gouverneur Morris":** Paine to James Monroe, Prison of the Luxembourg, September 10, 1794.

279 **"In place of that noble love of liberty":** *Moniteur,* January 25, 1797.

280 **"That which you did for the happiness and liberty of your country":** Conway, *Life,* 2:141.

281 **"I hoped soon to have got you all out of this":** Lefebvre, 3:415.

281 **"found a refuge from evil,":** Keane, 395.

281 **"I was one of the nine members":** Conway, *Life,* 2:135.

281 **"The state of things in the prisons":** Paine, *Letter to George Washington,* July 30, 1796.

282 **"My illness rendered me incapable of knowing anything that passed":** Declaration and Testimony Concerning Denis Julien, Luxembourg, 17 Vendemiaire, Year 3.

282 **"A violent fever which had nearly terminated my existence":** Paine, *Letter to George Washington,* July 30, 1796.

283 **"As soon as I was able to write a note":** Conway, *Life,* 2:142.

283 **"I have now no expectation of delivery":** Paine to James Monroe, Prison of the Luxembourg, August 17, 1794.

284 **"In a few days I received a message from Mr. Monroe":** Conway, *Life,* 2:142.

284 **"so honest that if you turned his soul inside out":** White House Library presidential biographies, http://www.whitehouse.gov/history/presidents.

284 **"It is unnecessary for me to tell you":** James Monroe to Thomas Paine, September 18, 1794; Philip S. Foner, *Complete Writings,* 2:1355n.

285 **"We have heard with regret that several of our citizens":** Edmund Randolph to James Monroe, July 30, 1794; Conway, *Life,* 2:155.

285 **"After some time had elapsed":** James Monroe to Secretary Randolph, November 7, 1794; Conway, *Life,* 2:161.

286 **"for some time the prospect of his recovery was good":** James Monroe to Joseph Jones, September 15, 1795; Conway, *Life,* 2:170.

286 **"till his death or departure for America":** Hawke, *Paine,* 307.

287 **"Time seemed to have made dreadful ravages":** Conway, *Life,* 2:301.

288 **"I am determined to speak the truth":** Conway, *Life,* 2:132.

288 **"The news of your being set at liberty":** Conway, *Life,* 2:442.

289 **"your observations on our commercial relations to France":** Edmund Randolph to James Monroe, March 8, 1795; Conway, *Life,* 2:151.

290 **"Whenever there are in a country uncultivated lands":** Philip S. Foner, *Complete Writings,* 2:605, citing Philip S. Foner, ed., *Thomas Jefferson: Selections from His Writings,* 56–57.

291 **"thinks that the President winked at his imprisonment":** Powell, 250.

292 **"[Washington] is fortunate to get off just as the bubble is bursting":** Thomas Jefferson to James Madison, January 8, 1797; James Smith, *The Republic of Letters,* 2:955.

293 **"Had it not been for the aid received from France":** Paine, *Letter to George Washington,* July 30, 1796.

294 **"Although he is soon to become":** Washington to David Stuart, Philadelphia, January 8, 1797, Papers of George Washington, Library of Congress.

294 **"never after that said one word to me":** Thomas Jefferson to James Madison, January 8, 1797; James Smith, *The Republic of Letters,* 2:955.

294 **"His patronage of Paine":** Rosenfeld, 465.

295 **"You can have but little conc[eption]":** Paine to Thomas Jefferson, Havre de Grace, France, April 1, 1797.

295 **"Our house was at No. 4 Rue du Théâtre Français":** Conway, *Life,* 2:443.

296 **"vain beyond all belief":** Williamson, 248.

297 **"In spite of his surprising ugliness":** Hawke, *Paine,* 339.

297 **"his blazing-red face dotted with purple blotches":** Keane, 388.

297 **"a well-dressed and most gentlemanly man":** Williamson, 248.

299 **"the intention of the expedition":** Conway, *Life,* 2:275.

299 **"a statue of gold should be erected to you":** Hawke, *Paine,* 333.

299 **"if the expedition should escape the fleet":** Conway, *Life,* 2:255.

299 **"only a feint to cover":** Conway, *Life,* 2:275.

299 **"the completest charlatan that ever existed":** Keane, 443.

299 **"the whole nation may be made as enthusiastic":** Conway, *Writings,* 2:293.

300 **"The English are all alike":** Keane, 445.

300 **"the police are informed that he is behaving irregularly":** Aldridge, *Man of Reason,* 264.

300 **"Bache is cursing and abusing daily":** Rosenfeld, 84.

301 **"A little patience, and we shall see the reign of witches pass over":** Rosenfeld, 136, citing Thomas Jefferson to John Taylor, June 1, 1798.

301 **"an unbounded thirst for ridiculous pomp":** Rosenfeld, 518.

302 **"the yellow fever arrested [Bache] in his detestable career":** Rosenfeld, 250, citing John Adams to Benjamin Rush, June 23, 1807.

302 **"Is there no pride in American bosoms?":** Durey's "Paine's Apostles" has the background for Paine's journalistic revenge on Adams.

303 **"revolution . . . on the public mind":** Talbot.

303 **"I am in hopes you will find us returned generally":** Conway, *Life,* 2:298.

11. Utopian Dissolves

306 **"nothing but a forest and woods on the way":** Rosenfeld, 680, citing Stewart Mitchell, ed., *New Letters of Abigail Adams,* Boston: Houghton Mifflin, 1947, 256–58.

306 **"I arrived at Baltimore on the 30th October":** Paine to Thomas "Clio" Rickman, New York, March 8, 1803.

306 **"that living opprobrium of humanity":** Keane, 451.

306 **"this loathsome reptile":** Aldridge, *Man of Reason,* 269.

306 **"a drunken atheist, and the scavenger of faction":** Keane, 451.

306 **"lying, drunken brutal infidel":** Keane, 451.

306 **"Be his religious sentiments what they may":** Conway, *Life,* 310.

306 **"he dines at the public table":** Hawke, *Paine,* 360.

306 **"Mr. Paine is not now":** Hawke, *Paine,* 360.

307 **"is too well entitled to the hospitality of every American":** Rickman.

307 **"Thomas Paine entered":** Keane, 470, citing William Plumer to Judge Smith, December 9, 1802, in William Plumer Jr., ed., *Life of William Plumer by his Son, William Plumer, Junior,* Boston, 1856.

309 **"by the only party that respects or does not hate him":** Aldridge, *Man of Reason,* 274.

309 **"an author might lose the credit he had acquired":** Paine, *Examination of the Prophecies.*

309 **"Would that the world had no Mississippi!":** Kukla, 107.

309 **"measures were already taken in that business":** Philip S. Foner, *Complete Writings,* 2:1431.

310 **"there never was a government":** Bernier, *World in 1800,* 217.

310 **"Damn sugar, damn coffee, damn colonies!":** Kukla, 282.

310 **"What would the U.S. give for the whole?":** Kukla, 284.

311 **"The Constitution could not foresee":** Paine to Thomas Jefferson, Stonington, Connecticut, September 23, 1803; Philip S. Foner, *Complete Writings,* 2:1447.

311 **"The United States is . . . now the parent of the Western world":** Paine to Thomas Jefferson, New Rochelle, January 1, 1805; Philip S. Foner, *Complete Writings,* 2:1453.

312 **"his principles avowed in his 'Age of Reason'":** Conway, *Life,* 2:318.

312 **"never saw him jollier":** Conway, *Life,* 2:325.

312 **"Mr. Paine was too much occupied":** Conway, *Life,* 2:318.

312 **"I'll be damned if he shall go in my stage":** Conway, *Life,* 2:328.

312 **"My stage and horses were once struck by lightning":** Philip S. Foner, *Complete Writings,* 2:xliii.

313 **"I shall be employed the ensuing winter in cutting":** Paine to Thomas Jefferson, Stonington, Connecticut, September 23, 1803; Philip S. Foner, *Complete Writings,* 2:1447.

313 **"though careless in his dress and prodigal of his snuff":** Vale, 145.

315 **"I always considered Mr. Paine a gentleman":** Vale.

315 **"probably the most useful man that ever existed on the face of the earth":** Philip S. Foner, *Complete Writings,* 2:788.

315 **"What you heard of a gun being fired into the room is true":** Paine to William Carver, New Rochelle, January 16, 1805; Philip S. Foner, *Complete Writings,* 2:1455.

316 **"I enclose the fifty dollars for Mr. Lewis":** Library of the American Philosophical Society.

317 **"nearly the color of tanned leather":** Hawke, *Paine,* 382.

317 **"[I] was struck with a fit of an apoplexy":** Paine to Andrew Dean, New York, August 15, 1806; Philip S. Foner, *Complete Writings,* 2:1483.

318 **"Elisha Ward and three or four other Tories":** Paine to Vice President Clinton, May 4, 1807.

319 **"I have had Tom Paine living with me for these five months":** Williamson, 271.

319 **"Mr. Paine's extreme parsimony":** Thomas Haynes to Robert Hunter, October 30, 1807, collection of the New York Public Library.

320 **"from tavern to tavern and from brothel to brothel":** Durey, "Paine's Apostles."

320 **"I, sir, never permit anyone to alter anything that I write":** Aldridge, *Man of Reason.*

320 **"is an ugly tempered man":** Aldridge, *Man of Reason,* 308.

321 **"His blue eyes were full, lucid":** Aldridge, *Man of Reason,* 315.

322 **"you, who were once the companion of Washington, Jay, and Hamilton":** Hawke, *Paine,* 385.

322 **"Do you wish to believe that Jesus Christ is the son of God?":** Rickman.

322 **"He was now become extremely weak":** Conway, *Life,* 2:452.

12. Provenance

326 **"Since Mr. Paine's arrival in this city":** Conway, *Life,* 2:418.

327 **"he had never seen the slightest indication":** Conway, *Life,* 2:402.

327 **"the cause of religion":** Conway, *Life,* 2:402.

327 **"Cheetham was a hypocrite turned Tory":** Conway, *Life,* 2:391.

328 **"the head was . . . small for a man, and of the Celtic type":** Williamson, 282.

328 **"My grandmother's first husband":** Powell, 264.

328 **"On Tuesday, January 27, 1833, I went to 11 Bolt Court":** Bressler.

329 **"the papers you speak of regarding Thomas Paine":** Conway, *Life,* xx.

330 **"if I had been alive during the Revolution":** Author interview with John Wright.

330 **"Tom Paine, the philanderer and an unmitigated scamp":** Williamson, 202.

331 **"a few who thought highly of his *Rights of Man* and *Age of Reason*":** E. P. Thompson, 498, citing C. Wilkins, *History of Merthyr Tydfil,* 1867. Thompson's masterpiece is the key source on Paine's influence in the history of Britain's labor movement and Labour Party.

331 **"if anybody bought a book":** E. P. Thompson, 498, citing Henry Mayhew, *London Labour and the London Poor,* 1884, 1:318.

331 **"Facts are seditious things":** John Wilson, *The Songs of Joseph Mather,* Sheffield, 1862, 56–57.

332 **"At this time the writings of William Cobbett suddenly became of great authority":** E. P. Thompson, 620, citing Samuel Bamford, *Passages in the Life of a Radical,* 1893, 11–12.

332 **"a traitorous conspiracy has been formed":** E. P. Thompson, 634.

333 **"God gave [the rural poor] life upon this land":** *Cobbett's Weekly Political Register,* February 28, 1835.

333 **"by disseminating the principles propagated by that great philosopher":** Foot and Kramnick, 33.

333 **"I will not sit in the chair and hear that great man reviled":** Rock.

333 **"International arbitration, family allowances, maternity benefits":** Foot and Kramnick, 34.

334 **"The ruling class is the rich, who really command our industry":** *The American Ruling Class,* a film written and produced by Lewis Lapham and directed by John Kirby, 2005.

335 **"more enduring than all the piles of marble and granite":** Hitchens, "Philosophical Tinderbox."

336 **"the age of severance, of dissociation":** Emerson, "Historical Notes of Life and Letters in New England," *Lectures and Biographical Sketches, The Complete Works,* Boston, 1883.

336 **"had no relations or friends":** Wood, 341.

337 **"A new generation of democratic Americans":** Wood, 369.

337 **"This American world was not made for me," "Where is now, the progress of the human mind?" "into the hands of the young and ignorant,"** and **"All, all dead, and ourselves left alone":** Wood, *Radicalism,* 366 et seq., citing Rush to John Adams, February 19, June 29, August 14, 1805; April 2, 1807; June 13, 1808; October 2, 1810, June 27, 1812; in John A. Schutz and Douglass Adair, eds., *The Spur of Fame: Dialogues of John Adams and Benjamin Rush,* 1805–1813, San Marino, CA: 1980, 22, 28, 31, 32, 79, 108, 169, 227. Jefferson to Francis Adrian Van De Kemp, January 11, 1825, in Ford, ed., *Writings of Jefferson,* vol. 10, 77, 337.

337 **Joseph Priestley emigrated to Pennsylvania:** See Bashore for details on Priestley's emigration.

338 **"I wish you would write a poem in blank verse":** E. P. Thompson, 176.

339 **"May it be to the world":** Rahe, 375.

Sources

Archives

Ambrose Barker Paine Collection, Norfolk County Council Library, Thetford
Archives of the New-York Historical Society, New York
Bibliothèque Nationale, Paris
Institut d'Histoire de la Révolution Française, Université de Paris (Sorbonne), Paris
Library of Congress, Washington
Library of the American Philosophical Society, Philadelphia
Ministère des Affaires Etrangères, Paris
Musée Carnavalet, Paris
Musée de la Révolution Française, Vizille
National Portrait Gallery, London
National Portrait Gallery, Smithsonian Institution, Washington
New York Public Library, New York
Sussex Archaeological Society Library and the East Sussex Records Office, Lewes
Thomas Paine National Historical Association, New Rochelle

Publications

Adams, Charles Francis, ed. *The Works of John Adams.* Boston: Charles Little and James Brown, 1841.

Adams, John Quincy. *An Answer to Paine's "Rights of Man."* London: John Stockdale, 1793.

Aldridge, Alfred Owen. *Man of Reason: The Life of Thomas Paine.* Philadelphia: J. B. Lippincott, 1959.

———. *Thomas Paine's American Ideology.* Newark: University of Delaware Press, 1984.

———. "Natural Religion and Deism in America before Ethan Allen and Thomas Paine." *William and Mary Quarterly,* 3rd ser., 54:4 (October 1997).

Allen, Brooke. "Our Godless Constitution." *Nation,* February 21, 2005.

Anderson, Fred. "What Would George Celebrate?" *New York Times,* July 4, 2003.

———, ed. *George Washington Remembers: Reflections on the French and Indian War.* Evanston, IL: Rowman and Littlefield, 2005.

Appleby, Joyce O. *Liberalism and Republicanism in the Historical Imagination.* Cambridge, MA: Harvard University Press, 1992.

Ayer, A. J. *Thomas Paine.* Chicago: University of Chicago Press, 1988.

Ayling, Stanley. *George the Third.* London: John Murray, 1980.

———. *Edmund Burke. His Life and Opinions.* London: John Murray, 1988.

Bailyn, Bernard. *Faces of Revolution: Personalities and Themes in the Struggle for American Independence.* New York: Knopf, 1990.

———. *The Ideological Origins of the American Revolution.* Cambridge, MA: Belknap Press of Harvard University Press, 1992.

———. "Jefferson and the Ambiguities of Freedom." *Proceedings of the American Philosophical Society* 137:4 (1993).

———. *To Begin the World Anew: The Genius and Ambiguities of the American Founders.* New York: Knopf, 2003.

Barash, David P. "Unreason's Seductive Charms." *Chronicle of Higher Education* 50:11 (November 7, 2003).

Bashore, M. Andrea. "Joseph Priestley and His American Home." *East-Central Intelligencer: The Newsletter of the East-Central/American Society for Eighteenth-Century Studies* 16:2 (May 2002).

Beatty, Mary Lou. "The Past IS Unpredictable: A Conversation with Bernard Bailyn." *Humanities,* March/April 1998.

Becker, Carl. "The Memoirs and the Letters of Madame Roland." *American Historical Review* 33:4 (July 1928).

Ben-Atar, Doron. "Private Friendship and Political Harmony?" *Reviews in American History* 24:1 (1996).

Berkin, Carol. *A Brilliant Solution: Inventing the American Constitution.* New York: Harcourt, 2002.

———. *Revolutionary Mothers: Women in the Struggle for America's Independence.* New York: Knopf, 2005.

Berlinski, David. *Newton's Gift: How Sir Isaac Newton Unlocked the System of the World.* New York: Free Press, 2000.

Bernier, Olivier. *Lafayette.* New York: Dutton, 1983.

———. *The World in 1800.* New York: John Wiley and Sons, 2000.

Bernstein, Mark. "History, Letter by Letter." *Princeton Alumni Weekly,* May 14, 2003.

Bevir, Mark. "Republicanism, Socialism, and Democracy in Britain: The Origins of the Radical Left." *Journal of Social History* 34:2 (2000).

Blackburn, Simon. "Meet the Flintstones." *New Republic,* November 25, 2002.

———. "The Ethics of Belief." *New Republic,* December 1, 2003.

Blom, Philipp. *Encyclopédie.* London: Fourth Estate, 2004.

Blumenthal, Max. "Avenging Angel of the Religious Right." *Salon,* January 6, 2004.

Boorstin, Daniel J. *The Discoverers.* New York: Random House, 1983.

Bourne, Russell. *Gods of War, Gods of Peace.* New York: Harcourt, 2002.

Boyer, Pascal. *Religion Explained: Evolutionary Origins of Religious Thought.* New York: Basic Books, 2001.

Brace, Richard Munthe. "The Problem of Bread and the French Revolution at Bordeaux." *American Historical Review* 51:4 (July 1946).

Brands, H. W. *The First American: The Life and Times of Benjamin Franklin.* New York: Doubleday, 2000.

Bressler, Leo A. "Peter Porcupine and the Bones of Thomas Paine." *Pennsylvania Magazine of History and Biography* 83:2 (April 1958).

Bromwich, David. "Wollstonecraft as a Critic of Burke." *Political Theory* 23:4 (November 1995).

Bronstein, Jamie L. *Land Reform and Working-Class Experience in Britain and the United States, 1800–1862.* Palo Alto, CA: Stanford University Press, 1999.

Brookhiser, Richard. *Gentleman Revolutionary: Gouverneur Morris—the Rake Who Wrote the Constitution.* New York: Free Press, 2003.

Brown, Gillain. *The Consent of the Governed: The Lockean Legacy in Early American Culture.* Cambridge, MA: Harvard University Press, 2001.

Brown, Stuart Gerry. *The First Republicans: Political Philosophy and Public Policy in the Party of Jefferson and Madison.* Syracuse, NY: Syracuse University Press, 1954.

Browne, Stephen Howard. " 'The Circle of Our Felicities': Jefferson's First Inaugural Address and the Rhetoric of Nationhood." *Journal of World Studies,* Fall 2000.

Bryan, William Jennings, ed. *The World's Famous Orations.* New York: Funk and Wagnalls, 1906; New York: Bartleby.com, 2003.

Buchan, James. *Crowded with Genius.* New York: HarperCollins, 2004.

Bumsted, J. M. " 'Things in the Womb of Time': Ideas of American Independence, 1633 to 1763." *William and Mary Quarterly,* 3rd ser., 31:4 (October 1974).

Burke, Edmund. *Reflections on the Revolution in France in a Letter Intended to Have Been Sent to a Gentleman in Paris.* London, 1790.

Butterfield, L. H., ed. *The Letters of Benjamin Rush.* Princeton, NJ: Princeton University Press, 1951.

———, ed. *The Diary and Autobiography of John Adams.* Cambridge, MA: Harvard University Press, 1961.

Caesar, James W. "A Genealogy of Anti-Americanism." *Public Interest,* Summer 2003.

Calhoun, Craig. "The Class Consciousness of Frequent Travelers: Toward a Critique of Actually Existing Cosmopolitanism." *South Atlantic Quarterly* 101:4 (Fall 2002).

Cappon, Lester J., ed. *The Adams-Jefferson Letters: The Complete Correspondence between Thomas Jefferson and Abigail and John Adams.* Chapel Hill: University of North Carolina Press, 1988.

Carlile, Richard. *The Life of Thomas Paine.* London, 1820.

Chalmers, George. *The Life of Thomas Paine, the Author of Rights of Man, Age of Reason, & c., with a Defence of his Writings, by Francis Oldys, A.M., of the University of Pennsylvania.* Boston: Printed by Manning & Lorring, for David West, No. 36, Marlborough-Street, 1796.

Charles, Joseph. "Adams and Jefferson: The Origins of the American Party System." *William and Mary Quarterly,* 3rd ser., 12:3 (July 1955).

Chen, David W. "Rehabilitating Thomas Paine, Bit by Bony Bit." *New York Times,* March 30, 2001.

Christian, William. "The Moral Economics of Tom Paine." *Journal of the History of Ideas* 34:3 (July–September 1973).

Claeys, Gregory. "The Origins of the Rights of Labor: Republicanism, Commerce, and the Construction of Modern Social Theory in Britain, 1796–1805." *Journal of Modern History* 66:2 (June 1994).

Cobbett, William. *An Antidote for Tom Paine's Theological and Political Poison.* Philadelphia, 1796.

———. "A Letter to the infamous Tom Paine, in answer to his brutal attack on the Federal Constitution, and on the conduct and character of General Washington." *The Political Censor, or Monthly Review of the Most Interesting Political Occurrences, Relative to the United States of America, by Peter Porcupine.* Philadelphia, Published by William Cobbett, Opposite Christ Church, Price, One Quarter of a Dollar, December 1796.

———. *Porcupine's Gazette and Daily Advertiser.* Philadelphia, 1797–1802.

———. *Cobbett's Weekly Political Register*. London, 1802–1835.

———. *Rural Rides.* London: Penguin, 2001.

———. *Cobbett's Review of the Life of Thomas Paine.* London: R. Gilbert, Printer, n.d.

Cohen, Roger. "Change in the Middle East: What's In It for America?" *New York Times,* March 6, 2005.

Collins, Paul. *The Trouble with Tom: The Strange Afterlife and Times of Thomas Paine*. New York: Bloomsbury, 2005.

Conniff, James. "Edmund Burke and His Critics: The Case of Mary Wollstonecraft." *Journal of the History of Ideas* 60:2 (1999).

Conway, Moncure Daniel. *The Life of Thomas Paine.* New York: G. P. Putnam's Sons, 1892.

———. *The Writings of Thomas Paine.* New York: G. P. Putnam's Sons, 1896.

———. "The Adventures of Thomas Paine's Bones." *Journal of the Thomas Paine National Historical Association,* March 2002.

Craveri, Benedetta. *The Age of Conversation.* New York: New York Review of Books, 2005.

Damasio, Antonio. *Descartes' Error: Emotion, Reason, and the Human Brain*. New York: Avon, 1994.

———. *Looking for Spinoza: Joy, Sorrow and the Feeling Brain.* New York: Harcourt, 2003.

Darnton, Robert. *George Washington's False Teeth: An Unconventional Guide to the Eighteenth Century.* New York: W. W. Norton, 2003.

Davidson, Edward H., and William J. Scheick. *Paine, Scripture, and Authority: The Age of Reason as Religious and Political Idea.* Bethlehem, PA: Lehigh University Press, 1994.

Davidson, Ian. *Voltaire in Exile.* New York: Grove, 2005.

Davies, Paul. "E.T. and God: Could Earthly Religions Survive the Discovery of Life Elsewhere in the Universe?" *Atlantic Monthly,* September 2003.

Dawkins, Richard. "Creationism: God's Gift to the Ignorant." *Times* (London), May 21, 2005.

Del Veccio, Thomas. *Tom Paine: American.* New York: Whittier Books, 1956.

DeWan, George. "A Maverick's Rowdy Odyssey." *Newsday* (New York), September 12, 2005.

Dickey, Laurence. "Thomas Paine: Context, Text, and Presentism." *Reviews in American History* 24:2 (1996).

Dillon, Patrick. *Gin: The Much-Lamented Death of Madam Geneva.* Boston: Justin, Charles and Co., 2003.

Dowd, David L. "Jacques-Louis David, Artist Member of the Committee of General Security." *American Historical Review* 57:4 (July 1952).

Durey, Michael. "Thomas Paine's Apostles: Radical Emigrés and the Triumph of Jeffersonian Republicanism." *William and Mary Quarterly,* 3rd ser., 44:4 (October 1987).

———. *Transatlantic Radicals and the Early American Republic.* Lawrence: University of Kansas Press, 1997.

Dyck, Ian, ed. *Citizen of the World: Essays on Thomas Paine.* London: Croom Helm, 1987.

Edison, Thomas. "The Philosophy of Paine." *The Diary and Sundry Observations.* London: Abbey Publishing, 1968.

Einstein, Albert. "Religion and Science." *New York Times,* November 9, 1930.

Eisenstein, Elizabeth L. "Who Intervened in 1788? A Commentary on the Coming of the French Revolution." *American Historical Review* 71:1 (October 1965).

Ellis, Joseph J. *After the Revolution: Profiles of Early American Culture.* New York: W. W. Norton, 1979.

———. *American Sphinx: The Character of Thomas Jefferson.* New York: Knopf, 1997.

———. *Founding Brothers.* New York: Knopf, 2001.

———. *His Excellency: George Washington.* New York: Knopf, 2005.

Englund, Steven. *Napoleon: A Political Life.* New York: Scribner, 2004.

Ferguson, Niall. *Empire: The Rise and Demise of the British World Order and the Lessons for Global Power.* New York: Basic Books, 2003.

Ferguson, Robert A. "The Commonalities of Common Sense." *William and Mary Quarterly,* 3rd ser., 57:3 (July 2000).

Ferling, John, and Lewis E. Braverman. "John Adams's Health Reconsidered." *William and Mary Quarterly,* 3rd ser., 55:83–104 (1998).

Fielding, Henry. *An Enquiry into the Causes of the Late Increase of Robbers, &c.* London, 1751.

Fischer, David Hackett. *Albion's Seed: Four British Folkways in America.* New York: Oxford University Press, 1989.

———. *Washington's Crossing.* New York: Oxford University Press, 2004.

Fiske, John. *The American Revolution.* Cambridge, MA: Riverside Press, 1891.

Fitzgerald, Jim. "Reburial of Thomas Paine Sought." Associated Press, March 31, 2001.

Fitzpatrick, John Clement, ed. *The Writings of George Washington from the Original Manuscript Sources.* Library of Congress and the University of Virginia Library, http://etext.lib.virginia.edu/washington/.

Fliegelman, Jay. *Declaring Independence: Jefferson, Natural Language, and the Culture of Performance.* Palo Alto, CA: Stanford University Press, 1993.

Foner, Eric. *Tom Paine and Revolutionary America.* New York: Oxford University Press, 1976.

———. "The Meaning of Freedom in the Age of Emancipation." *Journal of American History* 81:2 (September 1994).

Foner, Philip S., ed. *The Complete Writings of Thomas Paine.* New York: Citadel Press, 1945.

Foot, Michael, and Isaac Kramnick, eds. *The Thomas Paine Reader.* London: Penguin, 1987.

Franklin, Benjamin. *The Writings of Benjamin Franklin.* The History Carper Online Resources. http://www.historycarper.com/resources/.

Fruchtman, Jack, Jr. *Thomas Paine: Apostle of Freedom.* New York: Four Walls Eight Windows, 1994.

———. "Classical Republicanism, Whig Political Science, Tory History: The State of Eighteenth-Century Political Thought." *Eighteenth-Century Life* 20:2 (1996).

Garber, Marjorie. "Our Genius Problem." *Atlantic Monthly,* December 2002.

Gay, Peter. "Rhetoric and Politics in the French Revolution." *American Historical Review* 66:3 (April 1961).

———. *The Enlightenment: An Interpretation: The Rise of Modern Paganism.* New York: W. W. Norton, 1996.

———. *The Enlightenment: An Interpretation: Volume II: The Science of Freedom.* New York: W. W. Norton, 1997.

George, Phillip Brandt. "George Washington: Patriot, President, Planter and Purveyor of Distilled Spirits." *American History,* February 2004.

Gleick, James. *Isaac Newton.* New York: Simon and Schuster, 2003.

———. "Isaac Newton's Gravity." *Slate,* October 21, 2004.

Goldberg, Michelle. "The New Monkey Trial." *Salon,* January 10, 2005.

Gopnik, Adam. "American Electric: Did Franklin Fly That Kite?" *New Yorker,* June 30, 2003.

Gordon, Sarah Barringer. "Blasphemy and the Law of Religious Liberty in Nineteenth-Century America." *American Quarterly* 52:4 (2000).

Graetz, Michael, and Ian Shapiro. *Death by a Thousand Cuts: The Fight over Taxing Inherited Wealth.* Princeton, NJ: Princeton University Press, 2005.

Grant, James. *John Adams: Party of One.* New York: Farrar, Straus and Giroux, 2005.

Greene, Jack P. "Paine, America, and the 'Modernization' of Political Consciousness." *Political Science Quarterly* 93:1 (Spring 1978).

Gross, Daniel. "Goodbye, Pension. Goodbye, Health Insurance. Goodbye, Vacations." *Slate,* September 23, 2004.

Gustafson, Sandra M. "Morality and Citizenship in the Early Republic." *American Literary History* 15:1 (Spring 2003).

Hague, William. *William Pitt the Younger.* New York: Knopf, 2005.

Hawke, David Freeman. *Paine.* New York: W. W. Norton, 1974.

———. *Everyday Life in Early America.* New York: Harper and Row, 1988.

Hill, Mike. "The Crowded Text: E. P. Thompson, Adam Smith, and the Object of Eighteenth-Century Writing." *English Literary History* 69 (2002).

Himmelfarb, Gertrude. *The Roads to Modernity: The British, French, and American Enlightenments.* New York: Knopf, 2004.

Hitchens, Christopher. *The Days of the French Revolution.* New York: Harper and Row, 1980.

———. "Philosophical Tinderbox of Two Revolutions." *Newsday* (New York), April 12, 1989.

———. "Reactionary Prophet." *Atlantic Monthly,* April 2004.

Hobbes, Thomas. *Leviathan.* London: Penguin Classics, 1982.

Holifield, E. Brooks. *Theology in America.* New Haven, CT: Yale University Press, 2003.

Holt, Jim. "The Big Lab Experiment." *Slate,* May 19, 2004.

———. "Unintelligent Design." *New York Times,* February 20, 2005.

Hunt, Lynn. "The World We Have Gained: The Future of the French Revolution." *American Historical Review* 108:1 (February 2003).

Hunz, Jabez. *Thomas Paine's Bones and Their Owners.* London, 1908.

Hyneman, Charles S., and Donald S. Lutz, eds. *American Political Writing during the Founding Era, 1784–1822.* Indianapolis: Liberty Fund, Inc., 1983.

Ignatieff, Michael. "Who Are Americans to Think That Freedom Is Theirs to Spread?" *New York Times,* June 26, 2005.

Ingersoll, Robert G. "A Vindication of Thomas Paine." *The Works of Robert G. Ingersoll.* Dresden, 1877, V:447.

Isaacson, Walter. *Benjamin Franklin: An American Life.* New York: Simon and Schuster, 2003.

Jacoby, Susan. *Freethinkers: A History of American Secularism.* New York: Metropolitan Books, 2004.

James, Clive. "The Good of a Bad Review." *New York Times,* September 7, 2003.

Johnson, Paul. *Napoleon.* New York: Penguin, 2003.

Johnson, Samuel. *A Dictionary of the English Language: In Which the Words are Deduced from their Originals, and Illustrated in the Different Significations by Examples from the Best Writers. To which are Prefixed, a History of the Language, and an English Grammar.* London: W. Strahan, 1755.

———. *The Works of Samuel Johnson.* Troy: Pafraets & Co., 1913.

Jones, Gareth Stedman. *An End to Poverty?* London: Profile Books, 2004.

Jordan, Winthrop D. "Familial Politics: Thomas Paine and the Killing of the King, 1776." *Journal of American History* 60:2 (September 1973).

Kaiser, Robert G. "In Finland's Footsteps." *Washington Post,* August 7, 2005.

Kates, Gary. "From Liberalism to Radicalism: Tom Paine's *Rights of Man.*" *Journal of the History of Ideas* 50:4 (October–December 1989).

Katz, Jon. "The Age of Paine." *Wired,* May 1995.

———. *Virtuous Reality: How America Surrendered Discussion of Moral Values to Opportunists, Nitwits, and Blockheads like William Bennett.* New York: Random House, 2003.

Kaye, Harvey J. *Thomas Paine and the Promise of America.* New York: Hill and Wang, 2005.

Keane, John. *Tom Paine: A Political Life.* Boston: Little, Brown, 1995.

Kertzer, David I., and Marzio Barbagli, eds. *Family Life in Early Modern Times, 1500–1789.* New Haven, CT: Yale University Press, 2001.

Kimball, Roger. "Friends of Humanity?" *New Criterion,* November 2003.

Knott, Sarah. "Sensibility and the American War for Independence." *American Historical Review,* February 2004.

Kramnick, Isaac. *The Rage of Edmund Burke: Portrait of an Ambivalent Conservative.* New York: Basic Books, 1977.

———. "The 'Great National Discussion': The Discourse of Politics in 1787." *William and Mary Quarterly,* 3rd ser., 45 (1988).

———. *Republicanism and Bourgeois Radicalism: Political Ideology in Late Eighteenth-Century England and America.* London: Cornell University Press, 1990.

———, ed. *The Portable Enlightenment Reader.* New York: Penguin, 1995.

Kukla, Jon. *A Wilderness So Immense: The Louisiana Purchase and the Destination of America.* New York: Knopf, 2003.

Langguth, A. J. *Patriots.* New York: Simon and Schuster, 1988.

Larabee, Leonard W., ed. *The Papers of Benjamin Franklin.* New Haven, CT: Yale University Press, 1959.

Leckie, Robert. *George Washington's War: The Saga of the American Revolution.* New York: HarperPerennial, 1993.

Lefebvre, Georges. *The French Revolution.* Princeton, NJ: Princeton University Press, 1962–64.

Lewis, Joseph. *Thomas Paine: Author of the Declaration of Independence.* New York: Freethought Press, 1947.

Lind, Michael. "In Defence of Mandarins." *Prospect,* October 2005.

Lindholdt, Paul. "Luddism and Its Discontents." *American Quarterly* 49:4 (1997).

Linton, William James. *A Brief History of the Remains of the Late Thomas Paine, from the Time of Their Disinterment in 1819 by the Late William Cobbett, M.P., Down to the Year 1846.* London: J. Watson, 1847.

Lipscomb, Andrew A., and Albert Ellery Bergh, eds. *The Writings of Thomas Jefferson.* Washington, D.C.: Thomas Jefferson Memorial Association, 1905.

Locke, John. *The Reasonableness of Christianity, as Delivered in the Scriptures.* Stanford, CA: Stanford University Press, 1958.

———. *An Essay Concerning Human Understanding.* New York: Prometheus, 1994.

———. *Two Treatises of Government and A Letter Concerning Toleration.* New Haven, CT: Yale University Press, 2003.

Lossing, Benson J. *Pictorial Field Book of the Revolution.* Philadelphia, 1850.

McCullough, David. *John Adams.* New York: Simon and Schuster, 2001.

———. "The Argonauts of 1776." *New York Times,* July 4, 2002.

———. *1776.* New York: Simon and Schuster, 2005.

McDougall, Walter A. *Freedom Just Around the Corner: A New American History, 1528–1828.* New York: HarperCollins, 2004.

McLemee, Scott. "A Conservative of the Old School." *Chronicle of Higher Education* 50:35 (May 7, 2004).

McMahon, Darrin M. "From the Happiness of Virtue to the Virtue of Happiness: 400 B.C.–A.D. 1780." *Daedalus* 133:2 (Winter 2003).

Manjoo, Farhad. "The Man Who Saw God's Plan." *Salon,* June 4, 2003.

Mann, Charles C. *1491: New Revelations of the Americas before Columbus.* New York: Knopf, 2005.

Marsden, George M. *Jonathan Edwards: A Life.* New Haven, CT: Yale University Press, 2003.

Martin, Joseph Plumb. "Selections from the Diary of Private Joseph Plumb Martin." http://www.ushistory.org/march/other/martindiary.htm.

Massachusetts Historical Society. *Adams Family Papers: An Electronic Archive.* http://www.masshist.org/digitaladams/.

Meier, Christian. *From Athens to Auschwitz: The Uses of History.* Cambridge, MA: Harvard University Press, 2005.

Michelet, Jules. *History of the French Revolution.* Chicago: University of Chicago Press, 1967.

Montesquieu, Charles de Secondat. *The Spirit of the Laws.* Cambridge, UK: Cambridge University Press, 1989.

Moore, Judy. *Thomas Paine's Lewes.* Seaford, UK: S.B. Publications, 2000.

Morgan, Edmund S. "Poor Richard's New Year." *New York Times,* December 31, 2002.

Morris, Anne Cary, ed. *The Diary and Letters of Gouverneur Morris.* New York: Charles Scribner's Sons, 1888.

Morris, Gouverneur. *A Diary of the French Revolution.* London: Harrap, 1939.

Mossner, Ernest Campbell. *The Life of David Hume.* Edinburgh, 1954.

Murphy, Cullen. "The Path of Brighteousness." *Atlantic Monthly,* November 2003.

National Institute of Mental Health. "Bipolar Disorder." www.nimh.nih.gov/publicat/bipolar.cfm.

Noll, Mark A. *America's God: From Jonathan Edwards to Abraham Lincoln.* Oxford, UK: Oxford University Press, 2002.

Nordlinger, Jay. "Impromptus." *National Review,* November 13, 2002.

Packer, George. "Wars and Ideas." *New Yorker,* July 5, 2004.

Pain, Stephanie. "Waterloo Teeth." *New Scientist,* June 16, 2001.

Paine, Thomas. *A Brief History of the American Revolution Written by Thomas Paine While He Was at the Head of the American Army with General Washington, During the Seven Years' War with Great Britain, from 1776 to the Close, 1783.* Philadelphia: James A. Bliss, 1881.

Penniman, Howard. "Thomas Paine—Democrat." *American Political Science Review* 37:2 (April 1943).

Perroud, Claude, ed. *Lettres de Madame Roland.* Paris, 1900–1902.

Picard, Liza. *Dr. Johnson's London.* New York: St. Martin's, 2000.

Pilbeam, Pamela M. *Themes in Modern European History, 1780–1830.* London: Routledge, 1995.

Pocock, J. G. A. *The Machiavellian Moment: Florentine Political Thought and the Atlantic Republican Tradition.* Princeton, NJ: Princeton University Press, 1975.

Pole, J. R. "In Machiavelli's Fading Footprints." *Historical Journal* 38:3 (September 1995).

Pollan, Michael. "The (Agri)Cultural Contradictions of Obesity." *New York Times,* October 12, 2003.

Porter, Roy. "Enlightenment Pleasure." *Pleasure in the Eighteenth Century.* New York: New York University Press, 1996.

———. *The Creation of the Modern World: The Untold Story of the British Enlightenment.* New York: W. W. Norton, 2000.

Postel, Danny. "The Age of Reason." *Chronicle of Higher Education* 49:25 (February 28, 2003).

Postman, Neil. *Building a Bridge to the Eighteenth Century: How the Past Can Improve Our Future.* New York: Knopf, 1999.

Powell, David. *Tom Paine: The Greatest Exile.* New York: St. Martin's, 1985.

Prochaska, Franklyn K. "Thomas Paine's *The Age of Reason* Revisited." *Journal of the History of Ideas* 33:4 (October–December 1972).

Radford, Tim. "Science Cannot Provide All the Answers." *Guardian* (UK), September 4, 2003.

Rahe, Paul A. *Republics Ancient and Modern: Classical Republicanism and the American Revolution.* Chapel Hill: University of North Carolina Press, 1992.

Randel, Fred. "The Political Geography of Horror in Mary Shelley's *Frankenstein.*" *English Literary History* 70:2 (Summer 2003).

Ratliff, Evan. "The Crusade against Evolution." *Wired,* October 2004.

Reid, John Philip. *The Concept of Liberty in the Age of the American Revolution.* Chicago: University of Chicago Press, 1988.

Richard, Carl J. *The Founders and the Classics: Greece, Rome, and the American Enlightenment.* Cambridge, MA: Harvard University Press, 1995.

Rickman, Thomas "Clio." *Life of Thomas Paine.* London, 1819.

Rock, Howard B. *Artisans of the New Republic: The Tradesmen of New York City in the Age of Jefferson.* New York: New York University Press, 1979.

Rose, Jonathan. "The Classics in the Slums." *City Journal,* Autumn 2004.

Rosenfeld, Richard N. *American Aurora.* New York: St. Martin's, 1998.

Rothenberg, Molly Anne. "Parasiting America: The Radical Function of Heterogeneity in Thomas Paine's Early Writings." *Eighteenth-Century Studies* 25:3 (Spring 1992).

Rousseau, Jean-Jacques. *The Social Contract and Discourses.* London: J. M. Dent, 1913.

Rudolph, Lloyd I. "The Eighteenth-Century Mob in America and Europe." *American Quarterly* 11:4 (Winter 1959).

Sale, Kirkpatrick. *Rebels against the Future: The Luddites and Their War on the Industrial Revolution: Lessons for the Computer Age.* Reading, MA: Addison-Wesley, 1995.

Saletan, William. "Unintelligible Redesign." *Slate,* February 13, 2002.

Saville, John. *1848: The British State and the Chartist Movement.* Cambridge, UK: Cambridge University Press, 1990.

Schama, Simon. *Citizens: A Chronicle of the French Revolution.* New York: Knopf, 1989.

———. "The Unloved American: Two Centuries of Alienating Europe." *New Yorker,* March 10, 2003.

Schiff, Stacy. "Vive l'Histoire." *New York Times,* February 6, 2003.

———. *A Great Improvisation: Franklin, France, and the Birth of America.* New York: Henry Holt, 2005.

Sharp, Andrew. *The English Levellers.* Cambridge, UK: Cambridge University Press, 1998.

Shorto, Russell. *The Island at the Center of the World: The Epic Story of Dutch Manhattan, the Forgotten Colony That Shaped America.* New York: Doubleday, 2004.

Shulim, Joseph I. "Robespierre and the French Revolution." *American Historical Review* 82:1 (February 1977).

Simon, James F. *What Kind of Nation: Thomas Jefferson, John Marshall, and the Epic Struggle to Create a United States.* New York: Simon and Schuster, 2004.

Smith, Frank. "New Light on Thomas Paine's First Year in America, 1775." *American Literature* 1:4 (January 1930).

———. "The Authorship of 'An Occasional Letter on the Female Sex.'" *American Literature* 2:3 (November 1930).

———. *Tom Paine, Liberator.* New York: Frederick Stokes, 1938.

Smith, James Morton, ed. *The Republic of Letters: The Correspondence between Thomas Jefferson and James Madison, 1776–1826.* New York: W. W. Norton, 1995.

Smylie, James H. "Clerical Perspectives on Deism: Paine's *The Age of Reason* in Virginia." *Eighteenth-Century Studies* 6:2 (Winter 1972–1973).

Sparks, Jared. *The Life of Gouverneur Morris.* Boston: Gray and Bowen, 1832.

Spater, George. *William Cobbett: The Poor Man's Friend.* Cambridge, UK: Cambridge University Press, 1982.

Sprat, Bishop Thomas. *History of the Royal Society,* 1667. St. Louis: Washington University Studies, 1958.

Stourzh, Gerald. "Reason and Power in Benjamin Franklin's Political Thought." *American Political Science Review* 47:4 (December 1953).

Striner, Richard. "Political Newtonianism: The Cosmic Model of Politics in Europe and America." *William and Mary Quarterly,* 3rd ser., 52:4 (October 1995).

Sydenham, M. J. *The Girondins.* London: University of London Press, 1961.

Talbot, David. "I Shall Not Burn My Press and Melt My Letters." *Salon,* September 2, 2003.

Taylor, Royall. *The Algerine Captive: or the Life and Adventures of Doctor Updike Underhill: Six Years a Prisoner among the Algerines,* 1797.

Teichgraeber, Richard F., III. "'Professionalism' and the Publishing Boom in British History." *Journal of British Studies* 30:2 (April 1991).

Thomas, Isaiah. *History of Printing in America.* Worcester, MA, 1818.

Thompson, E. P. *The Making of the English Working Class.* New York: Vintage, 1966.

Thompson, J. M. *The French Revolution.* New York: Oxford University Press, 1945.

Thurman, Judith. "Eminence Rose." *New Yorker,* October 7, 2002.

Tocqueville, Alexis de. *Democracy in America.* New York: Signet, 2001.

Tucker, Tom. *Bolt of Fate: Benjamin Franklin and His Electric Kite Hoax.* New York: Public Affairs, 2003.

Twigger, Robert. *Inflation: The Value of the Pound, 1750–1998.* House of Commons Library, Research Paper 99/20, 23 February 1999.

Uglow, Jenny. *The Lunar Men: Five Friends Whose Curiosity Changed the World.* New York: Farrar, Straus and Giroux, 2002.

Urovsky, Melvin I., and Paul Finkelman, eds. *Documents of American Constitutional and Legal History. Volume 1, From the Founding through the Age of Industrialization.* New York: Oxford University Press, 2002.

Vale, Gilbert. *The Life of Thomas Paine.* New York, 1841.

Voltaire (François Marie Arouet). *Letters on England.* London: Cassell & Co., 1894.

Wakefield, Mary. "The Mystery of the Missing Links." *Spectator,* October 25, 2003.

Ward, Adolphus William, A. R. Waller, William Peterfield Trent, John Erskine, Stuart Pratt Sherman, and Carl Van Doren, eds. *The Cambridge History of English and American Literature. Volume 9, From Steele and Addison to Pope and Swift.* New York: G. P. Putnam's Sons, 1907–21.

Wecter, Dixon. "Thomas Paine and the Franklins." *American Literature* 12:3 (November 1940).

Weintraub, Stanley. *Iron Tears: America's Battle for Freedom, Britain's Quagmire: 1775–1783.* New York: Free Press, 2005.

Weisinger, Herbert. "The English Origins of the Sociological Interpretation of the Renaissance." *Journal of the History of Ideas* 11:3 (June 1950).

Wells, William V. *The Life and Public Services of Samuel Adams.* Boston: Little, Brown, 1860.

Wessel, David. "Sad Little Rich Country." *Washington Monthly,* November 2003.

Whitman, Walt. "Specimen Days." *Prose Works.* Philadelphia: David McKay, 1892.

Williamson, Audrey. *Thomas Paine: His Life, Work and Times.* London: George Allen and Unwin, 1973.

Wilson, David A. *Paine and Cobbett: The Transatlantic Connection.* Kingston and Montreal: McGill–Queen's University Press, 1988.

Windschuttle, Keith. "Edward Gibbon and the Enlightenment." *New Criterion* 15:10 (June 1997).

Wollstonecraft, Mary. *A Vindication of the Rights of Women: With Structures on Political and Moral Subjects.* New York: W. W. Norton, 1988.

Wood, Gordon S. *The Radicalism of the American Revolution: How a Revolution Transformed a Monarchical Society into a Democratic One Unlike Any That Had Ever Existed.* New York: Knopf, 1992.

———. *The Americanization of Benjamin Franklin.* New York: Penguin, 2004.

Zakaria, Fareed. *The Future of Freedom: Illiberal Democracy at Home and Abroad.* New York: W. W. Norton, 2003.

Index

Page numbers 341 and above refer to notes.

ILLUSTRATION CREDITS

Frontispiece: Pain signature, wedding banns, courtesy East Sussex Record Office. **Insert, page 1,** *top:* Author's collection; *middle:* Unknown, *A General View of the City of London, Next to the River Thames,* 1760?, Emmet Collection, Miriam and Ira D. Wallach Division of Art, Prints and Photographs, The New York Public Library, Astor, Lenox and Tilden Foundations; *bottom:* Sir Godfrey Kneller, *Joseph Addison,* The National Portrait Gallery, London. **Page 2,** *all:* Author's collection. **Page 3,** *top:* Unknown, *View of Several Public Buildings in Philadelphia,* Emmet Collection, Miriam and Ira D. Wallach Division of Art, Prints and Photographs, The New York Public Library, Astor, Lenox and Tilden Foundations; *bottom:* Unknown, *Benjamin Franklin,* Print Collection, Miriam and Ira D. Wallach Division of Art, Prints and Photographs, The New York Public Library, Astor, Lenox and Tilden Foundations. **Page 4:** *Common Sense,* first edition cover, The Library of Congress, Washington, D.C. **Page 5,** *top:* Charles Willson Peale, *Portrait of George Washington,* 1780, The Colonial Williamsburg Foundation; *bottom:* An artist in the studio of Allan Ramsay, *George III,* The National Portrait Gallery, London. **Page 6,** *top:* Author's collection; *bottom:* Sir Joshua Reynolds, *Edmund Burke,* The National Portrait Gallery, London. **Page 7:** Portrait by Winkler, circa 1865, courtesy of the Col. Richard Gimbel Collection of Thomas Paine Papers, American Philosophical Society. **Page 8,** *left:* Francis Oldys, *Life of Thomas Pain,* courtesy of the Col. Richard Gimbel Collection of Thomas Paine Papers, American Philosophical Society; *top right:* James Gillray, *Thomas Paine,* publ. 23 May 1791, The National Portrait Gallery, London; *bottom right:* Unknown, *Tom Paine's Nightly Pest,* courtesy of the Col. Richard Gimbel Collection of Thomas Paine Papers, American Philosophical Society. **Page 9,** *top left:* William Brockedon, *Marie Joseph, Marquis de Lafayette,* The National Portrait Gallery, London; *right:* Unknown, *J. P. Brissot,* Print Collection, Miriam and Ira D. Wallach Division of Art, Prints and Photographs, The New York Public Library, Astor, Lenox and Tilden Foundations; *bottom left:* Unknown, *Jean-Antoine-Nicolas de Caritat, Marquis de Condorcet,* Print Collection, Miriam and Ira D. Wallach Division of Art, Prints and Photographs, The New York Public Library, Astor, Lenox and Tilden Foundations. **Page 10,** *top: Les deux ne font qu'un,* MRF 1989-182, Musée de la Révolution française, Vizille; *middle: Le ci-devant roi a la Barre de la convention Nationale,* September 1792, Division of Rare and Manuscript Collections, Cornell University Library; *bottom: L'exécution de Louis XVI,* MRF 1986-182, Musée de la Révolution française, Vizille. **Page 11,** *top left: L'ami du people: Marat,* MF 1988-112, Musée de la Révolution française, Vizille; *right:* Gravedon, *Robespierre,* Emmet Collection, Miriam and Ira D. Wallach Division of Art, Prints and Photographs, The New York Public Library, Astor, Lenox and Tilden Foundations; *bottom left:* Unknown, *Georges J. Danton,* Print Collection, Miriam and Ira D. Wallach Division of Art, Prints and Photographs, The New York Public Library, Astor, Lenox and Tilden Foundations. **Page 12,** *top:* Author's collection; *right:* Ezra Ames, *Gouverneur Morris,* ca. 1815, John Wesley Jarvis, 1809, accession number 1817.1, Collection of the New-York Historical Society; *bottom left:* Jacques-Louis David, *The Emperor Napoleon in His Study at the Tuileries,* 1812, Samuel H. Kress Collection, The National Gallery of Art, Washington. **Page 13,** *top:* Author's collection; *middle:* John Joseph Holland, *A View of Broad Street, Wall Street, and the City Hall,* 1797, I. N. Phelps Stokes Collection, Miriam and Ira D. Wallach Division of Art, Prints and Photographs, The New York Public Library, Astor, Lenox and Tilden Foundations; *bottom:* Robert L. Bracklow, *Bleecker Street Showing Thomas Paine's Residence,* Photo Collection Alexander Alland, Sr./CORBIS. **Page 14,** *top:* John Wesley Jarvis, *Thomas Paine,* 1806/07, gift of Marian B. Maurice, Board of Trustees, National Gallery of Art, Washington, D.C.; *bottom:* Portrait bust by John Wesley Jarvis, 1809, accession number 1817.12, Collection of the New-York Historical Society. **Page 15,** *top:* Death mask by John Wesley Jarvis, 1809, accession number 1926.56a, Collection of the New-York Historical Society; *bottom:* Author's collection. **Page 16:** Unknown, *A Radical Reformer,* 1819, courtesy of the Col. Richard Gimbel Collection of Thomas Paine Papers, American Philosophical Society.